THE VIKING HEART

THE
VIKING
HEART

HOW SCANDINAVIANS
CONQUERED THE WORLD

ARTHUR
HERMAN

Houghton Mifflin Harcourt

Boston   New York   2021

For information about permission to reproduce selections from this book,
write to trade.permissions@hmhco.com or to Permissions,
Houghton Mifflin Harcourt Publishing Company,
3 Park Avenue, 19th Floor, New York, New York 10016.

hmhbooks.com

Library of Congress Cataloging-in-Publication Data
Names: Herman, Arthur, 1956– author.
Title: The Viking heart : how Scandinavians conquered the world / Arthur Herman.
Other titles: How Scandinavians conquered the world
Description: Boston : Houghton Mifflin Harcourt, 2021. | Includes bibliographical
references and index.
Identifiers: LCCN 2020057689 (print) | LCCN 2020057690 (ebook) |
ISBN 9781328595904 (hardcover) | ISBN 9780358536734 | ISBN 9780358536840 |
ISBN 9781328595201 (ebook)
Subjects: LCSH: Civilization, Viking. | Vikings. | Northmen. | Civilization, Modern—
Scandinavian influences. | Scandinavian Americans—History. | National characteristics,
Scandinavian.
Classification: LCC DL65 .H47 2021 (print) | LCC DL65 (ebook) | DDC 948/.022—dc23
LC record available at https://lccn.loc.gov/2020057689
LC ebook record available at https://lccn.loc.gov/2020057690

Book design by Greta D. Sibley

Printed in the United States of America

1 2021
4500828305

Frontispiece art (*Leif Erikson*): HelloWorld Images / Alamy

Maps on pages viii and 277 by Mapping Specialists, Ltd.

Excerpts from *100 Pieces of Advice for Emigrants* by
Holger Rosenberg, translated by the Museum of Danish America.
Used with permission from the Museum of Danish America, Elk Horn, Iowa.

For Beth, my magic talisman and guiding spirit

CONTENTS

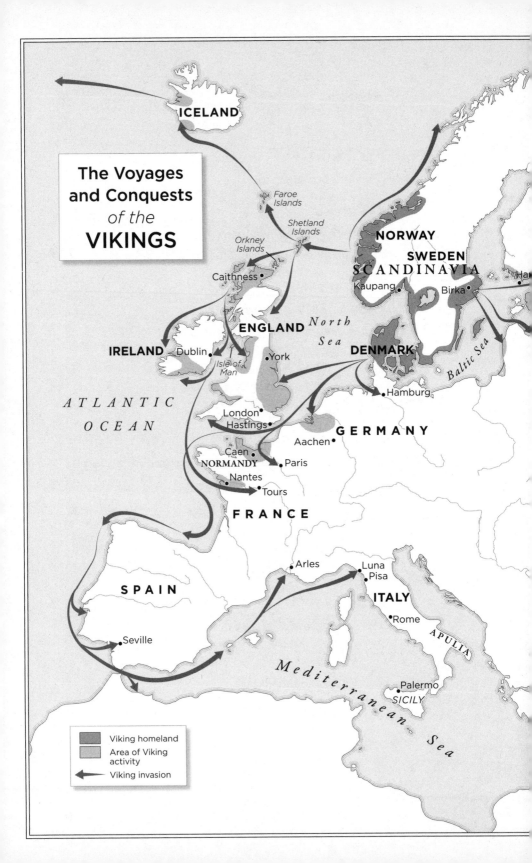

The Voyages
and Conquests
of the
VIKINGS

ICELAND

Faroe
Islands

Shetland
Islands

Orkney
Islands

Caithness

IRELAND Dublin

Isle of
Man

ENGLAND

York

*North
Sea*

ATLANTIC

OCEAN

London
Hastings

Caen
NORMANDY
Nantes
Tours

FRANCE

SPAIN

Seville

NORWAY

SWEDEN
SCANDINAVIA

Kaupang   Birka   Ha

DENMARK

Hamburg

Baltic Sea

GERMANY

Aachen

Paris

Arles   Luna
Pisa

ITALY

Rome

APULIA

Palermo
SICILY

Mediterranean Sea

Viking homeland
Area of Viking
activity
Viking invasion

PREFACE

MY PARENTS HAVE a photograph of my Norwegian grandmother on the plains of Montana, not long after she arrived in America. She is surrounded by her brother and her cousins in front of a barbed-wire fence set against the flat bleak landscape. It's a hunting party. In my grandmother's arms is a Winchester rifle, and a row of rabbits dangles from the wire fence.

I've never forgotten that photograph since the first time I saw it as a boy. In one way, it was hard to reconcile with the grandmother I knew, who baked cookies and made Thanksgiving dinner when we came to visit in Brainerd, Minnesota, with the intrepid hunter in the picture. But increasingly I came to realize this was indeed the same woman, a quiet but strong Norwegian lady for whom Montana (where my mother was born) was just one stop on a journey that took her from her village of Ulefoss to Kristiania (now Oslo) to board a ship for America.

That was in 1910 (my mother still has the trunk her mother brought with her, with the sticker for the steamship line attached to the side). At the time, Anna Carlson was just one young girl in a mass exodus of Norwegians, Swedes, Danes, and Finns from their Scandinavian homeland to America, which is sometimes dubbed the Great Migration. In just under two decades, more than 450,000 of them came to the United States. Together they would transform America and the American Dream forever. Neither would be the same again.

Anna Carlson's part in that transformation was, compared to others, admittedly rather small. But her journey showed off many of the qualities that made her distant ancestors, the Norsemen Vikings, famous: physical and moral courage, determination and adaptability, a deep loyalty to family, and a commitment to cultural heritage, which for her included the Lutheran Church.

The only persons more revered in my grandmother's house than Franklin Roosevelt were Martin Luther and Leif Erikson, the Viking discoverer of America.

In fact, both she and Leif had taken long journeys to arrive at their chosen destinations. In Leif's case, the trek took him from Norway to Greenland, and ultimately to somewhere along the coast of Labrador. In the case of Anna Flaaten (née Carlson), it took her from Ulefoss and Kristiania to New York City and then Lansing, Iowa, where she shared a home with Norwegian cousins. Then she was off to Montana, where she married fellow Norwegian Carsten Flaaten, and then to Minneapolis. Minneapolis was the mecca of Scandinavian Americans in those days, a place where Swedes and Norwegians and a sprinkling of Danes and Finns chose to make their homes in hustling, bustling America. My grandmother worked as a maid in the city's hotels. Her journey finally ended in Brainerd, Minnesota, a town made up almost entirely of Swedish and Norwegian American families. There, at the top of a rise well-suited to her grandchildren's downhill sledding, she lived in the tiny white house where she had raised three children, including my mother, and where we would occasionally gather for Thanksgiving dinner. For dessert, a cake would come out from the kitchen with a tiny Norwegian flag stuck in the middle to remind us of her homeland, and her brothers and other family who were still there.

You are about to read a book that ranges over several centuries. It's a story of epic journeys and battles, longships and steamships, buried treasures and pagan rituals, kings, queens, warriors, and heroes. Some are armed with swords and battle-axes, and others with a plow and an awl or perhaps nothing more than a pen — and some with a Winchester rifle on the Montana plains. But you will soon discover that a single thread runs through them all. It's a thread that connects my grandmother, and the members of my family, to the original settlers of the land she left at the beginning of the past century. Those were the people we call the Vikings. The connection is more than just genealogical, a happenstance of DNA and biology. It does, as we'll see, run deeper.

This is a book about a frame of mind, a way of life, a way of doing things and making things, including making things happen in the face of the worst adversity. It's about loyalties that burrow down into the most granular of relations, to immediate family and kin, relations that sometimes cut against the grain but that, in a harsh, unforgiving environment, a land of ice and snow and forbidding mountains and forests, make survival possible — even meaningful.

It's about a willingness to venture out into the complete unknown, as Leif Erikson and my grandmother and grandfather did, with the confidence that somewhere on the other side of the far horizon, freedom and a new home wait. It's the quality I call the Viking heart, and it lies at the core of this book — the people it describes, the journeys they take, and the significance of their legacies.

These characteristics of the Viking heart have been an essential part of Scandinavian culture almost from its beginning. They are by no means the exclusive property of Scandinavians or of Scandinavian immigrants to this country. In truth, they did not completely define the Vikings themselves, whose more rapacious and brutal exploits have been handed down in history and legend. But over the centuries, Scandinavians have figured out how to make the most of this constellation of human virtues.

Many historians see the Vikings as a one-act drama. They make their contribution to civilization with their raids and voyages, including those reaching as far as North America, and then they conveniently exit the historical stage. This book takes the opposite tack. Studying Viking history reveals that the defining characteristics of the Viking heart have actually survived through the centuries and still shape our world today.

The other crucial mistake many make is to insist that the defining legacy of the Viking heart is somehow racial. This is the error the Nazis made (and in this book we'll learn why), and the one that their fringe neo-Nazi offspring still make, with sinister consequences. In truth, the Norsemen of the Dark Ages never formed a single race or even one national identity. What defined them was a way of life and an outlook that we can delineate as cultural and spiritual, and they still have relevance and meaning today.

The first half of a book about the Viking heart, obviously, has to be about the original Vikings themselves. The history herein reflects the contributions that recent scholars have brought to our understanding of the Vikings. This deeper comprehension of who they were only makes their achievements, from the Dark Ages to the early Middle Ages, that much more impressive, exceeding what the myths and legends have described.

The first of these notable contributions came to light through recent archaeological discoveries, which have tremendously expanded our knowledge of the Vikings. These new findings follow in the footsteps of the spectacular ones that first fired the imagination of Scandinavians, and the rest of Europe, in the nineteenth and early twentieth centuries, weaving the romantic myths of the Vikings that linger today. This growing archaeological record makes it clear: The real Vikings were neither superheroes nor rampaging, bloodthirsty savages. They were farmers, herders, and fishermen who turned to war and plunder to enrich themselves in a world where wealth was scarce and where ethical standards about how to get it were even scarcer. The Vikings were, in most ways, like people elsewhere: men and women looking to better their lives through finding new land and opportunities. The temptation of taking loot from people who were defenseless and vulnerable, and who in fact despised the Vikings, was irresistible.

Another way to deepen our perspective on who the Vikings were, and what made them who they were, is to take a fresh look at the original texts of Viking history, the Icelandic sagas. The sagas are far more than just folk literature or bardic recitals. As a body of literary art, they are for their era unparalleled in their exploration of the secrets of the human heart, while also providing invaluable insight into the nature of Viking culture during its heyday.

The third and final contribution to our revised view of the original Vikings is the science of DNA. This innovative investigation into the impact of the Norsemen's world is still very much underway. But it has already shown that the Scandinavians who set off on their incredible journeys from the British Isles and France to Russia and North America were interested in far more than loot and plunder. Their lingering genetic presence in the communities living in these places today shows that the Viking expansion was driven by people seeking new homes and new lives for themselves and their families. That search would eventually take them across the Atlantic to Iceland, Greenland, and then the shores of America — just like their modern counterparts nine hundred years later.

Possibly the greatest result of these DNA investigations has been demolishing the myth that the Vikings formed a single race or nation. That myth underlay the Nazi ideology of Nordic racial purity — the same ideology whose racist adherents are even now operating on the fringes of Scandinavian and European society, as well as in America. If the study of the real history of the Vikings has contemporary political value, it is first of all in undermining those racist ideologies that, from time to time, raise their ugly heads in various corners of today's world — they triggered an unspeakable atrocity in Norway in 2011. The Norsemen themselves, and their offspring, represent a greater genetic melting pot than anyone could have guessed. More still, the Viking legacy is genetically more widespread in Europe than previously imagined.

One consequence of white nationalism's appropriation of Scandinavian heritage is that it has consistently obscured the real role that Scandinavians have played throughout history. Far from being a master race or, alternately, slinking off the historical stage when they were done with terrorizing Europe, the Vikings and their descendants have had, as the distinguished medievalist R. W. Southern once put it, "a knack for being in the right place at the right time." They would continually change the course of world history as a result.

The Vikings first displayed that knack, of course, at the end of the eighth century, when they seized on Europe's vulnerability after the death of the emperor Charlemagne to launch a series of daring overseas expeditions. Their raids reached east to Russia and as far west as Ireland, with the goal of not only enriching themselves at others' expense but also finding new homes for their families — a constant theme in Scandinavian history.

After acting as a largely destructive and disruptive force for two centuries, the Norsemen suddenly pivoted and became a galvanizing presence in European civilization. They helped shake Europe out of its Dark Age malaise, finding innovative ways to transmit ancient Greek and Arab knowledge and science to the West, while expanding and fortifying the boundaries of Christendom, thereby laying the foundations of the medieval West. Starting in the eleventh century the Normans, descendants of the Norsemen, became living conduits of astronomical, medical, mathematical, and physics texts and instruments, including the astrolabe, bringing them from Italy and the Mediterranean to northern and western Europe. By doing this they triggered an intellectual renaissance that would sustain European civilization for the next four centuries.

In fact, an informal title for this early history, from the Middle Ages onward, might be "Scandinavians to the Rescue." The descendants of the Vikings came to the aid of the papacy in the 1000s, when the Catholic Church most needed help. In the 1100s they transformed their earlier paganism into a powerful cultural force that would inspire Western music, art, and literature for centuries, right down to today.

Then, having rescued Latin Christianity, the men and women of the North went on to save the Protestant Reformation, when it seemed doomed to be swept into the dustbin of history. They also turned Protestantism itself into a powerful force for reshaping the future of humanity — what I have described as the Lutheran work ethic, which still characterizes the men and women of contemporary Scandinavia.

The story of the Viking heart doesn't end there, however. Having conquered and reshaped Europe, Scandinavians would then descend on the new republic of the United States. There they came to the rescue of the American frontier and the Union cause in the Civil War, opening up the prairie states and winning a war for liberty, a cause that Scandinavians deeply identify with. A commitment to freedom is buried deep in their own history and reflected in many of the institutions of the Vikings centuries before.

Scandinavian Americans went on to transform the American self-image at a critical time in the twentieth century, while back in Europe their former countrymen rallied against tyranny and stopped in its tracks the Nazi effort to build an atomic bomb — while also working, at home and from far away, to save Jews from the Holocaust.

The impact of Scandinavian Americans on America, I will finally argue, goes far beyond their actual numbers — even though today the eleven million Americans who claim Scandinavian heritage would, if they formed their own nation, outnumber the population of any one of the countries where the Vikings originated.

In fact, more than any other group of American immigrants, Scandi-Americans pointed the way toward a new paradigm for the American "melting pot," one that featured a robust cultural assimilation without a full shedding of their ethnic identity or their roots in the homeland. Like my grandmother, they were proud to be Americans. But as her tiny Norwegian flag reminded the rest of us, a part of her still remained in the country of her birth, a place where members of her family could still be found. In a profound sense, Scandi-Americans have managed to use their pride in their ancestral home and its history — including its most famous inhabitants, the Vikings — to embed themselves *deeper* into American culture, to become important contributors to American society as farmers and businesspeople, as philanthropists and engineers, as artists and politicians and leading figures in sports and entertainment.

That sense of belonging to America but while retaining pride in the past, even a once-violent past, remains an outstanding example for how immigrants can still shape the future of the American Dream in the shadow of American exceptionalism.

In that sense, the second half of this book could almost be called "The Tale of Two Grandmothers." This is because my paternal grandmother, Helen Sorlie Herman, was the descendant of Norwegians who came to America in a much earlier wave of immigration, in the 1850s. That was when fleeing poverty and the specter of starvation drove thousands of Scandinavians to make the almost impossible journey to America on sailing ships — vessels the Norwegian dramatist Henrik Ibsen once dubbed "coffin ships." Many lost their lives on those ships, from disease and hardship as well as natural disaster. They arrived in an America that was rougher, less civilized or forgiving, and — when my great-great-grandfather Oscar Sorlie arrived — on the verge of civil war.

All the same, this earlier generation of immigrants made this America their own and became fully assimilated a generation before the Great Migration. By the time my maternal grandmother reached the American shore, the Sorlies were comfortable and wealthy North Dakota gentry — with the largest farm, it was rumored, in the Red River Valley. Oscar Sorlie's granddaughter Helen Sorlie went on to marry one of Minneapolis's most promising young surgeons. In fact, Anna Flaaten (née Carlson) was probably stripping beds and cleaning sinks as a maid in the same hotels where Helen Herman (née Sorlie) was attending dinner parties and banquets.

In the end, theirs is a story of cultural assimilation by stages, like the story of America itself. Anna Flaaten had few books in her house, but one was John F. Kennedy's *A Nation of Immigrants*. She was deeply proud of her status as an immigrant *and* her status as an American.

• • •

The story of the Viking heart has many byways and twists.

Most recently, Scandinavians have come to the rescue of modern life and culture by providing a new model of how to organize one's political economy — and how to confront the worst pandemic in more than a century.

We'll also see that the Viking myth itself has become embedded in the heart of our popular culture; its characters and lessons permeate the world of superheroes, fantasy, and science fiction, from J.R.R. Tolkien's *Lord of the Rings* trilogy to George Lucas's *Star Wars* movies and J. K. Rowling's Harry Potter stories.

This can't come as a great surprise. *The Viking Heart* tells the story of how a people not only transformed the world but also in the process transformed themselves. Step by step, the descendants of the Vikings shed the vestiges of their primeval savagery, superstition, and ruthless greed while retaining the virtues of courage, trust in family and community, and willingness to risk it all to achieve their destiny as individuals and as members of a community. It's the story of how they passed those virtues on to their offspring and ultimately to the rest of us. They offer a model of how to be both modern and human, to combine the compassion and sophistication that we usually associate with the so-called Scandinavian model, yet to retain certain qualities that made the Vikings the scourge of civilization, and then its saviors.

Again, in displaying these qualities, the Scandinavians are not unique. Other cultures and peoples and immigrants to America have demonstrated them as well, in different times and places. They're certainly not racially rooted or DNA-bound. But what does make Scandinavians unique, from the Vikings onward, is the uncanny ability to bring all these qualities together and translate them into concrete action.

From that point of view, the recent Nordic revival — in fashion, food, popular culture, and fascination with the story of the Vikings — has gotten one thing right. Nordic culture has an inner vibrancy that persists to this day. In the end, this cultural revival charts a clear path for the future of liberal nationalism in Europe and elsewhere, as Scandinavians themselves are discovering for themselves, somewhat (it must be admitted) to their own surprise.

That Nordic revival has made its way to America and offers powerful lessons for this country as well. It shows how elements of the Scandinavian American experience can provide inspiration for keeping the American Dream alive and helping us stay on an even cultural and spiritual keel (a metaphor the Vikings themselves would appreciate, since they invented the ship's keel). A deeply polarized community can look to the story of the Great Migration, and those who made it happen, for a parable of hope, future direction, and resolve.

But the story of the Vikings offers another message that's even more universal. Throughout history, these remarkable people and their descendants have exhibited a fascinating level of courage and resilience, which enabled them to venture into the unknown, explore and settle the most remote and hostile environments on earth, and enjoy the freedom to make a satisfying life for themselves and their families. And they did this not just for themselves but also to give back to their fellow human beings, through the fruits of their labor. Their scientific discoveries, philanthropy, and works of art and literature and philosophy have changed how we think and feel about ourselves and nature and our community — even about our relationship with God.

It is said that all of life is a journey. The Vikings and their Scandinavian offspring are among the world's most powerful and important journey makers, and we can still identify with and learn from them.

In today's world of Facebook and Instagram, the Vikings may seem superhuman. In truth, they embodied a quality of human spirit that can live in all of us.

It's called the Viking heart.

—Arthur Herman
March 13, 2021

THE VIKING HEART

1

The Wrath of the Norsemen

Hungry wolves take big bites.

— Traditional Viking saying

ON A BRIGHT June day in the year of our Lord 793, the thirty or so monks at the island monastery of Lindisfarne in northeastern England noticed a row of ships on the horizon.

Some of them may have gone down to the beach to greet what they assumed were friendly visitors. Theirs was a peaceful world, remote from turmoil and suffering. Their lives were dedicated to prayer and meditation, and grateful local nobles donated gifts of gold and silver and precious gems to the monastery as gestures of devotion. The monks on the beach probably didn't notice the shields mounted along the ships' sides or the dragon's-head carvings at the prows.

As the ships came ashore one by one, and fierce men leaped over the sides, armed with swords and battle-axes, the monks of Lindisfarne realized their mistake. But it was too late.

The English chronicler Simeon of Durham, in his *Historia Regum Anglorum,* described what the men from the ships did next: "They came to the church of Lindisfarne, laid everything waste with grievous plundering, trampled the holy places with polluted steps, dug up the altars and seized all the treasures of the holy church. They killed some of the brothers, took some away with them in fetters, many they drove out, naked and loaded with insults, some they drowned in the sea . . ."

The raiders were gone almost as soon they had arrived, but the damage had been done. The sacking of Lindisfarne sent shock waves across England and the rest of Europe. Everyone in Christendom was suddenly aware of the people who had done this: the Northmen, as they became known, from the remote and hitherto obscure lands of Scandinavia. Contemporaries called them Northmen or Norsemen, and a variety of other names. The modern world knows them as Vikings. With their shock-and-awe landing on the beach at Lindisfarne, the Vikings announced their arrival as the scourge of civilization for the next two centuries.

The Lindisfarne raid actually wasn't their first. The *Anglo-Saxon Chronicle* reports attacks by "Northmen" in Wessex four years before — one on the town of Portland in 789 consisted of just three ships. A church record from 792 mentions defensive fortifications being built in Mercia, on England's east coast, for protection against "pagan seamen," meaning the same Scandinavian raiders.

But the raid on Lindisfarne struck at the vulnerable heart of civilized Christendom, signaling the beginning of a campaign of relentless pillaging and plundering across the British Isles. In the following year, 794, the Anglo-Saxon double monastery of Monkwearmouth and Jarrow near the town of Newcastle came under similar attacks. And in 795 the monastery of Saint Columba, on the Scottish island of Iona, became the next to fall to what churchmen called "those valiant, wrathful, purely pagan people."

The term "pagan" was right. To this day, no one knows who those very first Viking raiders were, or who led them. But they clearly had no respect for the sanctity of Christian rites and artifacts. In fact, the Vikings seemed to actively seek them out, as well as their caretakers, with the utmost savagery. Looting, destroying altars and holy relics, slaughtering civilians or, alternatively, selling them into slavery — this became the standard modus operandi for the Norsemen marauders. The terror they must have struck into the hearts of civilized Europeans is hard to fathom. According to one horrified chronicler, the Norsemen "spread on all sides like fearful wolves, robbed, tore, and slaughtered not only beasts of burden, sheep, and oxen, but even priests and deacons, and companies of monks and nuns."

Alcuin of York, one of the emperor Charlemagne's closest advisers and English by birth, wrote this chilling diagnosis: "Never before has such a dreadful deed come to pass in Britannia as the one we have now been exposed to in the hands of a pagan people, nor was it thought possible that such an inroad from the sea could be made." Deemed the wisest man in the West, Alcuin was reduced to quoting Jeremiah 1:14: "Then the Lord said unto me, Out of the north an evil shall break forth upon all the inhabitants of the land." In the decades after the Lindisfarne attack, it was easy to believe Jeremiah was speaking directly to the Vikings' victims.

The Norsemen were breaking out in three streams from three different parts of their northern homeland — today known as Denmark, Sweden, and Norway. By 834, seventeen years after Charlemagne's death, the Viking raids had grown into full-scale expeditions involving dozens and scores of ships, as every summer chieftains from Scandinavia led their followers to the sea. Raiding parties of Norsemen were able to set up permanent camps at the mouths of strategic rivers, from which they could sail — or even carry — their boats farther and farther upstream.

Every monastery, church, and town in the British Isles with any treasure or stealable goods, so long as it was reachable by sea, suddenly lay at the mercy of the raiders from Scandinavia — and there was nothing kings or popes or local authorities could do to save them.

In short order, Danes sacked London (in 841), Nantes, Rouen, Paris, and, deep in the heart of Gaul, Toulouse. By that date Swedish raiders had penetrated up the Volga and founded a settlement at Novgorod. They captured the town of Kiev, where one chieftain, Rurik, would go on to establish a permanent capital, raiding and enslaving the Slavic inhabitants nearby. Danish raiders attacked Seville in Spain in 844, and then Nîmes and Pisa in the Mediterranean. Over the next two decades, Viking raiders from Kiev ranged across the Black Sea. They reached Constantinople in 860. By then, another intrepid band had reached Baghdad, home of the caliphs.

By 878 more than half of England, as well as large portions of the rest of the British Isles, was under Scandinavian occupation. Ireland and Scotland had ostensibly become Norwegian colonies. Before the Norsemen were done, they would expand their range west into the Atlantic, even as far as North America.

Eleven centuries later, Winston Churchill would write: "When we reflect upon the brutal vices of these salt-water bandits, pirates as shameful as any whom the sea has borne, or recoil from their villainous destruction and other cruel deeds, we must also remember the discipline, the fortitude, the comrade-ship and martial virtues which made them at this period beyond all challenge the most formidable and daring race in the world."

In fact, the more we reflect on the Viking breakout, the more astonishing it becomes. Never before in history had a part of the world with so small a popu-lation (barely a hundredth of humanity today, and even less then) made more of an impact on human civilization in so short a time. It's no wonder they have been celebrated in myth and legend, in fiction and nonfiction, as well as film. And it's no wonder, in retrospect, that the Vikings seemed to take on the aura of superwarriors, even superheroes.

But who were these extraordinary people, destined for such extraordinary deeds? What did the Northmen achieve, and why did they set out on their world-changing journeys in the first place? These questions aren't just for his-torians. They are at the crux of grasping Scandinavia's lasting impact on the world, including America, as well as its impact on the modern imagination. To begin to answer these questions, we first have to know something about the lands from which the Vikings came.

One of Scandinavia's earliest observers from the world to the south, the Roman naturalist Pliny the Elder, described it as "a world unto itself." Its harsh environment made severe demands on those daring and strong enough to live there. Scandinavia is a land of sweeping contrasts, from ice-frozen mountain ranges stretching above the Arctic Circle, to innumerable lakes and forests of fir and birch, together with wind-swept pastures that fast-moving rivers cut across. From the Northern Cape of Norway to the southern border of Den-mark, Scandinavia measures half the length of Europe from north to south — with a total landmass bigger than that of Britain, France, and Spain put to-gether. Yet much of that landmass is virtually uninhabitable.

When many non-Scandinavians think of Scandinavia, they visualize a dra-matic mountain-lined coast fractured into deepwater fjords, shielded from the fury of the North Atlantic by a line of small islands and rocks. In short, they picture Norway. Most of its west coast is indeed serrated like a knife by sea inlets known as fjords, some driving as much as a hundred miles inland. Just off the coast is the Skerry Guard, a line of islands and reefs that offer a sheltered, safe passage out to sea. Hence the name "North Way," or Norway, which harks back to the centuries when ships, including those of the Vikings, used the Skerry channels to make their way seaward.

Most of Norway is ruled by the formidable line of mountains rising up from the sea in the west and sinking slowly to the east, to the Gulf of Bothnia, which separates Sweden from Finland. The Vikings characteristically gave the mountain range a nickname derived from shipbuilding: "the Keel." A large part of the Keel lies above the tree line, while thick coniferous forests blanket most of the rest. Only 3 percent of Norway, along the fertile plains around the Oslo and Trondheim fjords, is actual arable land, even today. The rest is one-quarter forest and more than two-thirds bare mountain ranges, including the Hardangervidda, or Hardanger Plateau, where one of the most important dramas of World War II played out — it would in fact determine the outcome of the conflict.

Farther east is Sweden, slightly larger than Norway, at 173,860 square miles (roughly the size of California) versus the 148,729 square miles of its western neighbor and long-time rival. Sweden has a northern coastline very similar to Norway's, with fierce mountain ranges permanently blanketed in ice and snow. Farther south, however, the landscape opens up to innumerable lakes and dense spreading forests, a fertile land for those strong enough and willing to carve out a farm or pasture from the intervening strips of bog and marsh. But the alternating lakes and forests also made most of inland Sweden almost impassable until modern times. Even farther east lies Finland, geographically similar to Sweden but ethnically distinct. Forests, lakes, and bogs dominated its landscape, making overland travel there even more challenging.

The fourth part of Scandinavia, Denmark, is by contrast flat and relatively unforested. In the remote past it was host to great deciduous forests, but these were cut down during the Viking Age. Then as now, its narrow northerly peninsula, called Jutland, extends into the North Sea and the Baltic and nearly touches Sweden on its eastern shore; its southern base is joined to the main European plain. Denmark's relatively open geography is one reason why it was the first part of Scandinavia to be politically unified, while its physical connection to the rest of Europe made it, over the centuries, the part of Scandinavia most exposed to influences from the Continent.

But even here, in Scandinavia's traditional farm belt, the temptation to travel overland was limited by southern Jutland's sparse and infertile soil — for centuries an empty buffer zone between the world of the Danish Vikings and the non-Scandinavian south.

The rest of Denmark consists of no fewer than six hundred islands, the largest being Fyn, or Funen (slightly smaller than New York's Long Island), Sjaelland, or Zealand, where Denmark's capital, Copenhagen, is situated, and Lolland. At Hoby in Lolland, a pre-Viking Danish chieftain had been buried with great ceremony, surrounded by splendid presents from the local Roman imperial commander, including two large silver cups decorated with scenes from Homer's *Iliad* — a sign that the Romans already sensed it was best to stay on the good side of the men from the North.

Whether it's Norway, Sweden, Finland, or Denmark, the Scandinavia we see today largely reflects the geography carved out by the last great Ice Age. Until thirteen thousand years ago, the entire region was almost completely covered by a sheet of ice. Then a wave of global warming slowly opened the landscape to humans. As the ice receded, bands of Mesolithic hunters spread across a topography evolving from barren frozen steppes and tundra into deciduous and coniferous forests, framed by an expansive seacoast rich in shellfish and opportunities for fishing; islands and harbors offered secure bases for fishing craft.

Stone Age Scandinavia was defined by bodies of water, especially the sea. In a profound sense, water has defined the life of the inhabitants of Scandinavia ever since. As the dramatist Henrik Ibsen once said, Norwegians live under the spiritual domination of the sea. Even today, the majority make their living by and through the sea. So do sizable numbers of people in the other Scandinavian countries.

Around 8000 BCE the peoples perched along the Baltic and North Sea coasts started navigating their way through the fjords of Norway, up into the lakes and rivers of Sweden, and around the six hundred separate islands of Denmark. They fished and hunted seals and whales in little boats or canoes made of ash, rubbed down with whale blubber or oil to make them seaworthy and held together with strips of leather, with cowhides stitched together over the frame. These were the primitive ancestors of the formidable longships that would carry Viking adventurers as far east as Russia and Turkey, and eventually west to North America.

Then a catastrophic event interrupted the Scandinavians' aquatic wanderings. In about 6000 BCE a massive earthquake shoved a two-hundred-mile stretch of mountainous ridge on Norway's west coast into the ocean, creating a tsunami that inundated the land bridge connecting what would become the British Isles to the mainland. Known as the Storegga Slide, this geologic event completely remade the map of northern Europe. Two great primeval rivers — the Thames and the Rhine — once shared the same estuary but now were pulled apart by the North Sea. This in fact was Scandinavia's first major contribution to the history of the rest of Europe. By giving the British Isles their "splendid isolation," the Storegga Slide ensured that the course of English, Scottish, and Irish history would follow a pattern very different from that of continental Europe — and that the history of the British Isles would also be constantly connected by water to the Nordic world to the east.

Two thousand years later, in about 4000 BCE, rising sea levels forced another change to the way of life in Stone Age Scandinavia. The inhabitants had to move farther inland. A migratory life built around hunting and fishing slowly changed into a rooted life based on farming. This shift laid down an enduring demographic foundation for the Vikings. For all their long-distance travels and overseas wanderings, they remained a people of farmers. Then and later, where a Scandinavian could find a place to build a farm, he or she had found a place to stay.*

Those Stone Age farmers had their work cut out for them. As the geographer W. R. Mead has pointed out, "the characteristics of the frontiersman have

---

* Or almost all of them. A hardy few, later known as the Sámi, pushed their way in from the coast and farther north. Close to the Arctic Circle, they found a way to preserve their nomadic lifestyle, following herds of reindeer native to the region. This is the origin of Scandinavia's Lapland people, whose lands are spread across the northernmost parts of modern Norway, Sweden, and Finland. They kept alive an essentially Neolithic way of life until well into the twentieth century.

persisted longer in parts of Scandinavia than in any other part of Europe." Perhaps this made the American frontier seem in many ways more like home to their descendants, like my grandmother Anna Carlson Flaaten and my great-great-grandfather Oscar Sorlie, than it was for other European immigrants.

In the lands that would become Denmark, tiny communities laboriously carved out strips of arable land from the bogs and marshlands. Neolithic Swedish farmers focused on clearing land in the fertile land around three lakes: Mälaren, Hjälmaren, and Vättern. In Norway, farming settlements sprang up in the small patches of low-lying land found at the neck or along the steep sides of deepwater fjords. In Norway, however, more than in the rest of Scandinavia, fishing still predominated as an essential way of life, just as it does today. And Norwegians quickly learned that what miserly Mother Nature refused to provide, they would have to go out and get for themselves.

As for the Finns, although ethnically and linguistically distinct, their way of life became indistinguishable from that of their Swedish neighbors. History meanwhile would turn the Swedes into Finland's rulers until the rise of Russia — ironically, another outpost of Swedish conquest — made that brave and tough people a bone of contention between the two empires right up to the twentieth century.

Altogether the population of Scandinavia slowly but steadily grew until 1700 BCE or so, when for the first time implements made of bronze — the fusion of copper and zinc — became available. The Scandinavians were roughly a millennium behind southern Europe and the Mediterranean in the manufacture of this metal, and all bronze had to be imported from their southern neighbors. So did the gold that turns up in small but precious quantities in early Bronze Age grave sites in the region.

This time lag would be typical of Scandinavia's technological progress, or lack thereof, for the next thousand years. Wherever their contemporaries were in terms of the progress of civilization, whether in Egypt's New Kingdom, Mycenaean and Homeric Greece, or later, Republican Rome, Scandinavians would always be several centuries behind the curve. Later, they would make up the difference (except in their development of writing, which would have important cultural consequences). But this situation did make it hard for their more civilized neighbors to treat the men and women of the North as equals — that is, until it was too late.

In the end, the water surrounding the Vikings shaped them the most. In fact, the word *Viking*—which means "people of the Vik"—comes from the Norse word *vik*, which signifies "bay" or "creek." Bronze Age Scandinavia was, above all, a world of sea voyagers and sea warriors almost two thousand years before the first Viking appeared off the shores of the European continent or the British Isles.

We get an indication of how important the sea was when we look at the Bronze Age stone carvings at Tanum in Sweden. The vessels they depict look amazingly like Viking longships, though they date almost a thousand years before the first Viking voyages. We can get a similar sensation when visiting another Swedish site, the extraordinary Gotland graves, more than four hundred of them on the island of Gotland alone, each one made of upright stones (some as high as three feet) laboriously set out in the shape of a ship. The

Bronze Age carving, Tanum, Sweden. Anders Blomqvist / Getty Images

tallest stone was often used to demarcate the ship's prow and stern. Similar ship-shaped graves are found elsewhere on the mainland and along the Baltic coast, but archaeologists think they had a special meaning for the inhabitants of Gotland, whose island is itself in the form of a longship — and it would be a major jumping-off point for Scandinavian migration over the centuries.

Water aside, the early inhabitants of Scandinavia had a life carved out of perpetual scarcity and an unforgiving climate, even for those living in the most fertile parts of the region. Clinging to family and clan and tribe wasn't just essential to political and social life — it was crucial to survival. We have to imagine the ancestors of the Vikings as clusters of families and clans at the southern foot of Scandinavia and its neighboring islands, all speaking early variants of Old Norse and all holding stubbornly to the land they'd cleared from the wilderness. Like the warriors of Homer's poems from about the same time, they fought endless tribal quarrels by day and caroused by night, as bards by the fireplace sang epic stories of heroes and gods — the prototypes of the sagas of the Norsemen.

The events shaping the civilized world were taking place far away to the south and east. The rise of Greece and Athens, the conquests of Alexander the Great, the rise of the Roman Republic and Empire, and the birth of Christianity: all echoed distantly and indistinctly across the forests, lakes, and fjords — if they penetrated at all.

Beginning in the third century BCE, some tribes of southern Scandinavia began a slow but steady migration toward the Roman imperial frontiers. A period of global cooling may have encouraged them to think about finding a less icebound environment. Or they may have been drawn by the occasional trade in objects from their more advanced southern neighbors, the Romans and the Celts. But, whatever the reason, other tribes clung stubbornly to their homeland and refused to move. These are the true ancestors of the Vikings. The others — one could argue the more sensible ones — chose to retreat from the cold and move southward, where they found new forests to clear and, still farther south, open pasture for sheep and cattle.

Among the first to migrate were the Teutones and another tribe from their Danish homeland, the Cimbri. Both the Teutones and the Cimbri collided with Roman armies in Gaul, as well as Spain and northern Italy, in about 150–

100 BCE. That collision set in motion a pattern of sustained contact between people originally from Scandinavia and the more populous and settled groups to the south. A new chapter in European history, as well as Roman and Scandinavian history, was about to be written.

A Roman historian later gave a scarifying account of the aftermath of a battle between the Cimbri and their Roman enemies near Orange, after the Cimbri had captured the Roman camp. It sounds ominously like the Norsemen raids of the future. "They set about destroying everything which they had taken," the historian wrote. "Clothing was cut to pieces and cast away, gold and silver was thrown into the river, the breastplates of the men were hacked to pieces . . . The horses were drowned in whirlpools, and men with nooses round their necks were hanged from trees. Thus there was no booty for the victors and no mercy for the vanquished."

Momentarily knocked off balance by this aggressively militaristic society out of Scandinavia, the Romans recovered and dealt swiftly and decisively with the threat. The Roman consul Gaius Marius routed the Teutones at Aix-en-Provence. And when the Cimbri crossed the Brenner Pass, Marius and his consular colleague Quintus Lutatius Catulus defeated them as well, on the plains of northern Italy.

But the Teutones and the Cimbri were here to stay. Following in their footsteps and wagon tracks, other tribes began a similar journey out of Scandinavia. There were the Marcomanni, the Langobards from Skåne, the Burgundians possibly from Borgundarholm (Bornholm), and the Goths from Oster and Västergötland in Sweden. The most important of these early migrants would become known as the Goths. They reached the boundaries of the Roman Empire somewhat later than the Teutones and the Cimbri, and farther east. Eventually they would migrate to the Oder and the Vistula Rivers and eventually beyond. But all of them sprang from the same Scandinavian stock.

The Romans realized at once that these different peoples, with their strange guttural language (descended as we now know from Old Norse), their outlandish religious rites involving blood sacrifice, and their fierce warrior ways, were all related. The name of the original invaders from Scandinavia, Teutones, or Teutons, would stick to their successors. Others would call them Germani, or Germans. But it was obvious to all observers that they stemmed from the same place, namely, Scandinavia. It is why, four centuries later, the chronicler Jordanes would call these raiders' original home "the womb of nations," the mother matrix from which the German impact on Europe would descend.

Julius Caesar had to deal with them early in his career, as governor of Gaul. "They spend all their lives in hunting and warlike pursuits," Caesar tells us, "and inure themselves from childhood to toil and hardship." In fact, Rome's traditional enemies, the Celtic Gauls, "do not even pretend to compete with the Germans in bravery." It was these men (and women) from Scandia who now posed the real threat to Rome.

Julius Caesar's successor, Augustus Caesar, learned firsthand just how big a threat the Germans could be when their chieftain Arminius, or Herman, the precursor of the great heroes of German and Norse myth and legend, destroyed three crack Roman legions in the Teutoburg Forest in 9 CE. Ninety years later, the Roman historian Tacitus would pen his own description of the German tribes in one of the most influential works in ancient literature, *De Germania*, or *On Germany*. The German in Tacitus's time was still a warrior first and foremost: "No business, public or private, is taken up except in arms." The German's wife and slaves handled the business of the household, while he spent his time carousing, gambling, and above all, fighting.

According to Tacitus, in German society no man ranked higher than another except through prowess in battle. "The power even of the kings is not absolute or arbitrary," he declared. "It is their example rather than their authority that wins them special admiration — for their energy, their distinction, or their presence in the van of fight." Given this heroic model of leadership, a chieftain would be shamed if he failed to be as brave as the rest in battle, while his chosen companions had to be no less brave than the leader they followed. In fact, the companion who survived his leader in battle was disgraced for life. To defend and support the chief or leader, even unto death, was the sacred obligation of the companion band — or *comitatus* in Latin.

Courage in battle, loyalty, leadership through example rather than birth or status: these are the first qualities of the Viking heart, German style, to be recognized in Western literature. The Romans called it *virtus*, or virtue, or the quality of being a man (*vir*). But German women had their role as well in this aristocracy of the brave. "It stands on record that armies wavering on the point of collapse have been restored by their women," Tacitus wrote. "They have pleaded heroically with their men, thrusting their bosoms before them and forcing them to realize the imminent prospect of their enslavement—which they fear for their women far more than for themselves." He noted that the Germans had an almost reverential regard for their women and "believe that there resides in women an element of holiness and prophecy, and so they do not scorn to ask their advice or lightly disregard their replies." This respect for women would be typical of their Viking cousins as well, and would later be reflected in their laws.

But ancient Roman and then Renaissance thinkers would all conclude that without manly virtue, no society or institution could survive the steady drumbeat of unexpected and disruptive events that the world throws at all of us. Shakespeare called them "the slings and arrows of outrageous Fortune," including disasters both man-made and natural, from wars and bankruptcy to earthquakes, hurricanes, and deadly pandemics. For the Norsemen, this manly virtue would be the foundation stone of the Viking heart. To Romans like Tacitus, however, it was the Viking's cousins, the Germans, who seemed the embodiment of this robust quality. The question was, Would it be a constructive or destructive force in the future?

By the mid-third century CE, the Romans had their answer. Two great restless conglomerations of German tribes had emerged on their frontier. One, centered in southeastern Europe, consisted of Goths, Vandals, Burgundians, Gepids, and Lombards facing onto the Danube. The other, made up of Frisians, Saxons, Alamans, Thuringians, and Franks, was entrenched along the Oder and the Elbe Rivers, with their restless war bands poised to strike from the eastern banks of the Rhine.

In 245 the Roman effort to keep the Germans out and the frontiers firm suddenly collapsed. That year Gothic tribesmen trapped and destroyed the emperor Decius, along with his army in the marshes of the Dobrudja, in the Balkans. Soon after, Frisian and Frankish longships moved out from the Rhine estuary to attack the exposed coasts of Britain and Gaul, while their Gothic counterparts set out from Crimea in their seagoing vessels to raid the helpless cities of the Aegean, even laying siege to Athens itself—exploits that anticipated the feats of the Vikings six centuries later.

Nonetheless, the bulk of the German threat might have stayed more or less permanently on the other side of the Rhine and Danube frontiers if another far more deadly menace had not come thundering out of the steppes of Asia. This was the Huns. Under their great chieftain Attila they would set in motion an avalanche of German peoples westward that the Roman Empire was helpless to contain — it would change the face of Europe, and civilization, forever.

Tribes rounded up their flocks, packed their families and belongings in ox-drawn carts, and abandoned their homes to stream for the borders of the Eastern Roman Empire — a mass migration of refugees the Romans were completely unprepared and unwilling to deal with. An armed confrontation was inevitable. It occurred on August 9, 378, near the town of Adrianople. After Teutoburg Forest, it was the second great decisive battle between the Germans and the Romans, and again the Germans won, this time destroying not only the Roman army but killing the emperor himself. The Eastern Romans were able to save their capital, Constantinople, but only by deflecting the Visigoth and Ostrogoth invaders — and other German tribes in their wake — westward toward Rome itself.

One by one the German tribes pulled apart the ancient provinces of the Roman Empire and settled their families. One grouping of West Germans, the Franks, seized northern Gaul, and the Visigoths seized the south — the two halves of what would become France. Other Visigoths crossed the Pyrenees, occupied the Roman province of Spain, and crowned themselves kings. The Vandals moved on even farther and crossed to North Africa. The Ostrogoths made their homes in Italy, as would their German successors, the Lombards.

After a series of bloody conflicts with the Huns (memorialized in the German epic poem *The Nibelungenlied*), the Burgundians headed for the mountain slopes of today's Savoy and Switzerland. The Alamans would settle there too, leaving their distinctive linguistic mark on Swiss German pronunciation to this day.

Still another tribe, the Saxons, joined forces with the Angles from Slesvig and its nearby islands, and they turned the Roman province of Britain into a conglomeration of separate Anglo-Saxon kingdoms, each led by a powerful warrior chieftain and his followers. In fact, the Angles of Slesvig would leave their Scandinavian tribal name — Angli in Latin, Angelcynn in Welsh, and Englisc in Gaelic — to the domain they conquered: England.

England, France, Spain, Italy, Switzerland: the modern map of Europe, with its eventual separate nation-states, was taking shape under German leadership. Still other German tribes that sprang to life in the wake of Attila's invasion and retreat — Thuringians, Bavarians, the Saxons themselves — would settle across the forests and clearings of Germany proper. The Roman Empire in the West ended in 476, and Europe found itself with a new ruling class and a new destiny.

At the center of this Germanized Europe were the Franks. Nomads originally rooted in Holstein, in southern Denmark, they broke out into the Continent in the Huns' destructive wake. The Franks' migration from Scandinavia had carried them steadily south and west, until they reached the banks of the Rhine and the sand dunes of the Rhine estuary. It wasn't until they hit the great Roman road running from Boulogne to Cologne that the Franks finally halted — a pause still reflected in today's Belgium, divided into two languages, Flemish and French. Later still, some surged farther south, a few as far as the river valleys of the Seine and the Loire. But the majority made the territory of modern Belgium their homeland, with Tournai as their capital.

The Franks were above all warriors. Like their Viking cousins, they chose their kings by vote in their warrior assemblies. In 451 the king they chose was one Meroveus, or Merovech (meaning "the sea fighter"). It was Meroveus who made the momentous decision that year to join his people with their traditional rivals, the Visigoths, to help the Roman governor, Flavius Aetius, defeat the Huns and their fearsome chief, Attila, at the battle of the Catalaunian Plains. It was Meroveus's grandson Clovis who then converted his kingdom to Catholicism, while the Franks slowly consolidated their power. Then events in Spain suddenly thrust the Franks into the leadership of Europe. Muslim Arab invaders and their Moorish allies overran Visigoth Spain in 711 and thrust across the Pyrenees into the heart of Frankish Gaul. A Frankish chieftain named Charles Martel, or Charles the Hammer, on account of his warrior prowess, checkmated the Muslim advance outside Poitiers in central Gaul.

Then in 771 one of Charles Martel's descendants, Charlemagne, or Charles the Great, took up the title of king of the Franks. He would turn the Frankish conquests into a thoroughgoing empire, the backbone of medieval civilization, and dedicate himself to restoring a sense of internal order that western Europe had not known since the end of the Roman Empire.

Charlemagne himself is one of the most extraordinary figures in history. With his blond hair, broad shoulders, and walrus mustache, he might also have been the very picture of a Viking chieftain, captaining his longship through uncharted stormy waters. The comparison is not fanciful. The values of personal loyalty, and the bonds between a king and his warrior companions, were as important to Charlemagne as they were to any Viking king. Charlemagne "treated those to whom he had bound himself in such friendship with the greatest reverence," according to his biographer Einhard. His entourage of devoted friends and drinking companions, both laymen and clergy, was the kind that an Icelandic bard would have celebrated. In fact, one poet did so a century or two later, in *The Song of Roland*.

In addition to internal reforms within the broad boundaries of his empire, Charlemagne spent his reign shoring up its frontiers, to the south and west, against the Basques, Moors, and Saracens. To the north, however, lurked an even deadlier threat: the pagan Saxons and their neighbors, the Danes.

Almost as soon as his reign started, Charlemagne launched a series of campaigns to the northeast against the Saxons, who conducted repeated raids into Frankish territory for loot and slaves. The northern boundary of Saxon territory, the river Eider, was also the southern boundary of the Danes. Inevitably Charlemagne's nearly thirty-year war against the Saxons was bound to have reverberations across the Eider.

By 800 Charlemagne's war against the Saxons had, at huge financial and human cost, largely succeeded. The leading Saxon chiefs had all submitted to baptism, and the Saxon threat had been largely dispersed by means of a series of mass deportations in 794–95 — the Carolingian version of ethnic cleansing, which was more humane than the German tribes' usual method of dealing with a recalcitrant foe: mass extermination.

But the subjugation of the Saxons, and Charlemagne's scouring out of Frisian pirate dens along the North Sea coast and the Scheldt estuary, eliminated the last remaining buffers between Charlemagne's empire, the mainstream of civilization, and the Scandinavian tribes. The first great Scandinavian hero in history, King Godfred of the Danes, was just the man to take advantage of this.

All contemporary evidence reveals Godfred as a man of enormous energy and ambition — a prototype of the Viking leaders to come. Sensing early on that trouble was headed his way from the south, he began building a long defensive wall across the southern border of his realm, which became known as the Danevirke, to seal off threats from Charlemagne and the Franks. It was a remarkable achievement, consisting of "a rampart, so that a protective bulwark would stretch from the eastern bay, called *Ostarsalt,* as far as the western sea [that is, the North Sea], along the entire north bank of the Eider River and broken by a single gate through which wagons and horsemen would be able to leave and enter."

The Danevirke would be one of Godfred's key claims to fame,* providing a convenient defensive barrier for Danish rulers over the centuries, including its Viking kings.

King Godfred's other major achievement was to seize the port of Hedeby, on the eastern side of the Jutland peninsula. His goal was to make Hedeby the biggest trading center in Scandinavia and the Baltic region. The port was located at the confluence of two major trade routes, one flowing west to east, linking the Frisian coast of northwestern Europe with the eastern Baltic and Russia, and the other leading up from the border with Saxony to Norway and the Kattegat, a waterway between Denmark and Sweden. To ensure Hedeby's monopoly of northern trade, Godfred descended on the neighboring Abodrits (who also happened to be Charlemagne's allies), wiped out their wealthy trading post at Reric, and administered a crushing defeat to their chieftain, Drosuk. From that point on (808 or thereabouts) Hedeby quickly exploded into economic prominence, with merchants exchanging everything from walrus tusks to amber, furs, and slaves — individuals who were dragged in almost

---

* This is still true, even though archaeology has shown that it incorporated an earlier barrier of felled trees that, judging from the age of the timber, were cut down in the summer of 737, perhaps in anticipation of Charles Martel's war against the Saxons the following year.

certainly from farther east, from among the Danes' fellow pagans along the Baltic. The port would be one of the most important entrepôts of the Viking Age, filling the coffers of every Danish king from Godfred onward.

To service this growth of seaborne trade came a Scandinavian revolution in shipbuilding. The classic large longship, with its raised prow and stern, lined with the shields of the warriors who formed its crew, had been a fixture in the surrounding seas for centuries. But around this time new features were added, namely, a large square sail and a mast. These additions made it possible for Scandinavian merchants to venture farther out than ever before, to bring goods from northern Norway and the Gulf of Finland to the markets in Francia (the former Roman province of Gaul) and even England.

For coastal and riverine trade, or for voyages along narrow waterways like the Kattegat, the standard Scandinavian longship, powered by rowing, worked fine. But the sail gave that vessel a boost in propulsion and power, which facilitated travel not only for merchants but also for royal navies, not to mention independent-minded pirates. An important technological foundation for the Viking Age had been laid, and King Godfred showed just how potent it could be by taking on the most powerful ruler in Europe, Charlemagne himself.

Godfred had already had a major confrontation with the Frankish ruler in 804, after waging a successful campaign against his Frisian neighbors at the northern doorstep of Charlemagne's empire. In a brazen show of strength, Godfred deployed a large fleet of ships off Sliesthorp, on the border between his kingdom and Saxon territory. It was a challenge Charlemagne did not dare to ignore, although he had numerous troubles to deal with along his southern borders in Spain and Germany. He took his stand with his army on the south bank of the Elbe. Although an effort to organize a personal summit with Godfred failed, the armies did not clash that day, or the next. But with no peace treaty finalized, war between the Germans and their Scandinavian cousins was inevitable.

According to Einhard, the arrogant Godfred began to talk about conquering all of Germany, even watering his horses in the well of Charlemagne's palace in Aix-la-Chapelle. The threat convinced Charlemagne it was time to build his own naval fleet, which he reviewed in the Scheldt estuary and off Boulogne in preparation for a Trafalgar-like decisive battle with the Danish king. He also assembled whatever troops he could and established a camp at the confluence of the Aller and Weser Rivers under the protection of his ships, where he waited for Godfred's next move. According to the annals, Godfred, "intoxicated by the hope of victory," bragged that he would fight Charlemagne hand-to-hand on the field of battle. Even at age sixty, Charlemagne was ready to meet Godfred in mortal combat if that's what it took to destroy the Danish menace.

But the great showdown between Frank and Dane didn't happen. In 810 Godfred was murdered by a member of his entourage (some sources claim the killer was one of his own sons), and his son Hemming ruled in turn for only one year before he himself was murdered. It was the kind of internecine quarrel that would be the plague of Viking politics for the next three centuries. At the time, it meant the Danish threat to Charlemagne's empire had vanished, seemingly overnight.

Still, Charlemagne felt a premonition that what he had created might not survive the threat to come. He himself had no fear of these "dog-headed fiends," as he called the Danes. "But I am sad at heart to think that even during my lifetime they have dared to touch this shore," he confessed to his companions, "and I am torn by a great sorrow because I foresee what evil things they will do to my descendants and their subjects."

He was right. Even as Charlemagne was being crowned Holy Roman emperor in the church of the Lateran in Rome in 800, a menacing new sight had appeared on the fringes of his empire, off the North Sea coast of Frisia and Gaul.

It was a ship with a raised prow and stern, and a square, blood-red sail. The Vikings were at last on the move.

Danes, Norwegians, Swedes: all three nations would "go Viking" in their own distinct way, and along their own distinct routes.

The Danes were the first Scandinavian people to enter the annals of mainstream European history, starting during the reign of Charlemagne. Their proximity to the Continent gave them easy access to the river basins of Francia proper and the England of their Anglo-Saxon cousins, as well as Spain and the western Mediterranean. The initial raiders on Portland and Lindisfarne were almost certainly Danes, or possibly Norwegians, who tended to push their expeditions farther north into Scotland and west to Ireland, and eventually even as far as the Atlantic.

The Swedes, the Scandinavians least familiar to western Europeans, directed their energies eastward along the Baltic route, pushing their longships up German and Russian rivers until eventually their capital and trading post at Kiev put them within reach of Constantinople, the greatest city in Europe.

On voyages and expeditions, however, all the evidence indicates that there was no sense of national exclusivity. A Danish raiding party would probably have Norwegians on board, and a Swedish longship would have a crew that included Finns and even Slavs. Virtually anyone who sailed off on a raid thereby became "a Viking." Later, even some Scots and Englishmen would accompany the Norwegian adventurers who colonized Iceland. Diversity was the rule, not the exception, during the Viking Age. Even at its outset the Viking spirit was a matter of intention and execution, not blood or race.

Danes, Norwegians, Swedes. In all three cases, the aim was the same: to grab loot and plunder while the getting was good. Every spring, when the snow and ice at home had melted, the ships would set out from their respective homelands. Then weeks or even months later, the longship would cruise into a foreign harbor or river basin. Armed men would leap over the side and, with pounding hearts and furious yells, throw themselves onto their victims.

> *Wolf-battening warrior,*
> *Wield we high gleaming swords.*
> *In snake-fostering summer*
> *Such deeds well beseem.*
> *Lead up to Lundr:*
> *Let laggards be none!*
> *Spear-music ungentle*
> *By sunset shall sound.*

Europe had of course seen violence, even piracy, before, but never so sudden and far-reaching in scope. A sense of shock and disbelief pervaded Europe's educated and political elite. Here was a threat that Charlemagne and his heirs, and rulers as far away as Spain and Byzantium, found themselves helpless to stop.

Charlemagne's heirs did what they could to fight off the Vikings. The Carolingian emperors, among them Charlemagne's son Louis the Pious and grandson Charles the Bald, were hardly weak or incompetent men. Both personally led armies to contain the Norsemen threat. Their heir Louis III was a true warrior hero; he defeated firsthand a Danish invasion at Saucourt in 881.

But they had other threats to worry about. There were Saracen raiders coming up from the south, who were virtually the equals of the Vikings in maritime skill and daring. For almost two centuries the central and western Mediterranean were highly vulnerable to Muslim intrusion following the Moorish conquest of Spain in 711. No community facing onto the sea was safe. At one point, Saracen raiders even sacked Rome itself, using Saint-Tropez as their main hideout. Louis III, the victor of Saucourt, also had to fight a series of rearguard campaigns to keep Italy from becoming, like Spain, a Muslim province. But despite his prowess in battle, he couldn't hold Sicily.

Then, thundering out of the central Asian steppes to the east came Magyar horsemen, as fierce as their kinsmen the Huns. They would sweep almost unopposed across the exposed Slavic and Germanic lands, and within sixty years they were striking as deep as Francia, the heart of the Carolingian Empire, and Italy, where they collided with the Saracens, completing the utter humiliation of Charlemagne's heirs. The darkest era of what we call the Dark Ages had descended on Europe. The Viking raids were a crucial factor, but hardly the only factor, contributing to the bleak outlook on the ground.

Besides, there didn't seem to be much that Charlemagne's heirs could do against the Norsemen's incessant raids from the sea, unpredictable and swift and ubiquitous as they were. Far too often, by the time the emperor learned what was happening, it was already too late to retaliate. The Norsemen's siege of Paris in 845 proved just how helpless the central government had become against the Viking onslaught.

By that date Danish marauders had harried the coastline of the Carolingian Empire for years, and even penetrated its river valleys, in search of loot. The key to unlocking the wealth of western Francia, the former Roman province of Gaul, was Paris. Once the ancient Roman settlement of Lutetia, it had never been the capital of Charlemagne's empire, nor of his successors. But Paris guarded the approaches to the Marne, Seine, and Yonne Rivers: the Carolingian heartland. As the archbishop of Rheims had once warned Emperor Charles the Fat, if he lost Paris to the Vikings, he would lose everything.

The first Viking who grasped this was Ragnar the Dane. Ragnar may or may not have been the real Ragnar Ladbrok, the most celebrated Viking hero of them all, star of sagas and even a television series. His historical reality is permanently shrouded in legend. But future TV star or not, Ragnar sailed up the Seine in March of 845, eager for battle and confident in victory. He had more than two hundred ships and four thousand men headed up the river for plunder. To stop him, Emperor Charles the Bald pulled together an army, which he split in half in order to guard both banks of the river. Ragnar saw his chance. He quickly sprang on the smaller force before the other troops could come to their aid and destroyed it, taking (the chronicle says) 111 prisoners. He decided to hang all 111 on an island in the Seine, in plain sight of the second force, as a form of psychological warfare. Ragnar's ruthless cruelty worked. Charles's remaining troops retreated in disorder as Ragnar triumphantly entered Paris and sacked the city on March 28 — Easter Sunday, as it happened. It was a symbolic victory over the Christianity Ragnar despised as well as a literal victory over a hapless Carolingian emperor.

As his men gathered their plunder and slaves, Ragnar was in no hurry to return home. Charles had to resort to paying him seven thousand pounds of silver to force the Viking chieftain to leave. Charles was much blamed for paying this ransom — the first instance of the extortionate payment that came to be known as danegeld. But what could Charles do? He had war with the Bretons brewing in the west, raids by Saracens in the east, and another Viking chieftain with 150 ships to contend with who had sailed up the Garonne River and attacked Toulouse. That contingent, by the way, would soon make its way to Spain and up the Guadalquivir River to Seville.

By now those who yearned for order and stability in the Frankish territories were close to despair. A monk in the island monastery at Noirmoutier wrote this as the 860s began: "The number of ships grows; the endless stream of Vikings never ceases to increase. Everywhere the Christians are victims of massacres, burnings, plunderings; the Vikings conquer all in their path, and no one resists . . ." He recounted the doleful list of cities that had fallen into Viking hands: Bordeaux, Périgueux, Limoges, Angoulême, Toulouse, Rouen, Beauvais, Meaux, Chartres, Angers ("annihilated"), Tours (ditto), and Orléans (ditto).

Even allowing for some despairing exaggeration on the part of a recluse viewing these tribulations from behind the monastic walls, the description painted a frightening picture. Even worse, the path to Paris still lay open for the next adventurous Viking. Forty years after Ragnar's raid, another Dane, a ruthless chieftain named Sigfrid, set out with an expeditionary force so large (according to one chronicler, the abbot of Paris's monastery of Saint-Germain, some seven hundred vessels) that it filled the Seine for nearly six miles.

It was late November 885, a good time for a Viking army to escape the frigid cold of the North for the outskirts of Paris — with the promise of fresh loot and glory. A good time too for the former victims of the Vikings to finally take a stand.

The second day after he arrived outside Paris and beached his longships on the river's shore, Sigfrid approached the city walls and presented the bishop, Joscelin, and the count of Paris, Odo, with his demand for ransom. With his heavy Norse accent, he mockingly beseeched the prelate: "Guazelin, have compassion on yourself and on your flock. Allow us only the freedom of the city. We will do no harm and we will see to it that whatever belongs to you or Odo" — gesturing to the count — "shall be strictly protected."

Bishop Joscelin must have smiled at this cynical offer. He replied, "Paris has been entrusted to us by the Emperor Charles . . . If like us you had been given the duty of defending these walls, and if you had done what you ask us to do, what treatment do you think you would deserve?"

It is easy to picture the Danish chieftain scratching his head and smiling ruefully in his turn. "I should deserve to have my head cut off and thrown to the dogs," he admitted. But, he added menacingly, if they did not give in to his demands, he would destroy the city and make sure pestilence and famine stalked the land for years to come.

The bishop and the count were unmoved. They took up the defense of the main tower, joined (according to the chronicler) by Odo's brother Robert and the bishop's nephew Abbot Ebolus — after all, the church did not prohibit a clergyman from willingly taking up the sword against a pagan enemy, especially one like the Vikings.

As morning broke the Norsemen began their attack. With a terrible cry, Sigfrid rushed the city walls and the stone tower. We have to assume his men used some kind of catapult, as well as volleys of arrows. The bishop himself was struck down by an arrow. "There perished many Franks" but also many Vikings, as Odo and his brother and companions distinguished themselves in the fierce hand-to-hand fighting.

It wasn't until dusk that the Vikings withdrew, carrying away their dead and wounded. "The tower had been sorely tried, but its foundation was still solid." Working through the night, the townspeople repaired the damage with planks and boards, and built a wooden tower, even taller, next to the battered one, made of stone. Their work done, the Parisians grimly braced themselves for a renewal of the battle in the morning.

Sure enough, at daybreak the Vikings swarmed the field again and rushed the two towers. "On every side arrows sped and blood flowed." Citizens and soldiers rushed back and forth to repel the invaders, as church bells rang and attackers and defenders shouted fierce war cries. At the center of the resistance was Count Odo, "who surpassed all the rest in courage." He rallied the soldiers and townspeople when their strength flagged, and he cleared away Viking attackers with his sword. When the tower was most threatened, he ordered "oil, wax, and pitch, which being mixed and heated, burned the Danes and tore off their scalps. Some of them died; others threw themselves into the river to escape the awful substance."

The tower, and the city, had stood firm once again — even though, the chronicler tells us that "within the walls there was not ground in which to bury the dead." Instead of renewing the attack, Sigfrid and his men settled down to a siege, besetting the city from both sides of the river. For eight months the Parisians endured starvation and the outbreak of disease. Twice Count Odo managed to slip past the Viking encirclement and reach Emperor Charles to beg for help — only to fight his way back into the city. It was the second visit that finally prompted Charles to take action. He realized that if Paris fell, it could doom his entire kingdom.

Charles assembled an army that reached the heights of Montmartre—then the outskirts of Paris—by October that year. By then Sigfrid had had enough. Looking for a way out of the deadlock, he offered the Parisians relief for a paltry sixty pounds of silver, which they proudly refused. For once, they felt they had the upper hand against the Norsemen, especially with Charles's army poised to strike. Still, the standoff continued until spring, with disease decimating the ranks of both armies and inflicting more suffering on the inhabitants remaining in the city.

In the end, Charles preferred to strike a deal rather than fight. Instead of sixty pounds, to everyone's amazement (especially Sigfrid's) he offered seven hundred, along with free passage over the Seine for any Viking vessels—exactly what the Parisians and locals had fought so hard to prevent. They were so furious about the deal, in fact, that they blockaded the Seine, shutting down the Vikings' escape route. Sigfrid and his men had to laboriously haul their ships overland—all under Charles's protection, by the terms of the agreement—until they finally reached the Marne, to begin the voyage home.

The Danes at last were gone, but the politics of the siege lingered. It had ruined Emperor Charles's credibility for good, and in 887 he was unceremoniously deposed. The western half of his empire, Neustria, found a new king, Count Odo himself, the hero of the siege and the strong face of resistance to the Danes. His sword had given Europe new hope, and his example a new role for men of power.

But the Norsemen's menace to the Frankish world was by no means over. The Vikings still roamed Europe's rivers at will: the Seine, the Marne, the Loire, the Maine, the Aisne, and the Vire, as well as the Scheldt and the Moselle. They had virtually become Viking inland waterways. In less than thirty years, a fresh wave of raiders, this time from Norway, would descend in large numbers on Francia's northern coast and play a large role in shaping the future of the Continent.

But Paris would never see a Viking fleet again. The siege of Paris marked a turning point in Europe's resistance to the seagoing raiders from the North. It also prompted the passing of the dynasty that had ruled the heart of Europe for more than a hundred years, and the rise of a new one—the descendants of Odo and the counts of Paris, whose great-nephew Robert Capet would be crowned the king of France in 987.

The wrath of the Norsemen was forcing Europe in a new direction. The power to shape events, which seemed to elude Charlemagne's heirs, was making a comeback as local rulers and communities took destiny into their own hands. Meanwhile, resistance to the Viking onslaught had found another testing ground among the Norsemen's Anglo-Saxon cousins in England.

The Vikings' attacks there had begun as early as 789, at Portland, with just three ships — the Norsemen's first recorded overseas raid. Their attacks quickly grew in fury and effectiveness from the Lindisfarne raid onward, until by 865 a Viking army of perhaps as many as ten thousand warriors — an immense host to keep fed and armed — was roaming the northeastern portion of England almost at will. Contrary to legend, which portrays them as superwarriors, the Vikings proved to be far from invincible in battle. In fact, over the next two centuries in England they lost about as often as they won.

But the overall margin of victories over defeats was enough to keep the Norsemen in virtual control of England, off and on, for more than a century, until their English opponents learned what the inhabitants in Francia did in the siege in Paris: the art of self-help. It was a skill first mastered by one Alfred, king of Wessex, whose success against the Danes helped earn him the honorific by which he has been known ever since: Alfred the Great.

In 871 he took the throne of the West Saxon kingdom, or Wessex, a land that had been severely pounded by Viking raiders for more than six decades. The attacks had been gradually mounting in number and daring until, in 841, London itself was sacked.

It did not help that England was divided into no fewer than five kingdoms; its northernmost, Northumbria, lay the most exposed to Viking attack from bases in Denmark. The Danes in particular were the bane of a peaceful life in England in the 800s and later years, as bold leaders and crews descended on unprepared coastal towns, taking hostages as slaves and whatever loot could be extracted from a confused and cowed population.

By the 860s the Danes had seen their chance for not only loot but also outright conquest, and the Anglo-Saxon kingdoms became their permanent prey. A "great heathen army," as the *Anglo-Saxon Chronicle* dubbed the invaders, had arrived under the command of two Danish brothers, Halfdan and Ivar Ragnarsson — supposedly the sons of the same Ragnar who had conducted the raid on Paris in 845, though there's no way to prove it.

The king of East Anglia had managed to buy off Ragnar's boys with a liberal offering of horses, but when the Great Army turned north, it was able to enter the kingdom of Northumbria virtually unopposed and occupy its capital, York. By 876 York had become in turn the capital of a Viking kingdom. The city would remain the main hub of Norse activity in England until the very end of the Viking Age.

In 867, four years before King Alfred assumed his throne, Halfdan and Ivar struck south into the kingdom of Mercia. A joint force of Mercian and West Saxon warriors — the one time that Anglo-Saxon kings banded together for protection — managed to rebuff the Viking advance, but the Norse warriors only swung south and east to East Anglia, which they overran in 869, killing its king, Edmund.

Now two English kingdoms were under the Vikings' control. A renewed invasion of Mercia in 873 increased the count to three, as Mercia's resistance collapsed. But the conquest of Mercia came only after the Danes had to confront the ruler of Wessex, Ethelred, and his younger brother Alfred, in pitched battle.

Ethelred was a warrior king with a strong and able English host under his command; his brother Alfred was an equally canny subordinate. Together they met Halfdan and the Danes in battle no fewer than nine times in 870. The Englishmen's most dramatic success was at the battle of Ashdown, after which Halfdan sued for a truce. His attention was shifting to the more vulnerable kingdom of Mercia. Certainly, when Ethelred died later that year, no one suspected that the Vikings were about to meet their match.

Ethelred was succeeded not by his infant son but rather his brother Alfred, a clear indication that the Wessex political elite knew they were facing a major crisis: the survival of Anglo-Saxon England was at stake. Fortunately, the Vikings' Great Army evened the odds somewhat by splitting apart after the conquest of Mercia and the capture of its capital, London. Halfdan took one half back north to consolidate his hold over York, while the other half, led by a Danish warrior-king named Guthrum and two other warlords, headed for Cambridge in East Anglia. King Alfred and the inhabitants of Wessex were about to have a respite. Meanwhile the full-blooded Viking settlement of England was about to begin.

What is today Yorkshire, Nottingham, Lincoln, Derbyshire, and Leicester were all now under Danish rule and ceased to be part of England proper. Soldiers from the Great Army broke off from military life to start plowing and farming. In Cambridgeshire, for example, they occupied the land "between the dykes and the Ouse, as far north as the fens." Although relatively few in number, the Danes were able to settle in rather comfortably with the local Anglo-Saxon population. Old Norse and Old English were, after all, fairly similar. Lack of communication was rarely a problem between Danish and English neighbors as it would be, for example, between Norman and Frank, or Rus and Slav. Besides, by seizing the land of the local nobles who had fought them, the Danes easily stepped into the role of landlord as well as farmer and livestock cultivator. And whatever disagreements over land or water rights might arise, a former soldier of the Great Army always knew his sword or broadax was available for final appeal.

Alfred used the pause in the action to good effect. He organized a large local militia, dubbed the *fyrd,* and fortified key points along the Wessex-Mercia border. It was not until 875 that Guthrum and his Vikings crossed to strike the West Saxons, who suffered a bad defeat; Alfred had to flee and hide in the Somerset marshes. But he regrouped and Guthrum's army proved weaker, due to the number of warriors who had remained at home to farm instead of going off to plunder.

Alfred and Guthrum finally met again in battle at Eddington in May 878, seven weeks after Easter. Alfred had gathered soldiers from Somerset, Wiltshire, and Hampshire, and after a furious battle, the Danes finally broke and ran. Alfred pursued them back to Chippenham, which Guthrum had occupied almost without opposition, and after a tense two-week siege Guthrum finally submitted. He agreed by formal treaty to withdraw from Wessex, and even to submit to Christian baptism, although it's fair to be skeptical about how serious this conversion really was.

What mattered to Alfred was that his kingdom and, more broadly, southwest England were finally safe from the Viking invaders. Guthrum was able to return unmolested to East Anglia, where he partitioned the land once more among his Danish warriors. Nearly two-thirds of today's England was in effect a Danish colony; later records would refer to it as the Danelaw (Denelagu). Huntingdon, Cambridgeshire, Bedfordshire, and the rest of Northamptonshire became Viking territory, along with Norfolk, Suffolk, and Essex, not to mention London itself. For the next two centuries these lands would have a different law, a different language, different personal names and place names, and different customs and cultural attitudes than the rest of England. In fact, traces of this Viking legacy survive today.*

Outside the Danelaw, pressure from the Vikings began to wane, thanks to Alfred's victory at Eddington and the resulting truce. Already — less than a century after their longships had burst onto the scene at Lindisfarne — the men (and increasingly the women) from the Norse lands to the east were shedding the role of conqueror and settling down as colonists. Though much turmoil and bloodshed lay ahead, a major shift had occurred. In both France and England, the Norsemen had suffered their first major checks, even as the Swedish arm of their invasion of Europe had shifted from marauding the Baltic coast and Slavic Russia into asserting outright rule.†

One Europe, Dark Age Europe, was passing. A new Europe was taking its place — all thanks to the Vikings.

---

* See Chapter 3.
† See Chapter 4.

2

Being Vikings

When spring came, and the snow and ice were loosed, then
Thorolf launched a large warship of his own, and he had
it made ready, and equipped his house-carles, taking with
him more than a hundred men; and a goodly company
there were, and well weaponed.

— *Egil's Saga*

WHAT WAS IT like to *be* a Viking?

First of all, they never called themselves Vikings. That term became popular in the nineteenth century, when Victorians discovered the allure and charisma of the Norsemen. Among the Norsemen themselves, calling someone a *vikinr* (in the masculine form) simply referred to someone embarking on a long sea voyage. Under the circumstances, however, and perhaps inevitably, the term came to refer to a pirate or robber — or in West Norse, the linguistic ancestor of the Norwegian word *vikingr*.

Other Europeans, who had to meet them face-to-face in sometimes very grim circumstances, had other names for them. Their German cousins called them Ascomanni after the ash timbers from which their longships were built. The Irish dubbed them Finngail (meaning "fair and dark strangers") and the Scots Lochlannach ("lake people"), while the Arabs and Slavs called them Rus, a word derived from a term from rowing—another tribute to the Vikings' maritime skills.

The ship lay under the cliffs. On board the armed men climbed,
Warriors ready; waves were churning
The sea with sand, as the sailors
Stowed their arms and armor amidships, then set their well-fitted ship
Off on its eager journey. They moved along the seas
With the strength of the wind behind them, the ship moving
Like a great bird, until in time,
On the second day, their curved prow had run its course
And the sailors see the land before them,
Bright rock shores, steep sea-cliffs,
Broad wide headlands. The deep ocean had been travelled,
Their voyage was at an end.

We can still feel the power behind the images in this passage from the most famous poem from the Viking Age, *Beowulf.* They evoke an era of seagoing marauders from the North, ranging far and wide until the sight of land promises new adventures ending in plunder, glory, or death. That's been the standard image of the Viking Age for centuries. But what was the reality behind it?

Set aside for a moment the heroes we encounter in the epic poems and Norse sagas. If we want to meet a real Viking, a good place to start is the warrior grave at Repton, England. Repton was a key strategic location for controlling one of the Anglo-Saxon kingdoms, Mercia, which the Vikings' Great Army had overrun in 873. Inside the fort built there by the Danes are a number of graves, including one containing two men. One had died in his twenties and other between thirty-five and forty-five years of age: well-seasoned, for a Norse warrior.

The younger one had died violently, probably in battle. His skull bears the marks of a massive blow to the right side of his head by a sword or ax. The older man died in an even more horrible way. In addition to two mortal injuries to his skull, he sustained a cut to his leg, right down to the femoral artery.

There are also indications that he may have been disemboweled or even cas-
trated.

However terrible his death, the warrior and his young companion were
buried by the fort's guardians with full honors. The older man's sword lay beside him, together with a fleece-lined wooden sheath and a pair of daggers,
one of which was folded in half: a Viking switchblade. Around his waist was a
leather belt, of which only the bronze buckle survives. Around his neck hung a
tiny silver hammer of Thor — an amulet to protect him in battle (in this case,
not very successfully).

Perhaps even more evocative, and even cinematic, are the very recent
finds in Salme, Estonia, of two Viking ships and their dead crews. These mass
graves date from the beginning of the Viking period, around 750, when Estonia was the scene of constant fighting between Swedish Norsemen and local
tribes. The two boats were buried side by side. In the first, smaller vessel, the
bodies of six men were placed in pairs, seated and gripping their oars, with
another seated at the stern — as if they were sailing together into the afterlife
in Valhalla.

The second, bigger ship contained the bodies of thirty-four Vikings —
most in their thirties and forties, and all bearing terrible battle injuries. They
had been placed carefully side by side, their swords laid beside them and playing pieces from a chesslike game strewn over the scene. One other man, obviously their leader, was settled in the ship's center, alongside the finest weapons.
He too was buried with a gaming piece — this one the figure of a king. It had
been placed delicately inside his mouth.

Viking graves like these, or like the one found at the remains of the big
Norsemen barracks at Sjaelland in Denmark, which contains the skeletons
of more than 154 young warriors, many of them buried with their weapons,
give us a vivid glimpse into the real human beings of the Viking Age. It's a
world of weapons, warriors, and warships, obviously. But it was also a realm in
which men and, as we'll see, women constantly ventured into the dangerous
unknown; sharing with others whatever fate awaited them, whether death or
life, made the journey worthwhile. Physically the Vikings were certainly distinct. People, especially those who weren't Vikings, tended to note their strong
stature and fair skin, their blond or reddish-bronze hair, and their blue eyes.

One Arab trader who encountered them described them as "tall as date palms, blond and ruddy . . . I have never seen more perfect specimens."

Tall, it seems, is a matter of dispute. The archaeological record indicates that the average Viking male was only about 1.70 meters tall (five feet, seven inches) — not exceptionally large for that time. And though blond hair may have been considered the ideal, the physical remains at gravesites show that many Scandinavians had to resort to bleaching their hair with lye to achieve those golden locks. Foreigners knew that the Norsemen came in more varieties than the stereotypical blond beast. They were all too familiar with Vikings with darker, almost Mediterranean features — the physical type that would later be known as "black Norwegian" or "black Swede."

The Vikings themselves paid close attention to these physical differences, and like people everywhere, they attributed character traits to physiological appearance. For example, in *Egil's Saga* the patriarch Uluf's son Grim is described as "swarthy and ugly, resembling his father in both appearance and character" — although at the same time Grim is "a cheerful, generous man, energetic and very eager to show his worth."

Still, we have no evidence that the Vikings ever considered themselves one people or race, any more than modern scientists can find a single "Viking" DNA profile. Throughout their history, they demonstrated a great intermingling of ethnicity, leading to a highly varied DNA pool, which flowed from trading posts as far flung as the Middle East and the eastern Mediterranean; Vikings likewise intermarried with the local population in the various places where they settled. As one expert, Dr. David Reich of Harvard Medical School, has recently concluded, "The findings from ancient DNA leave little solace for racist or nationalistic interpretations." This is especially true of the DNA of the Vikings.

In sum, the Scandinavian conquerors of Dark Age Europe were hardly superhumans, or racial supermen of the kind that neo-Nazi ideologues like to imagine. While their DNA remains do indicate a genetic link to the German tribes that had left their shared homeland to spread across Europe, what made the Norsemen stand out from their German cousins was rooted in culture, not race. The Vikings were the Scandinavians who had stayed behind, to be born and bred in the homelands and inured to their harshness. They also all spoke the same language, Old Norse, whereas the German tribes used dialects so distinct, they could barely understand one another.

The Norsemen shared the same way of life too, fishing on rivers, lakes, and seas and farming on their primitive farms. And they worshiped the same pagan gods. Given this cultural and linguistic unity, the differences that came to distinguish Norwegians from Swedes, and Danes from both, would emerge only gradually.

But by the year 700 all these communities faced the same challenge: a growing population that could no longer be supported by the meager resources of the land and sea around them. A millennium earlier, global cooling had driven from Scandinavia the people who became the German tribes; now an era of global warming ushered in more movement. In this climate, more children could be fed and thus survive the harsh winters, along with their father and the many mothers in a single family (the ancient Vikings were polygamous). With a growing population, local chieftains came under pressure to find wealth to reward followers and display status. In short order, the sea-rovers among them discovered the place to get it — the northern littoral of Charlemagne's great empire.

From the start this widespread migration was an entirely entrepreneurial, almost spontaneous movement. Interestingly, the reigning kings of the day, men like Charlemagne's rival King Godfred of Denmark and semi-legendary Norwegian dynasts like the Ynglings, seemed to play no role in the original Viking breakout, although they did nothing to prevent it either. Yet year after year for two centuries, shiploads of Norsemen left their Danish, Norwegian, and Swedish homes to set out across dangerous seas and distant latitudes until only China, it seems, eluded their grasp (though it appears they *almost* made it that far — in the grave of one forgotten Viking chieftain at Helgö, archaeologists found a splendid bronze Buddha from Kashmir).

Climate change and demographics no doubt motivated these people to venture out from Scandinavia. But a more wide-ranging and penetrating explanation for this diaspora comes from the great French historian Georges Duby: "They were seeking adventures by which to earn their reputation, treasure from which to replenish their hospitality, slaves with whom to furnish their homes, and lands upon which to quarter their weapons." In that sense, the Vikings weren't that much different from the earlier wave of emigrants from Scandinavia, who became the Franks and Goths and Teutones, or the other peoples of the medieval and premodern world who left their homelands behind.

But one stunning difference made the Norsemen unique. That was the incredible speed at which the Viking expansion happened. The Vikings managed to overrun western and eastern Europe, and a good part of the Mediterranean, in just a few decades; by contrast, the German migrations had taken two to three centuries. The Vikings weren't just a migration. They were a revolution — one that shook Europe from end to end.

What made it possible, first and foremost, was their ships.

The ships the Vikings built were a revolution in maritime design. The general structure of their ancient predecessors can be seen in the stone ships of Gotland and the Tanum ship carvings from the Bronze Age, roughly 1800 to 500 BCE. An actual pre-Viking boat discovered at Hjortspring in southern Denmark dates from about 350–300 BCE, just about the time the Teutones, the Cimbri, and other German tribes had begun their move south. As preserved, it already has all the characteristics of the ships the Vikings would use. Sixty feet long and eight to nine feet wide, the Hjortspring boat was clinker-built, meaning it was constructed with overlapping planks to prevent seawater from getting in, even on the high seas.

This oak-planked, iron-bolted, clinker-built construction became the principal design for ships sailing the northern waters for almost the next millennium. It was certainly on boats like these that the Goths raided the Black Sea and crossed the Aegean, and the Frisians terrorized the North Sea coast during the age of Charles Martel.

The big change came when Scandinavian sailors introduced the square sail, which, when combined with oars for propulsion, turned the Viking ship into an unsurpassed maritime instrument. It made for swift and sure navigation across large bodies of water: comparisons with the flight of birds, made by poets and others, were inevitable. Also, unlike the Mediterranean galleys of the same era, Viking ships were built to last. They were broad in the beam, as buoyant as giant water lilies, and equipped with a new nautical technology:

the single oaken plank running along the bottom of the ship, from stem to stern, known as the keel (in Old Norse, *kjǫlr*), which the Vikings invented in the seventh century.

It was the keel that gave the Viking ship its stability in any kind of sea and any kind of weather. A single sixty-foot pine mast (from the Norse word *mastr,* meaning "tree") raised in the dead center of the vessel, with a three-hundred-square-foot sail attached, gave the vessel the wind power it needed to travel anywhere. A ten-foot oak rudder stretching down from the right side of the ship (known as the starboard side, from the Norse word *styra,* "to steer") allowed it to be steered any which way, including backward when necessary. When a Viking vessel had to make its way up a river such as the Seine or the Thames or the Volga, its mast could be struck and laid aside and the oars lowered, so that the crew's muscle power could take over. Viking ships, with a draft of eighteen inches fully loaded, were well designed for these waterways.

That shallow draft was important. Though we often imagine Vikings going on great sea and ocean voyages, including those that eventually reached North America, their most devastating raids were riverine. It was their ability to navigate inland waterways — and unexpectedly spring upon towns that supposed their distance from the sea made them safe — that made the Vikings the terror of Europe. This was the essence of the Vikings' "shock and awe": the ability to travel where they pleased and when they pleased, by any waterway they pleased. Communities far and wide learned this bitter lesson: London in 841, Nantes in 843, Seville in 844, and Paris in 845.

The Norsemen built their vessels to fit their different needs and missions. Given the relatively short radius of the Viking raiding zones from their Scandinavian base, big oceangoing longships, like the one unearthed in the Gokstad find in Norway in 1880, were rare. Most were much smaller, perhaps no more than eighty feet long — large enough for a crew of forty, who ate and slept on deck (Viking ships had no hold), but small enough to be carried overland, or even rolled over a series of downed tree trunks, as the raiders sought the next inland watercouse.

Equally useful was the Vikings' version of a seagoing freighter, the *knarr.* A fine specimen was found at Skuldelev, Denmark. Fifty-four feet in length, with a crew of a dozen or two, the average *knarr* had a broader beam than a wartime longship and was capable of carrying cargo of up to twenty-four tons. But though mainly a trade vessel, the *knarr* could still go great distances. It was very probably the craft that carried passengers and settlers to Iceland and Greenland, as well as to North America.

The other secret to the Vikings' success was their time-tested navigational techniques. These included reckoning by the moon and stars as well as employing a crude device similar to the astrolabe later used by Mediterranean sailors. This instrument was a wooden bearing-dial that could cast a shadow at noon; its measurement could give a Viking captain a rough-and-ready guide to latitude during a voyage.* Finding a ship's longitude was a different problem, one that remained unsolved until the eighteenth century. But even more important was information from other Viking raiders, who came back at the end of each summer with fresh news about coasts and tides and navigable inlets and rivers, which chieftains would use the next summer to expand the range of their voyages to acquire fresh plunder. Viking raiding was a cumulative process. Each wave of marauders learned from the previous one, as their ventures probed farther and farther and became bolder and bolder.

To be clear, the Vikings had no monopoly on seaborne raiding and piracy. The Frisians, the Saxons, the Goths, and even the Franks had been adept at the same skills. The key difference was the Vikings' staying power and their ability to turn quickly from piracy to trade and settlement — then, if necessary, back to piracy again. And that staying power sprang from the second secret of Viking success: the Scandinavian people themselves.

Their homeland's northern latitude, long winters, shortage of fertile land, and lack of good routes of transport except by sea made for tightly knit communities scattered across the barren landscape. Each village was populated by men and women who would spend five months of the year literally keeping one

---

* Did the Viking captain know about the light-polarizing quality of calcite (or Iceland spar), which would allow him to sight the sun even when it was obscured by clouds? Speculation is rife. A reference in a fourteenth-century Icelandic manuscript to a voyage made by Saint Olaf, two centuries earlier, suggests that he did.

another warm: an impetus toward strong communal solidarity and a fundamental toughness.

Family and clan ties mattered far more than anything we could describe as national or ethnic difference. Sweden, for example, at the beginning of the seventh century was only beginning to emerge as a distinct society, thanks to the union of two tribes, the Gotar and the Svear, whose home was Uppsala. The Danes (their name, *Dana,* means "creek" or "bay") were scattered along a series of inlets facing onto the North Sea, while the Norwegians lived in isolated communities separated by great stretches of empty wasteland.

But whether Danes, Norwegians, or Swedes (or later, Icelanders), Vikings were farmers and fishermen first, warriors second. In all three kingdoms, "the free peasant, peasant proprietor, smallholder, farmer," notes the historian Gwyn Jones in his history of the Vikings, was "the realm's backbone."

His and her typical farm was the longhouse, which brought humans and animals together under one roof. Smaller buildings tended to have a sunken floor, with the first floor half-buried in the ground — a practice Norwegian and Swedish immigrants would bring with them to their homesteads on the American prairie. Where lumber was easy to find, as in Norway and southern Sweden, builders used timber logs. Where it wasn't, as in Danish Jutland, walls of clay-plastered wattle or even turf rose up around timber frames. Thatch was the ubiquitous roofing material, unless the farmer could find birch bark to make the home proof against rain, ice, and snow.

We can get a good visual fix on what these structures were like at the farm village excavations at Vorbasse in Jutland. The sites there are dated from 700 to 1000. The settlement consisted of at least six farms, all growing grain in the surrounding fields, with livestock kept in a fenced enclosure. The archaeology of Vorbasse reveals another surprising feature of Viking farms: they moved over time. The ones at Vorbasse changed location just about every century or so, perhaps as the land gave up its fertility or as its owners changed hands — or simply out of Scandinavian restlessness.

The most respected members of a Viking community were of course the ones with the biggest farms, large enough to include multiple tenants. The opening chapter of *Egil's Saga* provides a vivid picture of what a prosperous farmer was like. "Ulf is said to have been a very clever farmer. He made a habit of getting up early to inspect what his farmhand or craftsmen were doing and to keep his eye on his cattle and cornfields." His son Grim was even more gifted: "he turned out to be an active man; he was gifted in working in wood and iron, and grew to be a great craftsman. In winter he would often set off on a fishing boat to lay nets for herring, taking many farmhands with him."

If this seems too peaceful a picture for a Norse saga, look again. In the very next passage, the author mentions almost casually that Ulf's eldest son, Thorolf, is about to go raiding with a longship that is a gift from his father. It's a useful reminder that in Scandinavian communities, "going Viking" did not mean "going rogue." It was an extension, not a rejection, of farming and the normal rural life. The exception would be the farmer or chieftain driven into formal exile (the institution known as *uluk*) for whom setting out for the distant horizon on his ship was a matter of necessity. Many of those exiles became the most intrepid Vikings, men who literally had nowhere else to go. It's the image we get of Ingolfr Arnarson, the first settler in Iceland, and of Erik the Red, the future discoverer of Greenland.

Even so, such men were treated with a respect that radiates from the pages of the Scandinavian sagas. It suggests that, far from a disgrace, exile simply opened a new chapter in life, one that might stimulate others (as with Erik the Red's companions) to join in the adventure. What's more, exile was never treated as permanent. The possibility of an eventual return to home always loomed, especially if the ruler or chieftain who had imposed the sentence died or was driven into exile himself. Nor did exile necessarily entail a solitary existence. Ties of family constantly kept a Viking exile thinking of his homeland and the prospect of return — and revenge. Or, barring that, he looked forward to the day when his family would join him in the new homeland he had found, on the other side of the ocean.

Roving raiders and exiles aside, the farmer and the farming life remained at the center of Viking culture. The farmers themselves ranged from very poor, with a handful of acres and a cow or two, to men of authority like Egil's grandfather Kveldulf, whose farm is the envy of his neighbors. Many a young Norwegian or Danish farmer would have to live with parents and family until he was able to afford a farm of his own (marriage to a woman with a sizable dowry helped). Families attended religious ceremonies together. They did their own carpentry and blacksmithing, made and wore their own weapons, manned and navigated their ships, and at the end of a voyage were able to demand their share of the booty. And all of them, rich and poor, also had rights, both legal and political.

Above all, as landowners they participated in the most important and characteristic Viking political institution, the Thing, whose vestiges lay among the German tribes, such as the Anglo-Saxons. In Old English, the Thing's regular meeting place was called a "thingstead" (*þingstede*) or "thingstow" (*þingstōw*), which are direct cognates of the Thing, or Althing, prevailing among the Vikings.

In these meetings the free men of a particular tribe would deliberate on matters affecting the entire community. These might include accepting or rejecting a newly proposed law, deciding the guilt or innocence of persons accused of crimes or leaders accused of malfeasance, or determining the next target for their collective search for revenge or booty. Most important, the Thing was the place where Norse tribes elected their kings. This practice was also known among German tribes such as the Franks. Centuries earlier, the Roman commentator Tacitus had recorded the astonishing fact that these tribal assemblies elected their chieftains and also served as courts of law, dispensing justice and punishing the guilty — with death in the case of murder, or with drowning, in the case of cowardice or unnatural vice.

The best-known Thing, and the best surviving example of this form of Germanic or Norse democracy, still exists in Iceland. There, in 930, the thirty-six leading landowners, known as *gothar,* meaning "chieftains," came together to create an assembly for collective decision making, which they named the Althing. What made Iceland's Althing unique was its lack of a king or supreme chieftain; in fact, though they called themselves *gothar,* the landowners gathered in this assembly had very limited authority to command the other free farmers on the island. Thingvellir, their meeting place in the rocky wilds of Iceland's west coast, with its Law Rock, became a symbol, the ideal of the self-governing polity. As the medieval chronicler Adam of Bremen put it, "They have no king, only the law." Even after Iceland swore allegiance to the crown of Norway (by majority vote, we note, at the Althing), the Althing remained the instrument of self-governance, making Iceland the oldest continuous democracy in the world.

All the same, the Viking Thing, in its various locations in the Viking world, was far more than a political institution, let alone a rudimentary form of democracy. It served as a combination of legislative assembly, supreme court, and judge and jury of a leader's actions and proposals — as well as a place for social networking and displaying social status. Attendees at the tribal assembly included the very rich and the very poor: men whose wealth was won by the sword, or inherited from their fathers; men whose flocks were increasing and others troubled with dwindling fortunes and unhappy marriages or family quarrels. The important point was that, in the Thing, they met as equals, with one vote for each household, which were not separated by status or function (as happened in Greece and Rome, where self-governance came with multiple assemblies with different functions).

The Thing formed the collective voice of the community, and no individual man, no matter how rich or powerful — not even the king himself — dared contradict it. The West Gautish Law in Viking Sweden specifically pointed out that the Things "have the right to elect and likewise reject a king . . . When he [that is, the king] comes to the *Thing* he must swear to be faithful to all the *Gotar* [nobles and chieftains], and he shall not break the true laws of our land."

It would be foolish, and historically inaccurate, to wax overly poetic about Viking "democracy," however. Later in this chapter we'll see why. All the same, the average Viking man's legal rights were considerable compared to those of the rest of the population of Dark Age Europe. He could bear witness, produce verdicts as part of a legal inquiry, and vote on matters of general importance in the Thing, including weighty considerations such as the election of a king or, somewhat later, whether a change of religion, from paganism to Christianity, should become official. Apparently the latter decision was in fact taken in the Althing in Iceland. Local Things played a significant role in Sweden. For example, a prospective king had to make the rounds of all the local Things, a tour called the Eiriksgata, in order to secure popular support for his title.

As the historian Gwyn Jones has emphasized, the free man's importance was reflected most vividly in the laws governing man-money, or wergild. Like

their German cousins, Scandinavians put a monetary price on the taking of
a life as a way to limit the blood feud. Every person's life, even a slave's, came
with a price based on the person's perceived social worth, which, if paid by the
perpetrator or his or her relatives, closed the case — with no need for the victim's relatives to settle scores by taking a life in their turn. To the historian, the
wergild price is a good guide as to who was highly valued in Viking society,
and who was not. In Danish law, for example, writes Jones, any Danish free
man "was equated with the English peasant farming his own land," someone
who would normally be considered that Dane's social superior, and "his wergild set with that of Danish and English noblemen at the high figure of eight
half-marks of pure gold."

The Viking status of free man contrasted sharply with that of a tenant bound
to the land by contract, or a servant, or a slave — the latter known to Scandinavians as a *thrall*. In an economy that depended heavily on muscle power, those
who could provide it, whether willingly or unwillingly, made up the majority
of the population. Lest we become too starry-eyed about Viking "democracy,"
it's worth remembering that in Iceland in 1094, for example, out of a total estimated population of 80,000, the fully free men numbered only 4,560. The rest
found themselves in various states of subordination or servitude.

To Scandinavian contemporaries, this fact seemed too mundane to bear
noting. For anyone other than a very poor free man, working a farm was unimaginable without slaves. In the heyday of the Viking expansion, these un-
fortunates largely consisted of booty captured in raids or wars. Most came
from the British Isles or from Slavic lands — so many of the latter, in fact, that
their ethnic name (*Slavi*) became synonymous with the Latin term for "slaves"
(*sclavi*). As distasteful as the idea is to us today, for the Vikings slaves were an
important source of labor as well as indicator of wealth. Nor was it unusual
for a thrall to accompany his master on a river raid or a seaborne expedition.
The Saga of Erik the Red notes in passing that two of the passengers on the first
voyage to North America were two of Leif Erikson's slaves: a man named Haki
and a woman named Hekli, both of Scottish origin.

Women belonged to a special category in Scandinavian culture. Although
they were never considered equal to free men, a status encoded in Viking law,

they did have a surprisingly large number of rights — certainly more than their sisters did on the European continent or in the British Isles. Viking society was organized along gender-specific lines, as we would put it today, with men handling the realm of war and politics and women tending to the household and other domestic priorities. But a Viking woman always knew she could never be taken for granted. Judging both men and women by the content of their character rather than solely by their sex was a key element of the Viking heart.

Take divorce, for example. In Christian or Muslim societies at the time of the Viking Age, the idea of a woman suing her husband for divorce was unimaginable. But as a traveler from Muslim Spain, visiting a large Viking settlement, remarked with some disgust, "Women have the right to declare themselves divorced; they part with their husbands whenever they like."

That's an exaggeration. But as the historians Peter Foote and David M. Wilson remark, during the later Christian era in Scandinavia, "the sources preserve some evidence of an older, native system under which it was only necessary for a formal declaration to be made before witnesses by either husband or wife for divorce to be legally effective." Among the Vikings, arranged marriages were largely the norm, but yet the union of man and woman was always seen as a kind of business contract, with obligations to be upheld by both parties. Either party's declaration that the contract had not been honored apparently was enough to annul the deal, especially, in a woman's case, if her family backed up her claims.

Or take the inheritance of property. Later, Norwegian, Icelandic, and Swedish law excluded women from the line of inheritance, as was largely done across the rest of Europe. But Danish law allowed a daughter to inherit half of a brother's portion. That system percolated into the rest of Scandinavia during the thirteenth century, after the Viking Age. But it probably reflected a preexisting mindset that made such a provision seem less than outrageous. In the district of Varend in south Sweden, for example, local custom gave sons and daughters equal portions, a tradition that even a national law couldn't stamp out.

In general, wives had very little leverage over property, including a dowry that they brought to a marriage. On the other hand, once an unmarried woman reached the age of majority (twenty, in Iceland), any property that was meant to pass to her became entirely hers. Similarly, when a woman became a widow, she could take complete control over her property and administer the property of her children as well.

And if a wife's husband was absent — which, during the Viking Age, was pretty much the rule during spring and summer, especially for a man of standing and property — the farm and other business matters came firmly under her control, including the disposition of slaves and other members of the household.

By modern standards, these rights seem paltry. To contemporaries, however, the relative freedom enjoyed by Viking women was a matter of comment, and not all of it complimentary. One observer, a traveler and diplomat from ninth-century Muslim Spain named Al-Ghazal, quoted a pagan Norse princess (probably from either Denmark or Norwegian Ireland) as saying, "Our women stay with their husbands according to their choice. The woman stays with him as long as she wishes, and parts from him if she no longer desires him." This Moorish diplomat and poet found the princess's beauty and easy freedom in dealing with men to be intriguing, if not a little disconcerting. His account may reflect a certain degree of poetic license. But runic inscriptions and monuments from the Viking Age in some ways concur with his portrait of the women of the North.*

Certainly, judging by grave goods and inscriptions, the older that women got, the more status they acquired (something that would have pleased my Norwegian grandmother). We know that many of them amassed considerable wealth and took over the role of a missing or dead husband in the tight-knit rural communities in which they lived. This rune inscription from Hassmyra, Sweden, testifies to the respect they could garner:

> *The good farmer Holmgaut had this raised*
> *in memory of his wife Odindis.*
> *A better housewife*
> *Will never come*
> *To Hassmyra*
> *To run the farm.*

---

*For the origin and nature of runes, see the Appendix.

Without a doubt the most impressive monument to a Viking woman has to be the great Oseberg find, the Viking ship unearthed at Slagen, Norway, in 1904. The Slagen burial mound measured more than 40 meters in diameter, and was originally 6.5 meters tall. Inside was a ship 22 meters long and 5 meters broad, made from oak trees cut down in about the year 820 (thus giving the burial site a rough date). The ship itself was filled with a treasure-trove of goods: weapons, jewelry, ornaments including Buddha-like figurines from East Asia, and a host of sacrificial animals, including twelve horses. I first saw the Oseberg ship as a boy of fourteen in a visit to the museum on Bygdøy in Oslo, where it is still on display. The ship and its contents form a staggering projection of wealth and power.

But what's particularly impressive is that all this was done to commemorate a Viking princess. Her remains, along with that of a female companion (perhaps a slave), were lovingly and ceremoniously stowed at the center of the ship and its treasure: a magnificent sendoff for a voyage into the greatest unknown of all.

Still, evidence of women actually fighting alongside men in their raids or expeditions is scanty at best. The medieval Danish chronicler Saxo Grammaticus wrote of "shield-maidens" who dressed in men's uniforms and practiced sword fighting and knife throwing. More particularly, he and Irish sources cite the career of Rusla, the Red Girl or Red Maiden — from her Gaelic nickname, Ingean Ruagh — a Norwegian female warrior who was notorious for her take-no-prisoners ferocity and her equally ruthless female companion, Stickla. According to the (not always reliable) chronicler, Rusla, Stickla, and their fleet of pirate ships fought all across the Irish Sea, it seems, as well as along the coasts of Denmark. Rusla is even recorded as having fought against the Irish hero Brian Boru at the battle of Clontarf, where her two sons were killed.

The problem is, Clontarf is one of those military engagements that, in the historian Gwyn Jones's words, "was too important to be left to historians, so passed into the legend-maker's hand." Accounts of who was there, and who wasn't, are notoriously unreliable concerning the men, let alone any women.

Whatever the truth about the Red Maiden, we have a much better case for the existence of the shield-maiden from the Viking site at Birka, where, thanks to DNA testing, Professor Charlotte Hedenstierna-Jonson of the University of Uppsala made the startling discovery that a great Swedish warrior buried there was in fact a woman.

This Viking wonder woman was interred alongside shields, a sword, a battle-ax, a bow with twenty-five armor-piercing arrows, horses bridled for riding, and a game board with twenty-eight pieces resembling a chess set. All these indicate that she was a highly respected person, very likely in a position of leadership. Despite the lack of proof, it had always been assumed the remains were those of a man. But Hedenstierna-Jonson's DNA tests, published in 2017, showed otherwise.

Did this Viking woman lead troops in battle? The game board and pieces at least suggest "she was the one planning the tactics," according to Hedenstierna-Jonson, "and that she was a leader." In any event, the Birka discovery implies that other stories from chronicles and sagas telling of Viking women engaged in command in battle — including the Red Maiden — may well be true.

Probably the most vivid picture of Viking women comes from *The Saga of the People of Laxardal,* which is set sometime in the tenth century and was first written down in about 1250–70. Much of it centers on the women of an Icelandic dynasty, led by Unn the Deep-minded, the matriarchal settler of Dalir, in west Iceland. The main character, however, is the amazing Gudrun Osvifsdottir, who navigates her way through no fewer than four marriages and the rivalry between two brothers, Bolli and Kjartan, who contend for her love without success (in the end, Kjartan emerges as the love of her life). As a modern editor says, "The women in *The Saga of the People of Laxardal* are much more complex and memorable than the men, as if the men buckle beneath the weight of the heroic legacy they are forced to bear" — a predicament the women manage to transcend. How many Viking women in real life were able to do the same thing?

The portrayal of women in the sagas raises further questions. How much do the nuances of character and the male-female conflicts reflect the lived experience of Viking women (in this case, very affluent women) and how much the values of Christianity (Unn's decision to split her legacy among her children is portrayed as an act of Christian charity, and Gudrun ends her days as an abbess in a Christian nunnery). In their depiction of women, and all of Viking culture, the sagas reflect two worlds at once: that of the Viking past, which the poets and writers celebrated, and the Christianized present, which they inhabited.

In the end, it may not be necessary to definitively parse the two influences. As we'll see, the coming of Christianity did not change the ways of the North as much occurred elsewhere. In many unexpected ways, the Viking heart, for both men and women, ran deeper and extended further than the historians have led us to assume.

Women were also an important part of life in another vital part of the Viking ecosystem: the major trading posts, such as Ribe and Hedeby in Denmark, Birka in Sweden, and Kaupang (which means "marketplace" in Norse) in Norway. No major Scandinavian trading posts existed before the late eighth century. It was the Viking raids that put them on the map, literally, and made them valuable to Scandinavian rulers. Danish kings in particular played a role in founding and patronizing Hedeby, and the same seems true for the role of Swedish kings in founding and sustaining Birka.

Ribe was probably the oldest, but Hedeby was by far the biggest, numbering just under fifteen hundred inhabitants or so at the height of the Viking Age — still, quite tiny, even by the standards of Dark Age Europe. It housed a royal mint. Archaeological excavations have revealed the remains of a tollgate, which makes sense, since merchants would be charged a toll every time they entered or left the town. Residents were involved in a number of crafts, from metal and bone working, to bead and glass making, to pottery and boat repair. Hedeby's eastern edge opened to the sea, where docks were available for the loading and unloading of goods, many from as far away as central Asia and the Silk Road and transported via the river routes across Russia.

As a center of wealth, especially mobile wealth, Hedeby was inevitably also a target. It received a substantial defensive wall in the tenth century, which also linked it to the military complex of the Danevirke, built by Charlemagne's rival Godfred of Denmark. But its openness to the sea remained a vulnerability. Norway's Harald the Ruthless sacked it in 1050, and the Wends did the same in 1066. Over time, the Danish kings decided to abandon Hedeby and move their business interests farther south. Birka suffered the same fate, probably because of falling sea levels, which made it harder for large ships to dock and unload, along with a decrease in silver imports from the Near East. By 970 Birka was deserted, and by 1100 Hedeby was no longer a trading port.

By then new urban centers had sprung up, however, almost all thanks to royal patronage: Aarhus, Sigtuna, Trondheim, Oslo, Odense. Roskilde and Lunde came a little later. The Danes took the lead in urban development, with no fewer than fifteen towns established by the time the Viking Age came to an end. Norway had eight, and Sweden, more backward, only four. Unlike urban centers everywhere else in Europe, however, their presence did little to change the lifestyle or culture of Scandinavia, which remained invincibly rural. Instead, they functioned largely as gathering places for the wealth of kings and local nobles, the jarls. For them, the riches mattered, but not how they were gained: by theft or trade.

What merchandise did these Vikings trade? Some of it was raw materials from their own homelands, such as dried fish, furs, timber, beeswax and honey, and precious amber for jewelry and ornaments. Some of it was commodities that made up the bulk of commercial trade across Carolingian Europe, such as wine. Vikings learned how to buy low and sell high and also to charge tolls to distributors on the river courses they controlled.

In fact, the Vikings proved adept at doing business with every salable commodity. Grains, salt, glass, glue, hazelnuts, soapstone dishes, basalt millstones, iron and bronze weapons and implements, live bears and bearskins, falcons and horses and cattle: if a longship or *knarr* could carry it, a Norseman was ready to put it up for sale.

From the start, however, the most important commodity for Viking traders was slaves.

This fact strikes a jarring note with modern admirers of the Vikings. Most prefer to avoid discussing this topic, or at least try to paper over the bald truth: Vikings became world leaders in human trafficking, on a scale that awed contemporaries as it enriched the Viking chieftains and families that led the enterprise — and accelerated Scandinavia's emergence as Europe's newest center of wealth.

But as in any discussion of slavery, ancient or modern, context is needed. It will help us understand why the Vikings became involved in this detestable traffic in the first place, and how they carried it out.

As we've already suggested, slaves were a fundamental part of the domestic economy in Viking Age Scandinavia, as they were everywhere in the world at that time. It was only natural that the Norsemen would realize that the slaves they captured could be a useful commodity for a larger market. Dark Age Europe's other tormentors, the Saracens and Magyars, were just as guilty: the Saracens relied on slave-trading routes to the Middle East, which would eventually embrace sub-Saharan Africa centuries before any European thought of enslaving Africans.

What the Norsemen brought to this ugly reality was an entrepreneurial zest for turning seaborne routes, which they had used to obtain slaves for themselves, into a full-blown network for human trafficking across Europe. The most important source was the interior of Europe, where Vikings took the captives from the Slavic tribes. A slave-trade superhighway sprang up, ultimately stretching from Kiev in Russia to Prague in Bohemia, then across central Germany to the Frankish fortress town of Verdun, where Vikings also sold captives taken in raids in the British Isles.

Verdun in the west, Magdeburg in the north, Prague in the east: these cities grew into thriving slave marts, and the Vikings kept them well supplied with human captives. These traders preferred abducting individuals from heathen peoples like the Slavs, since the Franks and other Europeans could be squeamish about buying fellow Christians as slaves. At Verdun, according to the chronicler Luitprand of Cremona, in the ninth century boy slaves were regularly turned into eunuchs to be sold farther south, in Moorish Spain.

In their heyday, the Norsemen became suppliers catering to the insatiable appetite for slaves across the civilized world. Their customers included the Byzantines and the Islamic caliphates in Spain and Baghdad. In fact, the wealth and prosperity of the golden age of Islam were made possible in large part by the human labor supplied by Viking slave traders operating from trading posts in eastern Europe and Russia. These transactions no doubt brought in many of the Arab silver coins found in Viking hoards.

Today, of course, any appreciation of the return on investment in the slave trade — which was substantial, and why it was so immediately attractive a pursuit at the time — is dwarfed by its moral depravity. The Viking heart was still on a journey. It would reach a major turning point with the transition from paganism to Christianity, a religion that brought to the Norsemen's world a set of values that made enslaving other Christians, and eventually non-Christians, unattractive and then ethically repulsive. The slave trade went the way of human sacrifice and the mass slaughter of prisoners. At the same time, Europe's growing political stability made it harder for the average Danish or Norwegian adventurer to roam about and take slaves at will. Until then, however, Viking commerce was largely a slave commerce. For every intrepid voyage out from the fjords into the wide world, success meant coming home in a ship loaded with human captives in addition to wine, bolts of cloth, and precious metals and gems.

Within Scandinavia itself, mobile wealth, such as Arab silver, also bought slaves, of course. In addition it bought the loyalty of armed retainers, or housecarls, and every Viking king or chieftain relied on housecarls for his personal safety; they also served as a professional corps on seaborne expeditions. Riches likewise greased the bonds of loyalty that bound a ruler to his most powerful subjects.

Yet wealth, even substantial wealth, was never sufficient on its own to secure a position of leadership. Chieftains and kings relied on family and clan ties for a reliable core of followers — and it was assumed (often wrongly) that these particular followers could not be bought off by a rival's wealth. But even when that loyalty remained strong, leadership was never a matter of entitlement. In Viking society authority and power had to be earned — and kept. And the place where Viking leadership faced the ultimate test was the field of battle.

A successful leader, of course, gave his followers victory whenever possible and avoided defeat at all hazards. This demanded experience and skill combined with cunning, especially when (as often happened) raiding Norsemen found themselves outnumbered. The most successful Viking expeditions, like the attack on Lindisfarne or the siege of Paris, relied on the element of surprise, applying the time-honored principle of "hit 'em where they ain't." These Viking shock tactics often included a bracing dash of intimidation, violence, or even savagery. But the bloodshed was not gratuitous but rather a means to an end. Vikings preferred to intimidate an enemy into submission, as Ragnar the Dane had done with his ruthless execution of Frankish prisoners during his advance on Paris, rather than face off in a pitched battle.

But circumstance, and sometimes honor, dictated the fighting of a formal set piece. For a king or chieftain, commanding a small force, in which everyone could see him during battle, was by far the preferable way to engage an enemy. Leading an expeditionary force of a hundred ships, each one providing forty men for the battlefield, or some four thousand men in total, made tougher demands. The warriors were arrayed in a certain order. Front and center was the chieftain or king himself, often displaying his personal banner (one popular icon was the raven, sacred to the god Odin and the bird of blood, corpses, and battle). The soldiers closest to this leader would be his kinsmen, followed by the professional warriors of his bodyguard — the housecarls, who were sworn to fight to the death for their chieftain or king, and often did. As was the case for the Germans, according to the observations of Tacitus eight centuries earlier, outliving one's master was a mark of disgrace; for a true warrior, no fate could be worse. The soldiers' loyalty depended on the rewards they would receive for serving a successful leader, and not all of them were monetary. The Swedish king of the Rus, for example, kept a bodyguard of four hundred men, each one equipped with two slave girls. If the Arab traveler's account of his visit with the Rus is accurate, these men were unashamed of having sex with their slave women in public, so barracks life must have been chaotic, to say the least.

That core of bodyguards was reinforced by a band of berserkers. We don't know very much about the berserkers beyond their mention in the sagas: their irrationally violent behavior in combat may or may not have been fueled by drugs. Odin was deemed their sacred patron and protector, and they were certainly feared on the battlefield for their contempt for death and their willingness to take on any and all opponents in a kind of murderous frenzy. Like that of the housecarls, their ultimate reward, more often than not, was death on the battlefield — evidence suggests that neither friend nor foe regretted this fate.

All the same, the heart of a Viking *hirth,* or army, remained its free men, its *bondar* or thingmen; they were also the backbone of the Viking body politic.

A relatively wealthy farmer might bring along a retinue of relatives and tenants and laborers, as well as his own slaves, who would fight beside him when he joined other *bondar* in a raid or a battle. His female relatives, including his own wife, might be there as well, to cheer the men on, as the German women in Tacitus's day had done, or to help gather the loot after a successful battle, a task that included stripping the dead of weapons and finery. And, as we've seen in the case of the Viking woman warrior at Birka, a woman may even have fought and commanded forces in the field.

Who served in the Viking army was never left to chance. A chieftain or king might call on a half levy of his followers for offensive operations, such as a series of summer raids, or a full levy when he had to make a stand and defend his turf.

The Vikings' weapons reflected the lives they led in peace as well as war. "In the lives of the most prosperous free men," the historian Georges Duby has written, "war was closely interwoven with hunting, expeditions, and farm management." The housecarls and other professionals would carry iron-forged short swords and two-handed broad swords and battle-axes — and these axes were largely indistinguishable from the ones used on the farm. The Norse warrior also wore coats of iron mail, which protected him down to his knees, along with a conical helmet with leather or iron cheekpieces and a noseguard (contrary to legend, Vikings did not wear helmets adorned with animal horns). The average free man in the levy would in most cases be armed with shield, spear, and bow; a sword and a helmet less often made up part of his gear. The warriors' shields, made of wood or hide reinforced with iron bands, were also used to line the sides of a longship as it cruised, keeping high seas from sweeping the deck. They also helped repel any would-be boarder or any volleys of arrows during a sea fight (some of the Vikings' most decisive battles, especially against each other, were conducted entirely at sea).

In the end, the typical Viking leader and his followers were adept at meeting any opponent on any terms, whether at sea, on foot — or even on horseback. Other Europeans were often shocked to discover that these Norse sailors were also skilled equestrians. That versatility would enable Danes and Norwegians and Swedes to beat virtually any kind of armed resistance that other rulers could throw at them, even when outnumbered and far from home. Successive Frankish emperors and Anglo-Saxon kings discovered this, to their cost.

The average Viking was a part-time warrior, but a warrior nonetheless. We need to banish the idea that a Viking raid consisted of a boatload of muscle-bound thugs, armed to the teeth and eager to prove their prowess. Instead, it was a community of people who reflected Scandinavia's social order, from the leader and his brothers and their armed entourage at the top, to the slaves at the bottom, who did the heavy labor involved in building a boat landing or a fortified outpost. In the middle were the *bondar* and free men, who tended the ship while it was at sea and refitted it in harbor or on the beach; they also confiscated food and supplies, usually at the point of a spear or a sword, from the terrified locals.

It would also be wrong to assume that because they were Vikings, these men enjoyed killing. Some did, of course; some always do. But by and large scholars understand that the typical medieval soldier, including your average Norseman, was just as uncomfortable about taking the life of another human being as their modern counterparts are — probably more so. It's not easy terminating someone's life in the up-close-and-personal situation of a medieval battle — especially since one sword thrust or ax swing from an opponent could as easily take one of your limbs or end your life. At a time when, as Peter Foote and David M. Wilson vividly put it, fighting consisted of "bashing the hell out of the other side," most participants probably spent their time clinging tightly to their shield and trying to avoid getting within sword or spear reach of an enemy. Those who didn't, who willingly fought toe to toe with their foes, quickly stood out as champions. In fact, it's very likely that a large proportion of the casualties on a Viking battlefield were caused by a small number of men, those who did the bulk of actual fighting and who would be remembered as heroes in saga and legend — ironically, this brave but also foolhardy minority gave Vikings their enduring reputation for fearsomeness.

As mentioned, some of those champions were berserkers, or "bear-shirts"; the bear stood as a kind of totem of their wild, ferocious spirit. They exemplify an extreme form of the mental "psyching up" that every Viking fighter needed in order to risk his life in the punishing arena of battle. Berserkers were famous, or notorious, for the frenzy that would overtake them before and during combat, as they ran howling at the enemy, often with no protection other than animal skins, while wielding a sword in each hand. Some have speculated that alcohol or even secret psychedelic concoctions caused their delirious furor; there is, however, no evidence from historical sources, or even the Norse sagas, to back up these claims. We do know "such men were prized as warriors," as Foote and Wilson tell us, "and were evidently regarded with awe as manifesting supernatural powers." But these same men were prone to outlawry during peacetime. The typical berserker can't have been mentally stable, even in the best of times, and a chieftain must have been secretly relieved that, useful though such a warrior might be in a fight, a berserker's life was (not surprisingly) relatively short.

Like every fighting force before or since, a Viking army demanded unit cohesion, whether the conflict at hand was a tip-and-run raid on an English monastery or a head-on pitched battle against an equally armed foreign foe — or against a fellow Danish or Norwegian chieftain. Elaborate pre-battle rites and rituals, including ceremonies invoking the war god Odin, certainly played their part. The Vikings' long and perilous expeditions, however, built a particularly special bond between leaders and followers. There was no captain's cabin or officers' quarters on a Viking longship. Chieftain and warriors, farmers and tenants, and even slaves all shared the same shipboard space for mealtime, and they slept side by side on deck, night after night. They too shared in the same danger when they finally landed on some known or unknown shore:

I fought, nor feared vengeance;
Falchion there reddened
Blood of son of Bloodaxe,
Bold king, and his queen.
Perish'd on one pinnace
Prince with twelve his liege-men,
Such stress of stern battle
Against them I stirred.

In the end, Viking leadership rested on the sense of being one with one's subordinates, a bond that only death could terminate.

There is no trace in Viking history of a king or chieftain being some kind of divinely anointed ruler, let alone the head of an organized national state. The term for "chieftain" in Old Norse, *gothi* (plural *gothar*), is akin to the Gothic word *gudja,* meaning "priest," which signifies that Viking chieftains originally had sacred or religious powers. But that sanction had faded into oblivion long before the Viking Age. *Gothar* came to refer to the eminent persons who led the Thing, the standard assembly of the Viking community, meaning that what may have begun as an authority bestowed by religious function shifted over time to one bestowed by the authority of the community, especially the band of followers and warriors on whom the *gothi,* or chieftain, ultimately depended — and, one could add, vice versa.

Self-styled kings abounded on the ground in Norway and Sweden during the Viking Age, and later in Viking settlements in Ireland and on the Isle of Man. Yet the title of king (*kunungr* in Old Norse) signified nothing more or less than a chieftain who commanded the loyalty and submission of other chieftains, a first among equals at the banqueting table, in religious ceremonies, or on the battlefield. Throughout this period, acquiring this title also depended on the approval of the assembly of free men and warriors, an "aristocracy of the brave." It was even required by Swedish law.

So although some would come to regard their royal crown as the possession of a single family or dynasty, any member of that family could aspire to the title. As a result, succession disputes were common. Losers in the contest, assuming they weren't killed, often went into exile, where they might win enough wealth and support to make a future bid for the throne. This constant "game of thrones" was enough to destroy the Danish monarchy in the ninth century, and it persisted as part of the Scandinavian scene until very late in the Middle Ages.

Egil's Saga, for instance, describes the subtle process by which King Harald Finehair of Norway recruits Thorolf, who has become a successful sea raider on his own, to be one of the king's loyal retinue. In the saga, the king recognizes "what a great and generous man Thorolf was. He kept a large band of men which soon proved costly to maintain and was difficult to provide for, but the farming was good and it was easy to obtain everything that was needed."

Royal favor, of course, would make that support easier. But when Thorolf hosts a feast for King Harald, the monarch decides the presence of Thorolf's personal entourage is an affront to his own authority, and he leaves in a rage. It's up to Thorolf to smooth out the relationship, which he does in a face-to-face meeting at the end of the king's stay.

"On the day the king was due to leave, Thorolf approached him and asked him to come down to the shore. The king agreed. Offshore lay the dragon-prowed ship that Thorolf had had made, with its awnings up and fully rigged. Thorolf gave the ship to the king, asking him to respect his intention in having so many men at the feast simply as a gesture of honor towards him, not as a challenge. The king took this well and grew friendly and cheerful. Many people rightly added words of praise for the splendid feast and noble gift that the king was given on departing, and the great strength that he enjoyed in such men. They parted in friendship."

In the saga, the friendship doesn't last. In real life too, alliances between Viking leaders were likewise fickle. Expediency and contingency of events dictated the typical bond of trust, including its duration. The history of the Vikings is replete with examples of treachery and betrayal, including (perhaps especially) those involving members of the same family. When we are told that Erik Bloodaxe killed five of his brothers in his quest for the throne of Norway, only to be overthrown and driven into exile by the sixth brother, it's hard to know where fact ends and legend begins. But there's no denying that Viking leaders grew up in a hard school, where success could be dazzling but also fleeting. And while the soldier crouched beside you at the helm of your longship could be your loyal friend and even your relative, he might also be your bitterest enemy.

The earliest Viking kings mentioned in the sagas and the saga-like history of the Norwegian kings, the *Heimskringla,* are shrouded in legend and myth. For the historian, the first real king of Norway to emerge was Harald Finehair, or Fairhair. The date usually assigned to his formation of a unified Norwegian kingdom is set as 872, when he defeated the last petty kings who resisted him at the battle of Hafrsfjord, killing no fewer than five crowned heads that day. Consolidating control of his kingdom, which was only a fraction of present-day Norway, took decades, and upon his death the kingship was broken up again and shared among his sons.

In Sweden, most rulers whose names appear in sources such as the *Heimskringla* and *The Ynglinga Saga* belong to mythology, not history. From about the sixth century, these earliest kings are gradually succeeded by semi-legendary kings with at least some claim to historicity; they are all depicted as descendants of the house of Ynglings/Scylfings, either in direct royal line or through the house of Ragnar Ladbrok and the house of Skjöldung (Scylding), although here again the line between fact and fantasy gets blurry.

In fact, while there are literally thousands of runestones in Sweden commemorating the lives and deeds of commoners, only a handful even mention a Swedish king, and those come from the very end of the Viking Age. We have to wait until 1100 or so for a Swedish king to emerge as a genuine historical figure.

We are on firmer ground, historically speaking, in Denmark. The king of the Danes mentioned in *Beowulf,* Hrothgar, seems a largely mythical figure. But Kings Sigfrid and Godfred, who gets credit for building the Danevirke, do appear in the chronicles of the time, including Charlemagne's. But it is doubtful that they controlled much of modern Denmark beyond its southern borders and the neighboring islands. It's not until the tenth century that three figures emerge who can claim to be more than glorified tribal chieftains: Gorm the Old (in Old Norse, Gorm den Gamle), Sven Forkbeard, and the most famous of all, Harald Bluetooth. But the realm they ruled was probably even a couple of hundred years older than that.

In either case, chieftain or king, *gothi* or *kunungr,* one basic rule pertained to all of them: don't expect to be on top for long. According to a familiar saying, "A king is for glory, but not a long life." Death in battle, or death by treachery, was their common fate, both in fiction and reality.

Consider the fate of the kings of Norway during the Viking era. As Paddy Griffith details it in *The Viking Art of War,* out of sixteen kings, eleven were either killed by enemies or driven into exile. Only four — Harald Finehair, Canute the Great, Sven, and Magnus the Great — managed to die peacefully of natural causes. The record for the rest is grim:

Gudrod the Magnificent: murdered by the wife he had abducted.
Halfdan the Black: fell through a hole in the ice, and drowned.
Erik Bloodaxe: after being exiled to England, died at the battle of
   Stainmore.
Hakon the Good: killed in the battle of Fitjar.
Harald Greycloak: killed in the battle of Lymfjord.
Earl Hakon Sigurdarson: murdered by his own slave.
Olaf Tryggvason: drowned in the battle of Svold.
Olaf Haraldson: killed in the battle of Stiklestad.
Harald Hardarad: a violent death in England at the battle of
   Stamford Bridge in 1066.

As for Earls Erik and Sven, both were struck down by disease (in Sven's case, after being driven out of his own kingdom by rebels), and Earl Hakon Eriksson, rival to Canute the Great for rule of Norway, drowned at sea. To complete the picture, all sixteen faced at least one major rebellion at one time or another. All in all, it's debatable whether becoming king of Norway in the Viking Age was a boon or a curse.

Yet despite the high mortality rate, there was never any lack of candidates for the title of king, or for the similar title in Denmark or Sweden. That included candidates from the other kingdoms. In Norway's case, not once in the years from 793 to 1066 was it ever invaded, or even threatened by invasion, by a non-Scandinavian foe. But over the same period, it was attacked at least half a dozen times by its Danish and Swedish neighbors. Whenever they could, Norwegians were happy to return the favor.

Perhaps the most titanic of these clashes was the battle of the Helgeå in 1026 (although the *Anglo-Saxon Chronicle* dates it to 1025), when King Canute of Denmark confronted both of his rivals, King Olaf II of Norway and Anund Jakob of Sweden, in a massive sea battle, pitting Canute's 600 ships against 480 ships of the enemy. Although Canute lost more ships and men, it was Olaf and Anund Jakob (king of Sweden from 1022 to 1050) who withdrew from the battle, allowing Canute to subjugate the Swedish lands around Lake Mälaren and even mint his own coins at Sigtuna.

Mention of a mint suggests that big changes had come over the Vikings and their homelands. They were no longer just pillagers of empires. They were becoming makers of empires themselves. The heyday of tip-and-run raids and random piracy was over. A new relationship with the civilization around them was springing up, and Vikings would contribute to it decisively — influencing not only Viking society but all of Europe.

3

The World the Vikings Made, Part One

From Russia to the British Isles

> The island of St. Patrick was burnt by the Danes, they
> taxed ye Landes with great taxations, they took the
> Reliques of St. Dochonna & made many Invassions to
> this kingdome & tooke many rich & great bootyes, as
> well from Ireland as from Scotland.
>
> — *Annals of Clonmacnoise,* entry for 795

FOR THE BETTER part of two centuries, from 780 to about 950, waves of Scandinavians descended upon the rest of Europe and penetrated as far as the Mediterranean and the Black Sea.

Those from Denmark divided their attacks between the Anglo-Saxon kingdoms and the European mainland, from Frisia (the modern Netherlands) and Francia to Spain. Norwegian marauders traced an arc of destruction from the Faroe Islands to Scotland and Ireland. Swedes chose a more easterly route, across the Baltic to the rivers of present-day Germany and Russia.

Then, slowly, a change came over the Scandinavian conquest of Europe. As time went on, their role shifted from marauder to trader to settler, in a trajectory that would alter the face of western Europe and open new frontiers in the east. To be clear, these three roles were never completely distinct. The Vikings themselves could shift from one to another with a flexibility that baffled contemporaries, as it still does historians. But the Vikings' role in history was steadily moving from a destructive one to something more constructive.

As already mentioned, it does a disservice to the Vikings to exaggerate the savagery and violence of their raids. Of course the Norsemen were capable of great brutality. But in a world where rape, pillage, and the murder of war captives or their sale into slavery were largely the norm, the Vikings do not stand out as particularly bloodthirsty or ruthless, no matter what the chronicles of contemporary monks suggest.

A good example is the supposed violence and rapacity of the original raid on Lindisfarne in 793, which in one stroke made the Vikings both famous and infamous.* But looking more closely, beyond the propaganda and fake news of the day, it's likely that the Vikings' savage attacks on this and other Christian sites were actually a reaction against Charlemagne's ongoing genocidal war on the Vikings' pagan Saxon neighbors. The renegade Saxon rebel leader Widukind had taken refuge in the court of the Danish king Sigfrid. No doubt he wove horrific stories of the atrocities the Franks were committing on his people, stories that would have been passed along to Sigurd's successor, Godfred, and then *his* successors. The message would have been clear: these Christians were waging a war of extermination on their neighbors and kin, and it was time to hit back hard.

Viewed from their perspective, aspects of the Lindisfarne raid (which was almost certainly conducted by Vikings sailing from Denmark) make sense. The destruction of holy relics and the deliberate vandalizing of Catholic holy sites like the monasteries at Lindisfarne and Jarrow were very likely part of a "culture war" between two different systems of belief. Paganism was fighting back against an alien religion, Christianity, whose leaders were determined to wipe it out.

Part of the reason for the earliest wave of large-scale Viking raids, then, may have been to make Christians pay in blood and treasure for what they

---

* See Chapter 1.

had already done to the Norsemen's fellow pagans. Then, as they carried out these acts of retribution, the Vikings learned something valuable: their European neighbors were both wealthy and unable to defend themselves. Given the standards of the age, it was a tempting opportunity and one that most anyone might seize to their advantage. The Saracens and the Hungarians did exactly the same.*

Still, even after that discovery, the Norsemen proved to be interested in far more than plunder and wanton destruction. Their actions over the next two centuries reveal a deeper pattern: the desire to make better lives for themselves and their families, at first by bringing wealth home to Scandinavia but then later by acquiring land overseas. What happened in England with the Danelaw became increasingly the model for Viking adventurers and their followers. Wherever their longships could take them, they were prepared to put down stakes, establish an outpost or two, and hold their claim against all comers, as shown in this passage from *The Saga of the Greenlanders:*

> They then left to sail to the east of the country and entered the mouths of the next fjords until they reached a cape stretching out seawards. It was covered with forest. After they sheltered their ship in a sheltered cove and put out gangways to the land, Thorvald and his companions went ashore.
>
> He then spoke: "This is an attractive spot, and here I would like to build my farm."

This is the other side of the Viking Age, a contrast to the dangerous sea cruises and the raiding expeditions. It's actually the side that would make the

---

* Furthermore, much of the Vikings' use of violence was strategic more than reflexive. When towns like London or Chartres fought back, or reneged on an earlier promise to pay an agreed ransom, they suffered the worst from the Vikings in terms of punishment or reprisal. There are only a very few examples of Viking raiders completely destroying a town or other significant site. The Saracen raiders were, by contrast, quite capable of razing such a place, especially a Christian one.

more lasting impact on Western civilization. At first the Norsemen thought of their voyages as a way to steal anything they could carry — gold, silver, precious objects, wine — anything manufactured or crafted by others, as well as men as slaves and women as concubines, that could add to their status at home or circulate as an object of trade.

Eventually, however, trade took precedence, then settlement. The Norwegian and Danish and Swedish adventurers and warriors transformed themselves into merchants and entrepreneurs, and proved themselves adept in their new roles. The temporary shelters the Vikings used for wintering between raids gradually became permanent trading posts, doing business with the locals — sometimes the very folks they had ransacked the summer before.

As we've noted, for a long time this network's chief commodity was human chattel, drawn from the lands the Vikings raided. At the same time, it accommodated other goods, including the loot that Norse chieftains had stolen in earlier raids. As time went on, this would become the Vikings' chief contribution to the making of medieval Europe: their role as middlemen. They returned to circulation the wealth that had been stored up as church and royal treasure during the Dark Ages and made it part of daily commerce and trade.

This development was particularly crucial following the Muslim invasions of the seventh century, which had severed western Europe's access to the Mediterranean, its traditional source of wealth, particularly gold. From the ninth to the mid-tenth century — a time when Europe's traditional routes to the wealth of the east were almost entirely sealed off — any merchant looking for Arab silver could find it circulating in towns along the shores of the Baltic, thanks to the Vikings. Before the heyday of the Vikings was over, they had created new sea routes for trade across the North and Baltic Seas and the North Atlantic, circumventing the Mediterranean altogether. These new routes would eventually allow the countries of western and northern Europe to dominate an entire continent. One could even say they would eventually dominate the world.

The best example of how this change happened lies in Russia, far to the east of those early Viking raids on Frankish Europe. But the story begins in Birka, in south-central Sweden.

• • •

Birka is an island town off Sweden's Lake Mälaren. It had traditionally marked the dividing line between Gothic tribes and their fierce rivals, the Svear. Originally founded in the eighth century, when the trade routes through the Mediterranean to the rest of Europe broke down after the Arab invasions, Birka became a hub for securing the wealth of the east in new ways. Whereas the other major Viking trading entrepôt, at Hedeby in Denmark, had a tumultuous history of claims and counterclaims for the right to rule, as different leaders competed for power, Birka's affluence apparently grew without serious interruption, apart from the occasional brutal sack, such as the one mounted by Norwegians in the year 1000.

Archaeology at Birka reveals a settlement with population of seven hundred to a thousand, clustered around the harbor and protected by a wall. From time to time the community gathered in what's become known as Warrior's Hall, a large chamber some 19 meters long and 9.5 meters wide that is split into two rooms, with a massive fireplace at the end of each. As you look over the site, it's not difficult to imagine the walls lined with shields and swords (shield bosses and iron spearheads have been found along the remains of the walls) as a Swedish king or chieftain enters the hall to thunderous cheers. Then his followers and housecarls raise silver goblets in salute (many silver slivers from such goblets remain as evidence) while valuable gifts (such as a bronze dragon's head and more than forty comb cases, also found in the hall) are handed out to one and all. Adding to Birka's attractions was its location not far from Uppsala, the pagan cult center of Sweden: a convenient stop on some chieftain's ceremonial tour of his native country.

All the same, the comb cases may come as a surprise. They were almost certainly not for women. Viking males were famous for being meticulous about their long hair. And it wasn't just for vanity's sake. Like the Scandinavian penchant for bathing in hot water, personal grooming of the hair probably prolonged the men's lives, since the Viking comb was also useful for removing fleas and lice — major carriers of contagious diseases. Again, it's not hard to imagine a well-laden Viking traveler coming home to Birka, bruised and filthy from his long journey, and ready to settle in for a cup of mead, a hot bath, and an hour of grooming his tangled hair with a comb presented by his grateful chief.

For a long-distance merchant, Birka was a perfect base of operations. It was only five days' sail from the Baltic entrance to the trio of rivers — the Dnieper, the Volga, and the Dniester — that would give Sweden's Vikings access to eastern markets as far away as Constantinople. In addition, it was five days' sail from Hedeby, the main mart for Danish kings and the western end of a thread of trade connecting the two halves of the Norse world.

That thread consisted of many goods, including slaves. But most important, it included silver, almost all of it coming from the lands ruled by Islam. The coin hoards the Vikings left behind in their homeland suggest just how much silver was brought from Arab sources to Birka and then spread to the west — not only around Birka but to the island of Gotland, a major stop in the trade from the east. The first Arab silver dirhams started arriving in the ninth century. Their numbers steadily grew until 900, when the trade really took off, culminating in about 950, the approximate date that archaeologists associate with no fewer than eight major silver hoards — almost all of it in the form of Arab coins.

More than eighty-four thousand silver coins from Muslim lands have been found in what is now Sweden. Gotland itself grew so affluent that the Swedish king could charge every household an annual tax of twelve grams of silver without missing a beat. Even after taxes, the Gotlanders hardly knew what to do with their wealth. The most satisfactory solution was to bury it, a real convenience for the archaeologist and the historian.

Not all, but perhaps the majority, of this wealth came from means other than trade. This included payments of tribute from local rulers around the Baltic Sea to Viking mercenaries serving in their endless wars; they became known to the locals as Varangians (just as the Baltic itself became known as the Varangian Sea). Some coins were simply stolen during raids, as plunder. In the early stages of the Norse intrusion into the Slavic hinterland, we don't find much evidence of Swedish or Scandinavian goods being imported into Russia in enough volume to account for this heady flow of Arab silver into Scandinavia.

Nonetheless, the trade routes were there for the enterprising Norseman. The men who established them (and there doesn't seem to be much evidence of women accompanying them on their epic journeys east) would ultimately use them to reshape the region in their own image. These men became known to their neighbors as the Rus, or "the men who row" — a tribute to their amazing maritime enterprise along the rivers leading east.

The route they founded went all the way to Constantinople, home of the Roman emperor and the wealthiest city in the world. From the Gulf of Finland, Viking adventurers would make their way up the Neva River to its mouth at Lake Ladoga (the future site of Saint Petersburg). After rowing across Lake Ladoga, they passed through the Volchow River and Lake Ilmen, where they picked up the Lovat and the upper Dnieper Rivers (going from the Lovat to the Dnieper required some overland portage, a familiar undertaking for any intrepid Viking). Then they followed the Dnieper by easy stages down to the Black Sea, and thence to the gates of Constantinople, capital of the Byzantine Empire.

There was also an alternate route back and forth, passing from the Dnieper to the Dvina on the homeward journey, into the Gulf of Riga. And a third more easterly route ran to the Volga and the Bulgar. A merchant could use this route to get from Lake Ladoga along the Svir and Lake Onega, followed by a short overland route jogging south to Lake Beloozero. There he would pick up another river that led straight into the Volga, where he found an inviting waterway measuring almost one kilometer wide. Soon other Viking explorers managed to blaze still another route to the Volga, via Lake Ilmen.

Four routes, four paths to wealth but also danger. A Swedish merchant adventurer in those years regularly passed through local Slavic tribes — often hostile, sometimes not; at times friendly during a previous spring's visit and then murderously hostile the next. It was a way of life that demanded not the skills of a tip-and-run raider but those of a master negotiator and deal maker, backed with a firm, ruthless hand when it was needed, but more often by a friendly hand ready to cut a deal.

The Varangians were already showing their prowess in the middleman role when they agreed, in 839, to go to the court of the Holy Roman emperor for the sake of the Byzantine emperor. It must have come as a shock to Emperor Louis the Pious when "he investigated the reason for their coming here, [and] discovered that they belonged to the people of the Swedes." In short, they were the Scandinavian cousins of the same Norsemen who had been harrying his coastline year after year.

The settlements the Rus built, starting at Volkhov, where the Vikings had to switch from seagoing ships to river craft, sprang up as early as the seventh century. One of the most strategic was Staraja Ladoga on the Lovat, where an active Swedish community grew up among the Finnish majority. The most important, however, took shape at the northern end of Lake Ilmen, with its access by river and portage to the upper Volga, or the western Dvina, or the Dnieper: you could take your pick. Known to locals as Gorodsce, the Scandinavian settlement a little farther south became "new" Gorodsce, or Novgorod. By the start of the ninth century, it was the capital of an emerging Viking colony fifteen hundred miles away from Birka and Uppsala, and eight hundred miles from Constantinople.

For a truly intrepid Viking taking the journey to Constantinople on the Volga route, the eastern Roman capital was just his first stop. He could bank to the east and take the Volga to its mouth at Itil, the principal seat of the Khazars on the Caspian Sea. In 922 the Arab merchant Ibn Fadlan would meet Rus slave traders there. Then he would follow the shore of the Caspian Sea until he reached what is modern-day Rasht, where a river would lead him to the threshold of the western Zagros Mountains, and then over the Mesopotamian plain to Baghdad, the capital of the Islamic world.

How far Rus traders actually got, no record tells us.* Some scholars, however, do think that at least some reached Baghdad. They probably returned home via a circuitous westward route, since relations with their neighbors were never very stable. The archaeological remains of Novgorod and other settlements show constant efforts at fortification, reflecting sustained tension and warfare.

The real turning point in Scandinavian fortunes in the east, however, came in around 840, when the local Slavic tribes south of Lake Ilmen decided they needed a leader. After being at one another's throats for years, the tribes sensed that prosperity could be within their grasp if only they could put an end to enmity and anarchy. That would require a strong ruler, who could impose order, but no such person could be found in their own ranks. "Here was no

---

* One Rus adventurer, Svyatoslav, did try to lead a raiding expedition from the eastern Caspian shore into central Asia, but he met with disaster on the way.

law among them, but tribe rose against tribe," says the *Nikonian Chronicle,* a sixteenth-century Russian compilation of much earlier historical narratives, many of which are now lost. So "they said to themselves, 'Let us seek a prince who may rule over us and judge us according to the Law.'" And "they accordingly went overseas and ... then said to the people of the Rus: 'Our land is great and rich, but there is no order in it. Come to rule and reign over us.'"

So the Rus did so, in the persons of three brothers: Signitur, Thorvadr, and Hroeker. They are better known by their names as they came down in Russian history: Sineus, Truvor, and Rurik. The last would emerge as the most prominent — one of history's great Viking heroes.

Although we have few biographical details, Rurik was probably a typical Norse leader: brave, headstrong, and charismatic, combining strategic vision with ruthless cunning. His two brothers quickly disappear from the historical record — whether by means natural or not, or with Rurik's help or not, we do not know. What we do know from the Russian chroniclers is that Rurik soon founded a powerful kingdom based in Kiev, on the shores of the Dnieper. From there he cast his eye toward farther horizons.

It was two of Rurik's followers, Askold and Dir, who in June 866 led one of the boldest and most dangerous ventures in Viking history: a full-scale attack on the Byzantine capital, Constantinople. They commanded more than two hundred ships, and their arrival under the walls of the city came as a great shock to the Byzantines, much like the appearance of Viking longships at Lindisfarne or London. As the Greek chronicler Photios later wrote,

> Do you recollect that unbearable and bitter hour when the barbarians'
> boats came sailing down at you, wafting a breath of cruelty, savagery,
> and murder [and] when the boats went past the city show their crews
> with swords raised, as if threatening the city with death by the sword?
>
> What quaking and darkness held our minds, and our ears would
> hear nothing but, "the barbarians have penetrated the walls, and the
> city has been taken by the enemy"?

In fact, Askold, Dir, and their men never entered the city; they did not manage to breach Constantinople's walls, and so they had to content themselves with burning and pillaging its suburbs. This they did until a sudden great storm drove many of their ships up onto shore, killing many in the Viking ranks. And the survivors sailed away home.

The raid had been a failure. But it drove home to the Byzantines that there was a new power in the neighborhood, one "out of the furthest north," as the Greek chronicler phrased it, whose journey had taken its men "from the ends of the earth" and across "numberless rivers and harborless seas" to the gates of the greatest city on earth. It made Rurik and his Kiev-based dynasty a byword for Viking courage and daring.

It was also proof that a great power, and a great people, meant to stay.

Meanwhile, at the other end of Europe, Norwegian and Danish raiders were transforming the British Isles in ways that persist to this day.

Ireland, they say, is the isle of saints and scholars. It's a title earned in the darkest days of Europe, when its monks and scribes tirelessly copied the West's greatest books, including the Bible.

Then in about 795 came the Norsemen to disrupt those scholars' work with a series of raids on the most vulnerable monastic communities. Inishmurray and Inishbofin were among the first to be hit. Then the raids extended to southwest Ireland until, by the 820s, Viking marauders had circumnavigated the entire island.

In the 830s the raids became more frequent, and the fleets much bigger. The attackers were Norwegians in the main, but they were joined by others, including the Danes and even other Irishmen. The monasteries were undefended; even a small band of thieves could successfully pillage one. Armagh, a particularly common target, was raided three times in a single month in 832. Anything made of gold or silver or decorated with jewels and ornaments, such as the covers of great books, was purloined. Many of these artifacts would eventually wind up buried with their takers in gravesites in Norway.

The most celebrated of those raiders, according to Irish verse, was Turgeis, whose real name was either Thurgestr (in Old Norse) or Thorgis (in Old Danish). His actual history is smothered in legends that were written down centuries later, but he seems to have been the leader of several raids on Ireland in the early ninth century. For a time Thorgis was highly successful in the north-

east and made himself lord of all the Gall-Gaedhil, or the foreign Irish, in Erin
and northern Ulster.* The capture of Armagh was one of the exploits that
made him famous, or rather notorious, throughout Ireland. He was himself
captured and killed in 845, but his name and that of his wife, Ota, would live
on in Irish legend. The most sensational tale mentioned how she and Thorgis conducted pagan sacrifices on the high altar of the monastery at Clonmacnoise — although it seems likely that this is largely monkish fake news.

In any case, with or without Thorgis at their head, by the 840s the larger
Norse expeditions began staying in Ireland over the winter, a sure sign that
the Vikings were getting ready to plant themselves more permanently. Irish
chieftains fought back as best they could, handing their invaders four major
defeats in 847 alone. But the Norsemen were there to stay. The first things
to be unloaded from any longship, after its crew and other goods, would be
the *instafars,* large wooden posts taken from an abandoned house in Norway
or Denmark. The Vikings would use these stakes to build an enclosure for a
makeshift trading post and fort; eventually this would become the walls of a
settled community. The numbers of settlers would be small at first. But the
simple fact of their presence marked a major change in Irish society.

The Vikings' most important outpost was on the east coast of Ireland,
at the mouth of the River Liffey and bordered on the south by the Wicklow
Mountains. It became known as Dublin and was said to have been founded
by Thorgis himself, although a monastic settlement existed there prior to the
naval base the Vikings founded, on the River Poddle. The Poddle was a tribu-
tary of the Liffey, whose "black pool" (*dubh linn,* in Irish) of deep water provided a place where longships could moor. The area is now Wood Quay — one
of the busiest neighborhoods of modern Dublin.

What was Viking Dublin like? Archaeological excavations at Wood Quay

---

* They were called the Gall-Gaedhil because they had abandoned Christianity and
become allies of the heathen Norwegians; many were accounted half Irish and half
Norse, and they had become inured to the Viking way of life. A similar renegade
community, the Gall-Ghàidheil, grew up in Scotland in the same time, from the
same ethnic and cultural mix. Like the Gall-Gaedhil, this community was distrusted
and despised by both its peoples of origin.

and other sites give us a picture of a waterfront community grouped around the Viking shipyards, with a surprisingly large population. In fact, almost half of the total worldwide Viking burials containing weapons have been found within a short radius of Dublin. Four were found in 2003 at a site behind the Long Hall pub on South Great George Street. They revealed the bodies of men who were no doubt tough customers — strong and large-boned. The best preserved retained evidence of a highly developed arm, no doubt accustomed to wielding a sword or battle-ax and rowing the many miles from home — a typical trip from Norway to Ireland via Scotland's Western Isles could take as long as a month.

Viking Dublin of the 840s has left its traces all over the modern city, but its heyday was yet to come. In fact, the Irish retook the city in 874, and for more than four decades, known in Irish history as the "Forty Years' Rest," Viking activity in Ireland subsided. The Danes who had taken over from the Norwegians had been distracted by events on the English mainland: the desire to rule the entire island from York remained a great dream of the Irish Viking chieftains — one that ended only with the establishment of English sovereignty over York, in 954.

By then, the Vikings were back in Ireland with a vengeance. They captured Dublin once again in 917, and the city soon became "a flourishing international trade center," according to the historian Else Roesdahl. With trade came the expansion of other Viking-based settlements, such as Wexford (from the Old Norse *Veisafjorthr,* meaning "inlet of the mud flats"), Waterford (from *Vadrefjord,* or "fjord of the waters"), Smerwick (*Smor Vick,* or "butter harbor," after the butter the area's cows supplied to County Limerick), Wicklow, Cork, and Limerick.

Next, the Viking kings of the day tried to claim sovereignty over all of Ireland. In 995 they were even minting their own coins. But native Irish tribes still kept control of the hinterland, even though Dublin's king Olaf Sigtryggson commanded large chunks of the interior. But like most Viking kings, Olaf had a short career. He was decisively beaten at the battle of Tara in 980, which marked the end of the Viking ascendancy. There would be one more famous battle, at Clontarf in 1014. There, as Vikings fought on both sides, Brian Boru smashed a coalition of Irish and Viking foes at the cost of his own life, and put the stamp on a united and independent Ireland for the first time.

Dublin's king at the time, Sigtrygg Silkenbeard, did not even take part in the fight. By then, Sigtrygg had been paying tribute money to Irish rulers, rather than the other way around — a clear sign that Viking rule in Ireland was finally over.

The main written source on the battle of Clontarf is an Old Norse text titled *Brjanssaga* (*Brian's Saga*), penned by an Irish cleric living in Dublin around 1118. Together with *Cogad Gaedal re Gallaib* (*The War of the Irish with the Foreigners*), it represented the birth of a Gaelic literary culture that reached from Ireland to the Orkney Islands and the Viking capital of York in the twelfth century — a culture extending across the centuries to the Irish writer James Joyce and the Irish American author Frank McCourt. This long-standing literary ecosystem owes a great deal to the tradition of the Norse saga.

But the mark of the Viking on Ireland continues far beyond towns and place names and literary remains. It's also embedded in the DNA of the Irish people. Two very recent studies by Dublin's Trinity College and the Irish College of Surgeons have revealed that the Scandinavian legacy in Ireland's genetic pool is much greater than previously thought, with the largest concentration found (no surprise) in the island's north and west. No one is suggesting that their descendants give up celebrating Saint Patrick's Day for Olaf's Day. But it might be apt, on that day of March expressing Irish pride, to swap one of those pints of Guinness for a Carlsberg beer, or perhaps a glass of Norwegian *akevitt*.

No one exactly knows when the first Scandinavian turned up on the northern shores of Scotland, but it must have been well before the first Viking raids. The northernmost islands of Scotland, the Shetlands, are only a twenty-four-hour sail from Oslo — a trip hardly worth mentioning for the typical Viking. Indeed, archaeological remains found on the islands suggest that Norwegians were traveling there as early as the pre-Roman Iron Age.

All the same, Scotland never had the same draw for the Vikings that Ireland had — or that England would have. Scotland's wide semicircle of outlying islands, stretching from the Shetlands and Orkneys in the east to the Hebrides and the Isle of Man in the west, became important largely as staging posts for Viking raids farther south and west, ranging all the way to Iceland, in the mid-

Atlantic. But the mark that the Vikings left on Scotland ran deeper and reveals a great deal about the Vikings themselves.

The Shetlands were the first part of Scotland to be overrun by Viking raiders; the Orkneys, slightly to the south, followed in short order. The Shetlands consist of nearly a hundred islands, the Orkneys over seventy. Many are uninhabitable, and for the rest the climate and terrain must have reminded Viking travelers of their own homeland. In any case, their invasion and occupation of both were fierce and sudden. Almost no trace of the original inhabitants — ancient Picts in most cases, in addition to some Celts — survived in place names or descendants. The DNA traces of both peoples are miniscule compared to the Scandinavian heritage. Those island inhabitants had also been Christians, which probably made the Vikings even more determined to obliterate every trace of their existence — these were the years of the raids on Lindisfarne and other monasteries.

Were the original Shetlanders and Orcadians exterminated, or ethnically cleansed, in a Viking-style genocide? Were they simply sold into slavery, like tens of thousands of other victims of Viking raids? Did they manage to flee to the mainland, or were they simply too few in number to resist being completely submerged in the Viking tidal wave? We don't know. What is clear is that the Shetlands and Orkneys became virtual Norwegian colonies, with a lifestyle almost identical to that of the Norwegian Vikings (the remains of the so-called Jarlshof farm on the southern end of Shetland Island are a virtual clone of a wealthy man's holding in western Norway). Their inhabitants would continue to speak Norn, a Norse dialect, right down to the eighteenth century.*

The extensive Orkney and Shetland settlements, however, inevitably became staging posts for raids on the Scottish mainland. Their targets included not only Lindisfarne but also the wealthy and famed island monastery at Iona, which was sacked so many times, the monks finally withdrew into Ireland's interior. The real prize, however, was Caithness, on Scotland's northernmost tip. The name itself shows the Norse influence: *caith* being the Gaelic word for

---

* The Viking DNA legacy was more permanent, running to more than 44 percent in the Orkneys, and still more among residents of the Shetlands.

"cat" and *ness* the Norse word for "neck," as in "a neck of land." Vikings overran the place in the early ninth century, and they soon found they had a strategic gem on their hands.

Caithness served as a gateway for raids both west toward Ireland and east along Scotland's eastern coast to York and Northumbria. The advance west toward Ireland took place by stages, as Viking marauders seized one island after another in the Hebrides. The Inner Hebrides became steadily more Scandinavian in character, while the Irish and Scots living on the windswept outer belt of islands held out more successfully.

Nonetheless, by the mid-ninth century a large Viking-dominated political entity had emerged in Scotland. Dubbed the earldom of Orkney, it owed allegiance not to any Scottish ruler but rather to the kings of Norway. Its lands included a large swath of the western Hebrides. A later saga, *The Orkney Saga,* and Snorri Sturluson's history of Norway would credit the conquest of Scotland to a single Norwegian king, Harald Finehair, but this is unlikely. Once again, the sagas both lead and mislead. No doubt, Viking chieftains in the region such as Ketil Flatnose, who ruled in the Hebrides from 840 to 880, acknowledged the authority of the great Vestfold kings like Harald and his father, Halfdan the Black, back home. But conquest and control were entirely in these local chieftains' hands, not governed by some crowned head in Norway. By the end of the tenth century, the current earl of Orkney, Sigurd the Stout, was probably the single most powerful man in Scotland, as well as the richest.

Sigurd made the mistake, however, of choosing to fight on the losing side at the battle of Clontarf in Ireland, in 1014, where he managed to lose his life as well as his army. The Viking position in Scotland quickly deteriorated, and power progressively shifted to the Scottish rulers from the mainland. But even their success was, ironically, due to the Viking penetration of their domain. The Norsemen's incursions had shattered the traditional power structure that had prevailed in the northern kingdom since the Anglo-Saxon invasion: Picts dominating the highlands; Britons the area around Strathclyde; Scots controlling the Dalriada, or western seaboard; and the Angles and Saxons ruling Northumbria. The Scots managed better than the rest to weather the Scandinavian storm. Starting in 844, with their conquest of the Picts, the Scots would sweep over the remaining communities until by 973 they had created a united kingdom of Scotland based on the mainland. The Viking retreat after the death of Sigurd the Stout enabled the Scots to advance their influence still farther, laying the foundation for the medieval Scotland of William Wallace and Robert the Bruce.

The kings of Norway, however, continued to claim the farthest western islands until 1266, when they finally surrendered sovereignty to the Scots. Yet the outer islands remained centers of Scandinavian resistance. This was also true of the Orkneys and Shetlands to the north, which remained Norwegian territory until quite late in the Middle Ages, but also the western Hebrides. Those islands, also known as the Western Isles, became a formidable kingdom in their own right. There, Norse and Gael people had allied and intermarried; they were known on the mainland as Gall-Ghàidheil.

The Gall-Ghàidheil would fight and die as seagoing warriors well into the fourteenth century; their name would live on in the word *gallowglass,* the term for a Scottish mercenary who served far and wide in medieval Europe. The gallowglasses were a foe every Scottish king had to reckon with, just as every Scottish merchant sailing in the approaches of the Irish Sea had to fear the Gall-Gaedhil ships, which were called *birlinns.* They were Viking longships in all but name.

The most famous — or notorious — of the Lords of the Isles (whose lands included Kintyre, on the mainland) was Summerled, the son of a Gaelic father and a Norwegian mother, who first claimed the title for himself and for his descendants. Among them were the rulers of Clan Donald, the MacDonalds, who in turn would claim Summerled as one of their own. As Lords of the Isles, the chiefs of Clan Donald ruled the western reaches of Scotland for more than two centuries from their base on the island of Islay. Their doom came in 1480, when John MacDonald, chief of Clan Donald and Lord of the Isles, lost a vicious sea battle against his bastard son Angus Og MacDonald in Bloody Bay in the Sound of Mull, which shattered forever the power of the Lords of the Isles. Their lands soon reverted to the Scottish crown, and the last remaining Viking principality in the British Isles vanished. Only place names and some Viking graves, including one on the tiny island of Saint Kilda, bear witness to the Scandinavians who once dominated and terrified populations on the northern and western coasts of the British Isles.

One of those islands is the Isle of Man, which lies squarely between Ireland and Scotland. So it is no surprise that the isle became populated by Vikings coming both from Norway and the Viking settlements in Ireland and on the British mainland. Although the island is only fifty kilometers long and fifteen kilometers wide, in the words of historian Else Roesdahl, "the wealth of Viking evidence here is unequalled in any other Viking colony."

Although Vikings had been landing on Man from at least the early ninth century, shortly after the raids on Lindisfarne, legend has it that Viking rule began with a survivor from the great battle between the Vikings and the Saxons at Stamford Bridge, in 1066. This survivor was Godred Crovan, who took refuge on the island and established a kingdom there. In fact, the central political institution of Man rather closely resembles that of another Viking colony, Iceland, with its Althing. The Isle of Man's Tynwald still meets every July 5 — competing with Iceland's Althing for the title of oldest continuous representative body in the world.

More than thirty Viking graves have survived there, perhaps the most intriguing one near Peel Castle, built in the eleventh century on the remains of a former Celtic monastery by Vikings who acknowledged the rule of King Magnus Barefoot of Norway. The grave is older than that, dating from perhaps 950, and holds the remains of a woman of considerable means and status. The prize of her collection of burial goods is a magnificent necklace of precious stones from various parts of Britain and Europe, some dating back to more than three hundred years before this Manx woman first donned the necklace.

But who was she? There is no clue, although some speculate that she may have been not only the head of a wealthy household but also a wise woman or shaman. The grave does offer proof that the relatively high status with which women were held in Scandinavia was also true in some of their colonies, even though Viking women numbered fewer abroad than in their homelands — or later in Iceland.

The Isle of Man is also famous for its runic inscriptions, including crosses that combine both pagan and Christian symbols. In fact, Norse Christian graves outnumber their pagan counterparts, suggesting that the Vikings on Man converted earlier than their Scandinavian cousins — very likely voluntarily rather than as a gesture of political allegiance or submission.

Despite the absence of Celtic place names on the island, which were almost entirely supplanted by Norse names, other evidence suggests the Celtic influence remained strong on the Isle of Man, even with its Viking overlords. Manx, a Celtic dialect, remained the principal language for islanders, and runes reveal that some of the Vikings had sons with Celtic names. A DNA survey by University College, London, shows a relatively small Scandinavian genetic legacy, barely 15 percent, which declines in proportion to the physical distance from Norway.

All the same, the mark of the Viking remains indelible in Man's runes and carvings. One of them displays the earliest known representation of the legend of Sigurd, showing him slaying the dragon Fafnir and tasting the dragon's blood — created at least a century before the story was written down in the form of a saga.

The Norwegians and Danes together were the conquerors of Ireland and Scotland, and Swedes the makers of Russia. But the story of how England became the Vikings' most significant colony belongs entirely to Denmark and the Danes. Nowhere was the mark of the Viking more closely interwoven with the people they had tried to conquer, even though eventually those Vikings wound up conquered themselves.

The peace that King Alfred had sworn with Guthrum in 878 did not last long after Alfred's death, in 899. The border between Wessex and the Danish-ruled territory known as the Danelaw again became unstable as Alfred's successor, King Edward, faced a revolt by his cousin Athelwold, who turned to the Danes for support. The combined attack on Wessex in 903, however, backfired. Athelwold and the local Danish king, Eohric, were killed in the same battle, and a Danish counterattack was checkmated in another, at Tettenhall in 910. As the distinguished medieval historian Robert Southern once wrote, "It was a time when he who committed himself to open battle, threw his fortune to the winds." All at once, the power of the Danish rulers of the kingdom of York, which comprised the bulk of the Danelaw, was exposed as vulnerable.

Edward had two indispensable tools, left to him by Alfred, for taking the war to the Danelaw. The first was an English militia, or *fyrd,* which was a direct copy of the Vikings' own armies, with a core of professional soldiers and armed retainers supported by local levies that could stay on campaign for months. The second was the system of fortifications, or *burhs,* that Edward could fall back to for last-minute defense — the physical foundations of urban England in the future. In swift order Edward swept through Danish Mercia and captured East Anglia. In 918 his sister Ethelfleda was recognized as ruler of Northumbria just before her death later that year.

The conquest of the Danelaw had taken less than seven years, but King Edward's triumph wasn't yet complete. The reason: a new Viking invasion, this time from Ireland. As Viking influence in Ireland waned, emigrants found new outlets for their energies on the mainland to the east, especially in northwest England and Northumbria. The most prominent of them was Ragnald, a Viking warlord from Ireland who seized control of York and shored up the Danish resistance to a resurgent West Saxon offensive. Ragnald himself died in 921, and Edward in 924. Their successors, Sigtrygg and Athelstan respectively, never met on the field of battle. But Sigtrygg's son Olaf and Athelstan did, in 937, at the pivotal battle of Brunanburh, where Olaf was joined by his uncle Guthfrith, the titular king of Dublin and a close ally of the Scots of Strathclyde.

Brunanburh was a battle for all the marbles, as it were, to determine ultimate lordship over the north of England — and ultimately all of Britain. It pitted a Danish-Irish army backed by Scottish allies against an English army backed by Danish-English allies, as well as Viking mercenaries. Athelstan won a crushing victory, and *Egil's Saga* (written three centuries later) gives us a vivid picture of the battle. Perhaps surprisingly, the saga's hero, Egil Skallagrimsson, and his brother Thorolf fight on the side of the English king against the Danes.

After routing the Scots, Egil and Thorolf turn on their main enemy: "Egil and his men headed for the king's column [that is, King Olaf's column], came upon them from their vulnerable side and soon inflicted heavy casualties. The formation broke up and disintegrated. Many of Olaf's men fled, and the Vikings let out a cry of victory. When King Athelstan sensed that King Olaf's column was giving way, he urged his own men forward and had his own standard brought forward, launching such a fierce assault that they broke ranks and suffered heavy losses. King Olaf was killed there, along with the majority of his men, because all those who fled were killed if they were caught."

According to the *Anglo-Saxon Chronicle*, "The two brothers, the king [Athelstan] and Atheling, returned together to their own country, the land of the West Saxons, exulting in the battle. They left behind them the dusky-coated one, the black raven with its horned beak, to share the corpses, and the dun-coated, white-tailed eagle, the greedy war-hawk, to enjoy the carrion, and that grey beast, the wolf of the forest."

Never, according to the chronicle, "was a greater slaughter of a host made by the edge of the sword, since the Angles and the Saxons came hither from the east, invading Britain over the broad seas, and the proud assailants, warriors eager for glory, overcame the Britons and won a country."

It must have seemed that Brunanburh had settled the future of northern England for good. Nothing, however, could have been further from the case. Contrary to how the saga tells it, Olaf was not killed at all but survived to return to Dublin. By 939 he was back in England to renew the fight. In fact, he and other Viking warlords, including an exiled Norwegian king turned adventurer named Erik Bloodaxe, would continue their desperate bid for power over the kingdom of York until 954. By then, Danish and Viking rule over England really did appear to be in permanent eclipse, although it would have a rousing resurgence fifty years later, under Denmark's King Canute. Meanwhile, however, the Norse imprint on the land was emphatically, and permanently, in place.

The Viking legacy was apparent, first of all, in terms of place names. Virtually every one of the thousands of English town and village names ending in *-by* (meaning "farm or village"), *-thorp* or *-thwaite* (meaning "a clearing") betrays its Viking origin, or at least a Viking takeover. Nor was the takeover sudden or temporary. The main period of Scandinavian name production seems to have been the early 900s, well after the initial Danish occupation. Experts have identified no fewer than eight hundred place names south of the Tees (not even the heart of the Danish settlement) with the suffix *-by*, at the end of the eleventh century. Other Scandinavian suffixes such as *-gil* (a ravine or valley with a stream), *-ey* (island), *-holm* (islet), *-wick* (bay), and *-ford* (fjord) pop

Anglo-Saxon and Viking silver penny coins found at the Vale of York, South Yorkshire, England, tenth century. Tony Baggett / iStock / Getty Images

up all across the British Isles as well as along English coastal areas or river valleys. Some place names reflect the names of the original Viking owners, such as Kettlethorpe (Ketil's farm) and Grimston (the village of Grim, *-ton* being the Anglo-Saxon suffix meaning "village").

Nor was the Norse influence limited to geographic names. Many English words, such as *cast, egg, knife,* and *window,* have Old Norse origins. In fact, it's estimated that the total number of Viking loan words in modern English comes to more than six hundred. These include *they, their,* and *them,* which replaced the Old English *hie, heira,* and *him.* Throw in *husband, fellow, happy, ills, bank, knife, race, thirst, carve, cut, drown, scare, take, want, birth,* and *die* (as in "to die" or "pass on"), and it's easy to see how the *Donsk tunga* became part of everyday life for everyone in England, not just those within the Danelaw — a region that, as early as 962, English kings acknowledged was a law unto itself and its Danish residents. Even the word *law,* as in *Danelaw,* has its origin in the Old Norse *lag.* While the actual term *Danelaw* did not gain currency until the early tenth century, it denoted a world apart from the rest of England, not only legally and linguistically but culturally and economically as well.

The Danelaw itself was split into three different districts. The southern Danelaw extended from the Thames to the Welland, which flows into the Wash. The eastern Danelaw comprised East Anglia. The heart of the Danelaw, however, was its northern sector, between the Well and the Tees: an area larger than William the Conqueror's Normandy. This sector included the so-called Five Boroughs, where the inhabitants maintained their own courts and made laws in accordance with those they knew from their Danish homeland, not those of the Anglo-Saxons.

The capital at York, with a population of twenty thousand by 1066, was a center of inter-British trade (objects from Viking Ireland and Scotland have been found at archaeological sites in England) as well as international commerce. Among the goods that made their way to York were wine from northwestern Europe, silks from Constantinople, and even small cowrie shells, which can come from only one place on earth: the Red Sea and the Gulf of Aden.

As a distinct legal and administrative unit, the Danelaw would survive the Norman Conquest in 1066. William the Conqueror himself confirmed that local custom was to be recognized as law for the West Saxons as well as the Danes. The Danish were after all present in large numbers (a contrast to the handful of Norman warriors who established control in 1066). They'd descended from men who had brought their families and settled down on the land. By the time the Conqueror's officials surveyed the realm, gathering the statistics that appear in the Domesday Book, persons of Scandinavian origins made up 60 percent of the Lincolnshire peasantry, 40 percent of the East Anglian peasantry, and 50 percent of the northern Danelaw. Four hundred years later, they were still there.

The farms they occupied were also distinct. The rank-and-file Viking warrior himself was expected to cultivate the land he was given by his overlord. The large estates that the Vikings took over were broken up into separate holdings;

though the landlord kept control, he hardly held what could be called outright ownership. Instead, the key figures in these estates, or sokes, were their farmers. They gradually acquired the right to sell, lease, bequeath, or give away their land. These expanded rights soon came to be reflected in place names, such as in Woolston in Berkshire, which was the *tun* (homestead) of a Norse owner named Wulfric. He gained full rights over his property in the ninth century.

The contrast with the south of England was striking. Whereas in Kent large estates remained long after the Norman Conquest, in the Yorkshire Wolds (part of the Danelaw) such estates had been broken up into many units of private ownership well before the Norman Conquest. The rise of the sokemen, the free farmers who comprised a large part of the population, was a distinct feature of the Danelaw settlements and would remain so well into the future.

Ultimately, of course, the separate legal system of the Danelaw disappeared. Yet the sokeman continued to till his land as he saw fit and answered to no man except the king; he remained an important part of the social and cultural landscape of northern England in the Middle Ages and beyond. By the time of the Norman Conquest, these farmers made up half of the population in Lincolnshire, one-third (two thousand) in Leicestershire, and nearly one-third (fifteen hundred) in Nottinghamshire. Whether of Norse or Anglo-Saxon descent,* they saw the land they farmed not in the feudal terms of tenure in exchange for service but in terms of rights — we can even say individual rights.

---

* Deciding this issue, that is, who was a Viking descendant and who an Anglo-Saxon "native," hasn't been helped by the science of DNA. The geneticist David Goldstein of University College, London, launched a study in 2000 to try to determine to what extent the Vikings left their genetic mark on the British Isles, including the Danelaw. His effort was frustrated, however, by the belated discovery that the Anglo-Saxon and Nordic genetic signatures were too close to be distinguishable, since people of both groups came from the same original homeland (finding the difference between Viking and Celt provided easier). The University College study proved inconclusive, except perhaps to provide more evidence that Scandinavia was indeed "the womb of nations."

In 1978 the anthropologist Alan Macfarlane published a groundbreaking book titled *The Origins of English Individualism*. It offered an explanation, based on the historical record, of why, from the Middle Ages onward, England never became a true peasant society as did the societies on the European continent. The country instead fostered the idea of individual rights, including property rights, and eventually a form of representative government based on protecting those rights.

By tracking the data, Macfarlane was able to show that by 1200, or possibly earlier, a system of law and custom had grown up in England that recognized property as a personal possession to be sold or alienated at will. In contrast, in typical peasant societies, such as those of medieval France or Germany, property was treated as the possession of an entire family and could not be alienated or sold by any single family member. Furthermore, the system in England also endowed women with a higher legal status than was the case in typical peasant societies. The legal historian Richard Maitland states that, after the Norman Conquest and under English law, "a woman with no husband [was] a fully competent person for all the purposes of private law; she sues and is sued, makes enfeoffments, seals bonds, and all without any guardian." Compare that to the situation in France at the time, where women could not inherit property at all.

That legal status for women does, however, conform to the laws of the Viking homeland known to the Danelaw's inhabitants. It may be entirely coincidence, but many of the places where Macfarlane found evidence to support his case, such as East Anglia, Suffolk, and the West Midlands, had been part of the Danelaw.

Macfarlane's thesis remains controversial. No single explanation may account for the differences between English law and politics and the legal and political systems that developed on the Continent. A century or more ago, historians tried to explain this difference in terms of a romanticized "Anglo-Saxon democracy" or a Nordic racial mystique. The answer, however, may be simpler, rooted in historical reality. In short, a clear thread may connect the Viking sokemen of the Danelaw to the intellectual ferment that produced the Petition of Right of the English Parliament in 1628 and, ultimately, the Bill of Rights in America.

While this link between the Viking spirit and Anglo-American constitutional and legal theory remains controversial, the presence of a Viking legacy
in the institutions of the emerging English kingdom and its way of life is not.
Another branch of the Viking family, the Normans, drove that impact even
deeper. By then the Viking world had extended far to the west: farther, in fact,
than any other Europeans would travel for nearly another five hundred years.

4

The World the Vikings Made, Part Two

Normandy, the Atlantic, and North America

> Then that decree [to submit and pay tribute to the
> Norwegian king] was sent to Iceland on the advice of
> the Cardinal [William of Sabina], since he called it
> beyond belief that the land was not subject to some
> king, as were all the others in the world.
>
> — *The Saga of King Hakon Hakonarson,* thirteenth century

THE URGE TO settle rather than plunder was first made manifest in the Viking conquests of the British Isles. Eventually the same proved true of the Viking invasion of France. There, just a year after the battle of Tettenhall, a Norwegian warlord and his companions carved out an autonomous principality, with its own language and laws and customs — the duchy that was destined to become Normandy.

The Franks called him Rollo, but his real Scandinavian name was Rolf, son of Rognvald, earl of More. He had had a lively career as a Viking marauder, not only in Francia but in Scotland and Ireland too (although the story, circulated by a biographer who was paid by Rolf's grandson, that Rolf had been one of Ragnar's warriors at the siege of Paris in 885 seems very doubtful). *The Saga of Harald Finehair* says Rolf was so large, no horse could carry him, so he had to go everywhere on foot; this gave rise to nicknames such as Ganger Rolf and Rolf the Walker. Again, very dubious. But an additional claim, that he managed to offend King Harald and was therefore outlawed, has a ring of truth to it.

Like other exiles from the Nordic homeland, Rolf left to carve out his fortune with his sword. In his case, it was an armed expedition up the Loire River into the heart of Francia. Rolf fought his way eastward until he was beaten by the troops of Charles III, the king of West Francia, in 911, in a pitched battle outside the walls of Chartres — once again proving that the Vikings were far from invincible, especially against a well-armed and well-prepared foe. But the emperor evidently decided it was better to placate Rolf, or Rollo, than try to drive him out of Francia altogether, so he granted the Viking leader a large tract of land in the valley of the lower Seine River.

Rollo did, however, have to pay a price for this concession; conversion to Christianity (there are, however, indications that he reverted to his ancestral religion before his death). Whether a written treaty sealed this arrangement remains doubtful. But certainly, at some date before 918, Rollo and his followers took possession of considerable land holdings in the area, and Charles III formally recognized them. Peace with the emperor also gave Rollo the opportunity to expand his territory, which would include the city of Rouen, and his power. In short order he commanded an area bounded by two rivers, the Epte and the Orne, and the sea. The territory's center comprised the districts on both sides of the Seine between Les Andelys and Vernon, and reached westward as far as Évreux.

The Seine provided the central axis for Rollo's possessions, right in the middle of what would become the kingdom of France. That waterway gave him and his followers access even to Paris itself. They swiftly became masters of trade and commerce up and down the river, and thence out to the English Channel. Two ancient Roman roads connecting the Channel to Marseille, and then Tours to Bayeux, were conduits for overland travel through the territory Rollo and his henchmen controlled.

These were the lands of the *Nor manni*, or Northmen, as the other inhabitants of Francia called them. Eventually, the region became known as Normandy, a land of strong warriors, loyal friends, and treacherous foes. Starting with his son William Longsword, Rollo's successors would lead their warriors on one campaign of conquest after another, until finally they reached across the sea to England, and even to Italy and Sicily. One would lead the campaign to capture Jerusalem in the First Crusade.*

At the same time—in language, custom, and law—these Vikings would soon shed their Scandinavian heritage and become one with their Frankish neighbors (although Old Norse was still spoken and understood in Bayeux as late as the 1020s). Grave sites show that they adopted the burial customs of their Frankish neighbors very quickly. Their trade ties with Scandinavia, never very strong, had largely ended by the late 900s. More striking, there is no trace in the historical record of a Thing or any other tribal assembly. Perhaps the Norsemen of Rollo's day were too few on the ground for the institution to make any practical sense.

Nonetheless, they left their mark on the place names of the region, especially along the coast. In today's Normandy a slew of villages bear a compound name made up of the original Viking colonist's name and the suffix *-tot,* which comes from the Old Norse word *tomt,* or *toft,* meaning "plot of land." Bramatot, Coletot, Gonnetot, Herguetot, and Ketetot (Ketil's *toft*)—this mark of the Vikings in Normandy remained permanent. Other Norse names became Latinized over time, such as when Asbjorn changed to Auber, Asfridr to Anfray, Astketill to Anquetil, and Thorvaldr to Touroude.

Elsewhere the French suffix *-ville* was added to a Norse name or nickname such as Amundi (Émondeville), Blakkr (Blacqueville), Bosi (Beuzeville), Barni (Barneville-sur-Seine and Barneville-Carteret), Bondi (Notre-Dame-de-Bondeville), Kati (Catteville), Stali (Étalleville), Thori (Tourville), and Toki (Tocqueville), the ancestral home of Alexis de Tocqueville, author of *Democracy in America*—among numerous other examples.

By the end of the tenth century, the Normans already seemed almost indistinguishable from their Frankish neighbors. But in their fearlessness, restlessness, and "eager thirst of wealth and dominion," they remained Vikings at heart. The chronicles tell of William Longsword, Rollo's son, visiting Attigny, where the most powerful nobles in the land were gathered to greet Otto I, the

---

* See Chapter 6.

Holy Roman emperor, in 941. When William found that the doors had been barred to him, he simply broke them down and demanded his seat at the table. Otto responded to this insult by having William murdered a year later.

William's son Richard was only ten years old when the Frankish king Louis IV and the Capetian duke Hugh joined forces to try to stamp out the Normans once and for all. It was the supreme crisis of Norman history. The Norman warriors, potentially spurred on by a boost in patriotism related to a revival of paganism in the territory, rallied around William's young heir. But by happenstance, Hugh Capet and the French king fell out and became enemies. Hugh helped Richard recapture Rouen, and after their victory the duke gave his daughter Emma to the youngster, who then became duke — but at least one chronicle still dismissed him as a "pirate chief."

Richard I, duke of Normandy, now commanded a territory much larger than the one Rollo and his warriors had originally carved out. It stretched from the Cotentin Peninsula in the northwest to the town of Eu on the river Bresle in the northeast, and extended as far south as Sées and the Aure River. Rouen, Bayeux, Caen, Lisieux, and Pitres were its major local trading centers. And, if Richard and his successors ever needed to confront the king of the Franks in his own capital, Paris was an easy march across the county of Vexin and down the river Seine.

Here was a power base for any Norman ruler ambitious and ruthless enough to use it to full advantage — built upon a group of warriors too few to change the character of their new homeland but numerous enough to maintain independent rule. In many ways, the Viking conquest of Normandy prefigured the impact Scandinavian immigrants would have on America. They quickly assimilated, in terms of culture and language, with the majority population, yet they remained distinct enough that contemporaries perceived the difference — and came to look to their leadership when it counted.

Nothing illustrates the core character of the Normans better than the story of Rollo's confrontation with Charles III, also known as Charles the Simple, at the swearing of their treaty. Rollo was told it would be fitting and proper for him to kiss the foot of the king, his superior lord. It is said that he replied, "I will never bow my knees at the knee of any man, and no man's foot will I kiss."

• • •

While Viking adventurers were carving out territories and kingdoms for themselves abroad, others at home were transforming their raw, inhospitable homeland into its first truly unified kingdoms.

Earlier histories of Norway, Denmark, and Sweden traced this process back to the 800s and early 900s. The race of supermonarchs who reportedly carried out this heroic feat are duly celebrated in the sagas and the *Heimskringla,* as well as in Saxo Grammaticus's *History of the Danes.* They come with formidable nicknames like Harald Finehair, Erik Bloodaxe, Hakon the Good, and Erik Greycloak, and they are portrayed as kings who, through a series of epic battles, expedient marriages, and equally expedient murders worthy of an HBO miniseries, managed to impose some semblance of order on the disorderly territories they ruled. In time, their realms started to bear some resemblance to the modern nation-states of Scandinavia, which later historians would acknowledge and salute.

Great, stirring stuff. But is it true at all? A cold and sober look at the facts indicates that these figures hardly live up to their reputations in saga and legend. Some, in fact, may not be historical figures at all.*

Take Harald Finehair, or Fairhair (in Old Norse, *Haraldr inn hárfagri*). Widely celebrated in the sagas and the *Heimskringla,* he became an important figure in the Norwegian nationalism of the nineteenth century during the

---

* That's probably true of the most famous Viking of them all, Ragnar Ladbrok, or Ragnar Hairy Breeches, who is said to have lived between 850 and 900 and who is the star of today's graphic novels, movies, and TV shows. The most complete account of Ragnar's career comes from the thirteenth-century chronicler Saxo Grammaticus, in his *History of the Danes.* According to Saxo, Ragnar Ladbrok first surfaces raiding the Baltic around 840 or 850, then leads an enormous fleet of three hundred ships — meaning an army of no less than twelve thousand men — before emerging as the ruler of a Viking empire extending across Ireland, the Orkneys, and virtually all of Scandinavia. This is a physical as well as a historical impossibility. In *The Saga of Ragnar Ladbrok* (almost certainly the source from which Saxo drew his more sensational material) Ragnar rescues a princess from a dragon and saves himself from its venom by wearing a pair of leather breeches covered in pitch. Saxo adds that Ragnar stuffed these pants with hair beforehand, hence his famous nickname (*ladbrok* literally means "hairy britches").

country's struggle for independence from Sweden. According to the *Heims-kringla,* this son of King Halfdan the Black inherited a series of small and dispersed kingdoms in Vestfold, which he gradually consolidated into a single realm. The story of his empire-building exploits, particularly his victory at Helsingfjord in 872, in which he defeated five other contending Norwegian kings, provided a founding father narrative that seemed to herald Norway's emergence as an independent nation.

A national monument to Harald was erected in 1872 on Haraldshaugen, a prehistoric burial mound at the town of Haugesund, which, it was assumed, was Harald Finehair's burial place. Next to Saint Olaf, who doesn't appear on the scene for another two hundred years, Harald Finehair is probably the most popular and revered Norwegian monarch from the Viking era.

His legend begins with a love story. He proposed marriage to Gyda, daughter of Eirik, king of Hordaland, who said she wouldn't marry him "before he was king over all of Norway." Inspired by his love for her, as well as his love of power, Harald vowed not to cut or comb his hair until he was sole king of Norway. Ten years later, having accomplished his goal, he finally trimmed his locks, and changed his name. The former Harald Shockhead, or Harald Tanglehair (Haraldr lúfa), became Harald Finehair, the name by which he is now commonly known.

It's a lovely tale. But there may not be a word of truth to any of it. In 1976, the historian Peter Sawyer began to cast serious doubt on the entire legend. Since then, other historians have pointed out that no contemporary evidence supports the saga stories about Harald Finehair. For example, the late-ninth-century account of Norway provided by Ohthere to the court of England's Alfred the Great, along with the history by Adam of Bremen written down in 1075, don't mention any king of Norway who corresponds to the period when Harald was said to be in power.

With Harald's apparent successor, King Erik Bloodaxe, we are on somewhat firmer historical ground, although how unified his kingdom really was is hard to assess. No genealogical evidence supports the *Heimskringla's* claim that Erik was actually the son of the legendary Finehair. Erik does step into the pages of history because of his activities in England, where he crowned himself the king of Northumbria. But this took place after he supposedly had been expelled from his throne in Norway by another offspring of Finehair, Hakon Athelstansfostri (so-called because the ruler of England, King Athelstan, adopted him as a son — another highly dubious narrative).

The bottom line is, virtually every account of Norway's unification under its kings in the pre-Christian era comes from sources written more than two centuries later. Moreover, those accounts came from the pens of Icelanders, descendants of the men Harald had supposedly driven into exile — a useful narrative for stressing Iceland's independence from Norway. In fact, all the evidence points in the other direction — Norway remained a divided nation as its various Viking overlords, including its Vestfold kings, contended for a hegemony that always eluded them — even as their neighbors sought to exploit that weakness for their own ends.

One of those neighbors was Sweden, and here again the picture conjured up in sagas and later chronicles doesn't seem to coincide with historical reality. We do know that the region was sharply riven for centuries by two contending tribes, the Svea and the Gauts, or Geats (Beowulf, the hero of the Anglo-Saxon poem, was a Geat). The Swedes of both tribes were farmers, hunters, and fishermen like their Norwegian neighbors, although they added to their activities the extraction of bog iron and the expansion, to the south, of land under cultivation. They couldn't quite penetrate the great forests of Småland and Norrland, though. That would have to wait another three centuries.

By 900, Sweden was also the place where Viking wealth tended to accumulate the most, flowing east from Byzantium and even farther east from Baghdad. Overall, the Swedes were the first Vikings to shed their marauder ways and emerge as merchants, traders, and manufacturers, serving as middlemen between the trading entrepôts of Birka and Gotland and the riches of the east. Uppsala, a major pagan cult center, had perhaps at one time also been a political center. But the so-called kings of Uppsala simply remained tribal chieftains writ large until Erik the Victorious emerged, after a fierce battle in the 980s, with his own nephew, Styrbjörn the Strong, son of Erik's former co-ruler Olaf. It is not clear whether there were any genuine Swedish monarchs before Erik the Victorious appeared. One thing seems indisputable: he is the first

Swedish king to be cited in independent sources. Sweden's official list of rulers starts with him, rather than any of the odd names listed as kings in Swedish runic inscriptions.

Erik apparently married a Polish princess, a sign of the kingdom's increasing involvement in the Baltic regions, beyond the Atlantic world of Norwegians and Danes. He died around 970, and his son Olaf Sköttkonung may have been the first Swedish ruler accepted by both the Svea around Lake Mälaren and the Geats around Lake Vättern — a major step toward forming a single unified nation.

Of these early unifying leaders, the one with the firmest historical grounding is probably Harald Bluetooth of Denmark. A reference to his unification (or more likely, reunification) of the separate parts of Denmark appears on two massive carved runestones found at the town of Jelling, Denmark. It seems that Harald raised them in about the year 965, in memory of his parents, Gorm (sometimes known as King Gorm the Old) and Thyra. The stones are strongly identified with the creation of Denmark as a nation. The inscriptions mention "Danmark," in the accusative form "tanmaurk" (*danmɔrk*) on the large stone and the genitive "tanmarkar" (*danmarkaʳ*) on the smaller. The exact extent of Harald's kingdom is unknown, although it is reasonable to believe that it stretched from the defensive line of the Danevirke, including the Viking city of Hedeby, across Jutland, the Danish isles, and even into part of southern present-day Sweden, as well as Scania and perhaps Halland.

More controversially, the Jelling stones claim that Harald had also "won" Norway. It's an assertion that Norwegian patriots, and even some historians, will happily dispute. It is true there's no other hard evidence to support Danish chauvinism in this matter. The best physical evidence of Harald's reign is the series of large ring forts he built to secure his hard-won kingdom from attack. All the same, the remains of the great barrack camps at Trelleborg and Fyrkat, suitable for an army preparing for long-range and long-term raiding, hardly suggest that Harald expected his unification of Denmark to go uncontested. Nonetheless, his success in pulling together the disparate parts of Denmark, as well as some outposts in Norway, have made him a symbol of connectivity. The name Bluetooth was chosen, for example, for a company focused on wire-

King Harald Bluetooth's runestone, Jelling, Denmark. Niels Quist / Alamy

less communications technology. The king's runic initials on the Jelling stone have become the Bluetooth corporate symbol.

Bluetooth's son Sven Forkbeard is even more firmly rooted in history. He mounted a series of attacks against England, which were completed by Sven's son Canute, eventually known as Canute the Great, by the middle of the eleventh century. With Forkbeard (the forts at Trelleborg and Fyrkat may be as much his constructions as his father's) we finally see a man of the north who is more medieval monarch than Viking chieftain.

Harald Bluetooth's Jelling stone bears witness to another profound change that marked this transition from one era to the next. Its inscription reads, "Haraldr who won for himself all of Denmark and Norway and made the Danes Christian." It even includes an image of the crucified Christ. Harald and the dynasty he founded experienced the eclipse of paganism and the beginnings of the Christian faith in their lands. The whole of Scandinavia was on the verge of a new kind of adventure, one that would alter its own culture and change its interactions with the rest of Europe.*

Sometimes the Viking heart finds itself lost at sea or otherwise — which can end up being a good thing. That's what's striking about the case of Naddod, or Nadd-Oddur, who was thrown out of his native Norway in about 850 for dueling (or possibly murder) and then set off for a new life in the Faroe Islands.

Those islands lie roughly two hundred miles off the Shetlands, directly northwest of the archipelago's westernmost island. A couple of decades before Naddod's voyage, the Faroes had become a busy Viking colony. According to *The Faereyinga Saga,* Grimur Kamban was the first to arrive there. His name betrays his Irish origin; he was either from the Emerald Isle itself or the western Hebrides. Irish monks had been using these islands as a refuge from Viking attacks, but now they had to flee, because by 825 the first settlers had arrived from the Sogn, Rogaland, and Agder districts of western Norway. A few years later, the islands were home to more sheep than people — wool knits from the Faroe Islands are still famous today. The sheep grazed peacefully on the windswept lower slopes of the mountainous terrain until summer, when they could move upland to fresh grazing. Their Viking owners built stone huts there so they could keep watch over their flocks.

Naddod was simply following the route blazed by Grimur and the other Norwegian colonists when foul weather — or bad seamanship — got him thoroughly lost. When he finally did reach land, he found himself far from the Faroes, at a place with great ice-covered mountains and forbidding cliffs. Once ashore, he climbed one of the peaks and found that absolutely nothing within his view could make him want to stay. So he set off again and this time reached the Faroes safely. There he told the people of his strange adventure and how, when he had gone back to his boat, snow had started to fall unrelentingly. This led him to give the island its first name: Snowland.

That was in about 850 or 860. Over the next several years, at least three other intrepid Viking sailors would make landfall on Snowland. The second

---

* See Chapter 5.

or third one, Floki Vilgertharson, experienced such a harsh, bitter winter there that he was moved to give the island a new name, and it stuck: Iceland. It must have been a harsh winter indeed, to impress a Norwegian.

Floki's innovative method of navigation became celebrated as well. As the saga records it, he carried with him three ravens. "When he loosed the first, it flew aft astern; the second flew high in the air, then back to the ship; the third flew straight ahead in the direction in which they found land." He and his crew then arrived in a bay so well stocked with fish and seals that they became distracted and failed to make hay that autumn. Their sheep and cows starved, which doomed any hope of their making a permanent settlement there.

The man who first put down roots successfully in this forbidding landscape was Ingolfr Arnarson, again a Norwegian, and again an outlaw. Here was the typical Viking exile: a man seeking a new future when his present situation offered nothing. And the way to seek that future was to set sail and discover where the sea might take him.

Or not quite. Arnarson apparently brought enough lumber with him to build a small house. As legend has it, when his ship inched close to land, he threw his two *instafars* (main posts) overboard to see where the current would carry them. The posts came ashore at a spot near a geothermal vent, which was releasing great clouds of steam into the air. Thinking the steam was smoke, Arnarson named the spot Reykjavík — "smoky bay" — and there he built his house.

Once word of Arnarson's find got out, other settlers from the Faroe Islands followed him there. What these Vikings and their families found in Iceland was a place unlike any they had ever seen. It was a land, in the filmmaker Neil Oliver's words, of "active volcanoes spewing lava; barren, sterile expanses of newborn rock; geothermal springs of boiling water, belching steam; the rotten-egg smell of sulphurous gases." Geologically speaking, Iceland sits on the fault line between the Eurasian and North American tectonic plates. Its landforms are still a work in progress. In Arnarson's time, only human beings inured to making something out of nothing would want to call it home.

And by 930 there were enough of them to have well settled the place, or at least the parts where that was possible. Most of the interior was uninhabitable. But despite Iceland's proximity to the Arctic Circle, the Gulf Stream gave the coastline, along with the plains in the southern part of the island, a relatively mild climate. What Iceland managed to yield from the arable land there was enough wheat and barley, as well as pasturage for cattle and sheep (woolen cloth became Iceland's leading export), to support occupation by about 430 settlers and their families — at least according to the *Landamabok* (*Book of Settlements*), which dates to the twelfth century.

By then the largest landowners, known as the *gothar,* or chieftains, had decided they would need to convene the usual general assembly that Viking tribes used to establish a regular political order for a community. So they created the Althing, which met for two weeks every summer at Thingvellir to proclaim new laws, review the old ones, adjudicate disputes, punish the guilty, and acquit the innocent — and do some marketing. This rough form of representative government, with free Icelanders approving or disapproving the decisions of the *gothar,* would continue to meet at Thingvellir right up until the middle of the nineteenth century, establishing Iceland's claim to be the world's oldest democracy. The Althing's meetings finally moved to Reykjavík in 1844, but it wasn't until 1881 that Iceland's government had a permanent building. There is something in the Icelandic people, and in Scandinavians generally, that sees freedom as a privilege best exercised in the great outdoors.

Iceland in those early years certainly represented Viking society at its most concentrated. Interestingly, the Icelanders always referred to themselves as Vikings, even though they never engaged in piracy or overseas expeditions. And although the majority of settlers seem to have come from western and northern Norway, which was roughly seven days' sail away, many moved there from Scandinavian settlements in the British Isles, as well as the Faroes. That meant there was a fair smattering of Irish and Scots among the Viking settlements in Iceland. Slaves from the Celtic lands were also present. Like other Vikings, the settlers in Iceland could not imagine running a large farm without slaves to help. In any case, the Celtic strain is more evident in Iceland's DNA than one might imagine. Even the name of one of its celebrated saga heroes, Njal of *Njal's Saga,* is Celtic in origin.

The men who built the first farms and raised their families in Iceland's earliest days of settlement considered themselves aristocrats. As we've seen, the term they were known by, *gothar,* derived from the Old Norse word for "god," implies that they once had a role in religious functions. But they soon exchanged any such role for politics, though they had no power to compel other free Icelanders, the thingmen, to obey them. They were, in fact, the island's power brokers, and the thingmen clustered around them to secure their own interests. A leading *gothi* (the rank of Icelanders who had the right to vote in the Law Council, or *Lögrétta*) might act as their advocate in the annual Althing or offer protection in a dispute with another thingman farmer.

Icelandic politics probably resembled Tammany Hall more than politics in the rest of Europe. There is no sign that kings or thanes (*thegns*) or jarls ever ruled, or were chosen to rule. The Althing and the voluntary relationship between *gothi* and thingman were paramount to getting business done, creating a system unique in Europe: an entirely self-created nation in which the government was entirely in the hands of free men. It was also a nation with no foreign enemies and a government that imposed no taxes and did not engage in public expenditure. In this polity, the rights of individuals were considered inviolate, and the majority held this view. These principles are summed up in a maxim from the *Sayings of the High One* (*Hávamál*): "Each of the wise should wield his power in moderation; he will find no one is foremost when stout men gather."

There was only one flaw in this Norse utopia — an otherwise perfect home for the Viking heart. Since there were no foreigners to rob or prey upon, the earliest Icelanders tended to turn on each other. The Icelandic sagas provide plenty of details about blood feuds that pitted family against family for generations. Perhaps the most nuanced of these dramas, *Njal's Saga,* tells of one such feud lasting fifty years between two Icelandic families — the kind of conflict that must have had many parallels in real life.

Nonetheless, the main character, Njal Thorgeirsson, is hardly the typical Viking hero. He never kills anyone; he doesn't even draw a weapon (the short ax he carries is worse than useless in battle). His power is strength of character, a human understanding that at times seems almost modern — one reason the saga is a favorite among contemporary readers. His counterpart, Gunnar of Hlidarendi, *is* a great warrior, the greatest in Iceland in fact, who has served (as many Icelanders did) as a mercenary in service to various Norwegian overlords. However, he also hates killing, and he and Njal are drawn together as

friends. The fact that they become entangled in a family feud, which ultimately costs them their lives, is a true tragedy.

The advice Njal gives Gunnar would be worthy counsel for any Viking in
Iceland: "Never kill in the same family twice, and never break a settlement
which good men make between you and others." He adds that "if these two
things happen, you will not have long to live. But otherwise you will live to be
an old man."

Old age eluded both Njal and Gunnar. But every Icelander, and every Viking, had come to wish for this fate, far more so than in the past. Icelanders
now yearned for a way of living that would make a long life the rule rather than
the exception.

Christianity seemed to promise that happier ending. In about 1000 or so,
the Althing accepted Christianity as Iceland's official religion. But Icelanders still found no peace. The clashes between great families intensified until
law and order broke down in the early thirteenth century, and Iceland was
plunged into civil war. That conflict led, in the end, to direct rule from Norway, in 1263. The Icelandic Free State, as its inhabitants had called it, came to
an end.

But the memory of what Iceland had once been would linger in the written word, more durable than recitations around the fireplace. Iceland became
the home of the skalds, the epic poets of the courts of the kings of Norway.
The skalds' poems would be written down by numerous hands in the thirteenth and fourteenth centuries, giving us the earliest record of the history not
just of the Icelanders but of their Viking forebears too. These writings provide
glimpses of their pagan religion, which had been all but extinguished two centuries earlier. Vividly written, stunningly detailed, and historically unreliable,
the sagas (there are more than forty) live on as a record of a Viking culture that
was fast disappearing even while being preserved on parchment.*

"Iceland is the first 'new nation' to have come into being in the full light of
history," writes the historian Richard Tomasson, "and it is the only European
society whose origins are known." In a sense, Iceland was a test case for how

---

* For more on the sagas, see Chapter 7.

Scandinavians might build a new life in America, a place where they could live as they preferred: as freeborn citizens in a land that offered liberty.

But first, someone had to venture farther west.

It had taken one Norwegian murderer to find Iceland, and another would determine the next stage in the Viking march across the North Atlantic, to Greenland.

His name was Erik Thorvaldson. When he was accused of murder in his Norwegian homeland, he and his father fled to Iceland. There Erik, with his hair-trigger temper and general contempt for the rule of law, got himself into more trouble. In about 982 he decided to set out by sea for points farther west — in fact, no European was ever recorded as having sailed so far in that direction.

To say Erik Thorvaldson — known to his contemporaries as Erik the Red, on account of his flaming red hair — "discovered" Greenland would be a mistake. Other Icelanders knew of the island's existence. It is the largest island in the world; on a very clear day it can be seen from the summit of Iceland's highest peak, Snaefell. Others had landed there, including a Norwegian adventurer named Gunnbjørn Ulfson, who would later lend his name to Greenland's highest peak (Gunnbjørn Field). But Erik the Red was the first to decide to stay. This is because, after rounding what came to be known as Cape Farewell, at the island's farthest southern tip, he found something extraordinary.

Despite being covered almost entirely by a massive ice sheet and situated well above the Arctic Circle, Greenland's west coast was a land of fertile fields and inviting fjords — certainly lusher than Iceland. Erik headed back to the land that had driven him out and announced that he had found "a green land," with plenty of room for settlement. Those willing to live under the rule of Erik the Red set off for this new potential paradise in twenty-five ships.

The destination may have sounded inviting, but the voyage was not. The travelers had to make their way through the treacherous Denmark Straits in the winter, which proved so dangerous that only fifteen ships made it through: the rest either were wrecked or turned back. Those who persevered found that Erik's promises proved true. The land was covered with pasture, forest, and a host of animals whose fur, feathers, and tusks would be in high demand back in their native Scandinavia. Clever traders claimed that the long, slender tusk of the narwhal was the horn of the legendary unicorn, making it a famous and much sought after commodity, at least among the gullible.

As the millennium approached, Erik's colony had grown to some three thousand hardy souls divided into two large settlements. They conducted a brisk trade with Iceland, which was conveniently nearby (as long as one sailed in the spring to avoid the storms and icebergs of the Denmark Strait). And since Iceland is only five days' sail from Britain, and seven from Norway — hardly far enough to make a Viking break a sweat — a regular four-way trade was soon underway. In fact, archaeological evidence indicates that the Greenlanders enjoyed a virtual monopoly of the trade in walrus tusks across Europe. DNA analysis has also played a vital part in revealing the ivory's transatlantic origins. We now know, for example, that the most famous ivory chess set of the Middle Ages, which represents warriors of the Viking Age and now is on display in the British Museum, was made from tusks harvested in Greenland.

About the time that Erik's settlement had firmly taken root, with farms scattered up and down the coast, Christianity came over from Iceland. The burial grounds next to the tiny church at Brattahlid, almost certainly the first church built in Greenland, reveals something about what these bold settlers were like. The site contains the remains of forty-seven men, thirty-seven women, and thirty-four children, one of whom was buried, along with twenty of the men, in a communal grave. They had probably all died elsewhere and were moved to Brattahlid at a later date, though we have no clue as to why. These Greenlanders were strong and, for the time, fairly tall. The women averaged five feet three inches in height, and the men five foot eight. Not a few of the men were over six feet tall.

It was around that date, or shortly before 1000, that Erik's son Leif decided he would lead an even more intrepid band of settlers still farther west, to explore a coastline that one of Greenland's sailors, Bjarni Herjólffson, had spotted fifteen years earlier.

The Vinland Sagas, the primary source of information we have of Leif's voyage and the subsequent ones led by his brother Thorvald, state that after a day or two of sailing, Leif found the coastline Bjarni had first seen. Large glaciers covered the highlands, and the land was "like a single flat slab of rock from the glaciers to the sea." Leif decided to name this coastline Stone-slab Land, or Helluland. Then the explorers ventured a little farther south, where they saw a stretch of forest-lined shore with white sandy beaches; Leif dubbed it Forest-land, or Markland. Then they went farther south still, where after two days' sail Leif and his colonists landed on a shore "where a river flowed into a sea from a lake," where salmon swam in abundance, and where "the land was so good that livestock would need no fodder." It was also more temperate than Greenland or Iceland, with days and nights more equal in length.

It was here, the sagas relate, that Leif Erikson and his companions created a colony they named Vinland, after the wild grapes they found. They built log houses and, for at least three summers and winters, maintained a Viking settlement before returning home to Greenland. They were the first Europeans to set foot in America — more than four hundred years before Columbus.

Twin sagas, one named for the Greenlanders and the other for Erik the Red, tell the story of the American Viking settlement, but their details vary. One credits Erik's son Leif as the founder, the other a married couple, Thorfinn Karlsefni and Gudrid Thorbjarnardottir, who also happened to be parents of the first Scandinavian child born in North America, little Snorri Thorfinnson. Despite these inconsistencies, the historical truth of the settlement they describe is no longer in doubt. The circumstantial evidence has simply grown too strong (for example, the discovery of an Indian arrowhead at a Viking site in Greenland, which could only have come from a North American tribe). Now the big question is not *whether* the Vikings landed in America, but *where*.

The sagas' accounts have, of course, been scoured for evidence that would locate the place where Leif's party landed. The first author to advance the thesis that the Vikings, not Columbus, were the first Europeans to discover America identified the location of Vinland in Rhode Island, or perhaps Massachusetts. Others, more reasonably, opted for Martha's Vineyard. But most cited places much farther north, along eastern Canada's coast, which was much closer to Greenland, with natural features that conformed more precisely to the descriptions in *The Saga of Erik the Red* (for example, the presence of glaciers). Hence, Helluland is now generally identified with Baffin Island and Markland with the coast of Labrador, or perhaps Newfoundland.

As for the location of the most significant settlement of them all — Vinland — scholarly opinion ranges all over the eastern coast of North America, from Nova Scotia to as far south as Cape Cod. In historical terms, no site seemed more potentially momentous — or as tantalizingly elusive. Given this uncertainty, and the occasional hoax or two, some wondered if the entire legend of Leif Erikson in America was simply that: more fiction than fact.

In 1965 the debate dramatically changed. Helge and Anna Ingstad, a husband-and-wife team of archaeologists from Norway, found traces of what was undoubtedly a Viking camp at L'Anse aux Meadows in Newfoundland. They unearthed the remains of five buildings made of stone and turf, which had been large enough to shelter upward of a hundred people. In style they were similar to contemporaneous buildings in Iceland and the Faroe Islands. The Ingstads also found evidence that the settlement's inhabitants engaged in fishing and hunting — but, significantly, there was no sign of farming. Other remains reflected typical Viking life: an oil lamp carved from soapstone, a bronze brooch, and a spindle whorl. The latter item indicates that L'Anse aux Meadows was hardly an all-male enterprise.

But was this place the Vinland of the sagas? Today most scholars agree that it probably was not. More likely it was a temporary boat landing, a center for repairs and other maritime refitting, with provisions for travelers to stay there over the winter. The real Vinland, if it really existed as the sagas claim, was probably located farther south, in the Gulf of Saint Lawrence. This area also marks the farthest northern limit of the region's wild grapes, a detail that gives the name Vinland at least a ring of historical truth. But if Vikings indeed settled there, it seems they didn't stay long enough to leave the kinds of traces that archaeologists can find. Did Leif and his companions land there, discover grapes and other wild fruit, and then use that find to characterize the entire coast, including the settlement at L'Anse aux Meadows, in order to tantalize and encourage potential immigrants?

We simply don't know. In any case, Vinland still lacks its modern-day discoverer. On the other hand, evidence does suggest that the real center of activity in Viking North America wasn't Vinland but Markland, where enterprising merchants cut down trees to bring back to treeless Greenland for home building (again, DNA from Greenland burial sites proves the case).*

In the end, what doomed the entire Viking American enterprise — L'Anse aux Meadows and the rest — was the slow but steady demise of the Greenland colony. There are indications that relations with the local Inuit tribes had deteriorated badly. More critically, a shift in climate occurred in about 1300. The so-called Little Ice Age swept over Europe at this time and expanded the Greenland ice sheet southward. Eventually, even the coastal areas became more and more unhabitable. Sea ice would cut the colonists off from the outside world for years at a time.

By 1410 only the so-called Eastern Settlement (on the southwest tip of Greenland, stretching from Brattahlid in the north to Herjolfsness in the south) still survived. Inuit tribes had taken over the other sites. In 1540, when a ship stopped at the Eastern Settlement, the seamen found only desolation: some deserted farms and huts, and inside one of them, a single unburied body.

What had happened? Together with the lost Vinland site, it's one of the great unsolved mysteries of archaeology. Were the Viking colonists wiped out by the Inuit, or by disease? Did the settlers decide that if you can't fight the Inuit, you might as well join them, voluntarily merging with their more numerous neighbors? Perhaps, but studies of the DNA of Inuit remains from the same period show no sign of a Viking legacy. It's also possible that Erik the Red's descendants simply realized that staying in Greenland was no longer worth the trouble and packed it in to return to Iceland. The truth of the matter still eludes us.

But the epic importance of the Viking settlements in North America rests on this fact: the Vikings had set in motion an era of globalization unlike any-

---

* Unfortunately, when it comes to the Vikings, stupidity and counterfactual fantasy know no bounds. Vinland, or rather a fictional conception of it, is a case in point. According to news reports, neo-Fascists and neo-Nazis in Canada have used their historical reenactment group, Vinland Productions, to suggest that this vanished settlement somehow established a white supremacist claim to North America. Yet there's no convincing evidence of permanent Viking residents in North America, and Vinland's location is a total mystery. Jeremy Christian, the white supremacist who gunned down Muslim worshipers in Portland, Oregon, repeated this absurd claim.

thing seen before. From North America to Russia and Baghdad, and innumerable points in between, Scandinavians were connecting the dots with their longships and shaping the character of the places they visited and conquered. The repercussions were unfathomable at the time. Those enterprising sailors bringing timber from Labrador to Greenland, or walrus tusks from Greenland to Norway and Denmark, could not realize that they were triggering a global transformation.

Yet this important fact does not overshadow another significant development. Erik the Red, the founder of Greenland, was a pagan like his Norwegian forebears, but his son Leif Erikson, the putative founder of Vinland, was a Christian. By 1000 CE, the Vikings were embarking on a journey that was spiritual rather than physical. It would carry them far from the pagan pantheon of their forefathers and closer to mainstream civilization, transforming the Viking heart largely for the better.

It was not an easy transition. In some parts of the Nordic world, the acceptance of Christianity would take centuries. Nonetheless, once Danes, Swedes, Norwegians, Finns, and now Icelanders and Greenlanders set off for that luminous but unfamiliar shore, there was no turning back. On the contrary, the Scandinavian peoples would bring their own special gifts to medieval Christendom and Christianity.

5

Twilight of the Gods

Vikings, Kings, and Christianity

I see the Earth
Rise a second time
From out of the sea,
Green once more.

— *The Poetic Edda,* "Voluspa," stanza 57

THE COMING OF Christianity to the Vikings was a major world event — it triggered the integration of the Norsemen's culture and energies into the European mainstream. Christianity would transform the Viking heart in profound ways that would shape Scandinavia and release those energies in creative new directions. The impact on Europe would be equally profound, as a new confidence and drive became part of the making of the Middle Ages — and the future of European civilization.

The process began on the margins of the Viking world, with the Norsemen's Swedish offshoot known as the Varangians or the Rus. But before the Rus rulers could convert, they needed to consolidate political and economic power, a pattern that would be repeated in other Viking kingdoms.

In 879 the original Viking conqueror of Russia, the freebooter and adventurer Rurik, died. Because Rurik's son was very young, power passed to his son's regent, the powerful and shrewd Helgi, known in Russian history as Oleg. The heavy influx of Arab silver that had enriched the original Rus dynasty had come to a halt around 875, and Oleg was forced to look for new ways to reach the silver from Samarkand and Tashkent, where coins were being struck for the Muslim world. That required new trade routes and new ways of securing them. The skills of a raider, or even a Viking merchant prince, would no longer suffice. The times called for someone who could rule a unified political state.

By this time, Scandinavians had been involved in shaping European Russia for nearly 150 years. They almost completely dominated the trade with the Byzantines along Russia's major river routes. But they had not suddenly morphed into a nation of commercial travelers. Like their Danish and Norwegian cousins, they were unafraid of using force and intimidation to drive a bargain. That was certainly true of their most outstanding boss of bosses, Regent Oleg.

Oleg devoted his reign as regent to building fortresses and towns, drawing up laws and collecting taxes, and breaking the will of the Slavic tribes that still stood in his way. Then he decided that was not enough. In 907 he organized another armed assault on Constantinople, this time with ten times the number of troops Rurik had assembled — 2,000 longships instead of 220 — and backed by a confederation of local tribal nations and fellow Scandinavians who had come to recognize the sovereign power of the kingdom of the Rus.

Like the earlier Rus attackers, Rurik's forces raided the suburbs of Constantinople with great slaughter, burning churches and palaces and torturing and beheading the Greek prisoners they took. The Greeks managed to secure the city where it opened to the Bosporus strait, making a seaborne assault impossible.

But Oleg had a plan that would reinvent Viking warfare.

"Oleg commanded his warriors to make wheels," the chronicle tells us, "which they attached to the ships, and when the wind was favorable they spread the sails and bore down upon the city from the open country." When the Greeks saw that the Vikings had converted their longships into land tanks — a first in military history — they lost all heart. They sent emissaries to Oleg and "implored him not to destroy the city, and offered to submit to such tribute as he should desire."

The result was one of the great treaties in eastern European history. It allowed for the provisioning and housing of Rus merchants visiting the capital, with clauses that set out terms for the return of runaway slaves and the handling of shipwrecked merchants and their property. It also created rules for Rus warriors seeking employment with the emperor as mercenaries, the first reference to the Viking soldiers who would become world-famous as the Varangian Guard. The links of trade and politics forged between Byzantium and the kingdom of the Rus would last through the centuries, becoming the central axis around which the history of eastern Europe, as well as the Turkish and Russian Empires, would revolve for the next one thousand years.

After the years of glory under Oleg's rule, Igor, also known as Ingvar, followed. He was Rurik's son, according to the chronicles, although Rurik must have been an old man when this boy was born — by no means impossible. Igor consolidated power over his growing state through signing treaties and coercing tributaries. And then, like any good son of the Rus, despite the treaty of 912 affirming the "long-standing amity which joins Greek and Rus," Igor launched his own attack on Constantinople, in 941.

This time the Greeks fought back. After three years, during which military advantage had seesawed back and forth, Igor and the Byzantine emperor reached an agreement. The emperor even threw in a tribute equal to that paid to Oleg. Trade between the Rus and the Greeks resumed with customary vigor. Yet what is maybe most striking about this treaty is that, of the sixty Rus envoys who negotiated and ultimately signed it, almost all bear Scandinavian names. More than seventy years after Rurik established his power base, the mark of the Viking was still stamped upon the state he had founded.

And this wasn't true only in Rurik's capital, Novgorod. His descendants were just one of many Scandinavian families dominating the landscape. The treaty with the Byzantines mentions princes from Chernigov, Polotsk, Rostov, Liubech, and other towns scattered along the Rus's main water routes. It was not until forty years later, under Prince Vladimir — the greatest of the Rus princes, who moved his capital from Novgorod to Kiev — that the formation of medieval Russia was complete. Vladimir was able to survey a realm that extended from modern Belarus, Russia, and Ukraine to the Baltic Sea. By 980 its frontiers could stand firm against assault from Baltic tribes to the north, central Asian raiders from the east, and the Bulgar threat from the south.

By now the Rus were also largely assimilated into their Slavic neighborhood. They no longer spoke Old Norse, and their style of dress no longer reflected their Scandinavian homeland. Through intermarriage and alliances, they had lost their ethnic distinctiveness. Only one feature from their Viking past remained: their pagan religion. In or around 987, Vladimir decided it was time for something new.

The German peoples and the Vikings had shared the same pagan pantheon until the Germans turned to Christianity, beginning in the fourth century CE. Although the names of these two peoples' gods were not always exactly the same (Odin was Wotan to the Germans, for example), the deities' relationships and attributes were. Both sprang from a range of divine beings drawn from pre-Norse religion, and they were not so different from other Indo-European gods. There is the sky god Tyr, or Ziu, in Old High German, which is a cognate with the Greek Zeus; Ullr (in Gothic, *wulpus*), or "the glorious one," a god of warriors and bowmen (later, Scandinavians made him the patron of skiing); and Njord, the god of the seas and winds.*

But all the surviving evidence indicates that the peoples of the north built their gods' mythology into a profound poetic art, something their German cousins never did. Perhaps there was simply more time around the fire in the deep of winter to think about and embellish these ancient stories. Perhaps their wider range of voyages and experiences triggered a desire to understand the cosmos on a deeper level. One might say that, like today's fantasy fiction

---

*How deeply rooted are these pre-Norse gods? The village my grandmother Anna came from, Ulefoss, takes its name from the god Ullr and means literally "Ullr's river."

authors and fans, the Vikings were staunchly committed to "other-world building," or creating an imagined reality in such exquisite detail that it seems truly real. Certainly, world building as a literary and religious exercise radiates from the various Icelandic sources, and it enables, to a certain extent, an understanding of Norse religion. These writings, like the so-called *Poetic Edda,* have no parallel in anything we know from Germanic sources.

The Nordic version of Genesis starts with the Ginnungagap, a yawning abyss of fog and freezing ice — not an unfamiliar setting in real-life Nordic realms. From its frigid, slimy depths rise the giant Ymir and the first humans, a Scandinavian Adam and Eve, who live in Midgard, or Middle Earth. A series of struggles between gods and giants culminates in the victorious rule of Odin, king of the Gods, in his realm of Asgard.

Odin comes to play many roles in Nordic and Viking mythology. The Nordic peoples had more than two hundred names for him. He is king of the gods but also the patron of outlaws and thieves. He is the "All Father" but also a practitioner of magic, which is usually considered a feminine art. Odin is a warrior but appears more often as a rampaging killer than a disciplined soldier — his very name can be read as "The Furious One." His embodiment of inspired frenzy in battle also made him the patron god of berserkers. "[Odin's] men went without their mailcoats and were mad as hounds or wolves, bit their shields ... they slew men, but neither fire nor iron had effect upon them." This powerful savage state became known as "going berserk." The term survives today to describe certain kinds of irrational or bizarre behavior in addition to the Vikings' born killers on the battlefield. Its roots lie deep, however, in Norse religion, in the transformational moment when certain Norse warriors — even great kings — released their inner beast to prevail in combat. It was a power owed to the god Odin. And like Odin himself, it had its good side as well as its bad.

Odin loves war far more than he does peace — the perfect god for a society of warriors. He is also the giver of victory. One spectacular way for a Viking chieftain to secure Odin's favor in battle was to hurl a spear over the heads of his enemies while shouting, "Odin owns you all!" (*Óðinn á yðr alla*). Norse worshipers knew him by his nickname, Greybeard, a figure disguised under a cloak and eye patch, wielding his staff and accompanied by two ravens as he wandered among men. But today he is probably best known as the lord of Valhalla, the place where brave warriors go after dying in battle — and where they prepare for the final confrontation with the enemies of the gods on the great day of reckoning, the apocalypse of Norse religion: Ragnarok.

Odin is a deity of many moods: cunning and valiant, selfish and passionate, an adventurer and a poet and a magician, a compulsive womanizer who is also devoted to his wife and family. He embodies the Viking masculine ideal: the man whose excellence places him above and beyond the law and who demands the respect of his peers by being so. He epitomizes the Viking heart in its most flamboyant form.

Odin appears in song and literature as delightfully if infuriatingly human alongside the rest of the Norse gods — Frey, the god of fertility (his image at the cult center of Uppsala had an enormous penis); Freya, Frey's sister and Odin's wife, a formidable magician in her own right; Thor, Odin's son, the god of thunder, "winds and rainstorms, fair weather and the fruits of the earth," with his mighty war-hammer Mjölnir; and Tyr, the warrior god left over from pre-Norse religion. In the sagas, Viking heroes approach their gods almost as equals. They bargain with and even threaten the gods in order to get their way. Odin, in particular, is a god whose word a Viking hero quickly learns is not to be trusted.

In Norse religion, relations between humans and the gods is a reciprocal, almost transactional arrangement; respect for a deity is given on condition of the god's support and aid. A tribesman and his family members had a right to expect fair treatment from their gods, just as they knew the gods expected fair treatment from them. In the end, both parties knew themselves to be subject to the power governing gods and men alike: fate, spun out by the Norns under the great oak tree, Yggdrasil, which supports all creation.

The exception to this rule is Loki. He is the trickster in the Nordic pantheon, both the gods' resourceful helper and their treacherous enemy. He is also the father of a woman named Hel, who rules the shadowy world where the dead reside. Christians would adopt her name to denote the netherworld included in their teachings. Perhaps because of his unsavory reputation, Loki's name isn't commemorated in a day of the week, like the war god Tyr (Tuesday), Thor (Thursday), and Frigg (Friday), and of course Odin himself, with

Wodin's Day, or Wednesday. But like Odin's, Loki's persona is connected with the animal world — and man's inner beast. He is the father of the World-snake and Fenrir the wolf, monsters with an important part to play in the overthrow of the gods on the terrible day of Ragnarok.

Ragnarok is the catastrophe of catastrophes, for giants and gods alike. The disaster is triggered not surprisingly by Loki, who incites one son of Odin, Hod, to murder another, Hod's brother Baldr. The punishment that the gods mete out for this misdeed turns Loki into their implacable foe. Loki leads the Jotnar, or evil troll-like giants, against the gods, precipitating a terrible apocalyptic showdown.

> *Brother will fight one another*
> *And kill one another . . .*
> *The world will be a hard place to live in.*
> *It will be an age of adultery,*
> *An age of the axe, an age of the sword,*
> *An age of storms, an age of wolves,*
> *Shields will be cloven.*
> *Before the world sinks in the sea,*
> *There will be no man left*
> *Who is true to another.*

On that "dark day for the gods," Loki and the Jotnar sail into the east on Naglfar, the giants' ship made entirely from the fingernails and toenails of the dead. They disembark to fight Odin and the warriors he assembles from Valhalla under a dying, blood-red sun. Like the loyal companions of a Viking's war band, Odin, Thor, and Heimdal all fight to the death, as does Loki. The fire-giant Surt's flaming sword eventually consumes everything: Asgard and Midgard, along with Jotunheim, the realm of the giants. What's left is a grim scene of desolation and death.

> *The sun turns black,*
> *The earth sinks into the sea,*
> *The bright stars*

Fall out of the sky.
Flames scorch
The leaves of Yggdrasil,
A great bonfire
Reaches to the highest clouds.

But then, astonishingly, the cosmos is renewed. Two people, a man and a woman, have managed to survive the destruction. Under the shelter of Yggdrasil, they live to renew the human race. The land slowly rises up from the sea, and a new sun shines down. A new home, a golden-roofed hall called Gimlé (literally "fire shelter"), arises in Asgard, which had once been the abode of the gods; it now shelters the survivors of Ragnarok. In short, the violence of Ragnarok has swept away the world's evils and replaced them with something fresh and new and pure.

I see the Earth
Rise a second time
From out of the sea,
Green once more.
Waterfalls flow,
And eagles fly overhead,
Hunting for fish
Among the mountain peaks . . .
Fields will bear harvest
Without labor,
All sickness will disappear.

Here the essential lesson of Norse religion shines through: what seems to be decline and destruction is ultimately a source of renewal. The nineteenth-century German philosopher and admirer of Norse religion Friedrich Nietzsche dubbed it the "myth of the eternal return," an idea that has taken hold in places influenced by Nordic myth. It's the conviction that the world we know is fated to be eventually destroyed and then made anew — a place where human beings will once again find their rightful place.

I see a hall standing there,
More beautiful than sunlight,
Thatched with gold,
At Gimlé.
There bold men
Will dwell
And enjoy cheer
Throughout their lives.

If much of this story sounds familiar, it should — and not just because of the perennial fascination with Norse mythology reflected in TV series and comic books. The narrative of *The Poetic Edda* permeates two of the most influential works in Western literature: Richard Wagner's *Ring of the Nibelungen* cycle of operas (in which Nietzsche discovered his fascination with Vikings and Norse myth) and J.R.R. Tolkien's *Lord of the Rings.*

In Wagner's case, the influence of the *Eddas* was decisive in his artistic and musical formation.* As for Tolkien, his boyhood fascination with Norse mythology prompted him to found the Viking Club at his first teaching post, at the University of Leeds. His entire imaginative world rests on a bedrock of Norse myth (borrowing, for example, proper names such as Gimli and Middle Earth). Tolkien's most pivotal figure, the wizard Gandalf the Grey, bears many of Odin's characteristics. Tolkien at one point even called him "an Odinic wanderer."

In their stories, both Wagner and Tolkien drew from the story of Ragnarok, albeit in different ways.† Wagner saw the "twilight of the gods" as both an end and a beginning: a moment for rebirth and renewal, in which the passing of the old order, however traumatic and tragic, is also cause for celebration and new hope. For Tolkien, the Vikings' Ragnarok returned as an epic battle between the armies of good and evil; the forces of good ultimately prevail and the evil of Mordor is overthrown.

Both narratives capture something of the mythic power of the old Norse

---

*See Chapter 14.
† See Conclusion.

religion itself. All romanticizing by the modern Western imagination aside, the actual practices of the followers of Odin and the other Norse gods and goddesses were brutal in the extreme. They routinely included human sacrifice and the massacre of hundreds of captives in tribute to the Norse deities and the spirits of dead warriors and heroes dwelling in Valhalla. We know the sacred grove around the temple complex at Uppsala was decorated with the dangling corpses of sacrificial victims. "Even dogs and horses hang there," according to the chronicler Adam of Bremen. One eyewitness counted seventy-two bodies, in different states of putrefaction, suspended at one time in the grove.

The Rus were certainly no exception. The detailed description written by an Arab traveler in 992 of the horrific and bloodstained ceremonies surrounding the funeral of a Rus chieftain — including the ritual gang rape of a helpless female slave — leaves very little to the imagination.

Still, it was not an easy passage from the old religion to the new. It was more like a battle and was sometimes fought with spear and sword. In the end, we have to conclude that the forces for good finally won. Norse paganism may have reflected deep stirrings of the Viking heart — ones that still resonate. But it also failed to reflect an understanding of human possibilities beyond a lust for power, the caprice of the gods, and the random forces of fate. In its most primal form, the Viking heart rejected compassion, sympathy for others, and awareness of moral responsibility.

All of that began to change, however, with the advent of Christianity.

It's safe to assume that no humanitarian considerations entered Vladimir's calculations about finding a new religion for his people. What likely weighed on his mind instead was the need to find new sources of wealth, now that the flow of silver from the Islamic world had halted once again, in about 965. It was time for Russia to find its place in the larger world. And as neighboring nations continued to consolidate their identities around the dominant religious creeds of the day, it became clear that abandoning an alien paganism was the next crucial step.

But what religion should take its place? The sources tell us that, for Vladimir and the Rus, four possibilities loomed. One was Orthodox Christianity, represented by the emperor and patriarch in Constantinople. Another was

Latin Christianity, represented by the pope in distant Rome — the same Christianity that Vladimir's Norse relations had been preying on for more than a century. Rabbinical Judaism was the third option; Varangian mercenaries were quite familiar with it from their service in the armies of the Khazars, who had converted a century before. The final possibility was the faith of Russia's trading partners to the south: Islam.

As a means to decide, Vladimir chose a method that was distinctly Viking. He decided to hold a contest, in which representatives of all four faiths would present their case for conversion. Viking chieftains had once used this type of competition to determine who was the best poet at court, and German kings decided who was the best warrior in a similar challenge, the ancestor of medieval tourneys. This time, the contest would decide which was the best faith for the Rus to finally embrace.

The first emissaries in this "faith-off" were from the Islamic world. Vladimir liked the story about Paradise and the seventy-two virgins. But, according to the sources, when he heard that being Muslim meant no more alcohol or pork, he balked. "Drinking is the joy of the Rus," Vladimir declared; "we cannot exist without that pleasure." So the Muslim emissaries went home unrewarded.

The Jewish representatives from the Khazars did no better, for pretty much the same reasons. And when the representatives of the Latin church in Rome talked about the virtue of monkish abstinence, Vladimir completely lost interest. When the turn came for Eastern Orthodox Christianity, the best representatives turned out to be Vladimir's own soldiers and officials. Visiting Constantinople during a mission to help Emperor Basil put down a revolt in Cherson, they had been present for a major Orthodox festival (perhaps deliberately arranged to overawe the Russian visitors) and had been profoundly impressed.

"We no longer knew whether we were in heaven or on earth," they told Vladimir after describing a majestic Divine Liturgy at the basilica of Hagia Sophia, "nor seen such beauty, and we know not how to tell of it." It was hard, they said, having tasted something so sweet, to come back to something so bitter as their religion at home. Vladimir was sold. He agreed to be baptized in February 988. He personally oversaw the destruction of the old pagan statues, which were thrown into the Dnieper, and conducted a mass baptism of his warriors in the same river. Vladimir's conversion also opened the way for him to marry a daughter of the emperor himself — a magnificent match. Both French and German rulers had bid for it in vain.

Russia had now joined its fate to the orbit of Eastern Orthodoxy, not Latin Europe. This momentous decision would shape the fate of both worlds right down to today. But it also became a means by which Vladimir could confirm and consolidate his power as ruler of Russia. Breaking free from paganism wasn't simply a rejection of a fraught religious past. It was also a rejection of a decentralized, sometimes chaotic political history.

Vladimir's decision came as a series of rulers back in Scandinavia were making the same choice. At almost the same time, they were concluding that it was the right moment to move on from the religion of their ancestors and embrace the faith that was shaping the greater world around them. The choice did not come easily, not least for their subjects. And as had been the case with Vladimir in Russia, the reasons for making it hinged very much on politics and prosperity. But whether calculated or sincere, the decision to adopt Christian customs and values meant a major change in the Viking way of life. Although it's hard to imagine, the Norsemen were about to become a constructive, rather than destructive, force in Western civilization.

For starters, the coming of Christianity to Scandinavia ended the custom of grave goods, whereby the affluent deceased were buried with items such as jewelry and iron and bronze implements, along with cattle and horses and household slaves sacrificed for this purpose. This change was bad news for future archaeologists. But it was very good news for the people of Scandinavia at the time, allowing them to keep and recycle metal goods and other forms of wealth that in the past had been buried, lost to them forever.

What's more, Christianity spelled the end of the blood feud. Previously, all Vikings, as well as their German tribal cousins, believed that the murder of a kinsman by a member of another tribe or family demanded retribution: the death of a member of that same tribe or family. Left to its own logic, the blood feud system would have led to extermination. The one restraint pagan Germans and Vikings devised was the custom of wergild, by which the community assigned a material price for a person based on social status (with kings and nobles at the top, and slaves at the bottom) in hopes that receiving the payment from the murderer (or rapist or sexual predator) or the offender's family would be an acceptable substitute for blood revenge.

Christianity introduced a very different idea: individual responsibility for the crime of murder, as well as redemption and forgiveness for crimes of all kinds. Progress was slow. The historian Dorothy Whitelock has written that this shift of emphasis made virtually no impact in Anglo-Saxon England. In fact, across Frankish Europe, biblical maxims such as "an eye for an eye" and "vengeance is mine, sayeth the Lord" were understood as *reinforcing,* not ending the vendetta mindset. Nonetheless, by slow turns a new way of thinking began to take root, and it ended the cycle of violence and blood feud, moving Christianized Europe, including eventually Scandinavian Europe, in a creative new direction.

Finally, the Vikings themselves had already contributed massively to a major positive change in Europe, even during their most rapacious phase — a change that left an important impression on the Catholic Church, as well. This was the principle of self-help. Living under virtually constant assault from every quarter by Viking longships, Europe's kings and emperors had finally concluded that it was impossible to defend their territories against Norse raids with their large and unwieldy armies. So instead, Europe's rulers allowed a local lord or town, or even bishop, to summon their own warriors on the spot, local "boots on the ground" as it were, who could be counted on to assemble and respond quickly to a Viking assault. Dark Age Europe had plenty of warriors, thanks to the migrations of German tribes. The key was winning their loyalty. This was secured by giving each warrior a manor house or a farm with enough land, and enough peasants to work that land, in exchange for a formal pledge of service.

This was the birth of feudalism, named after the grant of land, or *feudum,* that underlay the system. Feudalism eventually came in many shapes and sizes and entailed many forms of service besides service under arms. It even included the church itself, one of Europe's most important landowners. Historians have ultimately judged feudalism to be a major retardant of Europe's social and economic progress. But in its early days it constituted the perfect solution for dealing not only with the Viking threat but also the ongoing attacks by Saracens and Magyars.

Feudalism soon spread from the former Frankish lands across central and eastern Europe. It steadily made Viking forays more costly for the sea-rovers, as had been proved by Robert the Strong during the siege of Paris. One response of the raiders was to launch larger, more heavily armed expeditions. But another was to shift from piracy to trade and settlement and to accommodate the values of the larger world, including Christian rites and beliefs.

The twilight of the Norse gods was indeed coming — but not because of the actions of giants and trolls at Ragnarok, as in Nordic myth. Instead, a handful of determined Viking leaders used their royal power to bring their kingdoms into the mainstream of Latin Christendom.

One of the first of these individuals was Anskar, or Ansgar, "God's Javelin," a Frankish monk based in Hamburg who ventured far into Viking territory to spread the word of God as early as 826; the pope, Gregory IV, entrusted to Anskar the pastoral care of all of Scandinavia. The Norwegian sack of Hamburg in 846 brought his work to a temporary halt. But before his death in 865, he had given the church a tiny toehold in the kingdoms of Denmark and Sweden, at the towns of Ripa and Birka respectively. The presence of obvious Christian graves in Ripa suggests that the new faith found some support among the town's mercantile community, despite the pagan customs and beliefs that guided society.

It would, however, be another 150 years before the church found more effective missionaries, in the persons of four Scandinavian kings. The first was Harald Bluetooth, who underwent conversion in about 965. By 986, before his son Sven pushed him off the throne, Harald could claim in his Jelling stone monument that he had "made the Danes Christians" — although how true that was in actual practice remains unclear.

The second was Olaf Tryggvason, king of Norway from 995 to 1000, who established the first Christian church in Norway, at Oslo, at the very beginning of his reign. It was King Olaf, according to *The Saga of Erik the Red,* who tasked Leif Erikson with converting the settlers in Greenland to Christianity. When Leif hesitated, worrying that the effort to overthrow the old pagan ways might be met with hostility, Olaf answered that he saw no man more suited for the job — "and you'll have the good fortune that's needed." Leif promptly replied, "If that's so, then only because I enjoy yours as well." In fact, according to the saga, Leif's proselytizing was a success. The text adds, with no apparent sense of irony, "Afterwards he became known as Leif the Lucky." True or not, the story underlines the fact that Olaf's converting his people to Christianity was also meant to be a boon to his royal status.

The third king was Norway's Olaf Haraldson, or Olaf II. Better known as St. Olaf, he unfortunately pushed the Christianizing effort with such fanatical and brutal zeal, it ultimately alienated enough of his subjects to spur them to strike an alliance with the Danish king, Canute, with the purpose of driving Olaf out. Even though Canute himself was a sincere believing Christian, who understood that amicable relations with the Catholic Church boosted his authority, the opportunity to seize the throne of Norway was too good an opportunity to pass up.

Defeated by a coalition of Canute's Danes, Norwegian rebels, and Swedish mercenaries, Olaf II died in the battle of Stiklestad in 1030, trying to regain his kingdom. According to the sagas, his battle cry on the field was "Christ's men." Despite defeat, his push to Christianize his people was not a wasted effort. Later he would be canonized a saint, and the church pronounced his death in battle a martyrdom. This Saint Olaf is still celebrated on a national holiday in Norway, and his tomb in Trondheim became a major pilgrimage site for Norwegians and also for other Scandinavians as the Christian faith began to take hold in the land.

The fourth king to push the Christianization of the Vikings was another Olaf, this time Olaf Sköttkonung of Sweden, son of Erik Segersall, the monarch known to Swedish history as Erik the Victorious. Erik had allowed himself to be baptized a Christian following his victory over the Danes in the 980s, but he reverted to paganism when he returned home to Uppsala, Sweden's traditional pagan temple complex. The old traditions were, it seems, too comfortable to be set aside so quickly. His son Olaf, however, became a Christian and stayed a Christian, even though he was instrumental in the defeat of Olaf Tryggvason, Norway's Christianizing king. Not coincidentally, Olaf Sköttkonung was also the first Swedish king to mint coins, and they bear Christian symbols as well as Olaf's title: *Rex Sv,* which stands for *Rex Sveorum.*

Yet even Olaf, whose domain included large parts of eastern Norway, faced limits as he attempted to purge his subjects of their heathen ways. When he proposed tearing down the great pagan complex at Uppsala, the intense opposition from the local Sveara population forced him to abandon the project. (Uppsala eventually became the seat of a bishopric, as did Skara in Västergötland, where missionary priests had been operating for some years.)

Nonetheless, Olaf adhered to a policy of prudent tolerance regarding his recalcitrant pagan subjects, which his German admirer and chronicler Adam of Bremen (a Catholic clergyman himself) summed up this way: "If he wished to be Christian himself he might choose the best part of Sweden and have full power there. He might build a church and introduce Christianity. But he must not force people to abandon the old faith. Only those who wished to should be converted."

Olaf's son and successor, Jakob, followed much the same policy. In fact he yielded to popular pressure, jettisoned his biblical name, and chose a traditional one, Anund; according to the chronicler his subjects made this change a condition of accepting his rule. Odin in Valhalla must have had a good laugh at the discomfort of his Christian enemies. The twilight of the gods in the Viking lands was going to take longer than originally forecast.

Nonetheless, most (but significantly not all) the kings of Sweden would be Christians after 1000. When one of them, Erik, was killed in battle in 1160, the church chose to treat his death as a martyrdom and graced him with canonization shortly afterward. The first archbishopric in Sweden was established in Uppsala four years later, in 1164. The destruction of the pagan temple complex would not be far behind. Adam of Bremen described this place as the center of human sacrifice, where "the bodies hang in the sacred grove that adjoins the temple," so sacred that "every tree in it is believed divine because of the death and putrefaction of the victims."

And yet the pagan ways remained strikingly strong and long-lasting in Viking Scandinavia over the following years — even though, astonishingly, the religion of Odin and Thor had no priestly class who might have resisted Christianity as a threat to their social or political standing. Modern archaeology has shown that even the main sacred sites like Uppsala were hardly very large or impressive — certainly not compared to Delphi or Karnak. All the same,

Christianization proved slow and arduous, far more so than among the German tribes. Adam of Bremen noted that at Uppsala, "those who have already adopted Christianity redeem themselves by joining in the mass pagan rites." We see this pull between the two faiths in grave markers from Sweden to Iceland, where images from the Nordic pantheon are mixed in with Christian symbols.

Why did this happen? An important clue can be found in the Christian churches the Scandinavians built for themselves, the famous stave churches. Most of the surviving examples are in Norway, where they are known as *stavkirker*.

Made from Norwegian pine, the stave church had design features borrowed from traditional *hofar,* or halls for Viking chieftains, and even temples to the Norse gods. The craftsmanship of the stave church also reflects the skills used in the making of Norsemen's longships, such as applying coats of dark-red tar, which made the Viking vessels watertight and seaworthy. This protective material also enabled a number of stave churches to survive. More than 250 of these structures remain standing, most of them in Norway.

Of course these enduring traditions of craftsmanship are also seen in the Romanesque and Gothic churches built in different parts of Europe in the same period. Likewise, church builders used the classical architectural elements — even the actual physical pillars and pediments — that characterized the pagan temples they replaced. The Pantheon in Rome, for example, was originally a temple to the Roman gods.

But most Catholic churches in France or Germany avoided using specifically pagan motifs as part of their decorations. Not so with the stave churches. Their towering structures loom skyward with dragons' heads perched on the roof, reflecting the strength and awe-inspiring power of the Vikings' seafaring past. The same is true of the wooden carvings incorporated into their designs. One of the most popular motifs, for example, was the Norse hero Sigurd slaying the dragon that protected the treasure hoard of the Volsungs. It was of course possible to interpret the story in Christian terms, as a Viking version of Saint Michael killing *his* dragon. But the simple truth was, the Scandinavians weren't quite ready to lay aside their pagan past so suddenly.

Most likely, the Viking pantheon and Norse myth manifested a deep understanding of Scandinavia's cultural roots — perhaps even, more broadly, an understanding of human existence. The rites and stories and parables recorded in the *Eddas* and other sagas taught life lessons about courage, loyalty, human vanity and ambition, and the life and hope that can spring up from the darkest night — or the desolation of Ragnarok. They express deep truths about the human heart, and not just the Viking version of it. The persistence of those myths more than a thousand years later, and their continuing popularity in the form of more recent epics like *Lord of the Rings, Game of Thrones,* the Harry Potter stories, and *Star Wars,* strongly suggests this is true.

But converting to Christianity did ultimately change the region, and Scandinavians, for the better. Centuries later it was a matter of nostalgic regret that once-celebrated pagan sites, like the temple complex at Uppsala, lay abandoned and forgotten. For centuries the songs and stories about Odin, Fricka, Thor, and Valhalla, the hallowed hall of dead heroes, disappeared from living memory — only to be rediscovered by scholars and artists like Richard Wagner in the nineteenth century, thanks to the sagas left by Icelandic poets and scribes of the 1100s and 1200s. Today, neo-Nazi groups have joined in this nostalgia for pagan rites, co-opting Nordic religion and tradition for their own political agenda.

This ignores the fact that Christianity introduced the idea of charity and compassion as moral obligations, and good works as necessary for personal salvation — in addition to banishing forever the concept of blood feud and the institution of wergild. Thanks to Christianity, the Viking ideal of loyalty and service to the community took on a new dimension: one of service to Christ and others as a Christian duty. And the message of hope conveyed in Norse cosmology, of rebirth following on the heels of disaster, found new resonance in the story of Jesus Christ and his resurrection as redemption for the human race.*

---

* This raises the question debated by some scholars, as to whether Christianity contributed to Viking culture by enabling Christian Icelandic scribes of the twelfth and thirteenth centuries, like Snorri Sturluson, to "clean up" the basic framework of Norse myth, by giving it a firmer teleology with a beginning and endpoint more parallel to the story of Genesis on the one hand, and Ragnarok and Armageddon/ Apocalypse, from the Book of Revelation, on the other. It may be impossible to

At that moment, the modern Scandinavian archetype we tend to admire today took shape. Cultural changes come slowly, especially in the frozen North. But far from suppressing or abolishing the Viking heart, the advent of Christianity progressively gave it a rich new dimension, instilling a greater regard for humanity. Eventually, Christianity spelled the end of the heyday of pillaging and slave trading — although King Olaf of Norway was quite capable of founding churches and overseeing baptisms one day and conducting raids on his Christian neighbors in England and along the Bay of Biscay the next.

Mention of King Olaf brings up another interesting fact about Scandinavia's turn to Christianity. Conversion never gave the emergent monarchs of Denmark, Norway, and Sweden the extra boost to their authority they had envisaged. Instead, they discovered what the kings of France, England, and Spain, and the Holy Roman emperor as well, had already found. Embracing Christianity introduced a new alien power into their territories: the Roman Catholic Church.

It would be another four hundred years or more before kings in the North learned to tame the church in their midst, and not through compromise but rather revolution.

By 1000, Danes, Norwegians, and Swedes were each separately fashioning a new identity as a unified nation. Though often in conflict, the three nascent countries were linked by history and culture. They had much in common: the Viking past and the acceptance of Christianity in the present. Also, each was settling down to a pattern of stability and settlement. They had abandoned the marauding and destruction of the past.

Viking England, however, was a different matter.

---

resolve the question definitively. Other than Snorri and the other skalds we have no sources to turn to. In the end, it seems best to follow Preben Meulengracht Sørensen of the University of Oslo and conclude that there are very good reasons "for regarding the myth of the recreated earth as genuinely pre-Christian" and that "Christian ideas were absorbed into the Nordic world-picture without changing its basis." (Preben Meulengracht Sørensen, "Religions Old and New," in Peter Sawyer, ed., *Oxford Illustrated History of the Vikings,* Oxford, UK: Oxford University Press, 1997, 212–13)

Very suddenly, starting around 975, the Norse raids revived. It was as if the aggressive spirit that had animated men like Rurik and Ragnar Ladbrok a century earlier had come back to life. These raids spelled doom to peace and stability in a land where, for the two and a half decades after the fall of the kingdom of York, men and women had been free from Viking attack.

What's more, this time the raids were starkly different. They weren't led by independent freebooters, but rather by Viking kings themselves. Surprising as it may seem, Scandinavia's crowned heads had played almost no part in the Viking breakout of the eighth and ninth centuries, or the conquests of Normandy and the British Isles. Those had been spearheaded by men who were outliers, or even exiles, in their own homelands, and they were happy to find new places to rule and plunder. Norway's Olaf Tryggvason and Olaf Haraldson were luckier than most. Each was able to become king of Norway after his career as a freebooter came to an end.

By the end of the 900s, however, newly established kings in the Scandinavian homelands began to take an interest in plunder and conquest as strategic goals, as an expression and extension of royal power. While both Norway and Denmark were becoming unified kingdoms, the men who assumed leadership needed wealth not only to reward loyal followers but also to consolidate control.

This had direct consequences for what might be called the foreign policy of the new kingdoms. For complicated reasons, the traditional sources of silver from the East, which had flowed from the Swedish Viking rulers in Russia as a principal source of royal wealth across Scandinavia, were drying up. By 960 they had ceased almost altogether. Kings like Olaf Tryggvason of Norway and Sven Forkbeard of Denmark needed to find a new source for the silver coins that kept their economies running. They found it in Anglo-Saxon England.

In 991 King Olaf landed with an army to ravage Kent and Sussex. He delivered a crushing defeat to an Anglo-Saxon army in East Anglia that the *Anglo-Saxon Chronicle,* and an anonymous Anglo-Saxon poet, would remember as the battle of Maldon:

> *Bows were drawn; spear points rained on shields.*
> *Bitter was the crush of battle; warriors fell;*
> *On either side, young men lay dead.*

Broken in defeat, the English king reacted by offering an enormous bribe — twenty-two thousand pounds of silver — for Olaf to leave his kingdom alone. Olaf agreed and took the money. But two years later he was back, this time in alliance with Denmark's king, Sven Forkbeard, and the two monarchs ravaged northern England and left only after the English had come up with another massive payment, this time eighteen thousand pounds.

For Olaf and Sven, the field seemed wide open. Their large royal fleets and armies gave them maximum flexibility to go where they wanted, with maximum impact. In the Danelaw they also had a built-in "fifth column" population who could support their operations. Moreover, after the death of King Edgar in 975, English monarchs simply didn't reach the same heroic heights of leadership as their predecessors. King Ethelred in particular was overwhelmed by the rapidly deteriorating security situation, as we would say today. Paying off the Viking invaders seemed to be the only clear course of action. These payments became so frequent and regular, they had their own name: danegeld.

Olaf of Norway's raids raged far and wide, from Northumbria and Scotland to Ireland and Wales, with an attack on France (Valland) thrown in for good measure. His attack on London in 994 was a failure. But it was now obvious that Olaf and his fellow Vikings were free to roam at will. Fresh raids led to another danegeld payment of twenty-four thousand pounds in 1002. Fighting then resumed in 1003 and 1004, and Sven Forkbeard returned in 1006–7 to secure yet another exorbitant danegeld ransom.

The significance of these sums should not be underestimated. For the Scandinavian kings and their subjects, it meant an instant infusion of cash that flowed into the royal economy but also enabled the kings to pay their soldiers and mercenaries, some of whom came from as far away as Russia. More than fifty thousand English coins, almost all of them dating from the period 980–1051 and the era of the great raids, have turned up in Scandinavian coin hoards. The loss of the silver that had flowed from the Islamic world was forgotten, and a new cash nexus was being forged between Scandinavia and the kingdom of England.

These danegeld payments were significant for England in another way. They were symbols not only of England's vulnerability but also its relative affluence. Those years of peace had not been wasted. England's economy had recovered and even thrived in the tenth century, and this was also the case in the Norse-dominated lands of the Danelaw. The fact that the king in London could provide such massive sums, year after year, was proof that the united Anglo-Saxon kingdom was an economic powerhouse, with trade links extending across northern Europe. That fact was not lost on the Viking rulers, whose links with England would harden over the next half century — and not simply in terms of conquest.

It was a good thing England was able to pay its danegeld ransoms because the raids did not stop. After the attack in 1002, a desperate Ethelred had ordered the massive ethnic cleansing of all Danes in his service. The "massacre of Saint Brice's Day," as it became known, was a hideous blunder. One story has it that Sven's own sister was among those murdered at Ethelred's order. Sven Forkbeard returned to England in a genuine fury, and the ravaging of England began afresh. He and his raiders sacked coastal towns from Norwich to Exeter, and in 1009 a Danish army under Thorkell the Tall landed at Sandwich and began a campaign of death and destruction without parallel.

By 1011, the Scandinavians had laid waste to no fewer than fifteen English counties or shires. The culmination of the destruction came in 1012, when the Danes sacked Canterbury, the holiest site in England, and murdered the archbishop, the primate of England. Sven of Denmark returned in person again the following year. King Ethelred was caught unprepared and without a single effective ally — not for nothing did he earn the nickname Ethelred the Unready. He fled, to Normandy, of all places. London still held out without its king, but shortly after Christmas it too surrendered to the Danes and joined virtually the rest of the kingdom in recognizing Sven Forkbeard as its king. Sven in turn demanded no less than 158,000 pounds in silver as tribute from his cowed new subjects.

It was England's lowest point in history, lower even than the darkest days of the Blitz in World War II. No one knew it, but a turning point had been reached: not only for England but for Scandinavia.

Sven had only five weeks to enjoy his triumph before he died suddenly, to be succeeded by his son Knut, or Canute — the same Canute who would later crush the forces of Olaf II of Norway and Sweden's Anund Jakob in the sea battle of the Helgeå.* With the support of two formidable warriors, Thorkell the Tall and Erik of Hlathir, Canute came to England in 1015 to claim his father's title. Ethelred had returned to England after receiving news of Sven's death; Ethelred himself died the following spring. His son Edmund, nicknamed Ironside, was an able soldier but plagued by bad luck. He and Canute waged a seesaw war of victories and defeats up and down England until finally their armies met outside Ashingdon in Essex — a very long way from the Vikings' original base in Northumbria. There Edmund was betrayed on the battlefield by one of his English allies, and his army was destroyed. Canute chased him as far west as Gloucestershire, where Edmund reluctantly agreed to divide the kingdom between them. A few weeks later, Edmund also died — whether from natural causes or not, we don't know — and Canute was able to claim the entire kingdom as his domain.

Canute stands out as one of the most extraordinary figures in European history. We can well rate him as the greatest Viking of them all. The well-worn legend about him — how with the encouragement of courtiers he commanded the sea to obey him — does him a grotesque injustice. In fact, he was far more than a vainglorious egomaniac or another Viking marauder. Except for just five years, for the nearly two decades from 1018 to 1035, Denmark and England were ruled by him, as sole ruler: no wonder he is called Canute the Great. He transformed England like no other sovereign and left his mark on the history of England and the history of Scandinavia alike.

Canute's rule in England began brutally enough. The son of Sven Forkbeard, as a boy of sixteen he had joined his father on a 1013 marauding expedition against England and fought at Sven's side for the next three years. When Sven died, the nobility in Denmark had acclaimed Canute's brother Harald as king of Denmark. But the Vikings and their allies on the other side of the North Sea, in England, chose Canute as their king. When he and Edmund Ironside clashed at Ashingdon, Canute was already a battle-hardened veteran. The devastating defeat of Edmund meant that Canute's rule was now

---

* See Chapter 2.

completely unchallenged. His career as a great monarch had just begun at only twenty-two years of age.

Three years later, in 1019, he succeeded his brother as king of Denmark. Bribery and war then won him the throne of Norway in 1028, which gave him formal rule over Greenland, the Orkneys and Shetlands, the Hebrides, and the Isle of Man, to add to his already established dominion over England and Denmark. This was truly a transoceanic Scandinavian empire, the first and last of its kind. Before his premature death, in 1035, Canute was unable to establish more than titular rule (by 1049, England, Denmark, and Norway once again subsided into separate kingdoms under different dynasties), yet he wielded what power he had with skill and effectiveness. He's a strong contender for the title of most underrated king of the Middle Ages.

In England, much of the fame and admiration later heaped on William the Conqueror — another heroic king sprung from Viking blood — truly belongs to Canute. Instead of imposing his rule through conquest, as King William was forced to do, Canute's governance came through the willing submission of his subjects. As king of England, Canute treated the tradition of good governance, established by Alfred the Great and the house of Wessex, with painstaking respect. It's true that he murdered the last adult son of his predecessor, Ethelred, to make sure he would face no competitor for power through hereditary succession. Canute was a Viking, after all. He also married Ethelred's widow, Emma of Normandy, so the Normans wouldn't be tempted to throw their support behind either of Emma's two previous sons as next in line for the throne of England. (One of those sons would ultimately rule England as Edward the Confessor.) And, following Viking tradition, Canute surrounded himself with a hand-picked, armed bodyguard of housecarls, who provided personal security and also put down armed revolts, though in fact almost none occurred.

In all other respects, Canute played it safe in his handling of his English subjects. He avoided confiscatory seizure of estates belonging to the nobles who had sided against him, and he did not impose Danish nobility on the land to act as garrison, as William the Conqueror would later do with his Norman followers. Instead, King Canute called an assembly at Oxford in 1018 and solemnly announced his intention to uphold and enforce the laws of his English predecessors. He issued a legal code that relied on earlier Anglo-Saxon law. He appointed Englishmen to the most important earldoms. And he made it clear that his reign would rest on the support of the higher English clergy. His use of his own fleet of forty ships to defeat a Viking fleet that had appeared off the English coast in 1018 won him additional support. Canute's rule ensured that the days when freebooters from Scandinavia could have their way with the English were permanently on the wane.

After the chaos and anarchy that had enabled Canute to take the throne, he gave his kingdom true stability and security, which subsequent rulers, including his successors Edward the Confessor and William the Conqueror, could rely and build upon. As the historian G. O. Sayles noted, "There is no doubt that England prospered greatly under him." In 1027, Canute negotiated a deal with the German emperor and King Rudolf of Burgundy to let English merchants do business in Italy. As a result, a series of English traders of Anglo-Saxon and Scandinavian descent set out on ships loaded with domestic wares, selling their cargoes far and wide. Many became rich. An Anglo-Saxon treatise estimated that just three voyages were needed to make a merchant a rich thane, a man of superior rank.

London became the main entrepôt for trade in Canute's day. The traditional husting there became a clearinghouse for agreements and disputes between foreign and English merchants — Anglo-Saxons, Danes, Norwegians, Flemings — it didn't matter who. Other sites also flourished, especially those within the Danelaw: York, Norwich, and the other Viking outposts on the east coast known as the Five Boroughs.*

Canute's reign was the heyday not only of the merchants but also of the Scandinavian free farmers, or sokemen. If it is indeed true that they played an important part in the future evolution of English life and law — perhaps even sowing the seeds of English individualism — it was due to their prominent role in rebuilding England's prosperity under Canute.

Nor should anyone overlook Canute's accomplishments in the rest of his Scandinavian empire. Back home in Denmark, he issued coins, on the English pattern, with his portrait, and for the first time the northern kingdoms shared

---

* These were the boroughs of Lincoln, Stamford, Nottingham, Derby, and Leicester.

a common currency. His respectful relations with the Catholic Church, which was taking root in Scandinavia, promoted domestic stability and social harmony. His careful diplomacy with the German emperor gave northern Europe a long-awaited period of peace. Canute's daughter even married the emperor's son. And in 1026, at the decisive battle of the Helgeå, he scored his sweeping victory over a combined Swedish-Norwegian naval force led by Norway's Olaf II and Sweden's Anund Jakob, enabling Canute, two years later, to win the Norwegian crown. Helgeå made Canute, without doubt, the dominant ruler in northern Europe — and without doubt he was the greatest Viking ruler of them all.

Sweden, however, eluded his grasp. The country was on track for a very different destiny. At the same time, another Viking power was on the rise across the water from England, but this time in the south. It was Normandy.

6

Conquerors

The Norman Transformation

When under the rule of a strong master the Normans
are a most valiant people, excelling all others in the skill
with which they meet difficulties and strive to conquer
every enemy.

—Ordericus Vitalis, *Ecclesiastical History,* twelfth century

ALMOST FROM THE moment they settled in Normandy at the start of
the tenth century, Rollo the Viking, his fellow Viking raiders, and their descendants had made the land run red with blood in a ceaseless struggle for power,
attacking their Breton neighbors to the west and the Franks to the east. It was
into this tough, competitive world that the future William the Conqueror was
born, in 1027 or 1028, the illegitimate son of the duke of Normandy, Robert II.
Here William succeeded as duke at the tender age of six.

No figure from the Viking legacy would rise as high in history's estimation,
not even King Canute, as William, duke of Normandy. Certainly none would
be as celebrated in the annals of medieval Europe. William the Conqueror
stands as a larger-than-life figure in the history both of France and Britain —
and, one could argue, in the history of Western civilization.

From that lofty perspective, it seems almost opportunistic to consider William strictly in the context of his original Scandinavian roots. In some ways, it's even a little misleading. Norway's last great Viking king, Canute, had already possessed the prize that William would one day risk everything to possess: the throne of England. In fact, William seemed destined by events to be the final scourge and destroyer of the Viking legacy in Britain.

All the same, William's Viking ancestors left their mark on him and his people. Norse was still spoken in parts of Normandy when William was born. His career, and the exploits of his Norman contemporaries, display the same courage, resourcefulness, and ruthlessness that characterized Canute the Great and Sweden's Erik the Victorious — and even Erik the Red. The Normans would use those salient qualities to remake Europe more decisively than even their Norse forebears had. The transformation of western Europe into a distinct civilization began with the Normans and William the Conqueror — much as the story of Rurik and his successors signaled the beginning of the unified history of Russia and eastern Europe.

But the similarities end there. The Norman impact on both northern Europe and the Mediterranean world — and on the Middle East too — follows a trajectory very different from that of the Viking conquerors. For starters, the Normandy of William the Conqueror was both a Christian power and a firm ally of the Roman Catholic Church. The church was one of its staunchest defenders, in fact. What's more, in language and culture, Normans had far more in common with their French neighbors than with contemporary Danes or Swedes or Norwegians.

And above all, the Norman Conquest is not a history of random pillaging gradually turning to trade and settlement. Though a warrior elite, an "aristocracy of the brave" in many ways like the Norsemen, undertook this military campaign, the Normans aimed to take advantage of, and even shore up, the patterns and institutions of civilized life. Despite any inherited propensity for savagery and ruthlessness in battle, Duke William and his contemporaries thrust Europe *forward* into the Middle Ages, not backward toward the Dark Ages. They were part and parcel of a new Christendom that was feeling confident and increasingly willing to take the initiative against its adversaries, including Islam. That new militant outlook would culminate in the Crusades. It owed a great deal to the Normans and their fearless, sometimes brutal, take on the qualities of the Viking heart.

The odds were against William, duke of Normandy, from the start. His mother was the daughter of a tanner from the town of Falaise, and the facts surrounding his birth were the source of his first nickname, William the Bastard. His father, Robert, was the first Norman duke to set out on a pilgrimage to the Holy Land. Before leaving, Robert decided it would be wise (wiser than he knew) to secure succession to his title for his natural offspring, just in case something happened to him en route. In a scene reminiscent of a Viking saga, Robert gathered his most powerful vassals around him to recognize little six-year-old William as his heir. They did so.

But when Robert died on his way to Jerusalem at the start of July 1035, almost at once Normandy collapsed into murderous anarchy. All four of William's guardians were murdered within the first five years of his rule, while private feuds broke out and the countryside descended into chaos. William had to be smuggled to safety time and time again by his mother's family, just in time to escape an assassin's knife or sword.

From those early days until his death in 1087, more than half a century later, William knew nothing but war. It was a hard school for a hard man, and he responded with vigor. When he turned sixteen, he had himself knighted. Two years later, his enemies became worried because he was asserting his authority too effectively, and so they united for a full-scale civil war.

Even at eighteen William was considered too formidable to confront face-to-face. Instead, his enemies planned to fall upon the teenage duke while he was asleep in order to murder him in his bed. But servants stirred William awake and warned him of what was afoot. The teenager grabbed a horse and rode all night and day until he reached the house of a friend, Hubert, in the town of Ryes. There he changed horses, swore Hubert to secrecy, and lit out for the safety of his mother's family in Falaise, with his enemies in hot pursuit. They first stopped at Hubert's house and demanded to know which way William had gone. Hubert gave them the wrong directions, and they galloped off. William never forgot this gesture, which had saved his life. Many years later, he would appoint Hubert's son Eudo as sheriff of Essex.

The center of the revolt was western Normandy, where independent Viking ways were still strong; the eastern part of the province had become more assimilated to French ways, and William's authority was strongest there. In fact, William quickly reached out to the king of France, Henry I, for help, and they joined forces to crush the rebels in 1047.

It was a turning point, but William's real work still lay ahead of him.

From 1047 to 1063, William had to wage constant warfare to secure his domain. He made doubly sure that the church in Normandy was loyal to its ducal overlord by handpicking every bishop and important abbot — an exercise in power that any other king in Europe would have looked upon with envy. He also imposed obedient submission on the members of the Norman nobility. The malcontents who didn't respond in the desired manner he drove into exile.

According to some sources, William interrupted this process of housecleaning and consolidation for a brief visit to England in 1051. This seems unlikely. He was hip-deep in shoring up affairs in Normandy at that time. It's more probable that the bishop of London, Robert of Jumièges, was sent that year to inform William of a momentous decision made by the sitting king of England, Edward the Confessor.

Edward was the last surviving son of King Ethelred, whose kingdom had been overrun by Canute and the Danes; he was also the last representative of the royal house of Wessex founded by Alfred the Great. Known to posterity as Edward the Confessor for his great Christian piety, he had returned to power and the throne thanks to a great Anglo-Saxon noble, Earl Godwin. But then the two fell out, and Godwin was driven into exile. Deprived of strong support from the nobility, Edward had turned in desperation to the dominion across the English Channel: William's Normandy.

Edward's court was full of Norman nobles. Even the churchmen to whom Edward was closest were Normans. After his quarrel with Earl Godwin and Godwin's banishment, and Edward's repudiation of his marriage to Godwin's daughter, it seemed that the childless Edward had only one place to turn to, in order to secure his legacy. As one modern historian has put it, England under Edward the Confessor seemed destined to be ruled by Normans.

So it must have come as no great surprise when William learned, from the Norman churchman Robert of Jumièges, that when King Edward died, the kingdom of England would be his. No witnesses were present for this conversation between William and his visitor when it occurred in 1051. But whatever was said or not said, when Edward, king of England, died fifteen years later, on January 4, 1066, William had no doubt of his legitimate claim to the throne. It was so strong, he was ready to defend it by force of arms.

The English themselves had other ideas. On the very next day, the fifth of January, England's most distinguished clergy and nobility assembled — ironically, the gathering resembled that hallowed Nordic institution known as the Thing. This Anglo-Saxon version, which the English called a *witan gemot,* met and acclaimed forty-two-year-old Harold Godwinson as king of England. Harold's father, Earl Godwin, had been Edward the Confessor's closest adviser for many years.

And Harold wasn't William's only rival. When news of Edward's death reached Harold's brother Tostig, who was exiled in Norway, Tostig struck a deal with that country's reigning king, known to posterity as Harald the Ruthless. If Harald would help Tostig regain his position as earl of Northumberland, the center of the old Danelaw (Tostig's constant quarrels with the Northumbrian nobility had forced him into exile), he would make sure the Norwegian monarch took possession of the throne of England. King Harald eagerly agreed. So, in the early weeks of 1066, William of Normandy learned he had not one, but rather two competitors for the crown of England, which he believed belonged to him alone.

In many ways it was a strange but crucial moment. For all their differences in background and experience, these three men, including William, descended from Vikings and boldly impressed their mark on the Europe of 1066.

William, of course, was the direct descendant of the Norsemen who had conquered and settled Normandy two and a half centuries before. But Harold Godwinson's Nordic roots, if anything, ran even deeper. His father, Earl Godwin, had been English. But Harold's mother was Danish, the sister of a jarl who had taken in the boy Godwin as an orphan and raised him like a son — even marrying him into his own family. In addition, Harold's wife, like his mother, was Danish, and he almost certainly spoke fluent Norse, as did his brother Tostig—unlike Duke William, whose first tongue was French.

As for Harald, king of Norway, he was the foremost Viking warrior of his age. Known by the sobriquet Hardrada, or "Hard Ruler," often rendered in English as Harald the Ruthless; and reputedly standing nearly seven feet tall, he led a life that reads like a Norse saga. War was his constant companion since he first served in battle, at age fifteen, beside his half brother, King Olaf II (later known as Saint Olaf). When Olaf was killed fighting rebels who had sworn fealty to the Danish king Canute—who also sat on England's throne at the time—young Harald was forced to flee the kingdom or face death.

In exile he had embarked on an epic journey that took him to Kiev, Novgorod, and "the land of Rus," where he served in the army of the king of Novgorod before taking up service with the emperor of Byzantium in the Varangian Guard. Later, some would claim, Harald became one of Empress Zoe's lovers. As captain of the Varangians, Harald had led his troops to places as far away as North Africa and Sicily. Then, when he and the empress quarreled and she had him thrust into prison, Harald escaped, put out the empress's husband's eyes in revenge, and returned to Novgorod with shiploads of war booty. There he made the king of Novgorod's daughter his bride. By this time many said that Harald was the richest Viking of them all.

Even so, it was not until 1042 that Harald felt strong enough to return to Norway and claim the throne, which he had always believed was rightfully his. (As it happened, in that same year the half-Dane Earl Godwin installed Edward as king of England.) Fearing an enemy as powerful and rich as Harald, the ruling Norwegian king, Magnus, boldly offered to divide his realm with Harald, and Harald accepted the offer. When Magnus died five years later, Harald took possession of the entire kingdom. The throne for which his father and brother had fought and died was his at last.

Harald's ambition, however, was not satisfied. He also aimed to inherit the kingdom of Denmark—Magnus had held the title after the death of the great Canute's last heir—but the Danes refused him. Harald retaliated by waging seventeen years of warfare up and down Denmark's coast, happily burning towns and villages and routing every army the Danes tried to throw at him.

Now came the opportunity to seize the crown of England in compensation. When the deal with Tostig was struck, Harald immediately began mobilizing his armies and a fleet of longships to take possession.

If William wanted his throne, he would have to fight for it against two men who were, in effect, Viking warriors by blood and breeding—more so than he could claim to be. But the duke of Normandy had two enormous advantages in advancing his claim to the throne of England. One was the element of surprise: no one expected him to fight for an inheritance that he alone believed was his.

The second was the backbone of his army: his mounted cavalry, the finest in Europe. Armed with beribboned lances and lozenge-shaped shields, and armored from head to toe in chain mail, the Norman knight had a decisive advantage over the foot soldiers who made up the Anglo-Saxon and Viking armies. The armored emblems of feudalism, William's knights reflected a military revolution that spelled the end of the old way of fighting and ushered in another. Viking hit-and-run tactics were no longer enough.

But William also faced one monumental disadvantage. Unlike Harald the Ruthless, whose sleek longships still plied the seas, as in the days of his Viking ancestors, and unlike Harold Godwinson, who could command a formidable fleet of English-built but Viking-designed ships when needed, William had no ships or navy.

Since settling in France, the Normans had lost the Vikings' love and knowledge of the sea. A crossing of the English Channel seemed an enterprise beyond their means—though their Viking forebears would have scoffed at the meager distance. Yet just such a crossing was essential to William's plan.

William refused to let this obstacle deter him. Over the spring and summer, through sheer force of will, and in the face of opposition from his own barons, who thought the entire undertaking too risky, he filled the six ports of Normandy facing onto the Channel with an invasion fleet of perhaps as many as seven hundred ships (some contemporary sources assert that there were three thousand, but this is pure fantasy). The ships he built, borrowed, or stole— probably including some from his neighbors the Danes—were not the sleek longships of the Vikings who first invaded Normandy. They were bigger and clumsier, many custom-built to carry large numbers of soldiers and horses—

something the Vikings had done, but never on the scale that William had in mind. He would be transporting an army of at least five thousand men, including heavy cavalry, into harm's way. A hostile English navy was guarding the shore.

But William had another, in some ways more powerful, weapon in his arsenal. That spring, he had managed to secure the blessing of the pope, Alexander II, as both the right and just successor to the English throne. This was thanks in part to William's representative, the archbishop of Lisieux, who argued that Harold Godwinson had violated his oath of obedience to King Edward, who had clearly appointed William as his heir; Harold had nonetheless seized the throne for himself. Pope Alexander was in no position to argue. He owed his position to William and the Normans in more ways than one, as we shall see. Besides, William had plans to bring the English church into closer obedience to Rome. The pope not only gave Duke William his blessing but presented him with two special gifts, which the archbishop brought back in triumph to William's court at Rouen. One was the pope's personal banner, emblazoned with the image of the keys of Saint Peter. The other was a bundle of holy relics for William to wear when he rode into battle. We don't know exactly which relics they were, but it was said that they once belonged to Saint Peter himself. Coming from the Vatican, they were sure to be profoundly sacred.

As a modern biographer of William has put it, "the venture had been, thanks to the visit to Rome, made to appear — and in Western Europe it was widely regarded — as something in the nature of a crusade." The relationship between Christianity and the early Vikings, as now represented by their heirs, had been completely reversed. No longer enemies, they had become allies. Instead of proud pagans, the sons and daughters of Rollo's marauders had become representatives of the new Church Militant. Nothing, it seemed, could stand in the way of this potent new coalition — certainly not the throne of England.

By summer's end, everything was finally ready at Saint-Valery in Ponthieu for the duke and his army to embark. All that was needed was a fair wind to carry them across the Channel.

So William waited. And waited. It was not until September that "at last the long-awaited breeze arose," as a medieval chronicler would write. "William and his men gave thanks to heaven with voice and hand, and all shouted together to encourage each other." He was ready at last to make the half-day journey to claim the kingdom that he — and now the pope — had declared was rightfully his.

Even as William got underway, however, his enemy Harold Godwinson was making his own decisive move to destroy the third candidate for the English throne, King Harald of Norway.

Harald and his Viking army had landed at Scarborough on the Northumbrian coast and burned the town to the ground, before moving on to Racall, twenty-five miles up the Humber and Ouse Rivers, on September 18. As the historian David Howarth remarks, "To take a large seagoing fleet so far inland, and in a hostile country, was something no one but a Viking would have thought of." There Harald unfurled his battle standard, known as Landeyda, "Land-Ravager," with a black raven set against a white field.

Two days later, Harald's Vikings crushed the local English levies in a short, sharp fight at Fulford. The city of York surrendered without a murmur, a major blow to the English Harold. The declared English king, however, was already leading a forced march from London, with his best and strongest nobles and their soldiers. On September 25 they caught up with Harald, Tostig, and the Vikings a short distance northeast of York, near the bridge at Stamford. The Norwegians, under-armored, were caught off guard. Thinking their fighting was done, most of them had left their chain mail in the longships. Nevertheless, Harald the Ruthless accepted battle. Like some Icelandic bard, he dictated an impromptu poem, taken down by a scribe at his elbow, to highlight his dilemma — "we march forward in battle array without our [iron] corselets to meet the dark blades; helmets shine but I have not mine, for now our armor lies down on the ships."

Then Harald swung into battle, with a sword in each hand — he was renowned as a brilliant berserker — but the outcome was never in doubt. According to the sagas, in his first charge Harald took an arrow in the throat and fell. The last of the great Viking chieftains was no more and, though no one knew it then, a whole era was over. Tostig gamely rallied the Norwegians' remaining troops, including his own two hundred loyal housecarls, but then he was killed, along with most of his men.

The English pursued the survivors as far as their ships, many of which they set alight. The biggest battle ever fought on English soil up to that point was over, with King Harold the overwhelming victor. Harold generously allowed the remaining Norsemen to set sail for Denmark, but there were only enough men left to fill twenty-four of the one hundred ships that had originally departed from Norway.

Harold spent a week sorting out the aftermath, including the burial of his rebel brother, who had died in battle. Then Harold hosted a great victory feast. It was during that celebration, surrounded by his housecarls, that he received the news that William and the Normans had landed at Pevensey, in the south of England, and were waiting for him.

Anticipating the Norman threat, King Harold had maintained a mighty fleet of ships in the English Channel all through the summer. But as luck had it, the fleet had been forced to repair to port as the first September gales began to blow. That had left the way open for the Norman invaders. After a short but harrowing crossing (at one point it was feared that William's ship had been lost), on the morning of September 28, the duke and his army landed safely at Pevensey.

From there, William searched for a more defensible position from which to receive Harold. His strategy was simple: force the victor of Stamford to march south again and attack the Normans on a ground of William's, not Harold's, choosing. William found just the place a few miles east of Pevensey, on a tiny peninsula ten miles long and five miles wide, where an abbey of Norman monks could serve as a base and the town, Hastings, could provide anchorage for his great fleet.

Over the next few days William's army moved to Hastings, laying waste to the villages in its path. At Hastings William drew up his final dispositions for battle. He divided his army into three wings. On his left was a strong contingent of soldiers from Brittany, which by William's time had become a virtual satellite of the dukes of Normandy. In the center were his Normans, including a large force of mounted knights under the command of his half brother

Abbot Odo, who, although a Catholic cleric, rode into battle; he carried a great wooden club so as not to violate the clerical injunction against shedding blood. On the right were French and Fleming mercenaries led by Count Eustace of Boulogne, along with a contingent of Normans under Robert Beaumont, one of William's most trusted vassals.

William commanded his troops to build a makeshift defensive wall around the town of Hastings, then waited for his enemies to approach. He did not have to wait long.

After two days Harold and his army arrived, a bit bedraggled and tired after another exhausting forced march. Harold had been in the saddle day and night. But the English king also came with a heavy heart. Before Harold left London, envoys from William had revealed that their liege duke had not only the pope's blessing but also the papal banner to unfurl during the battle and relics belonging to Saint Peter as gifts. According to one version of the history, Alexander II had even excommunicated the English king.

It was a stunning blow to Harold. The chroniclers tell us that the king's face became distorted with anguish. "He grew pale and for a long time remained as if he were dumb. And when the monk asked more than once for an answer, he first said, 'We march at once,' and then, 'We march for battle.'"

This was a grievous error. Instead of resting up and preparing for the engagement, Harold's bedraggled army made yet another forced march, this time to the outskirts of Hastings. By the night of October 13–14, they had reached the northern edge of William's position. Harold's men were tired and hungry; many had not eaten for two days. Even worse, several of his best soldiers were still far to the north. Instead, except for his loyal band of housecarls, who were prepared to fight on foot with the favorite weapon of the Viking, the battle-ax, his army consisted largely of hastily assembled levies and even local villagers. Few of the confident veterans who had fought and won at Stamford Bridge were with him now. It would be several days before any of them reached the battlefield.

Nonetheless, Harold pulled together his ragtag army, some seven to eight thousand strong, and planted his two banners, the Dragon of Wessex and his personal emblem, the Fighting Man, at the top of a slope overlooking

William's army. As dawn came up on the fourteenth, he and his men watched as William advanced toward them.

William had fewer men — perhaps no more than five thousand in all — but his army consisted of professional fighting men; his Normans rode on horseback with lance and shield. By contrast, Harold's men — including the king himself and his two brothers Gyrth and Leofwine — were dismounted and tightly packed, shield to shield, in a battle formation known as *shieldburh*. The English had learned this formation through years of combat against invading Norsemen, with housecarls and their broadaxes thrust forward in the front line.

It was as if all the lessons learned in two centuries of Viking warfare in England suddenly came together, to be put to the test in a single morning.

According to the chronicles, Duke William — covered from head to knee in chain mail, with the holy relics and papal banner exposed for all to see — spoke to his assembled troops and reminded the Normans of their great country and their many deeds — they had always been victorious in the face of great danger. "Now you must prove with your hands the stuff of which you are made, the spirit that inspires you," he said. "If you fight manfully, victory, honor, and riches will be yours; otherwise you will be slain or as captives, you will serve the whims of a most cruel enemy, and will be remembered for ever with shame."

Then with shouts of "Joyeuse!" and "Mountjoy!" from the Normans,* and "God Almighty!" and "Holy Cross!" from the English, the battle was on.

Whereas the English had never fought men on horseback before, the Normans and the Frenchmen had never seen the Viking broadax wielded by the English, and terror struck hearts on both sides. William's Breton allies fell back in disorder. Seeing the gap in the enemy's ranks, the English rushed forward to fill it. Instead they created a gap of their own. If Harold and his brothers realized what a serious blunder this was, it was too late to stop their men's impetuous charge.

In the meantime, William dispelled fast-spreading rumors that he had

---

* The chronicles tell us that the Normans went into battle singing passages from *The Song of Roland,* which includes Old French terms for Charlemagne's sword.

been killed in the initial fighting by riding boldly up the front ranks and lifting his helmet, with its protected nose- and cheekpieces, to show his face to his men. "Look at me!" he shouted. "I am alive, and will be the victor, with God's help!" When William's men realized their leader was not dead, but very much alive and in their midst, they took heart and surged forward.

Now it was Harold's troops who were in trouble. When William's warriors dropped back again (this time perhaps as a deliberate feint), Harold's compounded their earlier error by rushing ahead again, confusing and scattering their ranks even more.

Duke William, meanwhile, was in the thick of the fight. "With the strength of Hercules he withstood his opponents," according to one of the chroniclers. "Some he maimed, some he mutilated, some the sword devoured, very many souls he sent into darkness."

Even while fighting hand to hand, William saw he could take advantage of the growing chaos in Harold's ranks. He ordered his Norman horsemen to move up again, and systematically and mercilessly they began to pound the English line with charge after charge.

A grinding battle of attrition ensued. Harold's brothers were both killed early in the fighting, and Harold had no way to control or coordinate his troops without them. Instead, the English strategy was now reduced to stand and die. A wall of housecarls faced the Norman onslaught as the rest of the English army stood behind them, in some places as many as eight men deep.

None of this daunted William. He followed each Norman cavalry charge with volleys of Norman arrows, aimed deliberately high to drop down on the helpless ranks of Englishmen pressed together — some so closely jammed, the dead had nowhere to fall. Then would come another charge, with lances piercing the housecarls' wall of shields to find living victims, followed by another volley, then another charge.

It was a brutal contest. The most important visual documentation of the battle, the Bayeux Tapestry, presents a horrifying picture of the action, with hacked-off heads and limbs scattered across the battlefield and the ground thick with the dead, in their chain-mail armor.

Norman knights attacking the Anglo-Saxon shieldburh at Hastings.
From the Bayeux Tapestry. ilbusca

The grisly slaughter went on all afternoon. Slowly but steadily the English front line shrank away until the Normans were able to press in from around either flank. As the sun was about to set, warriors on both sides could see King Harold himself, valiantly fighting on foot to rally his dwindling army.

It was at about that time, it is said, that he received his famous fatal wound, an arrow in the eye — perhaps one of the arrows the Normans were volleying over the heads of the English front ranks.* Nothing could now save the English army. The survivors began a headlong retreat, with the Normans furiously following. A hardy few of the dead king's housecarls managed to rally and administer a punishing rear-guard attack in the twilight, but it was too little too late. Sunset and the coming of darkness finally ended the slaughter. William,

---

* Or did he? An Italian monk writing in the 1080s said he did. The Bayeux Tapestry shows a figure holding an arrow sticking out of his eye next to another English warrior being struck by a sword. Over both figures is this caption: "Here King Harold has been killed." It is not clear which figure is meant to be Harold. Other chroniclers say it was William himself and Eustache of Boulogne who came upon Harold, whether wounded or not, and killed him, dismembering his body in their fury while the rest of the English host fell back in confusion.

duke of Normandy, had won the second decisive battle on English soil that year — and the more famous.

The first, at Stamford Bridge, had finally broken the Viking yoke on England. The second, at Hastings, had swept away one great dynasty and established another — a Norman dynasty of Scandinavian descent that would go on to transform the kingdom, and all of history.

To the survivors still on the field, these issues mattered little. They knew only that they were still alive — although for many of the wounded, it would not be for much longer. It had been a brutal and bloody fight. Scholars estimate that as many as one out of three who appeared on the field in Hastings that day was either dead or wounded. The man most relieved to be alive, and the most satisfied at the battle's result, was undoubtedly William himself.

Not only was he unscathed, but his rival for the throne was dead. Nothing now stood in his way to crown himself king of England. The tidings that arrived shortly after the battle, that Harald the Viking king and Tostig Godwinson were also dead, only elevated the triumph.

But where was Harold's body? The sorrowful duty of finding it was left to Edith, King Harold's mother and Earl Godwin's widow. She scoured the ghastly scene for hours until she finally identified the mutilated body of her dead son. She begged to have the body returned to her, even offered to give Duke William its weight in pure gold, if he would yield it up.

William rejected her offer. Instead, he ordered Harold's remains to be gathered and buried under a mound of stones overlooking the sea. There, a fellow Norman, William Malet, composed an epitaph:

> *By the duke's command, O Harold, you rest here a king,*
> *That you may still be guardian of the shore and sea.*

Burial under a mound of stones was an ancient Viking ritual, a gesture of honor. William's and Harold's Norse ancestors would have approved.

Despite the decisive victory at Hastings, it was another two months before William and his men were able to enter London. After recovering from their wounds and burying their dead, the Normans began a slow advance. An attack by insurgents on some of his troops brought a savage retribution on the town of Romney. Other nearby towns, such as Dover, got the point and quickly surrendered.

But then an outbreak of dysentery, which also overtook Duke William, forced his army to pause for nearly a month near Canterbury. Canterbury surrendered. Winchester, the traditional capital of the West Saxon kings, was next to capitulate, which gave William control over the royal treasury.

When a detachment of William's cavalry found London Bridge heavily defended, William decided against a direct attack on the capital. Instead he launched a destructive march through nearby Surrey and Hampshire, with his soldiers burning and pillaging towns as they went. By mid-November, William's troops had crossed the Thames and were based at Wallingford.

Meanwhile, English resistance to the Norman invasion and its ruthless leader was quickly crumbling. Edgar Atheling, a grandson of an earlier king, Edmund II, was put forward as an alternative candidate. But England's most powerful nobles, including the queen dowager herself, and its leading clergymen were flocking to William's banner. In mid-December, the last remaining English leaders in London submitted to William at Berkhamsted. On Christmas Day, 1066, he was crowned king of England in Westminster Abbey, the church Edward the Confessor had built.

There was one mishap, though. When the crowd inside the abbey proclaimed William king, with shouts of acclamation, some of William's mercenaries thought a riot had broken out. They set fire to the buildings surrounding the abbey, probably to flush out any resisting troops. By the time they had corrected their mistake and put out the flames, billows of smoke had filled the abbey and William and everyone else were choking and wiping their eyes.

It would take another five years of brutal campaigning, especially in the north, where ironically the Norse legacy was strongest, before William was able to establish control over all of England. Still, his greatest source of anxiety was the other half of his realm, back in Normandy.

He set off to return as soon as he could in the early spring of 1067, even before his control over his capital of London was completely secure (to help with that, he had begun construction of the stone citadel that would become the Tower of London). Normandy would be his chronic problem child for the rest of his life. From 1073 until 1085, he would spend almost all of his time in that unruly land.

The truth was this: The Viking warriors who had occupied England and the Danelaw had, like their Scandinavian cousins before them, eventually settled down to a normal peacetime life. In Normandy, they never did. And whenever peace did break out, as occasionally it did, the young Norman noblemen, who had been raised for a life of combat, were eager to quench their thirst for adventure on other horizons. Even in the years before the battle of Hastings, their journeys had carried them and the Viking heart far away to the south and east, to southern Italy and Sicily.

In young Duke William's day, this cluster of sun-baked, sea-washed territories formed a rough borderland between Byzantine Greeks, Saracen Arabs, and Lombard counts and dukes — not to mention the occasional pope — and they were all engaged in a constant struggle for power and control, with a sort of Wild West lawlessness. There, a "have sword, will travel" attitude could become the ticket to fame and fortune — or sudden defeat and death.

We don't know exactly when the first Norman knights showed up in the boot of Italy. One story has it that a party of forty Norman pilgrims were journeying to the Holy Land when they stopped at Salerno. There they learned that the town was under constant siege by the Muslim Saracens. The Normans went to the local prince and asked for weapons and horses so they could help defend the town. They then went on to defeat the Saracens almost single-handedly, achieving an impressive degree of slaughter. That led the local people to beg the Normans to stay. When the victorious pilgrims said they had to go home, the residents of Salerno loaded them with gifts to encourage other Normans to come to the town, which they soon did.

Another completely different story about the first appearance of Normans in southern Italy tells of Norman pilgrims meeting a man named Melus, who asked them for help in a rebellion against the Byzantine Greeks — not the Arabs this time. In this story, the pilgrims declined to stay, but when they reached Normandy, they gathered together friends to return and help Melus in his assault on the town of Apulia, later to become a center of Norman activity. Yet another version of the story has Melus meeting the original forty

Normans—except they aren't pilgrims this time, but rather Norman exiles who had fled the wrath of their overlord. And when Melus asks for their support, they prove all too ready to join in.

Which story is true, or at least fact-based, is not clear. But clearly the situation in the region was chaotic enough that any help from outsiders against one's enemies was welcome, especially if those outsiders were skilled with sword, lance, and shield. The Normans were all of those things. By 1018 their numbers in southern Italy fighting against Arabs or Byzantines had grown from an original pack of 250 or so to nearly 3,000, according to one contemporary account. It was not until 1030, however, that the Normans secured a base of their own in the region. A local duke gave their acknowledged leader, Rainulf, the territory of Aversa. The duke also gave his widowed sister to Rainulf as his wife.

It was five years later that the first of the sons of Tancred d'Hauteville arrived on the scene. Together with his brothers he would transform the entire political and military landscape of Italy and the central Mediterranean.

Tancred the father was a typical Norman knight with land around the village of Hauteville, close to Coutances, who over the course of two marriages managed to raise twelve sons to manhood. There was not enough inheritance to satisfy all of them. "They saw that their own neighborhood would not be big enough for them," a contemporary account explains, "and that when their patrimony was divided not only would their heirs argue among themselves about the share-out, but the individual shares would simply not be big enough."

Such a situation was not unknown to their Viking forebears: too many sons and not enough land to go around. So when they learned about the opportunities along the frontier of southern Italy, two of the oldest, William and Drogo (and possibly a third, their brother Humphrey), made their way there, in the mid-1030s. In this instance they found themselves fighting for, not against, the Byzantines, during a raid on Saracen Sicily, where William is said to have distinguished himself by killing a Saracen emir in single combat. Then the d'Hauteville boys turned against their former employers and launched an invasion of Apulia in 1041. By the end of the following year, William d'Hauteville had established personal rule over Apulia, located on the heel of the boot of Italy, with a large war band of Normans under his command.

What made southern Italy such a magnet for ambitious young Norman knights? Lack of opportunity at home and a thirst for seeking one's fortune with one's sword played their part, of course. The d'Hauteville brothers were certainly not unique except in their numbers; at least seven would wind up in Italy as soldiers for hire. So did at least three of the eight sons of Guimund des Moulins, from nearby Mortagne on Normandy's southeastern border; they immigrated to Italy along with a bold and adventurous sister. Perhaps there was also some Roman Christian enthusiasm for defending the True Faith against the infidel, whether Muslim Saracen or Orthodox Greek.

But more likely the real issue was not the pull of Italy, but rather the push of events in Normandy, where constant political turmoil and revolts prompted a steady stream of banished exiles. Major rebellions in 1047 and 1051–54 had to be crushed by Duke William; the defeated rebels either fled abroad or received sentences of formal exile, exactly like the *uluk,* or sentence of banishment, prescribed in the past by Viking chieftains. Ralph de Tosny (his Norwegian forebears would have called him Rolf) was one of those knights. Initially driven into exile by Duke William's father, Duke Robert, he eventually wound up, like so many other Norman outliers, in southern Italy. His son Roger went on to Spain to join the predecessors of the celebrated Castilian warlord Rodrigo Díaz de Vivar, or El Cid, and a participant in the Christian Reconquista of the Spanish peninsula. Back home he became known as "Roger the Spaniard" — a tribute to another wandering Norman exile who made good.

We don't know if Robert d'Hauteville, the sixth of the d'Hauteville boys, or his younger brother Roger were among the rebels scattered to the four winds following the 1047 revolt. But Robert's arrival in Italy that same year did signal a new era in Norman domination.

By the time Robert arrived, his older brother William was dead. Drogo was now in charge, but he had no land to give to his younger brother. The other Norman enclave, at Aversa, owed allegiance to Richard Drengot, the younger son of Rainulf, who was not about to make room for a possible rival. So Robert realized he was going to have to cut his own way in this rough-and-tumble world.

Physically and mentally, he was well-equipped to do so. Tall and statuesque, "he had a ruddy complexion, fair hair, broad shoulders," wrote an observer, the

Byzantine princess Anna Komnene, who hated the Norman warrior yet could not contain her awe for him. "His eyes all but shot out sparks of fire," she wrote. Robert was famous for his ferocious temper and a voice loud enough to be heard from one end of his army to the other. "He was, as you might expect, no man's slave, owing obedience to nobody in all the world."

Nor was he ready to submit to a law imposed by others, even his own brothers. At the beginning of his career in Italy, he lived like a virtual bandit, looting the towns and villages of Calabria like his Viking forebears, with a cunning unscrupulousness that earned him the nickname Robert Guiscard, which some have translated as "Robert the Fox," but "Robert the Weasel" would be more accurate. Success followed his sword, and in just five years he was formidable enough to marry the heiress of a substantial land holding near Benevento.

Not far away, his brothers Drogo and Humphrey had become even more powerful, and Richard of Aversa more powerful still. "By the middle of the eleventh century," writes the historian David Douglas, "the Normans had most certainly become a power to be reckoned with by all the established authorities in Italy." These authorities included the new pope, Leo IX, who pulled together a coalition of Italian troops, with their Lombard nobles and German mercenaries, and marched in person to Benevento to press the Normans into battle.

Usually rivals, Robert, his brother Humphrey, and Richard of Aversa quickly pooled their men and resources and met the pope and his army outside Civitate, on June 23, 1053. Richard's horsemen quickly scattered the Italians, and after bloody hand-to-hand fighting with the Germans, during which Robert had to rescue his brother Humphrey from danger, the papal army was completely destroyed. Pope Leo found himself the Normans' prisoner, and he was marched off to captivity at Benevento.

With the pope their hostage and no army able or willing to stand in their way, the Normans continued their conquest of southern Italy unabated. Between 1054 and 1057, Richard overran the environs of Aversa and captured Capua, setting the stage for possession of his own principality. Robert continued to expand his domination of Apulia and Calabria. Humphrey had died, but another brother, Roger, had arrived in 1056 to lend his sword to the cause. By 1059, the Normans were so strong and influential that Leo IX's successor as pope, Nicholas II, had no choice but to recognize Richard of Aversa as the prince of Capua, and Robert Guiscard as the duke of Apulia and Calabria "by the grace of God," and both as formal vassals.

It was a turning point in the history of the papacy. Henceforth, popes and Normans were no longer foes, but friends and allies. It was also a turning point for Norman fortunes in Italy. The men from Normandy were now there not just to fight, but to rule.

Robert's brother Roger, meanwhile, had his own ambitions. He had set his sights on the big island to the south, Sicily. With the restless and ferocious energy of his brothers, he embarked on a series of bold amphibious lightning raids reminiscent of the Viking raids on Ireland. On one of the expeditions, in 1061, Roger captured Messina. Then, with his brother Robert lending help, he steadily pushed back the Saracens in a series of battles that culminated in a sweeping victory over the emirate at Cerami, in 1063. Palermo was the last and biggest prize. Roger and Robert joined forces for a five-month siege. The Muslim capital of Sicily finally fell to its new Norman overlords on January 10, 1072.

Palermo's half-starved population almost certainly expected the brothers to turn the prize of Sicily over to robbery, rapine, and massacre. Their army of Normans, Bretons, Frenchmen (still called Franks in the chronicles), and Italians probably expected the same. Both sides, however, were disappointed.

Instead, Roger "did not exile anyone, and ... didn't harm anyone, even though they were all pagans [that is, Muslims]," according to an admiring chronicle. "He treated all he conquered with fairness. And in place of the [city's] mosque he built a church to the Virgin Mary." It was Palermo's first real cathedral, the seat of a bishop who would now preside over the second-largest city in Christendom except Constantinople itself. One hundred years later, it would be rebuilt by Roger's heirs. Although it was still Palermo's largest church, it had been surpassed by the royal chapel, or Cappella Palatina, which was even more ornate and splendid.

Built by Roger's son Roger II between 1132 and 1140, the Cappella Palatina has to be the most extraordinary monument ever built to the Viking legacy. Along the narrow naves, the interior walls are covered from floor to ceiling with glittering gold mosaics. They display a complex iconographical program of saints and scenes from the Bible seemingly designed by Roger II himself, with a handful of close advisers.

What would Rollo or Olaf Tryggvason, or even William the Conqueror, have said, standing in the nave of the Cappella Palatina, which was lined with pillars and arches, with the slight hint of a point prefiguring the Gothic arch?* What would they have thought, gazing up at the ornate ceiling, with its golden honeycomb pattern and one of the finest examples of Fatimid decoration and architecture?

Two hundred years earlier, Roger's forebears had been burning down and pillaging churches. Now he and his heirs were building and enriching them. The Cappella and the cathedral in Palermo are powerful monuments to Norman achievement and the new Christian civilization they were raising up. A cosmopolitan culture was also taking shape, blending Arab, Norman, Frankish, and ancient Greco-Roman customs and institutions, and this culture would sweep from one end of the Mediterranean to the other, from the gardens of Córdoba to the shores of the Bosporus.

And at its center was the Italy the Normans built. In fact, the entire southern boot and Sicily were now under the rule of the Norman "3 R's": Richard of Capua; Robert Guiscard, duke of Apulia; and Roger, "the Great Count," ruling Sicily from his palace in Palermo, where he kept many of the Muslim ways, such as minting coins that used the Islamic calendar.

But it was his elder brother Robert Guiscard who held the reins of supreme power, not only in Italy but in the entire Mediterranean basin. In 1081, Robert even launched an attack on the Byzantine emperor on his home turf in Greece. When Emperor Alexios joined forces with Venice to check Robert's aggression, Robert crushed them both. Among those who fought to the death for their emperor in the final battle were Alexios's Varangian Guard, many of whom had been recruited from Robert's ancestral Viking homeland. Robert soon hurried back to Italy, however, to snuff out a rebellion in Capua, where both he and Roger faced constant revolts and conspiracies led by their Norman subordinates. Maintaining order in their territories was a tense and often

---

* It was probably from this Arab design that Western masons from Normandy and France picked up the art of the pointed arch.

bloody business. After suppressing that revolt, Robert found himself heading north to relieve Rome of its siege by the German emperor. The house-to-house fighting that ensued devastated the city. Many civilians died, and a large part of Rome burned to the ground. Nonetheless, Robert had rescued the pope, Gregory VII, and the German emperor retreated northward, his cause decisively broken.

For Robert Guiscard, the decisive defeat of both the Byzantine emperor and the German emperor, in less than four years, marked the culmination of a lifetime of fighting and conquest. "By 1085 Robert had become the greatest warlord in Latin Christendom," writes the historian G. A. Loud; "his support and alliance was courted by popes and emperors, and his armies could threaten the heirs to Charlemagne and Constantine." William of Malmesbury even claimed that William the Conqueror looked to the great feats of Robert Guiscard for inspiration, "saying it would be disgraceful to show less bravery than one whom he so surpassed in rank."

Maybe so, but the impact of Robert and his brother Roger on the future of Italy was their most lasting legacy. They had expelled the last remnants of a Greek influence that predated the Peloponnesian War, and they had brought Muslim rule to an end. It was the d'Hauteville brothers Robert and Roger who made Italy a Roman Catholic country — and made the papacy the peninsula's dominant political power as well as Europe's leading spiritual power.

This final achievement was steeped in irony because the Normans' relations with the papacy took a fateful turn just before Robert's death. With Gregory VII, the papacy gained a new authority in Europe, thanks to Norman conquests. The pope boldly pushed major reforms to extend that authority until other secular rulers, such as the Holy Roman emperor, balked. When the Germans laid siege to Rome, Robert Guiscard had come to the aid of the pope, but the excesses of his troops created a permanent break in relations. Gregory VII found himself in Norman custody and would die in bitter exile, on May 25, 1085, with a famous statement on his lips: "I loved justice therefore I die alone." Robert himself passed away two months later — remarkably enough, he did so peacefully, after a life marked by violence. Roger d'Hauteville, count of Sicily, died in 1101, but not before he had secured the last holdout to his rule on his island domain.

Three great men, destined to wind up at odds with the other great figures of their age, and even at times with each other. The legacy they left — a perennial tension between empire and papacy, between church and state, and ultimately between the sacred and the secular — would lend Western civilization its peculiar dynamic. If it's true, as the art historian Kenneth Clark has asserted, that Western civilization was basically the creation of the church, it seems fair to add that the church was basically the creation of the Normans — if by "the church" we mean not so much a repository of Christian piety and truth but rather an international corporate power.

Despite their militancy, however, the Norman rulers of southern Italy and Sicily also made their domains the transmission belts of ancient Greek and Arab learning to the West. The first European ruler to consciously model himself on the ancient Roman emperors, Frederick II of Germany, received knowledge of vanished Roman culture from those centers of learning to the south. Knowledge of Arab and Greek medicine (Salerno had one of Europe's leading medical schools), astronomy, and mathematics passed northward via manuscripts to enrich the intellectual life of Europe, while works of Arab poetry and history, including the now lost *History of Sicily* and an anthology of 170 Sicilian poets edited by Ibn al-Qatta (died 1121), made Count Roger's Palermo an epicenter of Greek, Latin, and Muslim literature and culture long after his death.

On Robert Guiscard's tomb, in the monastery of Venosa, where his elder brothers were also buried, the inscription reads:

Here lies the Guiscard, the terror of the world.

Yet Robert and his brothers proved to be far more than holy terrors. They were builders of empire and creators of dynasties; they helped make Europe richer culturally as well as monetarily, and stronger and more stable.

In fact, the real Norman terror was yet to come, with its bloodshot sights set on Christian Europe's enemies.

The last Norman to shape the Middle Ages was born in about 1050. His parents were going to baptize him Mark, but he was so big at birth that his father and mother, who happened to be Robert Guiscard and Guiscard's second wife, Aubrée, dubbed him Bohemund, after a legendary giant in local Norman myth.

The boy grew up into a legend in his own right. Bohemund "was the exact replica and living image of his father," wrote Anna Komnene, the daughter of Emperor Alexios; she knew and loathed both father and son. Bohemund also resembled his father in other respects: in his "daring, strength, bravery, and indomitable spirit." She added, with considerable bitterness, "Father and son you might liken to caterpillars and locusts, for what was left by Robert [Guiscard], his son fed and devoured."

Bohemund's baptism in combat and command came in the fight against the Byzantines, when he helped his father, Robert, in his campaign in the east in 1081, seizing the island of Corfu and capturing Durazzo. After his father left to save Rome from the Germans, Bohemund scored one success after another, dominating Albania and northern Greece and even threatening Constantinople itself. It was the high-water mark of the Normans' conquests in eastern Europe, almost matching their achievements in Sicily and Italy.

Then, with a magnificent effort, Emperor Alexios and his most seasoned general managed to stem the Norman advance and finally defeated the "barbarians" (as Alexios dubbed Bohemund's army) at Larissa in 1083. Within a couple of years, the Normans were driven out of Greece and the Near East, and Bohemund fell back to his patrimony in southern Italy.

The relations between father and son were now at a low point. Disappointed by Bohemund's loss of the family's empire in Greece and Illyria, Robert disinherited his eldest son. He left the entire patrimony to his younger son, Roger, nicknamed "Borso" because his father always noticed him checking his pocketbook (*borso* in Italian).

By the 1090s, a three-way contest for mastery was developing, pitting Robert's brother Count Roger Guiscard against Roger Borso, and Bohemund against them both. Then, one day as Bohemund was girding himself for battle during the siege of Amalfi, he learned that a large group of knights and fighting men had arrived from Normandy and other points west. They were shouting something strange as they approached the city, and strange markings, in the shape of a cross, could be seen on their tunics.

When Bohemund asked who these soldiers were, what the crosses meant, and what they were shouting, he was told: "They wear the badge of Christ's Cross on their right arm or between their shoulders, and as a war-cry they shout together 'God's will, God's will!'"

The men were in fact Norman and French knights who had undertaken the mission, at the pope's command, to free Jerusalem from the Muslims. They were the vanguard of what history knows as the First Crusade. The story of the Norman conquest of the Mediterranean was about to take its strangest twist yet, and Bohemund, son of Robert Guiscard, would be right in the thick of it.

The new arrivals happily offered the Normans at Amalfi the chance to join their crusade. Count Roger had no intention of abandoning his hard-won territories for a reckless adventure farther east. Roger Borso expressed sympathy for the cause, but he had no desire to embark for the Holy Land either. Bohemund, however, stopped to consider his options. Unlike his brother and uncle, he had neither land nor title. He had no future in Italy, at least not while they were both alive. The knights from Normandy were offering him an opportunity to carve out a fortune and a destiny of his own. It was an offer he couldn't refuse.

He broke off the siege of Amalfi and made his temporary headquarters at Taranto, where he gathered a formidable group of companions and set off for the east.

The men he brought with him were a tough lot. They were the sons and nephews of the Norman knights who had first won fortunes for themselves in the wars for southern Italy and Sicily — men who had been honed like fine steel in battle. They included Bohemund's own nephew Tancred; Hermann of Canne, son of Humphrey d'Hauteville, the original count of Apulia; Robert of Sourdeval from the Cotentin in Normandy and a vassal of Count Roger of Sicily; Robert Fitz-Toustan, scion of the Norman counts of Molise; two vassals of Bohemund's brother Roger Borso; Richard, son of Count Rainulf of Caiazzo, who had led more than one revolt against Bohemund's father; Count Godfrey of Ruscinolo; and another Godfrey, a Guiscard relative who commanded the fortress at Monte Scaliglioso, whose aunt later married the duke of Normandy himself, Robert II.

With this formidable group behind him, Bohemund had moved to the forefront of the crusade's leadership by the time he arrived in Constantinople, in March or April 1097. To the other crusade leaders, like Godefroy de Bouillon and the new duke of Normandy, the Conqueror's son Robert II, Constantinople's elegant streets, magnificent Hippodrome, and soaring basilica of Hagia Sophia offered a dazzling vision, accustomed as they were to the rough-hewn stone and half-timbered cities and towns of western Europe. To Bohemund, however, Constantinople was the lair of his former enemies, including the sitting emperor, Alexios himself. The big Norman was taking no chances.

Although Alexios greeted him warmly and offered him a splendid dinner, Bohemund remained cautious. In a scene worthy of an episode of *Game of Thrones,* he ostentatiously refused to touch any of the delectable feast. When asked later why, he said frankly, "I was afraid he [that is, Alexios] might arrange to kill me by putting a dose of poison in the food."

Alexios, however, couldn't afford to be offended. The imperial army had been destroyed at the battle of Manzikert in 1075 by the new masters of the Middle East, the Seljuk Turks. Alexios had lost all of Anatolia (modern Turkey), as well as Jerusalem, to the Islamic invaders. He had been so hard-pressed that he had pleaded with the pope, Urban II, for help from the west, to which Urban had responded with enthusiasm. The pope called for a crusade to free the Holy Places, and thousands of volunteers had answered. They poured across Europe, traveling by land and sea.

Unfortunately, the crusade had attracted enthusiastic amateurs rather than seasoned veterans like the Normans. The first wave of crusaders was slaughtered by Muslim opponents, who stacked their bones like firewood to be bleached by the hot sun of the Middle East. Then, according to one chronicler, they crushed the bones to use as mortar in the building of new fortifications.

Now, with Bohemund and his band of warriors, the crusade had a chance of success. He showed his bravery and skill at the battle of Dorylaeum. The Turks charged down on the crusaders "howling like wolves and furiously shooting a cloud of arrows," while "we were all indeed huddled together like sheep, surrounded on all sides by enemies so that we could not turn in any direction," one of them confessed later. They were paralyzed by the Muslims' mounted tactics. Except for Bohemund, that is, who urged his men to hold their line along a riverbank. "We passed a secret message along our line, praising God and saying, 'Stand fast all together, trusting in Christ and in the victory of the

Holy Cross.'" The battle that threatened to become a disaster became a success for the crusaders. Without Bohemund's leadership, it was doubtful that any of them would have come out alive.

Antioch, the richest city in Asia Minor, saw the next major victory of Bohemund and his men. They crushed two Muslim armies sent to relieve the Christian siege of the city, even though the siege had exhausted the besiegers as much as the besieged. On June 3, 1098, Bohemund personally led the final assault on Antioch's walls. Then he led the crusaders in defeating yet another relieving force, one of the signal victories of the entire history of the Crusades.

With Antioch under its control, the crusading army set off for Jerusalem. Bohemund was not among them, however. He had other plans. He had decided he wasn't going to hand over Antioch to the Greek emperor after all. Alexios had broken faith with the crusaders by not joining them personally, the Norman announced. Instead, Bohemund planned to keep Antioch for himself, as the capital of a domain he aimed to carve out from the surrounding territory.

It was an outrageous claim, but no one was in a position to argue with him. Least of all Alexios, who had no army left to enforce his will. God was, it seems, on the side of the bigger battalions: this impression was reinforced when an inspection of the city turned up what the bishop of Le Puy, who was part of the crusader entourage, declared to be part of the Holy Lance, the weapon that had pierced Christ's side when he was on the cross. The rest of the crusading army marched off as Bohemund watched from the battered walls of Antioch, his blood-red banner floating in the warm breeze.

He would miss the capture of Jerusalem the next year, and take no part in the subsequent sack, with its wholesale massacre of the city's Jews. But he was content. He was the sole master of one of the wealthiest cities in the east. In 1100, the archbishop of Pisa invested him with an official title: prince of Antioch.

Syria had a new master, a Norman master, who would leave his principality to his nephew Tancred upon his death, in 1111. Bohemund's domain would persist through six successors — longer, in fact, than any of the Norman dynasties in Sicily. Longer even than the dynasty founded by the greatest Norman conqueror of them all, in the kingdom of England.

• • •

When he conquered England in 1066, Duke William had anticipated some of the crusading spirit. He had raised images of the Virgin Mary on the prows of his warships and had himself worn holy relics blessed by the pope into battle at Hastings. His victory brought him spoils that equaled anything the crusaders would win in the Holy Land, including a vast quantity of gold and silver, which awed onlookers when he returned to Normandy at Eastertide in 1067. These riches included the solid gold shackles he had put on his English captives.

Although he had by then conquered only a portion of England, he felt secure enough to return to Normandy. From 1073 to 1085, he spent almost all of his time in the duchy. It was not a serene period. There was a constant threat of bloody incursions from the nobles of Brittany and nearby Maine. The French king was sometimes a good friend and sometimes a bitter enemy. Meanwhile in England, the trusted Norman knights he left to impose order struggled to extend firm control over his kingdom, especially along the borderlands with Wales and Scotland.

But throughout it all, the biggest threat still came from Scandinavia, especially Denmark. There were attacks in 1069 and again in 1070. The worst was the invasion by Sven Estrithson in the summer of 1069; he sailed in with 240 ships and anchored his fleet in the Humber estuary. Sven's arrival sparked a general uprising in Yorkshire, where memories of Danish rule were still strong. On September 20 of that year, Sven's army, with the help of Saxon nobles, took back York, the old capital of Viking Northumbria, which had surrendered without resistance to Harald the Ruthless exactly three years earlier. Sven's troops were feted in local villages, and a feeling of liberation permeated the air.

All at once, William's entire kingdom was in danger. He returned hastily to England, marching first westward to suppress a rebellion along the Welsh border. Then he conducted a merciless campaign to crush the heart of the Yorkshire resistance. He devastated the countryside and reduced the city of York to ruins. Sven and the Danes hastily departed. A relieved and triumphant William moved back to the south, reaching Winchester before Easter 1070.

As decisive as the battle of Hastings had been, it was the harrying of Yorkshire that finally made William's throne secure. Not that the Danes ever gave up. Sven's fleet sailed again in the spring of 1070 and raided Peterborough with the help of Saxon rebels. The Danes renewed their threat again in 1075. And rumors of an even bigger attack brought William back to England at the end of 1085, where he stayed until 1087 (what ultimately wrecked the Danish invasion plans was the murder of its chief instigator, King Knut IV, the son of William's Norse nemesis, Sven Estrithson).

But the hope that a Danish expedition could topple the Conqueror from his throne was gone for good. Never again would the British Isles be threatened by partition at the behest of a Scandinavian chieftain or king. More than three centuries after the first raid on Lindisfarne, Sven's troops would be the last Vikings to set foot in England.

Nonetheless, the last years of William the Conqueror were not happy ones. During the final twenty months of his life, he faced the threat of still another invasion of England from Scandinavia, this time by the king of Denmark and some Flemish allies, after William had barely beaten off an invasion by King Malcolm of Scotland. When this most recent Scandinavian threat faded, William had to return to Normandy in the spring of 1087 to defend the southeastern frontier of his duchy from the French king. During the attacks and counterattacks in the Vexin, the Conqueror received a lethal wound at Mantes. He died at Rouen on September 9, 1087.

From start to finish, William's life had entailed constant war and tension with his neighbors and kinsmen, even his own sons. It was a saga of soaring ambition and brilliant opportunism, punctuated by acts of savage ruthlessness. As for his Norman contemporaries, friend and foe alike, their most fitting tribute — an ambivalent one too — has to be this description by the English monk and chronicler Ordericus Vitalis: "When under the rule of a strong master the Normans are a most valiant people, excelling all others in the skill with which they meet difficulties and strive to conquer every enemy."

It's a pronouncement that many a monk or scribe might have made about the Vikings in their heyday. So is this characterization of the Norman knights by the eleventh-century scribe Geoffrey Malaterra: "They can endure with incredible patience the inclemency of every climate and the toil and abstinence of a military life."

Ordericus touched on these same themes in the speech he gave to Robert Guiscard on his deathbed (similar words could have been spoken by Scandinavian immigrants to America): "We were sprung from poor and obscure parents, and leaving the barren fields of the Cotentin, and homes ill-supplied with the means of subsistence . . . Only with much difficulty did we pass beyond that place," before adding, perhaps with a wan smile, "but afterwards, with God's aid, we got possession of many cities."

It was an impressive record, and a tribute to the Norman variant on the Viking heart.

But Ordericus had also added that, when Normans are not under a strong master, "they rend each other and bring ruin upon themselves."

William and Bohemund both managed to avoid that grim fate. For all their ruthlessness and cruelty, they and the Normans of Sicily had transcended their original Viking legacy. In the end, the Normans' transformation of their "aristocracy of the brave" from freebooters and mercenaries into dynastic rulers and cultural transmitters had laid the foundations for the unity of the medieval West.

7

Vikings into Scandinavians

From Games of Thrones to Mighty Fortresses

A mighty fortress is our God,
a bulwark never failing
Our helper He,
amid the flood of mortal ills prevailing.

— Traditional Lutheran hymn, text by Martin Luther

THE STORY OF Scandinavia in the Middle Ages diverges significantly from that of the rest of Europe. Having been the driving engine of change during the Viking Age, Scandinavia found itself on the margins once again.

This marginalization, at its core, resulted from a series of critical failures to adapt to Europe's changing political landscape. After the twilight of the Viking kings, Norway, Sweden, and Denmark failed to establish a strong royal authority. They failed to adopt feudalism, the institution that the rest of Europe had used to stave off the Viking marauders. And the Scandinavian church even failed to stamp out the last vestiges of violent paganism.

Rather than step into the medieval era with their trademark courage and energy, the Scandinavian nations retreated into an isolation verging on irrelevance. In the midst of this failure and fragmentation, three extraordinary women stepped forward to try to save the Nordic kingdoms from oblivion.

For nearly a century, these women best exemplified the evolution of the Viking heart, while the men at their sides watched as their kingdoms crumbled. These three attempted the impossible, and in many ways they achieved it. Their leadership pointed the way toward modern Scandinavia, and the success that its nations would ultimately realize in the modern era. They also set the stage for the next major transformation, the coming of the Reformation, which would give Scandinavian culture and society new direction and power.

Out of failure, success. Out of chaos, a new and more stable order.

Post-Viking Scandinavia's first important failure was the failure to unify. After the death of King Canute in 1035, and except for a short period toward the end of the Middle Ages, Norway, Denmark, and Sweden never managed to unite under a single crown or dynasty. France, England, Spain, and even Germany all took the opposite trajectory. They opted for the stability of a growing, ever-stronger centralized power wielded by a single noble house: the Plantagenets and Tudors in England, the Capetians and Valois in France, and the Hohenstaufens and Habsburgs in Germany.

Instead, the modus in the North was consistently centrifugal. Chaos, civil war, and disputes between competing dynasties — even within the same dynasty — were the norm.

Take Norway, for example. After the death of Harald Hardrada at Stamford Bridge in 1066, his family, under Harald the Peaceful (a highly un-Viking sobriquet, by the way), ruled Norway until 1130. But the demise of Sigurd I, known as Sigurd the Crusader as he was the first European monarch to set foot in the Holy Land, led to a century of civil war and anarchy that only the rule of his grandson, Haakon IV, managed to end.

Haakon's long reign brought Norway a brief golden age, with the annexation of Iceland and Greenland, but his son and heir Magnus had to trade away the Isle of Man and the Hebrides to the kings of Scotland. Possession of the Orkneys and the Shetlands did not last much longer, either. There was also a long quarrel with the church in Norway, which Haakon V healed, but he failed to provide a male heir to succeed him.

Sweden in the eleventh century endured constant turmoil and conflict as well, with a string of kings who could barely extend their power beyond the point of their swords. After the death of Erik the Victorious and then the extinction of the house of Stenkil, two more dynasties came and went in less than a century. The murder of King Sverker I in 1156 led to a century of civil war, the Swedish equivalent of England's War of the Roses, with the house of Erik and the house of Sverker by turns seizing the throne. The rest of Swedish history over the next centuries does not revolve around strong kings, but around strong nobles like Earl Birger, who was the power behind the throne of his son Valdemar. But under Earl's younger son Magnus there ensued a power struggle that by 1319 left the house of Birger, and royal authority in Sweden, in shambles.

By that date, Danish royal authority had also been reduced to chaos. Since the days of Harald Bluetooth, the impulse among its rulers had been to unify the kingdom to meet the present threat from the German emperors and the Slavic Wends in the south. The rulers also felt the need to expand eastward into the Baltic region, to reward loyal followers with land as in days of old. Danish kings invaded Finland at least twice, in 1191 and 1202, but each time lost out to their Swedish rivals.

Meanwhile, Denmark's efforts in the Baltic came to almost naught when their king, Valdemar, was captured and forced to give up everything the Danes had taken except Rügen and Estonia. Danish Estonia's capital was Tallinn (which in Estonian means "Danes' Town"), which had been founded in 1219 after a battle with local Baltic tribes — the setting, according to tradition, in which the Danes unfurled their national banner, red with a white cross, for the first time. Valdemar's defeat might have been worse; the pope himself had to intervene to win Tallinn back for Denmark. Even so, the town's German inhabitants remained firmly in control of the region. Denmark's dream of a Baltic empire proved to be just that: a dream. The monarchy, which had expended political and financial capital to build it, emerged weaker than ever.

By 1200 Scandinavia had fractured in yet another way. Old Norse had been its common language since the glories of the Viking Age. The language of runes and epic bards, it had maintained amazing stability and continuity across the centuries and across Scandinavia, even extending to Normandy and England. The Old English spoken by the Anglo-Saxons, including the creator of *Beowulf,* for example, was much closer to Old Norse than to modern English. As late as the twelfth century the so-called Grey Goose Law of Iceland could state that Swedes, Norwegians, Danes, and Icelanders all still spoke the same language (*Donsk tunga*).

But the next century saw the breakaway of Swedish (not modern Swedish, of course, but what linguists term Old Swedish) from its Old Norse roots, and then the same happened with Danish. Norwegian in turn would eventually break away from Danish, although it was viewed as a Danish dialect rather than a separate language almost until the dawn of the modern age.

Old Norse's last home, like so much of Viking culture, proved to be Iceland. The language that Ragnar Ladbrok or Harald Bluetooth recognized was preserved in Iceland's law courts, in the fishing villages and farms, but above all in the skaldic poems and *Edda*s. This had enormous cultural consequences for Iceland later on, as we shall see. But it couldn't disguise the fact that the emergence of distinct languages in the Vikings' original homelands pointed to three distinct destinies for three separate countries.

Denmark, for example, became a kingdom whose fate was now inextricably entwined with the peoples to its south, first with the pagan Wends and then the Germans and the Holy Roman Empire. As the Middle Ages advanced, the Danes would live in cultural and economic interdependence with the cities of the Hanseatic League adjoining its Baltic and North Sea coasts, while the indigenous Danish merchant class languished.

By contrast Sweden increasingly turned its energies to the east; its rulers and merchants found themselves irresistibly drawn along the same routes the Rus had followed centuries before, into the Baltic and Finland and beyond. Swedes competed for power not with the Germans, but rather the rulers of Poland and Russia — ironically, the latter being the political legacy of Swedish ancestors.

Norway's destiny was caught between its two Scandinavian neighbors like a fish in a net. But as in Viking days, its horizons continued to stretch to the west, starting first with King Harald's failed expedition to England in 1066 but then beyond, to the Norse settlements in Iceland and Greenland. Eventually its political history would be dwarfed by that of its two more ambitious neighbors, but throughout the next centuries it would remain one of the most precious homes of the Viking heart.

All three societies eventually emerged as monarchies that have endured to the present day. Iceland, then and now, was the exception. But everywhere else, the pattern was the same: chronic weakness at the top of society and a stubborn resistance to change from the middle to the bottom, especially if that change undermined local autonomy and community.

At its core, that weakness at the top stemmed from the failure to make the royal crown hereditary. The old Germanic tradition of elective kingship, which the Vikings had never abandoned, still had political bite. However much a sham in practice (aristocratic cliques in all three states, not the will of the people, determined who would, and would not, be the next monarch), this principle made the accumulation of power at the top almost impossible. The country's upper nobility retained the power to snatch the crown away from anyone they suspected of being too strong and to give it to someone too weak to challenge their authority.

The trend toward codification of law had the same effect. Instead of written law becoming an instrument for royal aggrandizement, as it did in Capetian France and Plantagenet England, in Scandinavia it became a way to preserve tradition and custom, like a dragonfly preserved in amber. It also kept alive ancient traditions of independent local government, which, as much as anything, checkmated the power of royal officials to act decisively in the name of the king.

Instead, the one source of unity the monarchies hoped they could use was Christianity and the institutions of the Catholic Church. One Swedish or Norwegian king after another seized on the church as a way to impose and build their authority. But even here, the story was one of unrealized goals and thwarted ambition. Like a submerged rock diverting a river's course, pagan rites and rituals survived and made the Christianization of Scandinavia a long, drawn-out exercise in frustration for contemporaries — albeit a source of fascination for the historian.*

As usual, it was Iceland that proved the exception to that rule. It became crucial to preserving the Viking heart's cultural and linguistic legacy in ways

---

* See Chapter 5.

that would enrich not only the mainstream of Scandinavian culture but that of Europe itself.

By 1200, Iceland had become the Norsemen's principal outpost in the North Atlantic. This island, which gently brushes the Arctic Circle at Grimsey Island, is about the size of New York State but has less than 1 percent of New York's population today. Whereas Vinland was quickly abandoned and settlement in Greenland slowly shrank away to extinction, the people and culture of Iceland found a very different path forward from the Viking Age. Icelanders had neither kings nor titled nobles. Its Althing remained a viable institution long after its German and Scandinavian counterparts had died away — viable up to the present day, even. In fact, it was the Althing, not a ruling monarch or family, that chose to replace paganism with Christianity almost by majority vote.

This meant that the transition from the rites of Odin and Freya to those of the Catholic mass went much more smoothly than it did in Norway or Denmark or Sweden. Strangely, it also meant that Icelanders were able to preserve a quiet pride in their ancient pagan past, *as* the past, while preserving Old Norse as their national language. That sense of pride in their roots is reflected in Iceland's most important contribution to Scandinavia and the world in general: the sagas, which Icelandic poets and scholars began writing down in the late 1100s. This literary industry would keep them occupied for the next two centuries. What else was there to do on an island where winter lasts more than seven months?

There are more than forty sagas preserved in multiple manuscripts. Their forms range from epic histories — like the *Heimskringla* and the sagas extolling, in sometimes sensational detail, the lives of Viking kings who had died centuries before — to descriptions of the lives and fates of Iceland's great families and their family feuds in the Viking Age, to works of pure literary fiction like *Njal's Saga:* Western civilization's first novels, in fact. The later sagas, composed in the fifteenth century, often were entirely fictional in character, looking back nostalgically to a Viking era that had vanished three centuries before.

The sagas also include two works that give us our most detailed look at Norse religions and cosmogony: *The Prose Edda* and *The Poetic Edda,* composed by the best-known of the saga writers, Snorri Sturluson. Most other saga authors remained anonymous.

Saga means "story" in Old Norse and in modern Swedish. The interweaving of fact and fiction that characterizes all the sagas, including the *Eddas*, had a simple goal: to tell a good story that commanded an audience's attention. Descended from the bardic recitations of the Vikings, these tales were preserved and embellished by the skalds, who became court bards for Norwegian kings and nobles. The skalds and their works grew into one of Iceland's primary export industries in the thirteenth century, when the island became a Norwegian dependency.

Many of the stories center on events in Iceland itself. They reflect the patronage of prominent *gothar,* the chieftains who looked to the bards to tell their family histories, many of which reached back to the heyday of the Viking Age. But what is most extraordinary is that patron and poet chose to write these stories down in Old Norse rather than in the lingua franca of the western Middle Ages, which was Latin. The fact that these stories were written down at all marked a sea change in Scandinavian history. In this way, the oral traditions that had preserved Viking culture and religion through the centuries — passed down through recitation from one skald to another — now found a more permanent form.

In fact, the Icelandic sagas are the only significant vernacular literature to emerge from Scandinavia for more than a millennium. It may seem incredible, but although the book and written word had been part of mainstream Christendom for more than a thousand years — for Judaism even longer — in Scandinavia, books were a relative newcomer. The very earliest example of a written religious text from Denmark (in Latin) dates from the eleventh century.

This tardy arrival of the written word, and the habits of mind that rely on writing for communication and connectivity, had a profound impact on the evolution of Nordic society and culture. In lieu of written texts, the North remain rooted in a Viking Age culture based on oral transmission. Even runes had been used for monuments and memorials, not for documentation or record keeping, let alone (like the Bible or Quran) for transmission of a religious belief system. What you said and did mattered more than what you, or someone else, wrote down. Instead of a culture of the book, a culture of deeds and spoken words shared with friends and neighbors, and even enemies, prevailed.

Written cultures, as the scholar Walter J. Ong has explained, strive for "a sense of closure," which reached its culmination in the printed word. Their people are comfortable with "a sense that what is found in a text has been finalized, has reached a state of completion." By contrast oral culture is constantly open to new additions and interpretations and iterations, based on the audience and the perspective of the speaker or reciter. "A typical visual ideal is clarity and distinctness, a taking apart," writes Ong. "The auditory ideal, by contrast, is harmony, a putting together." So whereas "sight isolates, sound incorporates. Whereas sight situates the observer outside what he views, at a distance, sound pours into the hearer."

Although the Norse sagas have come to us in written form, they preserve that sturdy oral tradition, with their strong narrative lines and steady flow of new but also familiar persons and events. They remain rooted in the rituals of storytelling around the hearth fire or on a ship's deck during a long, tedious voyage; those who tell the tale and those who listen are comrades and kin. That tradition would shape the character of the Icelandic sagas.

One reason why these works remain so readable today, whereas most medieval literature is of interest only to people in pursuit of a graduate degree (like myself as a budding young medievalist at the University of Minnesota), is because the sagas are the literature of a democratic community. There, as in modern Iceland, everyone knew one another and their families. These works include characters rich and poor, female and male, old and young, who have a familiar face.

Another reason for the sagas' continuing popularity is their consummate storytelling. The novelist Jane Smiley has said that the sagas represent the best training for an aspiring novelist: how to build a plot, memorable but also believable characters, and a narrative that reveals something profound about the characters but also about the audience of readers or listeners.

That storytelling tradition grew out of the circumstances in which they were composed. Iceland's small population and extreme cultural homogeneity meant a high degree of social mobility, with families and individuals rising and falling in wealth and dominance with surprising speed. The island nation's relative isolation also kept its people aloof from the disruptive trends sweeping over the rest of the Scandinavian world, while their well-remembered ancestry — as well as the island's rich Viking past — were passed down through the generations and remembered with both pride and nostalgia.

The sagas also reveal Icelanders at their most human. "People are always making rash commitments and foolish choices," writes Jane Smiley, "speaking unwisely, taking stubborn positions, ignoring the wise counsel of others, hoping to get something more on a gamble than what they are already assured of, refusing to submit or lose face." They are people we can relate to, which gives the sagas universal meaning and appeal. But they also reveal a world shaped by Icelandic, and more broadly, Scandinavian values. There, people take pride in work and what they do with their hands: building, cooking, washing, sheep herding, and horse breeding, as well as sailing and fighting.

Always fighting, in fact. Over land, over treasure, over women in marriage, and over children born in or out of wedlock. From a modern perspective, this literary universe combines the best of epic poetry with the best of soap opera. It's only surprising that their titles aren't better known, given that their themes, stories, and even characters live on in later Western literature. From Sigurd the dragon slayer in *The Saga of the Volsungs;* to Egil Skallagrimsson, the morally ambiguous hero of the most immediately readable of all the sagas, *Egil's Saga;* to Njal Thorgeirsson, the tormented central character in the saga with the most modern feel, *Njal's Saga;* and the gods, giants, dwarves, and elves who populate the *Edda*s: traces of these archetypal figures are scattered throughout the Western storytelling tradition — in Richard Wagner's operas, of course, but also in the works of J.R.R. Tolkien, not to mention *Star Wars* and the Harry Potter stories.

That is thanks, in large part, to Snorri Sturluson, the best-known of all the saga authors and one of the most famous Icelanders in history.

Snorri was no bookworm but something of a Viking warrior himself. Born in 1178 or 1179, he was the son of a hard-edged chieftain from western Iceland. When Snorri was two years old, Iceland's leading *gothi,* Jon Loptsson, offered to raise Snorri in his household as a way to settle a feud between Loptsson and the Sturlungs, the family of Snorri's father, Sturla. Snorri spent the next sixteen years on Loptsson's estate at Oddi, where he learned the art of storytelling as well as the art of war. The life of a skald was considered an exalted calling in thirteenth-century Iceland.

Snorri thrived. He married one of Iceland's wealthiest women and became a prominent *gothi,* or chieftain, in his own right. Twice he was elected as law speaker of the Althing, in 1215 and in 1222. The law speaker was the Icelandic equivalent of chief justice of the Supreme Court and Speaker of the House rolled into one.

At Thingvellir he built a magnificent hall for himself, which he named Valhalla; he and his cronies and allies both reveled and conducted official business there. We don't know when Snorri started writing sagas in his spare time. Surely he didn't have much time to spare, between supervising his large estate, presiding at the Althing, and making two lengthy voyages to Norway in order to leverage his power in Iceland with the help of Norway's most powerful families. But his works included not only the *Edda*s — among the world's most influential literary works — but also the semi-mythical history of the Danish kings, the *Heimskringla.*

All the same, as the commentator Jesse Byock has noted, "In the 1230's the number and reach of Snorri's enemies in Iceland and Norway grew enormously." In 1241 two of his former sons-in-law (the marriages of his daughters to Icelandic chieftains had ended disastrously, with ill-feeling all around) were recruited by the Norwegian king, Haakon IV, to rid Iceland of Snorri; Haakon considered him an arrogant and recalcitrant foe. The men surprised Snorri at his home at Reykjaholt, in western Iceland, and murdered him.

Snorri's death marked a turning point in Iceland's history. Yet Haakon IV was laboring to secure his grip over his island domain. Like the efforts of most Scandinavian kings when they tried to increase their power in the Middle Ages, Haakon's effort would fail. Snorri was his most prominent victim. But the losers in the struggle for thrones, whether in Iceland or at home, were the kings themselves: the sagas have survived, while the kings have vanished.

Another characteristic failure of Scandinavia during the Middle Ages was its failure to transition to feudalism. This fact separated it from virtually the rest of Europe — with huge implications for the future.

At the most basic level, there were simply too few people in Scandinavia for the system to work: too few to form the large masses of serfs and villeins, as tenant laborers were called in Norman England, to be herded about by their landlords, but also too few noble families to spread the code of military service as a matter of caste across the Scandinavian landscape. Instead, any king needing an army had to rely on free peasants, farmers, and townsmen to arm themselves and take up his cause. Denmark was the exception; some semblance of a feudal order sprang up there as it did in the rest of Europe. But even there, the Danish nobility lacked the one crucial element that made feudalism work among its German neighbors, for example: peasants willing to spend their lives — and to see their children follow the same pattern — working on land that was not their own.

Instead, an independent Scandinavian peasantry, tilling their own land and regarding their rights as hereditary, as the nobles did, remained a vital part of the Viking legacy. This dispersion of authority retarded Scandinavia's political development, as historians or political scientists might understand it — and probably its economic development as well. But it also imposed a natural system of checks and balances more ingenious than any that might be devised by a political scientist. In all parts of medieval Scandinavia, an entrenched nobility acted as a permanent restraint on monarchy, and a free peasantry acted as a permanent restraint on that nobility.

For example, unlike aristocrats elsewhere in Europe, the Swedish nobility had no hereditary fiefs. When a noble was granted a castle belonging to the crown, by law that noble's heirs couldn't later claim their ancestor's civil or military rights. The lands, however, belonging to the magnates who constituted the medieval nobility were their own, not "on lease" from a feudal king. If they wanted to use their own financial means to build a castle and arm it with a body of troops, that castle was theirs. But those troops were expected to serve as part of the army of the realm under the king's command, not in support of the aristocrat who recruited them, as happened in the rest of western Europe — where soldiers might take the side of a noble even against their king.

Monarchs in any other part of Europe would have been bewildered with delight at such a situation. It didn't mean that the rule of Swedish kings went unchallenged. Far from it. But it did mean that royal authority wasn't mortgaged to its most powerful enemies, as happened later in England under the

Plantagenets and in France under the Capets. The power struggle between king and aristocracy took place on a more or less level playing field. The situation also made it hard for either side to score a decisive win.

Also, in Sweden, outright serfdom never existed. Hence, at the end of the day, the Swedish nobility was basically a class of well-off citizens, not an elite caste whose power depended on owning other human beings. That included slaves. In the lands where so much wealth had been built on the slave trade during the Viking Age, slavery itself fell steadily into disuse, then outright abolition. By 1335, the last vestiges of slavery in Sweden had been swept away. The evolution of written law in Scandinavia, which by and large strengthened the autonomy of individuals, whether wealthy or poor and whether living on the land or living in towns, found no place for the status of slaves. From Sweden to Norway and Denmark, people who had been enslaved simply melded into the social landscape, like other tillers of the soil or servants in the towns.

Paralysis at the top, inertia everywhere else: this was no way to build a strong kingdom during the Middle Ages. In the later Middle Ages one Scandinavian monarchy after another buckled under constant pressures outside their control. By the end of the 1200s their economic fortunes lay in the hands of German merchants of the Hanseatic League, and their territories faced encroachment from neighboring competitors, such as the rising twin powers of Poland: Lithuania and the Order of the Teutonic Knights. By the mid-fourteenth century, Scandinavia faced a catastrophe of another kind: the Black Death, surging up from Germany and carried in by boat from England. That epidemic, which killed off perhaps as much as one-quarter of Europe's population, ravaged Norway, Denmark, and Sweden.

The result was a late medieval Nordic Europe distinguished only by its undistinguished and diminished kings and princes and prelates, a Catholic Church still struggling to stamp out the last vestiges of Viking paganism, and a political and social ecosystem mired in seemingly permanent decline. Then suddenly into the leadership vacuum stepped three extraordinary women who would transform not only their Scandinavian homeland but arguably the whole of Europe: Saint Brigitte of Sweden, Queen Ingeborg of Norway, and Queen Margaret of Denmark.

• • •

Women had always been prominent, if not entirely equal with men, in Viking society. The rise of written and canon law had eroded some of their freedoms, the laws governing divorce and property inheritance being one notable example. The advent of Christianity had also changed the respective roles of men and women, although not always for the worse, as some feminist scholars such as April DeConick contend. For example, Christianization ended the traditional Viking practice of infanticide, especially of female children. Not surprisingly, the three women who set the course of Scandinavia for more than a century came from the very top of society. Ingeborg and Margaret were both born to the royal purple, while Brigitte's father was a Lawman (in Swedish terms, a high-court judge) and very wealthy landowner.

But what made these women extraordinary was not their social status, but rather their single-minded commitment to transforming their fellow countrymen for the better. For Ingeborg and Margaret, this change would come in the political sphere; for Brigitte, the religious. Combining extraordinary intelligence with almost preternatural will and discipline, all three galvanized their contemporaries into taking unaccustomed positive action. If ever there were living embodiments of the Viking heart — boundless courage, a commitment to family and community, a deep personal resourcefulness — it was these women.

Brigitte's literal visions of a Christ who spoke directly to the hearts of common people, and in good Swedish too, left a permanent mark — on her beloved church and the continuing work of the Brigittine nuns, who perform good works in the straightforward, homespun spirit of their founder. Brigitte splashed onto the international scene earlier than the other two women discussed here; one of her daughters would eventually become a lady-in-waiting to Queen Margaret of Denmark.

Born in 1303, her father, Birger Persson, was *Lagman*, or Lawman, of Uppland, making him one of the most influential officials in the kingdom. He was also one of the most pious. Another future Swedish saint, Ingrid, was a close relative. Brigitte had a deep religious training from an early age, thanks to the strong-willed aunt who took charge of the girl after the death of Brigitte's mother. But though Brigitte showed clear signs of being destined for the monastic life, her father insisted on marrying her off, when she was only thirteen, to a prominent nobleman, Ulf Gudmarsson, who was only eighteen himself.

Fortunately for Brigitte, her husband was as devout as she was. Together they raised no fewer than eight children; their daughter Catherine would later be canonized as a saint. It was on a family pilgrimage to Compostela in Spain, the shrine of Christ's disciple James, that Ulf fell ill. He died in the Cistercian monastery of Alvastrâ in Östergötland, or East Gothland, in 1343, shortly after returning home. Ulf's death left his widow Brigitte free to cast aside the obligations of married life and devote herself completely to her religious convictions. She was already good friends with leading churchmen in Sweden, as well as King Magnus Eriksson; she gradually acquired great influence over the ruler as his spiritual adviser.

One of her first acts was to found an order of nuns: the Order of the Holy Savior, with its motherhouse at Vadstena, became known as the Brigittines. But Brigitte's main ambition was to meet with the pope, so she set off in about 1348 across a Europe that was still being devastated by the Black Death. When the two finally met, she told the pope about her ecstatic religious visions (later written down by a Cistercian monk from her original Swedish version) and asked him to authorize her order of nuns.

Such was her strength of will and persuasive powers that the pope gave way, authorizing the Brigittines as a branch of the Augustinian order. The order's motherhouse remained in Sweden, at Vadstena, where Brigitte's daughter Catherine would succeed her as head of the order. But Brigitte herself spent most of the rest of her life in papal Rome, advising various popes on issues such as how to end the Hundred Years' War between France and England and how to authorize a Swedish crusade against Novgorod, perhaps not knowing that the founders of Novgorod had been her fellow Swedes.

When she died in 1373, worn out from a pilgrimage to Jerusalem, Brigitte left an important legacy: her voluminous accounts of the many visions she had seen since childhood, with a sharp focus on the veneration of the Virgin Mary and inner dialogues with Christ himself. She was quite convinced that Christ had appeared to her and given her the power to predict future events — a conviction that earned her the respect and veneration of many (and not only in Sweden) but also the skepticism and suspicion of others. The decision to canonize her in 1391 was controversial, to say the least. Reading her *Revelations* today, however, she sounds less like a female Nostradamus and more like a typical outspoken Scandinavian grandmother, unafraid of speaking her mind and completely sure that she, not others, knows what's best.

Take this passage from Chapter 4, in which Christ speaks directly to Brigitte. It employs the homely (and very Scandinavian) metaphor of a strong and snug house:

> I want to explain to you the meaning of the house that I want to build. This house is the life of purity, and I myself, who created all things and through whom all has been made and exists, am its foundation. There are four walls in this house. The first is my justice, by which I will judge those who are adversarial to this house. The second wall is the wisdom, by which I will enlighten the builders of this house with my knowledge and understanding. The third wall is my power, by which I will strengthen them against the temptations of the devil. The fourth wall is my mercy, which receives everyone who prays for it. In this wall is the door of grace through which all, who pray for it, are accepted in. The roof of this house is the love with which I cover the sins of those who love me so that they will not be judged for their sins. The window of the roof, whereby the sun enters, is the thought and consideration of my mercy, and through it the warmth of my Divinity is let in to the builders of the house.

Brigitte's other legacy is, of course, her Brigittine order, which after her death expanded to more than eighty houses across Europe. It was her daughter who finally received papal approval for the order's official rule, with its distinctive double foundation of monks and nuns both under the authority of a single abbess: Brigitte would certainly have approved of this monastic matriarchy — as would the other strong women who followed her.

Ingeborg of Norway was born two years earlier than Brigitte, the only legitimate daughter of King Haakon V. Ingeborg was first betrothed to Magnus Birgerson, the son and designated heir of Birger, king of Sweden. But the engagement didn't last, as there were more compelling political reasons to give her to Birger's younger brother, Erik, the duke of Södermanland. The two were engaged in 1305, and the marriage took place in Oslo in 1312, in a double ceremony. Her cousin, Ingeborg Eriksdottir, went to the altar with Erik and Birger's other brother, Duke Valdemar Magnusson, at the same time.

The complicated political alliances that these marriages were meant to seal quickly fell apart. Ingeborg and her husband had barely time enough to bear two children before Duke Erik and his brother Valdemar were kidnapped by enemies and disappeared. Rumor soon had it that they had been murdered.

The two Ingeborgs sprang into action. On April 16, 1318, the women made a pact at Kalmar with the Danish duke Christoffer of Halland-Samsö and the archbishop Esgar of Lund to free their husbands, and to freeze peace negotiations with the sitting kings of Sweden and Denmark until the deal was done. In exchange, the duchesses pledged that their husbands would honor whatever promises their wives made to win their allies' support. The men never had the chance to back their ladies' pact. Later in 1318, the ugly rumors were confirmed: both husbands were dead.

The son of Ingeborg of Norway was now proclaimed king of the country, as Magnus VII, and Ingeborg was formally recognized as her son's regent. Then the nobility of Sweden elected him as their king as well, after deposing the despised Birger. Ingeborg became nominal regent in Sweden too, establishing her own court at her residence in Varberg. Her ally Mats Kettilumndsson presided over the Swedish regency council alongside the two "duchesses Ingeborg"; but Ingeborg Haakansdotter, as the regent mother was known, was the only one with a seat in both the Swedish and the Norwegian councils of state. She was also duchess of her own fiefs, which functioned autonomously under her rule, just as she also controlled a large number of strategically important castles and fortresses.

Her formal title was now "Ingeborg, by the Grace of God, daughter of Haakon, duchess in the Kingdom of Sweden." She was by far the most powerful person in either kingdom, Sweden or Norway. But in the chaotic political conditions prevailing in medieval Scandinavia, this type of success couldn't last. Ingeborg soon came under fire for running the government in a high-handed way, without consulting the Swedish and Norwegian councils. She was also criticized for using her son's royal seal to get what she wanted.

In 1322, open conflict broke out between Ingeborg and the Swedish regency

council. The male councilors struck an agreement that no order from Ingeborg should ever be accepted without approval from the entire council. The
next year she was forced to accept the terms of this loss of power and to give
up several of her most important castles and fiefdoms.

On February 20, 1323, the Norwegian regency council also rose up in revolt
against Ingeborg. By 1326 she had lost almost everything. The bulk of her castles
and fiefs was gone, as was her military power. She was also compelled to send her
right-hand adviser and not-so-secret lover, a petty noble named Canute Porse,
into exile. Even then, Ingeborg remained a formidable figure, feared by everyone
who dealt with her and a law unto herself. Eventually she married her lover, Canute, and made him duke of Halland and then duke of Estonia in 1329.

A year later Canute died. But by then, Ingeborg's eldest son, Magnus, was
nearly of age to become king — and Magnus was devoted to his mother. For
his coronation in Stockholm, in 1336, his mother had her own fleet of warships
to send to welcome guests, including her daughter, Euphemia; her son-in-law,
Albert of Mecklenburg; Rudolf I, duke of Saxe-Wittenberg; and Henry of
Holstein.

Ingeborg also never gave up on her dream of carving out chunks of Danish
territory for Sweden. She managed to incite her son to declare a war against
the rulers of Slesvig and Holstein, which were attached to the Danish throne,
and against the German cities of the Hanseatic League in Denmark in 1341.
She was still pushing her plans for conquest when death overtook her, in 1360.

By this time, her kingdoms' fortunes had reached a low point. Ingeborg's
dream of glory for Norway and Sweden, including hegemony over Denmark,
had dissolved into ashes. The Black Death had devastated a people who were
not very numerous to begin with. One in seven farms in Norway were left
abandoned, some forever. By some historians' calculation, almost two-thirds
of the nation's wealth had been wiped out. Nobles in Norway suffered alongside their tenants. The number of families formally ranked as knights shrank
from 270 to 60, and both Denmark and Sweden saw further diminution of
those who occupied the top of the social pyramid.

In Denmark, the plague hit independent farmers particularly hard, even as
the crown and the nobility demanded more taxes and rents from fewer people.
These years saw the introduction of a custom called *vornedskab,* by which a

son was forced to work on his father's farm as a form of debt payment to the land's lord. The goal was to prevent peasants from leaving a lord's estate, by force of law if necessary. The specter of serfdom haunted Denmark for the first time.

By the end of the Middle Ages, only one-eighth of Denmark's land was still in peasant hands. In Norway, the proportion was slightly better, at one-quarter, while in Sweden the peasants still maintained fully half of their holdings. The tax-paying free peasant was still important to Swedish society. These peasants also stayed busy carving out new farms from the forests of northern Sweden and Finland. Increasingly, Finland formed the brave new frontier for Swedes and the Swedish crown. The government encouraged settlers to venture to Finland's coastline and desolate regions to convert the heathen natives and earn a new life for themselves. In time the relationship between Swedes and Finns changed from antagonism to partnership in taming a vast wilderness. It was good training — later on, they would cross the Atlantic together to tame a different wilderness, in America.

But the key beneficiaries of the decline of the free peasantry in Denmark and Norway weren't the aristocrats. Even in Denmark, where the nobility never numbered more than 350 families before the Black Death had decreased their numbers, only a third of the land lay in the nobles' hands. In Sweden, the comparable number was 21.8 percent, and in Norway just 13 percent. The big winner in this shift in land ownership was the Catholic Church. By mid-century, it owned almost half of all arable land in Norway. In fact, the crown wound up as the biggest loser of all in the aftermath of the Black Death.

The shrunken population couldn't sustain the tax base that a king needed to arm himself and defend his kingdom. What's more, the landed aristocracy and the church were gouging out tenant dues and tithes, reducing what the people could pay in taxes.

Something had to give. If kingdoms couldn't make it separately, perhaps they could try doing it together. Duchess Ingeborg had managed to unify two lands. Then Queen Margaret of Denmark, for the fifteen years between 1397 and 1412, managed to bring together all three of the Scandinavian realms — something no person had done before or would do again.

· · ·

Even for Denmark, a country comfortable with powerful women, Margaret and her story demand some explaining.

Her father, Denmark's ruler Valdemar III Atterdag, the latter term meaning "New Dawn" because of his promise to maintain a strong and vibrant rule, was a commanding figure. He had lashed out at opponents in order to recover former Danish territory — at one point selling Danish claims to Estonia in order to buy back land Denmark had allowed to slip into the hands of Holstein. Margaret was sufficiently cowed by her father to obey his wish that she marry Haakon VI, king of Norway, even though the Norwegian court was so broke that Margaret had to borrow money from her father to pay her own servants.

But loyalty to her father's will only went so far. When her father died in 1375 and her elder sister's son Erik was set to inherit the Danish throne, Margaret moved quickly to have the Danish Council install her own five-year-old son Olav instead, with Margaret acting as regent. It was her first major political coup, but by no means her last. As it turned out, Margaret excelled in the role of regent. She was in fact so skilled at handling the men sitting on the royal council that they agreed to just about anything she proposed, no matter how bold or obviously self-aggrandizing. The "respect for that lady's wisdom and authority," as one admirer put it, not only led the Danish Council to approve her regency for little Olav but impelled its Norwegian counterpart to grant her a similar regency when King Haakon died and Olav, now ten, also inherited the crown of Norway.

Two kingdoms, one crowned head — and one very strong and determined regent queen. That left only Sweden outside the fold. Olav also happened to inherit the dynastic claims of the Folkung family, who had been driven from the Swedish throne in 1364, when its last remaining representative died. The moment seemed ripe to press Olav's claim and oust the sitting king, Albrecht. But before Margaret could make her move, Olav fell ill in 1387 and suddenly died at age seventeen. Any legitimate claim to the Swedish throne died with him.

A lesser mortal than Margaret would have been satisfied at getting the Danish Landthing to renew her title as regent, or as they put it, as Denmark's "sovereign lady, master and guardian," and having a convocation of Norwegian nobles proclaim her as their "mighty lady and master." A lesser mortal would have told herself that direct and unfettered rule of two kingdoms out of three isn't so bad. But Margaret was of a much stronger mettle.

The statesman Otto von Bismarck once said, "A statesman cannot create anything himself. He must wait and listen until he hears the footsteps of God sounding through events; then leap up and grasp the hem of His garment." Margaret's spirit is reflected in that statement. With consummate skill she now pulled together the Swedish nobles who controlled the estates left by the death of Sweden's wealthiest noble, Bo Jonsson Grip, and convinced them to sign a treaty transferring control of those lands and their fortresses to Margaret. They did so, and also agreed to recognize her as the "sovereign lady and rightful master" of Sweden, as she was of Norway and Denmark.

All that remained was to depose the sitting monarch of Sweden, King Albrecht, and take possession of her third kingdom — no small matter. And yet in February 1389, Margaret's army of Danish and Swedish nobles crushed Albrecht's forces at Falköping in Västergötland — one of the most decisive battles in Scandinavian history. Albrecht was led away from the battlefield in chains. Stockholm held out for another nine years, but eventually Margaret's triumph was complete.

What was won on the battlefield, she believed, now required a formal treaty. On June 17, 1397, a gathering of nobles, bishops, and royal councilors from all three kingdoms assembled under her watchful gaze at Kalmar, where they formally recognized her grand-nephew Erik, known as Erik of Pomerania, as the king of all three kingdoms.

It was a moment unprecedented in Scandinavian history, one could even say European history. In fact, the attendees at Kalmar might have been ready to give the three crowns to Margaret herself. The representatives at Lübeck even addressed her as "Lady King." But Margaret shrewdly decided it was better for a male to hold the royal title. Besides, Erik of Pomerania, the grandson of her sister Ingeborg, was still only fourteen, a perfect figurehead. Margaret could continue in her favorite role, as regent.

She didn't stop there, however. A few days after the Kalmar agreement was settled, Margaret had the attendees sign yet another document, which provided that the three kingdoms would be permanently united under one king, with a common defense and a common diplomatic policy. Norway, Sweden, and Denmark would, however, continue to have separate legal and administrative systems.

Signing the Union of Kalmar would become, in the words of one historian, "the most intensely discussed single event in Nordic history." What kind of document was it? A constitution in the modern sense, establishing a formal framework for governance? A merger binding the three kingdoms into one? Merely a set of agreements between the signatories, to observe certain protocols in the management of all three kingdoms? Or was it a blend of all three? Kalmar continues to baffle historians and constitutional scholars today, perhaps as it baffled the men who signed it.

But no matter what kind of document or treaty was drawn up, or what binding legality it claimed, the entire project of creating this union meant nothing unless it had something, or someone, to give it the force of reality beyond the paperwork. That someone was, of course, Margaret. For the rest of her life, she worked to make the Union of the Three Crowns a workable polity. Even after Erik came of age in 1401, Margaret continued to hold the reins of power. Bypassing the traditional council of each separate country, Margaret used an ad hoc body of political and ecclesiastical officials to make policy. The chief qualification for membership on this council was agreeing with whatever Margaret proposed. The council always said yes.

"This very cunning woman," as her political opponents the Holsteiners once described her, then dedicated herself to enlarging her political creation. She recovered Finland from the Poles and bought Gotland from its owners, the Livonian Order, for the Swedish section of what had in fact become her empire. She also began taking back the duchy of Slesvig to secure the southern border of her native Denmark.

She appointed Danes in Swedish and Norwegian bishoprics, and put Swedes in Danish posts; in fact, in her last years she spent more time in Sweden than she did in Denmark, putting the lie to the claim that she used the Union to promote Danish hegemony over the combined realm — the second largest political entity in Europe at the time, exceeded only by the Holy Roman Empire.

The focus of her time in Sweden, appropriately enough, was promoting the legacy of Saint Brigitte, whose canonization she secured in 1391. Margaret, like Brigitte, had a way of getting popes to do what she wanted. She made frequent visits to the Brigittine motherhouse at Vadstena, and some historians give her credit for spreading Brigittine houses from Sweden into Denmark and Norway.

What was this extraordinary woman really like? We don't know. She was described by contemporaries as beautiful, with dark hair and eyes, an intimidating gaze, and the confident aura of absolute authority. But this sounds like public relations boilerplate, medieval-style. Her official portraits — only a handful exist — do not betray any hint of personality. She never unburdened herself to a confidant, or in personal letters. Instead, she revealed herself through her public acts, which indicate an iron will, incredible shrewdness, and a certain ruthlessness.

One could add strategic vision to the list of her virtues. At the end of her reign she tried but failed to negotiate a double marriage alliance with King Henry IV of England, with Erik marrying Henry's daughter Philippa and Erik's sister marrying the Prince of Wales, the future Henry V. The result would have been the re-creation, four centuries later, of the empire of Canute the Great himself — a worthy legacy for "this very cunning lady."

Death came suddenly to Queen Margaret. She died in 1412, on shipboard in Flensburg Harbor, while preparing to lead yet another military expedition, this time against the duke of Holstein to complete her conquest of Slesvig. Whether her death was natural remains a mystery — and a good source of *Game of Thrones*–type conspiracy theories. Be that as it may, without doubt she ranks as one of the most extraordinary figures, male or female, in medieval history. All the other impressive women rulers of the age, including Eleanor of Aquitaine, look weak and vacillating by comparison. Margaret herself would have been a hard act to follow for anyone, man or woman. In fact, her successor, Erik, was hardly up to the standard set by his strong-willed and charismatic aunt. Although she had groomed him carefully and had given him a capital and a governing body at Copenhagen from which to watch over and rule his realm, the handsome, athletic, and intelligent Erik lacked one key quality: good judgment.

His ineptitude alienated the elites of one realm after another. Meanwhile, a large-scale peasant uprising in Sweden, led by a well-to-do minor nobleman (as most effective peasant revolts in the Middle Ages were) named Engelbret Engelbretsen, sapped Erik's authority as king. The concessions Erik made in order to restore civic peace earned him wide disrepute. But these missteps might have been forgiven if Erik hadn't proved a failure in foreign policy. He suffered a series of defeats and humiliations at the hands of the hated Hanseatic League, including a siege of Copenhagen.

By 1435 Erik had grown tired of war and made peace with the Hanseatic Germans. The Danes, Swedes, and Norwegians (or rather, their leading nobility) had grown tired too. The Danes were the first to boot him off their throne, in 1438, and the Swedes followed suit a year later. By 1441, Erik had been cast down from the Norwegian throne as well. Not surprisingly, he took these serial depositions badly. Now a royal rebel, he maintained himself under arms on the island of Gotland, trying desperately to negotiate his way back into power until death overtook him, in 1459.

In the meantime the three kingdoms had elected a successor, a German duke this time: Christopher of Bavaria, the son of Erik's sister Catherine. This connection gave Christopher some semblance of a claim by lineage. But he proved no better than Erik at making the Union work, and when he died in 1448, Margaret's great achievement — the union of the three Scandinavian kingdoms — existed only on paper.

The Danes meanwhile had reached out to another family of German nobles, the Oldenbergs, to be rulers over them. The first of them, King Christian, clung to a formal claim to sovereignty over Sweden, but the Swedes largely ignored it. They then picked out their own king, Karl Knutsen. There was little the Danes could do about the breakaway, although some Swedes tried to remain loyal to the Union. A vicious little civil war had to be fought before Karl's nephew Sten Sture won out and was recognized as Sweden's permanent Guardian of the Realm. The next inevitable step was the evolution of this guardianship into a royal house completely outside Copenhagen's control. By 1523, with the accession of Gustav I Vasa to the throne of Sweden, the formal breakup of the Union of the Three Crowns was complete.

Taken as a whole, the succession struggles of medieval Scandinavia can make for dreary, not to say confusing, reading. It is striking how, in royal genealogical trees, the end dates of the reigns of Scandinavian kings rarely coincide with their death dates. Your average late medieval Danish or Swedish ruler found it very hard to stay in office. It was more common to be deposed, to wind up dying in exile or in disgrace — or both.

In that sense, the story of Queen Margaret and indeed those of all three amazing women stand out for their dedication to success. They also show that the Viking heart is not limited by sex or gender. It is instead rooted in the human experience and a desire to shape events according to a personal vision. It's a striving for freedom of action reinforced by personal courage and rooted in community. Where the conditions are right, it can grow and flourish — whether in a royal fortress, a monastery, a fishing village on the Norwegian coast, or a farm on the American Great Plains.

But why didn't Margaret of Denmark's Union last? Its failure can't be entirely blamed on one or two leaders who lacked her charisma and judgment. Instead, it must be in part chalked up to the political dynamics of the time, which were dominated by the seesaw struggle of factions of nobles, whose view of the future extended no further than next year's landed income and their own family tree. To a large extent, this attitude characterized the rest of Scandinavian society, right down to the free peasant whose biggest worry was whether the next wheat harvest might be killed in a premature frost. In the end, the Union of the Three Crowns was the achievement of a single indomitable woman. When she died, the spirit that held it together died with her.

The price of a true and lasting union would have been high: the nobility, the merchant communities, and the stubbornly autonomous peasantry would have had to surrender some of their independence. This they were not prepared to do. In reality, Scandinavia was headed toward a future based on diversity, not unity. Three distinct societies would emerge, each with its own distinct national character.

The political union of Scandinavia was dead, never to be revived. But a new spiritual union was coming, thanks to the Reformation.

In late medieval Scandinavia, these were the building blocks of society: a powerful and recalcitrant nobility; the townspeople and merchants, including German foreigners from the cities of the Hanseatic League, jealously guarding their money and their privileges; and a free peasantry who, against all odds, had survived and even prospered since Viking times, and who were prepared, to the point of armed rebellion, to protect their right to be left alone. A clever king would have to look hard to find the weak link in the chains that bound his power.

That weak link turned out to be the Catholic Church. Two kings, in the wake of the breakup of the Union, discovered this at almost the same time. Ironically, they also deeply hated each other. But both found the same tool for advancing their ambitions: the Lutheran Reformation.

Despite the efforts of Brigitte and others, as an institution the Catholic Church had shallow roots in Scandinavia. The survival of paganism until quite late in the Middle Ages had something to do with this. The unsavory spectacle of ambitious churchmen, embroiled in power struggles with kings, aristocrats, and one another, didn't help. Perhaps above all, the hierarchical authority of an institution based in distant Rome, and dependent on a complex scholastic culture advanced by a lettered elite, seemed deeply alien to the inhabitants of the North.

All they needed was permission to throw off this church's bonds. In the early 1500s, they found it under Christian II of Denmark and Gustav I Vasa of Sweden.

The pair became bitter enemies, yet both realized that breaking up and seizing the Catholic Church's property was the surest way to secure their own power and to buy valuable allies. Their rivalrous ambitions shattered any hope of restoring the Union of the Three Crowns. But together they used a religious revolution to advance the monarchy as a state institution and to give a common face to the religious life of all three lands and their peoples.

The means at hand were the reformist ideas percolating up from the German south, specifically from Martin Luther and his followers. Luther had swept aside the Catholic Church's most important shibboleths, including its system of sacraments and obedience to the pope in Rome (whom Luther considered the Antichrist, no less), deeming them incompatible with the practices of the early Christian church as described in the New Testament. In place of the authority of the pope and the Catholic hierarchy, Luther preached a quasi-democratic doctrine. Its core beliefs can be summarized (somewhat inaccurately) as the priesthood of all believers, the idea that the Bible contained all that was needed for a person to become a true Christian, and faith in Christ alone as the ultimate basis of salvation.

All the rest of the Catholic Church as an institution — including its huge property and land holdings — could be swept aside as superfluous, and even contrary to true Christianity. The Scandinavian kings were the first monarchs in Europe to take Luther up on his proposition. They set an example that others, including England's Henry VIII, were excited to follow.

Religious issues were, however, caught up in political issues. Denmark's Christian II came to the throne in 1513 — four years before Luther nailed his Ninety-Five Theses to the church door in Wittenberg. He was determined to break up a growing movement in Sweden against the Union of the Three Crowns; Christian was its titular head. He struck with an army deep into Swedish territory in 1519–20, and after being crowned in Stockholm, he ordered the wholesale massacre of some ninety of his Swedish opponents, to crush any remaining resistance. It was the kind of cold-blooded act that would have made Machiavelli wince (he had published *The Prince* just seven years earlier). Ironically, instead of securing the Union, Christian's bloodthirstiness triggered its doom. Being Swedes, his enemies stiffened their resistance. A massive backlash precipitated Christian's fall, not only in Sweden but in Denmark as well — but not before he had set in motion a series of changes that sounded the doom of the Catholic Church in Denmark.

Christian had listened to the sermons of itinerant Protestant preachers from Germany. He may not have entirely understood their theological dimensions, but he grasped the essentials as far as his royal authority was concerned: the Catholic Church was a runaway corrupt institution, and secular authorities (himself included) needed to rein it in. In January 1522, he issued a royal decree that limited the Danish clergy's ability to claim jurisdiction from papal Rome and put a ceiling on their accumulation of landed property. The clergy, along with some opportunistic aristocrats, revolted. They deposed Christian and put their ally, Christian's fifty-three-year-old uncle, Frederick Oldenberg, in his place. He thus became Frederick I.

If Denmark's bishops thought Frederick would be their pliant tool, they were soon disappointed. Frederick completed the reforming of Denmark's

churches that Christian had begun. He turned the tables on his former patrons, deposed bishops he didn't like, and installed those who would do his
bidding. He went so far as virtually nationalizing church property across Denmark. Churches and monasteries were demolished (twelve alone in Viborg, in
1529), and Lutheran preachers were allowed to roam free and expound outrageous doctrines such as clerical marriage, salvation by faith alone, and the importance of the Bible as the sole basis for Christian belief. Danish translations
of the Bible proliferated, and a mass book in Danish (not Latin) was published
in Malmö in 1529.

The traditionalist clergy tried to strike back at the Copenhagen Assembly
of Notables, or Herredag, in July 1530, denouncing all these changes as her-
esy. When the usual tussle for the throne broke out after Frederick's death in
1533, the bishops made the mistake of backing the losing side. The new king,
Christian III, was sadly in need of money. He arrested the bishops of Roskilde,
Lund, and Ribe, and in a sweeping declaration abolished the episcopacy and
reorganized the property of the church — to Christian III's advantage, of
course, and the monarchy's.

In Sweden, Christian II's bitter enemy Gustav I Vasa had been elected king
in 1522, and soon he was following the same reformist course. His secretary,
Lars Andersson, introduced him to Lutheran ideas, which Gustav seized on
with a fierce enthusiasm. The Swedish assembly of estates, or Riksdag, formally endorsed his plans to radically cut back church property and the independence of the Swedish clergy, in June 1527.

By the 1540s the nationalization of church lands and the adoption of Lutheran doctrine as the official religious credo of Sweden were well underway,
as was the case in Denmark. Despite some initial resistance, Norway, Iceland,
and the Faroes soon followed the lead of the two senior kingdoms. In a mid-
century Europe increasingly divided by faith, Scandinavia was firmly in the
Lutheran Protestant column — a fact of momentous significance for the next
hundred years for Europe, as well as for Scandinavia itself.

The speedy and (relatively) bloodless shift in faiths is instructive. Whereas
the coming of Protestantism provoked decades of civil war in France and Germany, a long history of revolt and underground resistance in England and
Scotland, and wholesale massacre in Ireland, Scandinavia skirted the worst ex-

cesses of the so-called wars of religion. It was not the first time, and hardly the last, when Scandinavians would conform to apparently traumatic changes and adjust. The underlying strength of those national communities — a rock-firm common culture and heritage built up during the Viking Age and maintained despite differences — enabled them to survive and even use the massive changes to their advantage. The Viking heart's inner strength would be put to the test many times over the coming centuries — in all three Scandinavian countries as well as Iceland.

At the same time, the Protestant Reformation strengthened Scandinavia's two kings as they ruled their separate dominions, just as translations of the Bible into Danish and Swedish confirmed the separate destinies of those who spoke the two languages. No translation of the Bible into Norwegian appeared at this time, but the early translation of Holy Scripture into the town of Turku's southwestern dialect of Finnish helped establish it as the national language of the Finns.

Lutheranism also stitched onto the Viking cultural legacy a Protestant ethos that gave the Viking heart a new moral imperative: hard work equals the worship of God. Call it the Lutheran work ethic — Danish, Swedish, Norwegian, and Finnish immigrants would bring it with them when they arrived in America.

Its basis was Martin Luther's idea of *Beruf,* or a calling, which sprang from his reading of Jesus Sirach, Book of the All-Virtuous Wisdom of Yeshua ben Sira. The text is known by other names, including the Wisdom of Sirach, or Sirach, or the book of Ecclesiasticus. This Jewish document formed part of the Catholic Bible but was not included in Luther's Protestant one. Nonetheless, he considered it a "useful book for the ordinary man" for "showing what the relationship of such a man should be to God, the Word of God, priests, parents, wife, children, his own body, his servants, possessions, neighbors, friends, enemies, government, and anyone else." Luther added, "This indeed is the proper 'spiritual discipline,' and should be recognized as such."

This is the key passage, taken from chapter 11, verses 20–21: "Stand by your agreement and attend to it, and grow old in your work. Do not wonder at the works of a sinner, but trust in the Lord and keep at your job; for it is easy in the sight of the Lord to make the poor rich suddenly, in an instant."

What struck Luther about this passage was the idea that holiness leaves its stamp on even the ordinary occupations of life, such as mending a fishing net or carrying out the garbage. Lutheran doctrine imbued these humble duties with a special positive significance, as the sociologist Max Weber once observed: "the valuation of the fulfilment of duty in worldly affairs as the highest form which the moral activity of the individual could assume." In other words, the obligations we take on because of our position in the world, whether high or low, have an intrinsic value in the eyes of God.

This was an entirely Protestant idea, which Luther had arrived at during his first decade as a religious reformer and which he impressed on his congregations and followers. To quote Weber again: "Labor in a calling appears to him as the outward expression of brotherly love." The idea was also entirely new to European civilization: that the only way to live in accordance with God's will was *not* to withdraw into monastic retreat — the mistake the Catholic Church had made, in Luther's valuation — but to fulfill the obligations we all have imposed upon us by our place in the world, whether as the lowliest servant or the mightiest king. This idea of the division of labor forces every person to see his or her work as ultimately a work for others, in the eyes of God and our better selves. In fact, to renounce those duties, as the monk or nun does, becomes the highest act of selfishness. Instead, to work and toil where we are, with whom we share family ties and community, *and* to excel at that work, is to fulfill the will of God. Every kind of calling is equal in the sight of the Lord.

Luther's idea of the calling quickly spread to all Protestant populations. It became the moral justification for worldly activity, and success in that activity, a characteristic idea of the Protestant Reformation — even notoriously so. Yet Luther's message was distinct from that of John Calvin and those who are usually identified with the "Protestant work ethic," such as the Scottish kirk of John Knox and America's Puritans. Calvin's calling, after all, belonged to a chosen few, the Elect of God, who had been selected by him through the doctrine of predestination to succeed here on earth, and later, in heaven. Calvin's concept of a calling ultimately focuses on the welfare of the individual, whose moral worth rests on the ability to succeed — or to fail.

By comparison, the altruistic dimension of Luther's doctrine stands out. And though Luther was tolerant of capitalism, he was never its intimate friend or supporter. He was, for example, a fierce critic of usury and the charging of interest.

So while the Calvinist ideal swept through England and Scotland, and took firm hold in the English settlements of America, thanks to Martin Luther, the Scandinavian work ethic takes a different point of view. It sees good work not as a means to an end (that is, the creation of wealth) but as an end in itself. We will meet this ideal again in America, with Thorstein Veblen's notion of craftsmanship: a Norwegian American sociologist's worm's-eye view of the Lutheran work ethic. Before that, it found a perfect home in communities where the heroic effort to support kith and kin and community formed part of the Viking legacy.

In short, the primary goal of the Lutheran work ethic is *not* self-betterment — "liberation of energy for private acquisition," as Max Weber would put it — but the betterment of the community. That cultural mindset would leave a deep mark down through the next centuries, not least in the legacy of modern Scandinavian philanthropy, an effort built on not just funding good works but physically toiling to achieve them, even at the risk of one's life.

The need to risk it all had once led the Vikings to the farthest ends of the earth. After the Reformation of the 1500s, the Viking heart would once again lead its champions to do the same, only this time as a gift of love to their fellow human beings.

8

Viking Heart Empire

King Gustavus Adolphus and the Scandinavian Century

Let four captains
Bear Hamlet, like a soldier, to the stage:
For he was likely, had he been put on,
To have prov'd most royal; and, for his passage,
The soldiers' music and the rites of war
Speak loudly for him.

— William Shakespeare,
Hamlet, Prince of Denmark, act 5, scene 2

You may earn salvation under my command,
but hardly riches.

— King Gustavus Adolphus of Sweden

THE DATE WAS 1600, and London's premier theater group, the Chamberlain's Men, had a special treat for their audiences. It was a new play by William Shakespeare, with Richard Burbage, the Laurence Olivier of his day, in the title role. The title: *Hamlet, Prince of Denmark.*

Set at Elsinore Castle, the fortress that Queen Margaret's nephew Erik II had built to protect Copenhagen from the Hanseatic League, *Hamlet* proved an enormous success. According to the records, performances as far away as the coast of Sierra Leone took place in 1607, by the crew of a privateer called the *Red Dragon,* and in the Dutch East Indies two years later.

Most of the audience at the premiere, like most people today, probably assumed the story of Hamlet is fictional. What few realized then, or now, is that there was a real Hamlet — or at least a semi-real one — known to Danish history as Amleth. He was a figure who loomed large in post-Viking legend, thanks to the medieval chronicler Saxo Grammaticus. Whatever the dim historical truth underlying Saxo's version of the Amleth story, it breathes an atmosphere of family rivalry and revenge that must have drawn Shakespeare like a magnet. But unlike Shakespeare's self-doubting and introspective hero, Amleth, prince of Denmark, was a confident, swashbuckling warrior who not only avenged his father's death — including the killing of a spy who was caught hiding, Polonius-like, behind a tapestry — but went on to conquer England and Scotland. He returned home in triumph with not one but two trophy wives: in short, every Viking's dream. He was a Nordic superhero ready to rule the world.

As it happens, Amleth had a real-life counterpart in Shakespeare's day who really did want to conquer the world, and had the skills and the army to match his ambitions. His name was Gustav II, king of Sweden, the man posterity knows as Gustavus Adolphus and the "Lion of the North." More than anyone else, Gustavus Adolphus would make the seventeenth century the Scandinavian century — and rock the world as no one from the North had done since the days of the Viking raids, and never has since. Indeed, if anyone deserves to be titled the last Viking, it may be Gustavus Adolphus.

Yet he was far more than a typical Norse chieftain — or even a real-life Prince Amleth. His personality reflected the changes that came to characterize Swedish and Scandinavian culture after the end of the Viking Age. For one thing, he was deeply religious, a true believing Lutheran. He made it his primary mission, as monarch and commander, to save the Protestant Reformation from destruction by a resurgent Catholicism. For another, as king of Sweden he was a shrewd user of the royal authority that his predecessors, especially his Vasa relatives, had left him. His father had him trained in the minutiae of administration and handling the royal fisc at an early age. He was just fifteen when Charles IX put him in charge of the duchy of Västmanland. He learned early on how to use Sweden's slender resources in terms of wealth and manpower to maximum effect, eventually making Sweden the dominant military power of the age.

For yet another, his cultural and political horizons stretched far beyond those of any Viking warrior, or any of his medieval counterparts, including the great Queen Margaret. He not only managed Sweden's geopolitical competition with neighbors like Denmark, Poland, and Russia, but also built strong relations with France and the Netherlands in western Europe. In fact, it was from the Netherlands that he learned and mastered the new science of war pioneered by the Dutch commander Maurice of Nassau — a science to which, as we'll see, Gustavus Adolphus dedicated himself with all the care and attention that the Lutheran work ethic would demand of him.

Finally, Gustavus Adolphus foresaw that the power he had amassed during his brilliant military campaigns could win dominion of all of central Europe, from the Rhine estuary to the Danube basin. It would be his fate to lose the greatest prize of all, just when it seemed within his grasp — not unlike Shakespeare's fictional prince of Denmark. His failure would haunt Sweden, and the rest of the Scandinavian world, and eventually seal its future.

In that sense, Shakespeare's story does reflect the Scandinavia of Shakespeare's time. Arrestingly and very suddenly, after a long nadir, at the start of the seventeenth century Scandinavia reemerged as the pivot point of Europe. Both Denmark and Sweden were poised to rise to a prominence they would never see again, as they moved on a trajectory that was to shape the destiny of an entire continent. Together Denmark and Sweden triggered the two great geopolitical struggles that would dominate the heart of Europe until the end of World War II — France versus Germany and Germany versus Russia, with Poland caught in between.

But for their ambition and striving for power, both Scandinavian realms would pay a heavy price.

It was Denmark that stood at the pinnacle of its power when Shakespeare's play first appeared. Its monarch was an influential figure. Besides his own kingdom, he ruled over Norway and distant Iceland. He was master of the Swedish island of Öland as well as Gotland, the old Viking trading outpost. Even more important, the kings of Denmark controlled the Sound of Øresund, the narrow seaway that governed the world's trade with the Baltic economies. Seventeen miles at its widest, and just two and a half at its narrowest, the Sound would be the fulcrum of northern politics for the next two centuries.

For the English, the Sound gave access to Scandinavia as a major source for naval stores, especially masts from Norway's and Sweden's massive pine forests. For the Russians and the Poles, the Sound was their one outlet to the open sea and the increasingly prosperous Atlantic world beyond. As for the Swedes, the Sound poised them perilously between the Danes and the Russians, demanding a delicate diplomatic balancing act to avoid fighting a war on two fronts at once. Command of the Sound, in short, made Denmark the gatekeeper of a sizable part of the world's economy and geopolitics.

In addition, the ruler in Copenhagen was a heavyweight player in the German politics of the Holy Roman Empire because he was also the duke of Holstein, a title that gave him a seat in the imperial diet. As duke, he was without challenge the strongest prince in the Lower Saxon circle of the German states. This political network was dominated by Protestant princes who had won their independence from the Catholic Habsburg emperors in the first round of religious wars in Germany, which ended in 1555, with the Peace of Augsburg. The first round, but unhappily not the last. In the face of a threat from the Catholic Habsburg emperor, all the German Protestant princes looked to Copenhagen and its Lutheran ruler for support and protection.

Denmark also paid an ugly human price for this proximity to Germany. Of all the Nordic countries, it would be the one most caught up in the witch-hunting craze that swept across Europe in the sixteenth and seventeenth centuries; Germany was its epicenter. Nearly half of the two thousand witches put to death in Scandinavia during this hideous period were executed in Denmark. Even so, that number hardly compares to the tens of thousands of German, Swiss, English, and French people, mostly women, who suffered that terrible fate by hanging or burning or both. Of the witchcraft trials that took place in Norway, only 2 percent ended in a death sentence. One percent of Finland's trials resulted in death — even less than that in Sweden and Norway — compared to 42 percent in Germany and 35 percent in Switzerland.

Numerous explanations have been put forward for these low numbers. One is that torture and other coercive interrogation techniques weren't a standard part of Scandinavian legal codes. Another is that the paucity of printers and printed books meant that the popular how-to witch-hunting manuals, like the *Malleus Maleficarum* (which translates roughly as *The Hammer for Witches*), that circulated through the rest of Europe didn't have much of an audience in the North.

But the main explanation has to be that witch hunting cut against the cultural grain of the Nordic countries. Independent-minded women were part of the Viking legacy, and people were comfortable with them. But it was precisely these types of women, especially the older ones, who were the favorite targets of the big witch hunts in the rest of Europe. The misogynist instinct to put so-called wise women to the ducking stool, or the stake, or the hangman's noose, was simply not present in the North. Although notorious mass witch trials took place in both Denmark and Norway, the numbers of those accused and executed—thirty and twenty, respectively, in the case of the Vardø trials in Norway in the winter of 1662–63—were deeply disappointing to any truly dedicated witch hunter.* Even the impact of the Lutheran Reformation (Luther himself was a fierce persecutor of so-called witches) couldn't wipe away the respect for women or the sense of comradeship they shared with men as both faced challenges and dangers together over the centuries. In a larger sense, we can say that mass scapegoating and mass hysteria are generally not characteristics of the Viking heart. This virtue would shine through later, as we'll see, during the years of the Nazi Holocaust.

In any case, Denmark started the century as the more formidable of the two Scandinavian kingdoms. This was demonstrated when, for example, James I of England, the successor to Queen Elizabeth, was looking for a marriage to cement his power. He chose Anne, the daughter of Denmark's king, Christian IV. The arrival of the Danish monarch on a state visit in 1606 was the biggest diplomatic event of James's entire reign.

---

* Interestingly, witchcraft trials in Iceland wound up condemning twenty-one men and only one woman.

But Denmark's rival, Sweden, would quickly make up the distance, thanks to Gustavus II Adolphus Vasa, who came to the throne in 1611, at age seventeen. He inherited from his Vasa ancestors boundless audacity, self-confidence, and a willingness to risk everything for a goal worthy for his abilities — even if the resources at hand fell short of his ambitions. Gustavus also inherited from his father, Charles IX, a kingdom strapped with poverty and trapped in a losing war not on two but three fronts at once: against the Poles, the Russians, and the Danes. He inherited a Swedish nobility on the brink of rebellion — but then, Swedish nobles were always rebelling. It was practically their birthright.

Yet in a few short years, by a combination of brilliant soldiering and adroit statesmanship, the young Gustavus Adolphus had reversed the situation. By 1630, at age thirty-six, he had become the radiant hope of Protestants everywhere. Only then did he set his sights on the greatest prize of all: becoming Charlemagne's heir to the Holy Roman Empire.

That success did not come easy. The first fifteen years of his reign were spent waging a series of military campaigns back and forth along the Baltic coast, honing the Swedish army he had taken over from his father into the finest fighting force in Europe. At its core was a Swedish conscript infantry and light cavalry, bolstered by regiments of mercenaries; this military force ultimately numbered more than 130,000 men-at-arms. This was made possible by the domestic reforms that Gustavus and his chief adviser, Count Axel Oxenstierna, had used to turn Sweden into a modern state — in many ways the prototype of modern states everywhere. Through the judicious use of taxation and the manipulation of Sweden's nobility, turning them from recalcitrant would-be rebels into pillars of the army and the throne, Gustavus Adolphus blazed a trail for European monarchs for generations. No wonder that, only fourteen years after assuming the throne, his reputation was such that Germany's Protestants desperately turned to him to stem the tide of the Catholic Counter-Reformation.

In doing so, he led his countrymen on a great adventure. It almost culminated in raising Sweden, the colossus of the North, to the status of colossus of the entire world.

• • •

Gustavus Adolphus was born on December 9, 1594, the son of a noble, who would soon be crowned Charles IX, and Christina of Holstein. Sweden's throne at that time was both unstable and hotly contested. In 1600 — the same year Shakespeare was readying *Hamlet* for the stage — Charles IX deposed the sitting king, Sigismund, who found refuge in Poland and eventually became ruler there. Sigismund's efforts to regain his Swedish title created war and disturbance throughout Charles IX's reign, and beyond. Russia's efforts to gain a foothold in the Baltic by means of Finland was another source of trouble. Lastly, the Danes had secured control of both sides of the vital Sound: Halland and Skåne were now Danish territory. By the time Charles IX died, in 1611, his fruitless push to make the eastern side of the Sound Swedish again, including a blockade of Riga, then a Danish port, and the opening of an alternative route via the Arctic, had drained his treasury and left his heir at war with Denmark.

In his last letter to Gustavus, his father advised him to "be humane toward your subjects. Punish the wicked, love the good. Trust everyone, but not without caution." It would be excellent counsel in the turbulent years to follow.

Where anyone else would have seen a hopeless situation, the seventeen-year-old Gustavus saw an opportunity to make Sweden the dominant power in the region. In this, he had help from his closest and most trusted adviser, Count Oxenstierna, who over the next two decades would raise the money to build a Swedish war machine without equal in Europe. Gustavus would fine-tune it through a series of campaigns that checkmated Denmark's ambitions in the Baltic; forced Poland, which was twice the size of France, with six times Sweden's population, to sign a truce relinquishing Sigismund's claims to his throne; and gave Sweden its first territories on the European mainland — the first steps toward a Swedish empire.

Nonetheless, Gustavus Adolphus would be today remembered as a minor figure in European history, except for his role in a dynastic dispute in Bohemia (in the modern Czech Republic), far from Sweden. That dispute plunged Europe into the greatest of all its religious wars and opened the door for Sweden to emerge as a Protestant superpower. It allowed Gustavus Adolphus to emerge as the greatest soldier of the age.

It is worth remembering that for the people of Scandinavia, the Reformation had been a tonic, a source of political stability and spiritual renewal. For the rest of Europe, it left deep scars. It set Catholic against Protestant and Calvinist against Lutheran, and all three against a host of smaller sects they viewed as heretical. After Luther died in 1546, wars for religious supremacy raged for more than half a century. They quickly became entangled with rivalries for geopolitical supremacy, and Scandinavia's rulers and their neighbors played their part in an increasingly wider conflict.

The immediate issue in 1618 was who would sit on the throne of Bohemia and inherit the crown of King Wenceslaus (later canonized as a saint). By tradition, the title went to the heir to the Holy Roman Empire, who would inevitably be an Austrian Habsburg and a Catholic. But that year the Bohemians, Czech speakers and Protestants, decided they would prefer someone of their own religion, anyone really, even a foreign prince. This bizarre decision ran contrary to tradition but was popular in the religious climate of the time. It also demonstrated that those who choose principle over good sense usually wind up paying a heavy price.

The Bohemians needed a Protestant candidate to oppose the presumptive Habsburg heir. They found him in Frederick, prince of the Palatinate, on the Rhine River. Frederick was young, idealistic, and quite unprepared for the international crisis he was about to set in motion. His supporters in Prague threw the Habsburg representative out of a window in the town hall — or possibly he jumped, to avoid a worse fate. Either way, the so-called defenestration of Prague triggered an international conflict that no Catholic or Protestant country, not the Habsburg empire or France or England or Denmark or Sweden, could afford to avoid.

At first, things went very well for Frederick. On the battlefield, the Habsburgs proved ineffective, and Bohemian cavalry rode to the gates of Vienna. All of Europe held its breath as the balance of power between Protestant and Catholic seemed to shift permanently against Rome.

Then the tide of battle turned again, as the Catholic princes of Germany rallied to the Habsburg banner. The battle of White Mountain in 1620 destroyed Bohemian and Czech independence for three centuries; it was not restored until World War I. Prince Frederick became a hapless refugee. Like dominoes, one Protestant territory after another fell to the Habsburg armies, until the situation was so dire, in 1624 Frederick's father-in-law, King James of England, and the last remaining independent German Protestant magnate, George of Brandenburg, turned in desperation to the Lutheran kings of the North.

Not unnaturally, they turned first to Gustavus Adolphus. His campaigns along the Baltic had made him a soldier's king, tough, disciplined, and charismatic. At age thirty-two, he was clearly ambitious but also wise beyond his years. He was not opposed to entering a war in Germany that would save Protestantism and, incidentally, give Sweden new leverage on the European continent. But what he demanded in money and support was more than his prospective German allies could supply. So they turned instead to his neighbor and rival, Christian IV of Denmark.

At forty-seven years of age, Christian was in many ways a typical Renaissance monarch. He transformed Copenhagen with his magnificent palaces and churches. He spoke German, French, and Italian as well as Danish, and he was a brilliant patron of the arts. He constructed numerous strong fortifications, including battlements along the Sound, and built a Danish navy that was without rival, with more than sixty warships, and counting—some of them based on his own design.* He was in truth a Danish Henry VIII, with a sexual appetite to match. He managed to sire seven children with his first wife and twelve with his second, in addition to populating Denmark far and wide with his illegitimate offspring.

His wars with Gustavus Adolphus had failed to extend Denmark's imperial reach in the eastern Baltic. But Christian's strategic position in northern Germany was secure, so when the summons came to lead the forces resisting the relentless Habsburg advance, Christian was pleased to say yes.

Christian plunged into the war against Emperor Ferdinand and the Habsburgs with disastrous ardor. He found new allies. Despite their plight, the German Protestant princes proved unwilling to trade a conqueror they knew (Emperor Ferdinand) for one they didn't (King Christian). A near fatal fall from his horse put Christian out of commission during the crucial winter of 1624. It was his last opportunity to meet and defeat the advancing Habsburg

---

* He was also the founder (or rather, refounder) of the Norwegian city of Kristiania, restoring it after a devastating fire. Today Kristiania is known as Oslo, Norway's capital.

armies. When action resumed it was the imperial generals, Counts Johannes Tilly and Albrecht von Wallenstein, who were able to rally against the Danes and their German allies at the battle of Lutter, in August 1626. Christian suffered a catastrophic defeat. All of northern Germany, as well as Denmark itself, was left open to invasion.

The possibility of a Habsburg-dominated North Sea and Baltic coast, with a Habsburg navy to match, was more than the rest of Europe, especially its Protestant states, could tolerate. Certainly Sweden and Denmark shared this view — but Christian and the Danes were no longer masters of their fate. A series of military defeats forced them to abandon the Jutland mainland for the islands. By 1628 Christian was under siege in Copenhagen while imperial armies relentlessly occupied one Baltic town after another. Scandinavia's Renaissance monarch had all but lost his kingdom. But it was the impending collapse of Christian's domain, and the loss of any buffer between Sweden and the Catholic juggernaut, that stirred Gustavus Adolphus into action at last.

Sweden's soldier-king struck an alliance with Christian to last for three years, assuring the crestfallen Danish monarch that together they would crush anyone who opposed him, "king or emperor, prince or republic, or — nay, or a thousand devils," he proudly told him. But the deal came too late: Christian had already decided that his only remaining option was signing a separate peace with the Habsburgs. It was a hard peace. Denmark had to surrender all its northern German possessions and recognize Habsburg sovereignty over the duchy of Holstein. But Christian's throne was safe. He signed a treaty at Lübeck that marked the end of his hopes of being a Protestant champion and the leader of a dominant power. If Gustavus Adolphus had any such ambitions, he would have to pursue them alone.

Fortunately, he had the tools to do it.

As we've seen, feudalism — the system that had saved Europe from complete Viking domination — had never taken root in the lands of the Vikings. The Scandinavian nobility never managed to weaponize their land holdings by using them to support a large following of armed retainers the way their French, German, Polish, and even English counterparts were able to do. As was the case for their Viking ancestors, for Swedes military service was simply part of being a man. Gustavus Adolphus's Vasa forebears had turned this willingness to fight into a general system of conscription in the royal service. No one questioned or challenged it.

This gave the king the means to raise an all-Swedish army that could fight protracted campaigns against the Danes or the Poles or both, without the need for foreign mercenaries or hirelings, according to the standard practice of the day.

When "Gustavus came to the throne," writes the military historian Michael Howard, "he found to hand a national army which to contemporary eyes looked remarkably archaic but to ours appears no less remarkably modern." In Gustavus's army, military service was a twenty-year hitch. But only one man in ten was actually called to serve, and exemptions went out to the sons of widows, men whose brothers were already in service, workers in critical industries like mining or munitions, and members of the clergy (nobles were also exempt, but they served as officers anyway, as a matter of status and honor). Nonetheless, this service put pressure on Sweden's population, as village after village lost men in the prime of youth on the battlefield or to disease. Still, it was enough to give the king of Sweden a disciplined core of reliable professionals, an army unique for its time in being united by language and culture as well as by loyalty to a king. "My troops are poor Swedish and Finnish peasant fellows, it's true, rude and ill-dressed," Gustavus liked to say, "but they hit hard and they shall soon have better clothes" as their range of conquests grew.

Here was a new kind of army, much closer to the armies of modern democracies than the mercenary forces of the age. Thanks to Gustavus, it had new tactics to match.

Gustavus had learned from his father's foes, the Poles, how to use cavalry effectively, maximizing their shock value by having them attack at the gallop after musketeers on the ground had blown gaps through enemy lines with repeated volleys (another of Gustavus's innovations). Having his musketeers fight alongside the pike-wielding infantry, instead of as a separate body, marked a major change as well. In addition, he had learned from the Dutch and, in particular, Maurice of Nassau how to achieve a rolling fire, with ranks of musketeers firing in succession. Gustavus, however, improved on this by introducing a single devastating salvo as well, with all ranks firing at once.

The Viking hero Sigurd slaying the dragon Fafnir, from the Hylestad stave church, Norway, twelfth century. *Heritage Image Partnership Ltd. / Alamy Stock Photo*

"Blond was his hair, and bright his cheeks, / Grim as a snake's were his eyes." An ivory chessman depicting a Viking berserker, about twelfth century. *CM Dixon / Print Collector / Getty Images*

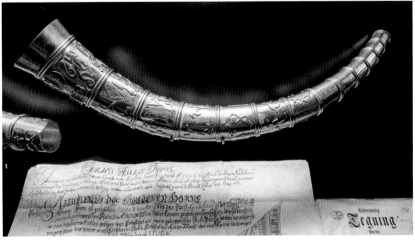

Replica of one of the two gold pre-Viking drinking horns housed in the Royal Museum, Copenhagen. Ironically, the destruction of the originals in 1802 triggered a fascination with Vikings and Viking culture that has lasted until today. *Hemis / Alamy Stock Photo*

The stave church in Borgund, Norway, thirteenth century. The *stavkirke* style preserved the traditions of Viking naval architecture long after the era of the longships. *Adam Major / Alamy Stock Photo*

Early-twentieth-century depiction of the Varangian chief Rurik being offered the throne of what would become the kingdom of the Rus, about 860–62.

Heritage Image Partnership Ltd. / Alamy Stock Photo

U.S. postage stamp marking the centenary of the voyage of the sloop *Restauration,* which carried the first Norwegian immigrants to America in 1825.

Courtesy of the United States Post Office Department

Thingvellir National Park, Iceland, the birthplace of the oldest continuous democracy in the world. *DBURKE / Alamy Stock Photo*

The interior of the Cappella Palatina, Palermo, Sicily. Commissioned by the count Roger II in about 1132, it is the greatest visual monument to the Norman achievement in Europe. *Paolo Paradiso / Alamy Stock Photo*

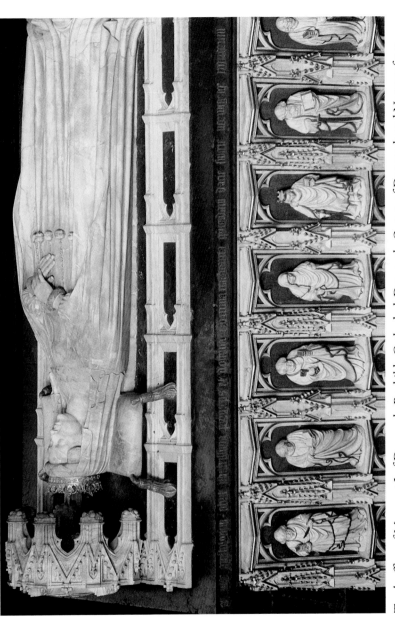

Tomb effigy of Margaret I of Denmark, Roskilde Cathedral, Denmark. Queen of Denmark and Norway from 1387 and queen of Sweden from 1389 until her death in 1412, she was the first and last person to unite all of Scandinavia under one rule. *Wojciech Stróżyk / Alamy Stock Photo*

A football trading card showing the legendary Notre Dame coach Knute Rockne, the son of Norwegian immigrants. Rockne's career as coach, from 1918 to 1930, laid the foundation for modern American sports. *Jefferson Burdick Collection / The Met / Art Resource, Inc.*

On the battlefield, all these elements came together as one. First there was the single musket salvo, which stunned and disrupted the enemy. Then, as the Swedish musketeers reloaded, Swedish pikemen (or alternately, Swedish cavalry) would charge into the gap, wielding death at the point of their pikes or the edge of their swords. If the enemy still stood firm, the pikemen would drop back and the musketeers would blast away again, while the pikemen or horsemen readied for another charge. After one or two rounds of this onslaught, few soldiers wouldn't choose to break and run, leaving the field to the Swedes — and a victory to their commander, King Gustavus Adolphus, who insisted on leading his troops in person.

When it came to battle, "it's necessary for me to see everything with my own eyes," Gustavus would tell those who questioned why he constantly risked his life on the front lines; without a helmet or a breastplate, and riding his own mount, he often led cavalry charges. His physical presence not only gave him firsthand knowledge of what was happening amid the clouds of smoke and the surging masses of soldiers; it also inspired his men. When they saw their king and commander, with his billowing blond hair and bright ruddy face, they knew victory would be theirs.

Still, all of this would have marked a minor change in battlefield tactics had it not been for the revolution in artillery that Gustavus Adolphus introduced. Like other European armies, Sweden's forces had deployed these weapons in a static fashion, keeping them entrenched in fortified positions. But now the Swedes transformed its artillery into mobile units, armed with lighter guns and fighting in conjunction with the cavalry and infantry. A new artillery piece, which fired a three-pound ball, could be used by individual regiments of infantry and cavalry. With an unprecedented 9.4 artillery pieces for every thousand men (most armies had less than half that number), Gustavus Adolphus had a military revolution on his hands, and his opponents were completely unprepared to deal with it. Sweden and Gustavus's army had become a well-honed instrument for victory and conquest, the best and most dangerous in Europe.

And it was about to become one of the largest too. In 1621, Swedish forces in Livonia numbered just under eighteen thousand men-at-arms. By November 1630, Gustavus Adolphus had more than forty-two thousand troops under his command. While his hardy and disciplined Swedish and Finnish troops re-mained the core of his army, as the range of his campaigns and conquests grew, he found he had to flesh out their ranks with foreign mercenaries — Dutch-men, Englishmen, Scots, Germans. Eventually they comprised more than eight of every ten men in the Swedish army.

Mercenaries brought advantages and disadvantages to army command-ers, including Gustavus Adolphus. They were a financial burden, first of all, and the more effective they were, the more they cost. Fortunately, Gustavus's war chest was full, thanks to his truce with Poland (although a real peace was not possible as long as King Sigismund still insisted on his claim to the Swed-ish throne). Even so, his invasion of Germany would not have been possi-ble without the covert financial support of two affluent geopolitical rivals of the Habsburg monarchy, France and Holland. They opened their purses and cleared the way for operations that otherwise would have been too large, even for Gustavus Adolphus.

Everything was ready for Sweden's foray into the biggest conflict Europe had seen in more than a century. In June 1630, with his four-year-old daughter Christina in his arms, Gustavus addressed the members of his Riksdag in the Hall of Assembly:

> I've not thoughtlessly engaged in this perilous war which calls me far from you. Heaven is my witness that it is neither for my satisfaction, nor personal interests that I go into this conflict. Ready to sink under the weight of oppression which hangs over them, the German Protes-tants stretch suppliant hands to us. If it please God, we will give them aid and protection. I'm not ignorant of the dangers that await me; I have already been in many others, and by the grace of God I have ever come happily out of them. But I feel that I may lose my life there, and this is why, before leaving you, I recommend you all to the protection of the omnipotent One.

He left Stockholm with a fleet of twenty-eight warships and an equal number of transports carrying thirteen thousand members of the infantry, cavalry, and artillery. On June 28, they landed on the sandy beach outside the village of Peenemünde, on Usedom Island in Pomerania — which was about to become a permanent Swedish outpost. While descending the gangplank, Gustavus stumbled and injured his knee. Propagandists instantly turned the accident into a good omen: on disembarking, they wrote, the new Protestant champion had fallen on his knees to seek God's blessing for his cause. As the historian C. V. Wedgewood put it, "The legend embodies a poetic truth, for whatever the forces behind the king of Sweden, his personal belief in his mission never faltered."

A formidable army and its leader were about to make history and remake the map of Europe. Once more — and for the last time — the other European powers were about to face a Scandinavian onslaught that they could hardly fathom.

What's more, this heir to the Norsemen had allies, and not only in France and Holland. They included the German city of Magdeburg, the richest port on the Baltic. When Count Tilly took revenge by besieging Magdeburg and burning it to the ground, it lit "a signal-flare for rebellion for the whole of Germany," as Gustavus himself put it. Brandenburg, Brunswick, Pomerania, Mecklenberg, Hesse-Cassel, Saxony: one by one the German princes had realized they faced one of two possible fates: domination by the Catholic Habsburgs, which meant persecution and confiscation, or by the Protestant Swedes. The majority chose the latter, and when Gustavus Adolphus at last confronted Ferdinand's leading general, Count Tilly, on September 7, 1631, at Breitenfeld, four miles north of Leipzig, he had an allied army that outnumbered the imperials.

The week before, he and his troops had marched triumphantly through Wittenberg, Luther's former home and religious base; there they were hailed as the champions of Protestantism against the forces of Catholicism. Now Gustavus Adolphus was ready to put Sweden's fate, and that of Protestantism itself, on the line before the God of Battles at Breitenfeld.

This was not a place where the imperial commander, Count Tilly, wanted to fight. It had been chosen by his second-in-command, Count Gustav Pappenheim, and if the battle went badly, they risked losing the strategic city of

Leipzig. "This fellow will rob me of my honor and reputation," Tilly is re-ported to have said when he learned what Pappenheim had done, "and our em-peror of his lands and people." His army was drawn up in the traditional style, with his infantry in the center and cavalry on the flanks, as Gustavus and his men cautiously advanced. The Swedes numbered some twenty-four thousand men, with eighteen thousand Saxon allies, versus an imperial force of thirty-five thousand. But Gustavus's numerical superiority soon vanished as Tilly's veterans routed the Saxons. Defeat stared the Swedish king in the face. Then Gustav Horn, commanding the Swedish left flank, launched a furious counter-attack while the Swedish cavalry halted, then reversed their mounted antago-nists commanded by Count Pappenheim, on Gustavus's right.

Suddenly the entire dynamic of the battle changed. Horn's counterattack quickly deprived the Habsburg forces of all their artillery, as the Swedish cen-

Gustavus II Adolphus, king of Sweden, at Breitenfeld, 1631. INTERFOTO / Alamy

ter under Gustavus's command triumphantly advanced under the cover of his formidable artillery barrages. Tilly himself was wounded and had to flee the field, leaving twenty thousand dead and wounded; the Swedes lost a tenth of that number. When the shattering news reached Vienna, the emperor considered fleeing to Graz, or even Italy. The art of war would not be the same again.

In the aftermath of Breitenfeld, the Habsburg tide, which had been rising so steadily, ebbed away. Even the emperor's cousins, the Spanish Habsburgs, found themselves on the defensive as Gustavus Adolphus's army swung through the Rhineland, brushing past the vital route that Spain used to supply and reinforce its army as it fought Protestant Holland. Then Gustavus pushed on to Bohemia, forcing an imperial evacuation of Prague. One Protestant town after another was liberated. Gustavus's processional continued through Bavaria to the gates of Ingolstadt, with an army that had swollen to more than eighty thousand men, under seven separate commands.

Gustavus Adolphus paid for all this with a method any Viking chieftain would recognize: by conquering foreign territory and imposing a levy on the inhabitants, in order to pay his soldiers and mercenaries. It made him and his army invincible, but it also earned him the suspicion and enmity of the German princes. Even the Protestants among them realized that Gustavus Adolphus, their apparent Protestant savior, had now become their Swedish taskmaster.

Still, they were not inclined to buck the geopolitical trend or the man behind it. At age thirty-six, the king of Sweden was at the height of his powers, both physically and intellectually. His bright florid face, clear blue eyes, and straw-yellow hair had become a popular sight across Germany. He regularly went into battle protected by only a leather doublet: "God will be my armor!" he would declare. His battle cry, "God is with us!" had reverberated over the battlefield at Breitenfeld. Gustavus had grandiose plans for the Holy Roman Empire he was in the process of conquering; they would ultimately make him more powerful than any ruler since Charles V, or even Charlemagne. With massive territories in northern Germany now under Swedish rule, Gustavus was organizing the Council of Churches for Protestant Europe under Swedish leadership, a geopolitical power network that would secure Europe's wealthiest nations — the Dutch, the French, and the English — as permanent allies.

The balance of power in Europe was being transformed, and the king of Sweden held the scales.

By Christmas 1631, Gustavus's successes had made him the most powerful man in Europe. Swedish armies were in command of half of Germany. "From Constantinople to Amsterdam, his agents were active, disseminating the story of his invincibility," writes his biographer Michael Roberts. His supporters regularly compared his exploits to those of the ancient Goths and the Vikings. They were building the perception that there was nothing the king of Sweden couldn't do, and no one who could stand in his way.

Gustavus Adolphus sent one group of emissaries to Constantinople and the court of the sultan, proposing they open a second front against the Habsburg emperor in southeastern Europe. The sultan turned him down, but Gustavus had more success with Russia. In fact, Gustavus Adolphus's Sweden was the first nation to establish a permanent mission in Moscow (the ghost of the long-dead Varangian adventurer Rurik must have smiled at the news). Gustavus and the tsar also had a common enemy, Poland. With Sigismund, the former Swedish king, at last on his deathbed (he would die in April 1632), an alliance between Swedes and Russians seemed in the offing, with a joint declaration of war against their rival. In the meantime, Gustavus's Scottish general Alexander Leslie was contracted to raise five thousand troops in Swedish-occupied Germany to strengthen the Russian forces.

To the west, Gustavus displayed a boldness, one might even say an arrogance, that startled the region's capitals. Sweden's king made it clear that he was unafraid of war with anyone, even with the mighty empire of Spain. France's prime minister, Cardinal Richelieu, who had been bankrolling Gustavus's drive into Germany, must have wondered what he had unleashed. He began to consider whether it was time to detach from some of the German magnates in Sweden's camp before Ferdinand and the Habsburgs suffered complete collapse, thus leaving all of central Europe to the colossus of the North. "Means must be devised to check this imperious Visigoth," the French cardinal is quoted as saying, "since his success will be fatal to France as to the Empire."

As for the Germans themselves, they had, it seems, little choice but to follow Gustavus's lead. Christian IV and Denmark were now too weak to intervene, even though Christian did intrigue in the politics of the Lower Saxon Circle to undermine Gustavus's influence there. Instead, everything was in Sweden's and Gustavus's hands. His trusted Count Oxenstierna came to join him in Mainz in early 1632 to assume control, and a central administration took shape for Swedish Germany. It included a chancery, a standing council, judicial powers, and a tax collection agency. Gustavus insisted on improvements in the local infrastructure, including a postal service, and announced a new church ordinance for Lutheran Germany. There was a frantic scramble for honors and offices among Gustavus's German clients. While those at the very top of German politics resented his rise to power, those in the middle saw an opportunity to advance their careers and the fortunes of their families — largely at the expense of a floundering Habsburg monarchy.

The prize that would truly solidify the Swedish king's power was becoming Holy Roman emperor. The title was, after all, elective. And at least four of the seven prospective electors were his allies, or at least had been reduced to neutrality.* Taking possession of the crown of Charlemagne would raise his status to something almost unapproachable and free his hand to conclude peace with the separate German states, both Catholic and Protestant, while ignoring the wishes of Vienna. A truly lasting peace, one to end nearly a century of religious and geopolitical conflict in central Europe, might be within his grasp.

But did he want to be Holy Roman emperor? Contemporaries certainly considered him a likely candidate, maybe even the inevitable choice. Some of his royal officials even took this outcome for granted. Apparently Gustavus Adolphus referred to the title only once in conversation, with Adolf Frederick of Mecklenburg in January 1632. "If I were Emperor," he exclaimed, "then would your grace be my prince." But the remark was likely made as an expression of exasperation with Mecklenburg's hesitancy to join the Swedish alliance more than as a serious proposition. So it's not clear if deposing Ferdinand, and being elected emperor in his place, was a serious part of the king of Sweden's plans.

---

* These were the Margrave of Brandenburg, Count Frederick of the Palatinate, and the (Protestant) bishops of Mainz and Trier. Opposing him were Bavaria, the Catholic bishop of Cologne, and the king of Bohemia — none other than Emperor Ferdinand himself.

What he was serious about, however, was securing Sweden's future security and interests. In that respect, he believed Sweden should become a member of the empire in order to safeguard its new German possessions. He also believed his *corpus bellicum et politicum,* or the Swedish-led German state he and Oxenstierna had set up—a kind of NATO, with Sweden acting as the United States—ought to have some formal status within the Holy Roman Empire. Certainly he thought of himself as far more than just another paid mercenary, like his opponents Tilly and Pappenheim. And if no one was able to stop him from reaching the highest summit of power, why should he put the brakes on?

In any case, if he did covet the title—as much for Sweden's future security as his own glory—one man stood in his way. It was certainly not Ferdinand, whose power was in shambles. Nor was it Cardinal Richelieu, although by now he was having second thoughts about his erstwhile client, whom he had helped raise to preeminent power in Germany and central Europe. Perhaps Gustavus Adolphus might soon pose a serious threat to the Bourbon dynasty of France, as he had done to the Habsburgs.

But the man who stood in the way of the Swedish king was Count Albrecht von Wallenstein, the greatest military entrepreneur of the age as well as the richest man in Europe. His factories and estates provided munitions and supplies for his master the emperor in unprecedented quantities, produced in the territories he controlled from the Baltic to Bohemia. He was working behind the scenes to weaken Gustavus by undermining his alliances—before a final showdown on the field of battle.

As the winter snows receded and Germany's rivers came into full spate, on March 2, 1632, the Swedish king and his army were on the move. They arrived in Nürnberg, where they were greeted with jubilation and gifts. Gustavus also picked up another forty thousand men before pushing on to Augsburg and then into Bavaria: the heart of Catholic Germany.

On April 12 he reached the river Lech. Tilly's army was parked on the opposite bank. Gustavus rode forward to reconnoiter possible crossings. Tilly's sentries didn't recognize him and hailed him with a mocking question: "Where's your king?"

"Nearer than you think," he shouted, and then cantered off.

Nothing was going to stop him. He had a pontoon bridge built overnight, then a handpicked force of three hundred Finnish troops to storm across and set up earthen ramparts for his artillery. Gustavus Adolphus personally led the charge up to Tilly's position. The imperial general took a bullet in the leg, and his second-in-command received a fractured skull. The Habsburg forces made yet another retreat, while, in desperation, Emperor Ferdinand struck a deal at last with Wallenstein to save what was left of his empire.

Gustavus made a stop in Augsburg on April 24. He spoke to the rapturous citizens about his duty to them and to God, signed an agreement for a subsidy of thirty thousand thaler, received a kiss from a local girl as the crowd roared its approval, then was off again. He stopped outside Ingolstadt, where his opponent Count Tilly lay dying and where a horse was shot out from under the Swedish king during a rapid skirmish. He then marched on, with Vienna, the Habsburg capital, as his final destination.

Then the advance slowed. Thanks to Wallenstein's machinations, one ally after another melted away, until only Gustavus's loyal Swedish forces and his mercenary bands remained. Throughout the summer Gustavus's army grew weaker while Wallenstein's grew stronger. The Swedish king even offered a deal to Wallenstein: peace in exchange for security for all Protestant princes, together with a formal role for "Gustavus's NATO" in a reconstituted empire. Wallenstein turned him down. The wily Westphalian sensed that his leverage over the Swedish juggernaut was increasing. Even the Protestant princes, who were deserting the Swedish cause, had come to the all-too-familiar conclusion that the devil they knew was preferable to the one they really didn't — especially one whom they now feared almost as much as his Habsburg opponent. No one was quite ready to exchange tyranny from Vienna for tyranny from Stockholm.

The only way for Gustavus to revive his cause was to score another decisive victory on the battlefield. There was a fierce fight at Alte Veste castle, overlooking the Rednitz River, in September. Gustavus tried to shove Wallenstein out of his heavily fortified camp but couldn't bring his cavalry to bear and had to withdraw, leaving four thousand killed and wounded. By now his German allies had fallen by the wayside one by one until just one remained, Prince Bernard of Saxe-Weimar. Gustavus's loyal Swedes, and his Finns and Scots, were the only reliable troops he had left. He had to bring about the decisive battle before winter came.

On November 6, Wallenstein and Pappenheim, the loser at Breitenfeld, joined forces. They had more than twenty-four thousand troops, while Gustavus had fewer than sixteen thousand. Then Wallenstein made a mistake. Thinking that the Swedes were too weak to launch an attack, he detached Pappenheim to try an end run at Halle. Croatian deserters passed this information on to the Swedes, and Gustavus saw an opportunity that he couldn't ignore — a chance to strike at his enemies while they were divided. So on the evening of the fifteenth, he surprised Wallenstein fifteen miles west of Leipzig, at a little town called Lützen.

November 16 dawned a wet, soggy morning, as Swedish drummers summoned the troops to their posts. Wallenstein had only twelve to fifteen thousand men with which to meet the Swedish assault. With Lützen on his right, he spaced his cavalry, infantry, and artillery in three separate groups, with a line of musketeers in a long ditch to repel the Swedish horsemen.

Gustavus's army was drawn up in typical Swedish fashion, with all three arms interspersed. Gustavus was himself in command of the right, and Bernard Saxe-Weimar was on the left — directly opposite Wallenstein's command post.

By ten o'clock, a thick fog covered the plain on which the battle was to take place. As the Swedish soldiers sang psalms to cheer themselves on, Gustavus raised his usual battle cry: "God is with us." He then rode along the lines and declared to his men: "The day has arrived on which you are to show what you have already learned in war. Hold yourselves ready; conduct yourselves as worthy soldiers; fight valiantly for your God, your country and your King." As they cheered, he added, "March with courage! . . . I myself will show the way. I am ready to risk my life and to shed my blood with you. Follow me, have confidence in God and bear away a victory whose fruits you and your posterity will gather forever."

The two sides could still barely see each other, thanks to the thick fog — perhaps the thickest that has ever enveloped a major battlefield. The future of Europe was about to be decided.

Gustavus and Wallenstein simultaneously decided to attack. Gustavus led a bold charge that swept aside the imperialist cavalry and seized the crucial ditch between the opposing forces, while Wallenstein's troops stormed Bernard's lines. Gustavus had doubled back to stiffen Bernard's resistance when

Count Pappenheim suddenly reappeared on Wallenstein's left wing, and shoved the Swedes back.

By noon, smoke had been added to the fog, thanks to Wallenstein's decision to set fire to Lützen. As buildings burned, clouds of smoke drifted across Bernard's lines, blinding combatants on both sides. Confusion reigned. A stray bullet struck Pappenheim in the chest, dropping him from the saddle. The cry went up for Gustavus to seize the moment and lead a final charge.

But where was the king? Some had seen him ordering up his elite Småland cavalry regiment and then leading a fresh charge on Wallenstein's wavering line. Then he had disappeared into the smoke and mist. Minutes later his charger came cantering back, its saddle empty.

The rumor spread through the stunned Swedish ranks: their king had fallen and was possibly even dead. The enraged army rallied and charged once again, scattering Pappenheim's cavalry while the Saxons pushed Wallenstein's men into the smoldering ruins of Lützen and beyond. Wallenstein, sick with gout and frustrated by his failure to break the Swedish line, fled. His army had lost its artillery; its retreat had barely avoided being a rout.

The battle of Lützen was over. It had been a stunning Swedish victory. Yet it wasn't until evening that the victors found their fallen king. He had taken a bullet in the back, which had blown him off his horse. Then two more had struck him in the arm, and someone had thrust a dagger into his chest. Then came the coup de grâce: a bullet in the head as he lay helpless on the ground. His enemies had taken his helmet, his ring, his watch, and the ornamental chain he wore around his neck, along with one of his spurs.

That night, Swedes, Finns, Scots, Germans, English, Poles, Frenchmen, and Dutchmen all mourned their dead leader. He was famed for sharing in their hardships just as they had shared in his glory. His concern for their welfare had been exceeded only by his lack of concern for his own safety. "He thinks the ship cannot sink that carries him," an English admirer had observed. Count Oxenstierna learned the terrible news on the twenty-first and spent the night pacing in grief and despair, mulling over the question that was on everyone's mind: could Sweden survive the death of its greatest king?

Perhaps, surprisingly, the answer would prove to be yes. The war machine Gustavus had built and perfected did in fact manage to preserve Sweden's hegemony for two more uneasy years. With Gustavus's death, the Habsburg cause recovered its nerve. Wallenstein got his revenge for the defeat at Lützen with a sweeping victory at the battle of Nördlingen in 1634, when the legend of Swedish invincibility was shattered forever. But even with Gustavus gone, and a girl of six inheriting the throne, Count Oxenstierna managed to keep Sweden in the game. Despite the severe defeat at Nördlingen, Sweden was still a formidable power, with a brilliantly professional army. It scored a textbook victory at Wittstock in 1636 where, despite a frigid winter that froze the Baltic and prevented supplies from reaching Sweden's commander, Field Marshal Baner, Baner was able to defeat the imperials with fewer than eighteen thousand men. Catholic fortunes were thus set back once again. As the distinguished historian Hans Delbrück put it, Wittstock "would have to be placed even above Cannae with the respect to the boldness of the plan and the greatness of the triumph."

Baner's successor, General Lennart Torstensson, scored a succession of victories culminating in a second success at Breitenfeld, on November 2, 1642, and then another at Jüterbog, on a freezing cold day (never an issue for Swedish soldiery) in December. The reversal of fortune triggered by Gustavus Adolphus's death had virtually been erased, and the possibility of Sweden's hegemony over Germany and central Europe seemed to beckon once again.

But this time, the Swedes had to deal with a second front: a war with the Danes. Conflict broke out between the two Scandinavian neighbors once again in 1642, and once again the Swedes came through with a smashing victory, this time at sea. Meanwhile, Lennart Torstensson was operating deep in imperial territory, where his Finnish engineers were bridging the Danube as his troops pressed on to Vienna. His victorious career might have eclipsed that of Gustavus himself: but once again Sweden's allies fell away, and despite the Swedish siege of Prague, Europe was now trending toward peace, not war.

The change in mood culminated in the comprehensive settlements signed by diplomats in Westphalia and Osnabrück, known collectively to historians as the Treaty of Westphalia, in 1648. It brought the conflicts of the Thirty Years' War to their conclusion, and although Sweden still would retain large chunks of Germany until the nineteenth century, the kingdom's bid for European hegemony was over, as was Gustavus Adolphus's thwarted ambition to be the Nordic Charlemagne.

It's almost impossible to remain neutral regarding the career of Gustavus Adolphus and its larger meaning. Throughout history, his admirers have outnumbered the detractors. The admirers include Oliver Cromwell, Napoleon I, and virtually every great military commander and strategist in the modern world.

For despite the tragedy of his death and the dashing of Sweden's hopes, Gustavus's legacy has to be listed as an overall success. He had prevented the victory of Catholicism over central Europe, and he saved the Protestant Reformation. His victories had also set the stage for the Peace of Westphalia and its most important underlying principle: that no single power — not the Habsburg Empire, not France, not even Sweden — would be allowed to control the center of Europe, including the heart of Charlemagne's old empire: Germany. This principle was the precondition on which a lasting peace could be built, founded on two new principles: nation-state sovereignty and a stable balance of power distributed among empires.

In addition, with the exception of Napoleon, no single person has had a greater impact on the evolution of modern warfare than Gustavus. His idea of the three arms — infantry, cavalry, and artillery — working together in close cooperation on the battlefield transformed European tactics. Swedish military discipline became the model for training troops. Light regimental artillery became widespread, and Swedish field artillery endured as the standard until the time of Frederick the Great.

Waging war by fighting and firing in line, so-called linear tactics, remained the rule on the battlefield until the end of the nineteenth century — or, one might argue, until the Battle of the Somme, in 1916. But European linear tactics would also become increasingly rigid and uncreative, unlike Gustavus's inspired use of mobile firepower, with his musketeers and the shock and awe brought to bear by his cavalry and pikemen, whose weapons were eventually replaced by the bayonet.

As for Sweden, the short but fateful reign of Gustavus Adolphus — "the king among kings, the captain among captains," as one of his English officers admiringly described him — created the first dim outline of the modern Swed-ish state, a country and a people transformed by the experience of empire, both for better and for worse. Even the Swedes who regret his squandering of their money and lives on his Protestant crusade across Europe recognize that his progressive reforms in Sweden itself were hugely significant. We can say that he would still be remembered as a great king if he had never fired a single shot in battle.

In a deeper sense, his career marks the striving of the Viking heart at its highest pitch. The same might be said of the ordinary Swedes and Finns who risked everything to follow him onto the battlefield for glory or death. Cer-tainly in Gustavus Adolphus, the dazzling qualities of the Viking heart — in-domitable courage, fierce loyalty, national pride and power, plus a religious zeal and a charismatic ambition — came the closest to turning military con-quest into permanent Scandinavian dominion over Europe.

There is, however, one other legacy we cannot ignore. The aftermath of Gustavus's reign also set in motion the first ships to head from Scandinavia to-ward North America in more than six hundred years. What began as a mere trickle would in time become a flood: a Great Migration that would transform two continents, as well as the people who took their places in it. The Viking heart would find a new home in the wake of its most charismatic exponent.

9

Scandinavians into Americans

We recall with gladness the day we left the chill cliffs of
Norway and praise the Lord whose wisdom guided us so
that our lot has been to dwell in the land where liberty and
freedom prevail, for here we can enjoy all the privileges to
which men are rightfully entitled.

— Voss Correspondence Society of Chicago, May 1, 1849

But America is not Norway. Here there is always a sense of
strangeness, something unlike home, and I don't suppose
we'll ever feel completely at home.

— Letter of Pastor Olaus Duus, July 30, 1856

IN 1636 COUNT Axel Oxenstierna was a busy man. He was still trying
to keep Sweden on an even keel after the sudden death of his beloved monarch, Gustavus Adolphus, on the battlefield at Lützen four years earlier. And
now, with an eleven-year-old girl, Queen Christina, on the throne, his duties
only increased.

But distracted or not, the chancellor of Sweden was never too busy for
Samuel Bloomaert. Oxenstierna had met him once on a visit to the Low Coun-
tries and had been so impressed by the Antwerp native and director of the
Dutch West Indies Company that Oxenstierna arranged for Bloomaert to be

Sweden's counsel in Amsterdam, in the very heart of Holland's blooming commercial empire. Now Bloomaert wanted Oxenstierna to meet his friend from the New Netherlands colony in America, Peter Minuit, who was in Stockholm for a visit. Oxenstierna was intrigued.

Peter Minuit was a persuasive man, as demonstrated by the (probably apocryphal) story of his purchase of Manhattan Island from the native people for a bundle of trinkets worth twenty-four dollars — the island where New Amsterdam now sat. His proposition to Oxenstierna was equally persuasive. Minuit wanted to create a new trading company, one that would establish an American colony similar to the one Minuit headed, but farther south, at the mouth of the South River, what we know today as the Delaware River. This time Minuit wanted to found the colony with Swedish capital. Minuit himself would lead it, but it would give Sweden the opportunity to engage in the kind of lucrative trade with local tribal groups that Holland was enjoying.

In the end they struck a deal: half the money for the enterprise would be Dutch, and the other half Swedish. Likewise, the personnel embarking for America would be half Dutch and half Swedish. But the ship carrying the first colonists and its escort vessel would both be Swedish. It was also understood from the beginning that the entire colony would be under royal Swedish control. With Oxenstierna's approval, the *Kalmar Nyckel* and the *Griffon* set sail from Stockholm in late August 1637. Thirty years after the founding of the settlement at Jamestown, and seventeen after the landing at Plymouth Bay, the Scandinavian experience in America was about to begin.

A storm nearly wrecked the *Kalmar Nyckel,* forcing it and its companion ship to put in at the Dutch port of Texel to make repairs. Not until almost New Year's Day in 1638 did the pair of vessels set out into the English Channel and point their prows, as earlier Viking longships had done, over the depths of the Atlantic.

After a stopover in the West Indies, they reached the North American coast in early March 1638. They landed on a promontory overlooking the Delaware River — today it is the location of Wilmington, Delaware. There, Minuit made the same kind of landmark deal he had struck to purchase Manhattan. Five local native chiefs agreed to give Minuit title to the land on the west bank of the Delaware River, from Bombay Hook as far north as the confluence with the Schuylkill River, where Philadelphia stands today. The Swedes then held an impromptu trade fair with the indigenous people to buy furs and other local products, while a dozen or so Swedish soldiers stood guard. By June 1638, they had enough goods to head home for Stockholm.

But they had to make the return voyage to Sweden without Peter Minuit. When the *Kalmar Nyckel* stopped over at Saint Kitts to take on supplies, Minuit disembarked to visit a Dutch friend on a neighboring ship. While he was gone, a hurricane descended on the island and blew the ship and Minuit out to sea. No one on board was ever seen again.

Despite the unexpected loss of their leader, the crew of the *Kalmar Nyckel* was able to bring back enough tobacco from Saint Kitts to give the Swedish government a net profit from the voyage. Another expedition set out from Stockholm with another Dutchman in charge, which rapidly expanded the colony's land holdings as far as Trenton. It wasn't until 1643 that a Swede finally arrived to take command of the settlement. He was Johan Printz, a giant of a man at nearly seven feet tall; he weighed nearly four hundred pounds. Printz was a veteran of several campaigns in Germany during the Thirty Years' War and former commander of the famed Västgöta cavalry regiment, which had fought at Lützen and Breitenfeld. Not one to shrink from a formidable task, Printz was determined to win Sweden its "place in the sun" in America.

"A remarkably beautiful country," he wrote rapturously to Count Per Brahe. "It has all the glories that any human being on earth can ever desire..." He had no doubt that New Sweden, and its capital, Fort Christina, named after Sweden's queen, "in time... would become one of the brightest jewels of the Swedish Crown."

Printz was wrong. In the end, Fort Christina was too small, too underfunded, and too undermanned to stop its neighbors, the Dutch and English, from squeezing the Swedes out. Printz himself built Elsenberg Fort Point to keep track of what the Dutch and English were up to nearby. But he could not prevent the changes outside its walls, which would ultimately overwhelm the colony.

Five years after Printz arrived, only ninety-four males were left in the colony, including a dozen or so Finns, four Dutchmen, four Germans, a Dane, and a single Black slave brought over on the *Griffon*. Printz had a foe worthy of his steel in the governor of New Amsterdam, Peter Stuyvesant; he made steady encroachments on the Swedish colony until, in the spring of 1654, Printz's successor, Johann Rising, tried to force a showdown by provoking a fight with a Dutch garrison, Fort Casimir. As a bid for regional hegemony, it was a complete failure. Rising lost the battle and the war. With the surrender of the remaining Swedish forces at Fort Christina at Wilmington, New Sweden came to an end.

Its unhappy history came as no surprise. The settlement was too weak to resist, the mother country too distracted to care. In any case, in a decade or two, rule by the Dutch would be replaced by rule by the English, and the remaining Swedes and other Scandinavians would merge into the larger European population. New Sweden was gone, barely a memory in the life of America. The Swedes themselves, even their historians, lost interest in its story for more than two hundred years. It became the "lost colony" in more ways than one.

But the impact of Scandinavians on the New World was just beginning.

After the death of Gustavus Adolphus, Scandinavia underwent some drastic changes, most of them bad.

The problems started with Sweden. Gustavus Adolphus's daughter, Queen Christina, was a remarkable character, another in a succession of strong and intelligent Nordic women, but she was a terrible monarch. She abdicated in 1654, having stayed on the throne just long enough to leave her kingdom in economic and political shambles. Her successors, including the brilliant soldier-king Charles XII, tried to revive Sweden's fortunes through endless wars against its neighbors: Poland, Russia, and especially Denmark.

Unfortunately, there was no disguising the fact that the costs of the Great Northern War (1697–1721), and other pointless conflicts that consumed the region to the close of the eighteenth century, reduced both Denmark and Sweden to second-rate or even third-rate status. The Scandinavian century had ended badly. Domestic political squabbling and turmoil became the grisly hallmarks of these twin Scandinavian kingdoms. Their permanent decline culminated in the assassination of a monarch, Gustavus III of Sweden, and the public beheading of Johann Friedrich Struensee, the intimate adviser of a Danish king.

The end of the next century was even worse. Both Denmark and Sweden became entangled in the global disruption of the French Revolution and the Napoleonic wars. In a series of disastrous decisions, rulers of both countries brought calamity to their kingdoms and their people. Denmark's once vaunted navy was crushed by its British counterpart in 1801, ending a maritime tradition that reached back to Christian IV. Soon after, the British army laid siege to Copenhagen and then occupied the city in 1805. In 1809 Sweden lost Finland to Russia, confirming that Sweden was no longer a great northern power.

Scandinavia's bleak decline was instantly obvious in 1815, at the Congress of Vienna. The last time Europe's diplomats had assembled to make peace and rearrange the map of Europe, at Westphalia in 1648, Denmark had been a major power and Sweden a great power. Both had controlled extensive holdings in Germany and around the Baltic. But when the diplomats met in Vienna a century and a half later, both Scandinavian countries had been reduced to voices that barely carried beyond the Sound.

Fortunately for them, the great powers assembled in Vienna were inclined to be conciliatory: not because Sweden and Denmark counted for so much on the world stage but because they counted for so little. Denmark was able to recover its former North American colonies in the Caribbean, such as Saint Bart's, and no one bothered to contest its sovereignty over the bleakness that was Greenland. Sweden's honor was saved by its new ruler, a former marshal of France and rival of Napoleon's, Jean-Baptiste Bernadotte, who was able to wrest control of Norway from Denmark as compensation for the loss of Finland.

Denmark and Sweden (now Sweden-Norway) had learned some hard lessons over the course of two centuries of war, conflict, and dislocation. Thanks to political mismanagement and the distractions of geopolitical struggle, all three Nordic nations missed nearly two centuries of economic and social progress. Poverty and underdevelopment became the norm from Telemark to Gotland and Jutland. The sudden shift to peace, however, brought another change to Scandinavia.

In 1769, the Lutheran clergy of all three countries — Denmark, Norway, and Sweden — organized a census to take a count of their populations. It was the first true census in the history of Europe. When they checked in again, in

1810 or so, the numbers hadn't changed much. But forty years later, by 1850, the surge in population was astonishing — and disturbing. In 1810, the population of Sweden stood at 2.5 million. At midcentury, it was closer to 3.5 million. Denmark had jumped from 1 million to 1.5 million, and Norway's numbers had nearly doubled, from 800,000 to 1.4 million. Since the Scandinavian countries had shown no appreciable urban or industrial growth to absorb the additional population, there was nowhere for the surge in people to go, and no way for them to be fed.

A Malthusian trap was looming. The population explosion of early-nineteenth-century Scandinavia led to rural proletarianization; a growing part of the population consisted of farm laborers and dairy maids who had little income and even fewer prospects. In Sweden, the rural working poor formed as much as 40 percent of the population by 1850.

Over the next six decades, immigration to America arose as the best solution for the average Scandinavian. The motives that drove Norwegians, Swedes, Danes, and Finns to set their hopes on the country across the Atlantic weren't so different from those that drove other immigrants from Europe: Germans, Scots, Irish, Poles, and Hungarians. For them too, the hardship of a transatlantic crossing and securing a new life in a strange land tended to pale in comparison to the hardships of the homeland.

But America had a special appeal for Scandinavians, and vice versa. Nineteenth-century America needed the energy and focus of a people willing to work hard in clearing virgin land, building a farm, and raising a family, often in a barren landscape, in order to create a lasting future for themselves and their posterity. Scandinavians happened to have these qualities in abundance. Like their Viking forebears, Swedish, Norwegian, Danish, and Finnish immigrants were looking for new horizons to conquer, but also new environments in which to make a home and shape a way of life that combined individual achievement with a devotion to family, church, and community — key ingredients of the American Dream.

Scandinavians brought other virtues with them as well. They were skilled in taming nature in ways that tap its abundance without destroying its bounty or its beauty. They believed in personal liberty — one reason America was particularly attractive — but they also respected social norms. A book on Scandinavian hipsters, past or present, would be very short indeed.

These new immigrants also saw education as important, even essential to a happy life, and they were as dedicated to building schools and colleges in their new country as the immigrant Scots were. The Scandinavians were true heirs to the Protestant self-scrutinizing conscience, sometimes to the point of morbidity, but always with the awareness that the finest actions stem from the noblest motives. They also retained a firm pride in the virtues and qualities of the "old country," including its Viking past, which could tinge with regret their new love for America, imbuing it with a spiritual depth.

They were adventurous, adaptable, and courageous, sometimes to the point of recklessness — among some of the Scandinavian immigrants, the legacy of the berserker lived on. Above all, these people embodied the Lutheran work ethic: the pursuit of excellence as an act of brotherly love for others, not just as a way to get ahead — although in the United States many would do both.

In short, the Viking heart had found a new home in America.

In outward appearance, the New Sweden colony had been a failure. But the handful of Swedes who had stuck it out to the end had managed to build the first colony in America that was free from famine or natural disaster. They also established the first Lutheran church in America, as well as the first flour mills and first shipyard, and they drew the first detailed map of the Delaware Valley. Not a bad legacy, taken together. And once they had settled down to a life of farming and logging, the Swedes were there to stay, regardless of who ruled: Swede, Dutchman, or Englishman. Eventually they became an integral part of the American colonial community.

Compared to the Swedes of New Sweden, the earliest Danes in America were men of substance and relatively wealthy — and relatively scarce. One exception is Jens Munk, the Norway-born sea captain and navigator-explorer who attempted to find the legendary Northwest Passage for the king of Denmark in 1619. The first European to explore the western reaches of Hudson Bay, he later succumbed to wounds suffered while fighting Wallenstein's army.

More typical were men like Jan van Breestede, literally "Jan from Breestede" in Slesvig, who settled in New Amsterdam and is listed as a member of Peter Minuit's council in 1626. Or Joachem Petersen Kuyter, who bought four hundred acres in the New Netherlands colony and was the first settler in Harlem, and Kuyter's friend Jonas Bronck, who bought five hundred acres along a bend in the Harlem River from the native people for six gold coins, two rifles, two kettles, two overcoats, two axes, two shirts, and a barrel of apple cider; he gave his name to the borough of New York on which his farm once stood: the Bronx.

By 1704, the Danish community in New York was large enough to build a church of its own, at the corner of Broadway and Rector. Danish merchants sailing to New York from the Caribbean islands of Saint Croix, which Denmark acquired in 1733, and Saint Thomas, which became a Danish crown colony in 1752, were able to attend Sunday services in Danish. Likewise, when Peter Kalm, a student of Linnaeus and an aspiring botanist, arrived in Philadelphia from the University of Uppsala in 1748, with a letter of introduction to Benjamin Franklin himself, he could attend services at the Swedish church on Water Street, which was built in 1698–1700 to serve the Swedes living in the city.[*]

Still, of the European newcomers to the American colonies in the eighteenth century, Danes, Swedes, and the occasional Norwegian formed a mere trickle compared to Germans, Scots, Dutch, and English — and certainly compared to the Scandinavians who would come over in the next century. For some, like the Danish Moravians who began settling around Bethlehem, Pennsylvania, there was religious dimension to their choice to live in the relative freedom of America.

Then there were Danish and Swedish soldiers who came over to join the

---

[*] Kalm published a work in three volumes describing his travels in America, which ranged as far west as the Great Lakes and as far north as Canada. The text became a European classic, translated into German, Dutch, French, and then English, as *Travels in North America, in 1770–1*. Kalm's work contains one of the first descriptions of Niagara Falls and one of the first predictions that America would achieve independence from Great Britain (Kalm was writing in the 1750s).

revolutionary cause when the War of Independence broke out. Some served with distinction, such as the Dane Christian Febiger, an immigrant from the Danish West Indies who fought at Bunker Hill, Brandywine, and Yorktown; he was known to his men as "Old Denmark." Similarly, Baron von Stedingk, who like many other Swedes served in the Revolutionary War as an officer in the French army rather than the Continental army, commanded a division under the marquis de Lafayette at the siege of Savannah in 1779, where he was badly wounded and had to be invalided home to Europe. This intrepid baron from Pomerania went on to lead Swedish forces against Napoleon and then served as Swedish ambassador to Russia. He died in 1837 at age ninety with the rank of field marshal.

But by the time the new republic was founded, however, Scandinavians barely registered in the demographics of the United States of America.

It was events, in particular religious events, in the mother country that triggered the first sizable wave of immigrants to America from Norway. The Danish sloop *Restauration* pulled into Long Island Sound on October 9, 1825, with forty-six passengers from Norway (including a child born at sea) and seven crew members. Interestingly, these Norwegians happened to be mostly Quakers. Embattled by the state-supported Lutheran Church in their homeland since its merger with Sweden in 1814, these Quakers had set off for America at the urging of one Cleng Peerson.

Peerson was born in Tysvær in the Norwegian county of Rogaland. "A Viking who was born some centuries after the Viking period," as one admirer called him, he would appear twice on Norwegian stamps (in 1947 and again in 1975) and become known as the William Bradford of the Norwegian migration to America — just as *Restauration* was the Norwegian *Mayflower*, although less than a fourth the size of the *Mayflower*, at just forty tons.

Their voyage had taken fourteen weeks, with a stopover at Funchal in Madeira, before the vessel docked in New York Harbor, where the immigrants were immediately hit with a fine for carrying too many passengers on so small a craft.

The six-hundred-dollar fine was far more than the Quakers, who had been taken in by the Quaker community in New York, could possibly pay, and it could have spelled ruin for them. But they and the ship owners appealed the fine by petition and received a presidential pardon, signed by John Quincy Adams, on November 15, 1825. The man who would later free the African slaves of the *Amistad* was also willing to help the Norwegians on the *Restauration*.

The "sloopers," as they became known, were still dependent on charity from their fellow Quaker New Yorkers when they moved upstate, to Kendall Township on the shores of Lake Ontario. It was not until the early 1830s that they could begin to make ends meet. By then their Moses, Cleng Peerson, had found their next destination, and a prime destination for future Norwegians it was: Illinois and the Midwest.

Peerson had achieved this by literally walking from the western portion of New York State through Ohio and Indiana and on to Illinois, which had become a state in 1818. There he finally stopped on a hillside overlooking a broad river valley, dropped to his knees, and thanked God. He had found the Promised Land for his fellow Norwegians.

He scrambled back to Kendall, where he convinced his fellow immigrants that the farmland they had all dreamed about now awaited them. Within a few years, most had left Kendall Township for the Fox River valley, sixty miles southwest of Chicago, and by 1836 nearly all the sloopers were out west. Peerson was joined by Gjert Gregoriussen Hovland, who by letter spread the word to Norway of the wonders of Illinois and America. Soon everyone who could read (and many who couldn't) knew what was awaiting them in the wonderland across the Atlantic.

Hovland's letters were filled with details not only about the marvelous land but also about the people and the American republic, where equality and liberty reigned. It was no idle promise to Norwegians living uncomfortably under Swedish rule. He counseled everyone to come who could, since "God had never forbidden men to settle where they pleased."

That was all it took, apparently, to start emptying out the Norwegian hinterland. In 1836 another shipload of Norwegian immigrants, 160 this time instead of 46, set out for New York on two brigs: the *Norden* and *Norske Klippe*. Almost all who landed made their way directly to Illinois and LaSalle County, which remained a hub of Norwegian settlement through the 1840s. Soon the immigrants were branching out into the wilderness of Wisconsin.

The Swedes were not far behind. The first party, consisting of sixteen families, arrived in 1841 and made their way to Wisconsin. For the Swedes, the immigration trail followed a more routine sea route: the one that carried Swedish iron ore to America. Soon those imports rivaled those to Germany and eastern Europe.

The Swedes' Wisconsin home at Pine Lake was a relatively miserable settlement of log cabins, one of them housing twenty-one settlers together. The single aristocrat in their midst, a Baron Thot, had to work as a cook to make ends meet. But the draw was irresistible. Another shipload from Sweden arrived in the autumn of 1844, and another in 1845, this time following a different route: running from New York to Pittsburgh, down the Ohio River, then up the Mississippi River. These immigrants also reached a different destination, the newly admitted state of Iowa. The Swedes made their home in Jefferson County, forty-two miles west of Burlington, which, as an expression of hope, they dubbed New Sweden.

Their leader was Peter Cassel, a millwright from Sweden who had once been manager of a large estate in Östergötland; he was the inventor of a hand-driven threshing machine. Paying twenty dollars apiece, he and his party had left from Gothenburg in the spring of 1845 and were probably headed to join the Swedes settled at Pine Lake. Then Cassel met Pehr Dahlberg, one of the first Swedes to venture out to the fertile lands beyond the Mississippi. He persuaded Cassel to forget about Pine Lake (which had been largely abandoned by that date) and push on to Iowa instead.

Unlike Pine Lake, New Sweden stuck. In January 1848, Cassel and his fellow pioneers formally founded a congregation, the first one in what would become the Evangelical Lutheran Augustana Synod of North America, and in 1860–61 the five hundred families living in New Sweden built a church in Lockridge Township, in the area known as Four Corners. It still stands.

All of this followed what was by now becoming a familiar pattern: One intrepid Scandinavian pioneer meets a fellow countryman who has ventured out even farther, and by word of mouth convinces him and his followers to strike out for the far horizon, to reach an even more abundant promised land. Then letters go out from one or both, encouraging folks back home to join them. In Cassel's case, his letters home to Sweden, extolling the virtues of life in America, drew fresh immigrants from the overcrowded farms and villages. Some set out for New Sweden; others headed for other stretches of Iowa, where they found a place near the Des Moines River they called Swedish Point, and settled there.

Another group, a party of seventy-five, made a harrowing journey from Stockholm, during which two women and three children died. They then headed for upstate New York via an equally harrowing trip up the Erie Canal, during which they were robbed of their money and their supplies. They soon found themselves stranded outside Buffalo without a cent and unable to speak a word of English. "Like a flock of frightened sheep," one later remembered, "we stood there helpless on the shore," as a cold, pitiless rain began to pour down from over the lake.

Then, almost miraculously, a man appeared. He recognized their accent and spoke to them in Swedish. Named Svedberg, he also was a recent Swedish immigrant, who had arrived with a friend and fellow native of Stockholm named Haglund. Svedberg found them shelter for the night, and enough food to keep the group fed over the weekend. Then a small Norwegian boy, from the nearby settlement in Lockport (founded in 1825), helped the Swedes find work as farmhands. For two years they stayed in Buffalo, the men working as laborers and the women as maids and laundresses, until eventually they made their homes around Jamestown, New York. Jamestown became the largest and most homogeneous Swedish settlement in the state. It also hosted one of the biggest Swedish churches in North America, and until World War II the community published a weekly Swedish-language newspaper.

But the biggest influx of Swedes came in 1846, a far cry from the early handfuls of families. This time they numbered more than a thousand. These so-called Janssonists had been inspired by their religious leader, Erik or Eric Jansson, to travel to America together.

Born in 1808 in an obscure farm community near Uppsala, Erik Jansson had taught himself to read and, from the age of fifteen, devoured religious works with gusto, from Luther to the Swedish pietist preachers. He fit the profile of the men and the women (rarer but not unknown) who became breakaway leaders of Protestant sects: an intellectually sharp but largely self-taught Bible reader who decided to interpret Scripture independently rather than according to the dictates of the established church. Jansson decided that the Bible was the only source of religious teaching needed and came to believe that God through Christ not only forgave sin but also wiped it away completely.

A doctrine like this was bound to attract followers, along with official disapproval. Within four or five years Jansson had stirred up enough controversy for the authorities to arrest him. This was due in part to his organization of a bonfire — a public burning of official religious texts — which in fact violated Swedish law. Jansson managed to escape and remained a fugitive. Soon enough he realized that he needed to leave Sweden and find a new home for himself and the growing number of the faithful. America was the obvious choice. Jansson turned to one of his most loyal followers for help.

He sent Olof Olsson to the United States to find a suitable spot to establish a utopian heaven on earth, a "New Jerusalem" that would eventually spread around the world. Olsson found it in Henry County, Illinois. On August 1, 1846, a title was signed in the name of Olof Olsson for sixty acres of land near Red Oak Grove. Olsson and Jansson paid $250, or just over $4 an acre. When he arrived, Jansson named the spot Bishop Hill after his birthplace, Biskopskulla, outside Uppsala.

The settlement grew apace, adding on a complete farm of 156 acres, with outbuildings, for $1,000. Then on September 26, the two purchased another 480 acres of federal land at $1.25 an acre. Everything was ready for the first group of settlers, who would arrive that fall. The first winter was a struggle. Many were struck down by disease, maybe contracted on the rough voyage over. But between 1847 and 1854, nine different groups made their way from Sweden to Bishop Hill, making it the single largest Scandinavian settlement in North America. At first it consisted of nothing but tents, then dugouts with wooden walls and dirt floors. Eventually there were homes built of handmade bricks, a flour mill, two sawmills, and a three-story church. The Norwegian Moses himself, Cleng Peerson, settled at Bishop Hill in 1847. There he found a virtual Norse commune, built on communistic principles (no private property) and the injunction to share all with all, according to the Bible (*The Communist Manifesto* had not yet been written).

"I take now pen in hand," one of the colonists wrote back home in 1847, "when I consider how God has blessed us here on this new soil by a hundred-fold in both spiritual and worldly goods over what we possessed in our father-land." They enjoyed a legacy "that could not be exchanged for a quarter of all Sweden."

But only three years after the start of the settlement, it had to get along without its messiah. Into this prairie garden of Eden there came a serpent in the form of John Root, who had married Jansson's niece. He had hoped to take her away from Bishop Hill, but Jansson prevented it each time he tried. Finally Root lost his temper and snapped, and shot Jansson down with a pistol.

It was a devastating blow, and many Swedes left, disheartened. But two disciples, Jonas Olsson and Olof Johnson, took over and held the community together until 1861 when, facing financial ruin, they abandoned the communistic system. The township of Bishop Hill formally disbanded, and its property was divided among the remaining residents. The New Jerusalem was no more.

But its legacy among history's Swedish immigrants to the United States remained. Several of its residents served in the Civil War, including Olsson's son, and letters home extolling the virtues of America kept the immigration spigot turned on. As for Bishop Hill, its spick-and-span brick-and-white-clapboard houses still stand, as does the church, serving a township with a total population of 125. Until 2004 Jansson's direct descendant, his great-great-grandson T. A. Mylross, still lived in the village; he died on a call for the volunteer fire department.

The Swedes of Bishop Hill had immigrated in 1846, a year after 400 Swedish and 150 Norwegian students, under the spell of Scandinavianism, gathered at Nytoldbod across the Sound from Malmö and made "a sacred promise" that they would be "faithful to the end, faithful in life and death" in their commitment to "our great common nation." An 1847 painting by the Danish artist Jorgen Sonne commemorates the event. But the dream of a great common nation uniting all branches of Scandinavia was already being realized — not in the north of Europe but in America.

California became another magnet for Scandinavian immigrants. While most were choosing to settle in what would soon be known as Homestead Triangle, between the Mississippi and Missouri Rivers and encompassing Wisconsin, Minnesota, Iowa, and the eastern Dakota Territory (Dakota got its first Norse settler in 1858), the 1849 gold rush in California drew many as well, along with other newcomers eager to strike it rich. But the Swedes and the Danes stood out.

Compared to Norwegians and Swedes, the Danes were relatively late to mass immigration. But California held a peculiar fascination for them, even before the discovery of gold there. In fact, the land adjacent to Sutter's Mill, where gold was first located, belonged to William Alexander Leidesdorff, a sea captain born in Saint Croix to a Danish father and a Creole mother. He had come to San Francisco in 1841 and stayed on, becoming a Mexican citizen (at the time California was part of Mexico) and a hotel owner while serving as president of the city's school board. The house he built, the biggest in San Francisco at the time, sat on the site of the current Bank of America tower.

Unlike John Sutter, Leidesdorff was no absentee landlord. When gold was discovered, Sutter invited the biracial hotelier to join him in the search for gold deposits on his own property: Ranch Rio de Los Americanos. Leidesdorff even hired James Marshall, who had made the original discovery at Sutter's Mill, to do the survey on his land.

Marshall found an enormous vein of gold at Ranch Rio, but Leidesdorff died that May before the news of the amazing find reached the public. By the time his estate was auctioned off, in 1856, it was worth more than $1,445,000, which did not include the value of the vast quantities of gold dug up from his holding. If Leidesdorff had lived, Ranch Rio might have become more famous than Sutter's Mill, and the history of the California gold rush might have a deeper Scandinavian tinge, and a Caribbean African one as well.

Other Danes in California opened sawmills and shipyards all along the Pacific coast, and this maritime world was, unsurprisingly, also a comfortable place for enterprising Norwegians and Swedes. But nowhere were Danes a bigger presence out west, or in all the United States, for that matter, than in Utah.

The reason was the Mormon connection.

The first Dane to convert to Mormonism was Peter Clemmensen; he was living in Boston at the time. He converted another Dane, Hans Christian Hansen, a sailor who had landed in Boston and then returned to Liverpool, where he was baptized a Latter-Day Saint.

Hansen was only the tip of what would become a very large Mormon iceberg. Then as now, Mormonism involved missionizing; Mormon elders continue to go from house to house, to spread the faith. In 1849, the church launched its first major outreach to northern Europe, including Scotland and Scandinavia. It selected one of the Hansen boys, Peter, and another Dane, Erastus Snow, as missionaries to Denmark. Both arrived in the spring of 1850, a propitious time. Denmark's new constitution, ratified by Frederick IV, had opened a new era of religious liberty (which was not extended to Roman Catholics). The Mormons joined Baptists, Methodists, and a range of other Protestant religious dissidents in enjoying this new freedom, although the Mormons did stir some controversy because of their acceptance of polygamy.

Conversions became common in places like Vendsyssel in Jutland. Mormonism attracted women as much, if not more so, than men, although the idea of polygamy hardly resonated with these staid Danes. Less than 10 percent of the converts, in fact, embraced the multi-wife option. (Their Viking ancestors would have viewed the issue very differently.) The Danish converts became missionaries in their turn in their home country.

But all felt the pull of the other side of the Atlantic, which offered what seemed to them an unprecedented spiritual freedom. Inevitably, their attention turned to Mormonism's original home in America. Until 1852, the numbers traveling in that direction were no more than a trickle. But soon they were swayed by a simple, compelling message: leave Denmark for "Joseph's Land" (meaning Joseph Smith, the founder of Mormonism) and a new life in Utah, where acres of land are waiting for you as a member of the Church of the Latter-Day Saints. Through the 1850s, no fewer than 2,898 of the 3,749 Danes who immigrated to America were Mormons. In the 1860s, 4,942 out of the 13,011 Danish immigrants were Mormons. Altogether they gave Utah the single largest Danish-born population in the United States.

Mormon missionaries found some success with other Scandinavians, including Norwegians and Swedes. But the Mormon message seemed to resonate more with the Danes, and not just for reasons of religious belief. Their home brand of Lutheranism was, after all, no different from that of other parts of Scandinavia. But becoming Mormon involved a change in language and culture as well as religious faith, and the Danes were perhaps better suited to this transition. A large portion of them were already bilingual, speaking both Danish and German, so perhaps the switch to services conducted in English, not Danish, was less jarring. Also, their homeland had been remarkably open to cross-cultural currents throughout the early modern age, so adapting to American culture may have seemed less challenging. Scholars of Scandinavian immigration to the United States generally agree on this point: the Danes proved the quickest to assimilate and merge into the larger population, whether they were Mormons or not. In the end, the Church of Denmark, the home country's official Lutheran church, never mustered more than 25 percent attendance in America.

Becoming Mormon posed risks, however. Many Danish converts faced fierce public opposition, even death threats. It was not forgotten that their founder, Joseph Smith, had been murdered by a lynch mob in Missouri. Perhaps the greatest threat was the wilds of Utah, where immigrant Mormons were to build a new life. Jens Nielsen, for example, converted to Mormonism in 1854 when he and wife, Elsie, met Mormon missionaries on a visit near their home in Aarhus. They didn't move to America until 1856, when they arrived in New York Harbor and set out for Utah. They gathered supplies for the two-thousand-mile trek, first by covered wagon and then, incredibly, by handcart.

The Nielsens estimated that the journey would take them seventy days. In fact, it took more than ninety. They ran out of food several times, and the cattle they acquired along the way stampeded as they were crossing Nebraska. They lost half their herd.

Then came snowstorms, and the death of their only son. They finally arrived at Salt Lake City on November 9, 1856, half-frozen. Their co-religionists carried them on stretchers because they could no longer walk. Once Jens had recovered, he proceeded to take on two more wives, for a total of three, including the faithful Elsie. Then he was called on to establish a Mormon community in Navajo country, in southeastern Utah. The Navajo called Nielsen "crooked feet," for the permanent injuries he had sustained during the journey across America. Jens managed to build two houses in Navajo country — one for Elsie and one for his second wife, Kirsten Johnson, whom he had baptized back in Denmark. He ate lunch at Kirsten's house every day. Jens died just two days short of his eighty-sixth birthday.

Jens Nielsen wrote one kind of American mini-epic in Utah. A different Danish Mormon immigrant, also named Jens, wrote another, roughly ten years later, in Idaho and California this time. Jens Borglum was headed to Utah when he first emigrated from Copenhagen in 1864, to find a new life in "Joseph's Land" by "the great salt city." He had married Ida Mikklesen, also a Mormon convert, as they were waiting to board their ship in Copenhagen Harbor, as part of a mass ceremony meant to reduce overcrowding (husband and wife could share one berth instead of taking up two) and to foster new families in advance of their arrival in America.

At first he and Ida got no farther than Nebraska. One of the women who accompanied them on the journey recalled how rough and dangerous the Great Plains could appear, to immigrants from Denmark. The land was "covered with buffalo grass. The road was crude, just a rutty, dusty, winding seemingly endless pair of ruts cut through which those before us had labored." At the first ford they came to, "the entire oxen and the wagon were lost. The driver barely escaped with his life . . ."

But eventually they reached Salt Lake City, with Ida's younger sister Christina. There Jens married Christina too, and the threesome set out for Idaho, to create a new Mormon community in the midst of what was a bleak wilderness. They made their home at Bear Lake Stake, in Ovid. Jens built a simple, two-room log cabin not much different from the kind a Danish or Norwegian farmer might construct in his home's neighboring uplands, where he could stay to tend cattle or sheep. Later, Ida and Christina's mother came out to join them on this Idaho farm.

It was here, on March 17, 1867, that Christina gave birth to a son, John Gutzon de la Mothe Borglum. Years later John would record an early memory of an encounter with a Native American when he was no more than three or four: "The first thing I remember was a Sioux Indian's face pressed closely against the window of our main room. I was sitting on my grandmother's knee, who had been telling me some Norse stories and I have never been able to disentangle the Vikings of Denmark from the Sioux Indians."

Gutzon Borglum and his family would travel to many places before they finally made a permanent home. But he always carried with him a desire to make beautiful things in wild places, a drive that eventually took him to South Dakota. There Gutzon Borglum sculpted the massive presidential heads of the monument on Mount Rushmore.

What drew Danes to Mormonism? Probably the same qualities drew them, and other Scandinavians, to America in general.

America was free of the traditional boundaries imposed by the aristocracy-dominated societies that they left behind. It also offered an escape from the material poverty that those societies had failed to address. Scandinavia did not adopt the land reform and industrialization experienced in other parts of northern Europe, especially Britain, Holland, France, and Germany.

That promise of freedom unlocked an inner drive in these immigrants, who were ready to meet vast horizons of the American heartland. Its great empty spaces could not be more dangerous than the great empty spaces their Viking ancestors had crossed in their ships or settled in the wilds of Iceland and elsewhere. Here the Viking heart had room to set down roots and start anew. In addition, it was a place that could accommodate the Scandinavian impulse to find the sacred in the secular, the exalted in the mundane, a transcendent connection in places that might be seen as inhospitable and empty, an awareness of the depths present in nature. Some, such as Leif Erikson, Fridtjof Nansen, Thor Heyerdahl, and Liv Arnesen, have explored its extreme outer reaches. Yet nearly all Scandinavians have sensed that wild and untamed places offer an inner freedom and peace.

But none of the early Scandinavian immigrants truly understood how wild and untamed this new home would be until they got there.

When Elizabeth Koren and her pastor husband moved from Norway to Washington Prairie, Iowa, in the winter of 1853–54, they arrived in a blinding snowstorm. Cold and snow presented no hardship to a Norwegian, of course. But the lack of a parsonage in a Norwegian settlement that was less than four years old meant sharing a single-room cottage, sixteen by fifteen feet in size, with another family, which had four members. The cottage's single room was separated by a curtain, so that each family had its own "bedroom." The Korens stayed there for three months. It was their cozy welcome to America.

As her diary recounts, they soon discovered they were among the more fortunate of Washington Prairie's residents. Elizabeth and her husband, Wilhelm, visited houses where the space between logs was so large that the walls couldn't keep out the snow or the cold, even when family members huddled around their most valuable family possession, the wood stove. She also learned that twelve to fifteen people might live in a house even smaller than the one they shared with their hosts. When they traveled on Wilhelm's pastoral rounds — a Norwegian Lutheran minister in America invariably had a wide-flung parish — they sometimes slept in an attic loft, where they could see the stars through the roof boards.

The one hardship they avoided were epidemic diseases like typhus and smallpox. In general, disease wasn't a common problem in Scandinavian American settlements. The standards of hygiene learned in the old country and passed down from Viking ancestors held up well in the new country — although when there was a cholera outbreak east of Washington Prairie in 1854, it caused plenty of local alarm.

The Korens' experience wasn't unusual for immigrants in the 1850s. In fact, as Elizabeth's diary frequently mentions, they were among the luckier ones. Many didn't even have to break into the American interior to have it hard. A Swedish clergyman who met a parcel of Swedish immigrants who had just arrived in New York in 1865 wrote this about what he witnessed:

"A great many are lying ill on Ward's Island; some have died and two women have given birth to children. One of them is reported dead, but I have been unable to visit her, as I live six miles away. The father is out west, and on Ward's Island there is said to be a deserted boy, who runs about dirty and full of vermin." He noted that the twenty or thirty refugees on Ward's Island, none of whom had a cent, would grab at his coat and cry, "Pastor, get me away from here so that we may escape the poorhouse."

But they still kept coming, especially (in those days) the Norwegians.

In just two years, 1849 and 1850, almost eight thousand people left Norway for America. The numbers continued to swell in the 1850s, reaching a peak in 1861, with eight thousand immigrants. A pastor in Sogn, Norway, by the name of Dean Hauge, wrote regular reports about the Norwegians heading out from his pastoral district to America. He found that almost all of them expressed the desire to find better circumstances for themselves, as well as "the noble thought" that they would find a better life for their children in America.

There was also the steady pull to join family members who were already there. If their kin could manage living in dugouts on a bleak and featureless prairie, or crossing miles of uncharted mountains and wilderness, or facing the threat of attack by native tribes (or by wild gangs of mountain men and others who resented the newcomers), then they could bear it. They were convinced by the fact that despite the hardship and danger, their predecessor immigrants praised the new land in their letters home. It seemed worth trying.

The number of Swedish immigrants never exceeded five thousand a year in the 1850s; by 1860 the numbers had dropped significantly. Norway, as we've seen, was a very different story. The depression years of 1849–50 were followed by a second wave, after the crop failures of 1859 and 1860, then the killer frost in 1861. A flood of Norwegians fled their impoverished country, nine-tenths of them passing through Quebec and then traveling to the American Midwest.

By then other Norwegians realized there was a thriving business in immigration, and the port of Bergen became its principal base. "So we rowed up the bay," one immigrant remembered, "and there lay the mighty ships, with masts hewn of the tallest trees in the forest — all ready to sail to America." One Norwegian ship owner alone in the 1850s built no fewer than six vessels to carry his fellow Norwegians across the Atlantic.

Tickets were fairly cheap. Thirty to sixty dollars (roughly thirty-five to seventy Norwegian dollars, the equivalent of two weeks' regular wages) would carry an adult to America, with children traveling at half fare and babies for free.

Though New York was still the destination for some, the chief port of arrival had become Quebec, with a further voyage up the Saint Lawrence to the Great Lakes, and then to ports like Detroit and Chicago. But whether to New York or Quebec, the journey was equally harrowing. Nine or ten weeks at sea was not uncommon. Months out of sight of land was typical. Every passenger had to provide his or her own bedding and food, and in bad weather the hatches were battened down, which shut out the light, and people felt as if they were living in a timbered tomb. Given the crowded and unsanitary conditions, even the hardiest Scandinavians could fall victim to epidemic diseases. Illness and death regularly stalked the passengers en route to America.

The playwright Henrik Ibsen gave the immigrant ships a grim name, "coffin ships." More than one lived up to that reputation. In 1861 a ship from Arendal reached Quebec with thirty-seven dead on board, and sixty more seriously ill. Another docked with thirty-three dead — mostly children under the age of six who had been cut down by an epidemic of measles.

Where did these new arrivals go? Unlike later immigrant populations, like the Irish or the Italians or the Poles, very few wanted to stay at their port of entry. There was no Little Bergen or Little Stockholm on the Lower East Side of Manhattan or in Brooklyn. The Norwegians wanted land to farm, and lots of it. So most new arrivals made their way to the Norwegian settlements in Wisconsin, founded in the 1830s and '40s. Its landscape would seem familiar terrain to a native Norwegian. She or he could easily spot familiar flora and fauna. Willow, alder, ash, maple, oak, and the ever-present birch in clumps of three: the trees weren't much different from those in Norway. "It brought them a greeting which made them feel that they were still on God's earth," a character remarks, in a Norwegian novel from later in the century, "and would be able to come to terms with the new land in the end."

But the new land was surprising in other ways. Olaus Duus was a minister for a parish in Wisconsin that stretched far and wide: from Waupaca and Neenah in the east, to a Norwegian congregation in Stevens Point, Portage County, to the west, and all the way to a Swedish congregation in Waupaca County. Arriving at Stevens Point, which sat on the banks of the Wisconsin River, he found that the waterway was "filled with rafts of logs and other timber which are to float down from the pineries via the Wisconsin and Mississippi to the southern states, where there are few pines." The men who worked the river, he found, "are unfortunately the scum of humanity, the dregs of both Europe and America. They live a life of constant drinking, gambling, swearing, and cursing; and even of occasional murder. They flee from justice, and since the language is all the same here in America they cannot be detected by their dialect."*

This was not true of Duus's parishioners, whose different Norwegian accents and dialects sometimes made communication among them impossible.

---

* I note in passing that Stevens Point is my hometown.

This was another advantage to being in America: by learning to speak English, Norwegians could talk to Swedes, Danes, and even other Norwegians without difficulty — something impossible at home.

Otherwise, Pastor Duus found that, despite the hard land that demanded hard work from his parishioners as well as himself, there was something strikingly beautiful about life on the Wisconsin prairie and in its forests. "On Christmas Day I preached in a rather large house that stands on a stretch of cleared land with a wooded ridge on one side and a fairly large lake surrounded by a thick forest of oak, aspen, and pine on the other. It was like a lovely April day in Norway, clear, sunny, and so warm that the melting snow lay in wide pools of water on the frozen ground."

But the weather wasn't the biggest surprise that day. When he and the congregation were singing hymns, Duus noticed someone was listening at the window. It was "a tall, powerful young Indian in his tawny deerskin garb, with a motley headdress" and his rifle at his side. "He listened intently during the singing of the hymns as though wondering what could be the reason for this gathering and this singing. For an hour he stood there, engrossed. After a long time, when my glance fell on the window, I saw him, his rifle on his shoulder, vanishing into the near-by forest."

Two tightly knit communities were brushing shoulders, one long settled in the land and one new to it. As for that new land, "I do not know anyone who does not live far better than in Norway," the pastor added in his journal.

And the Norwegians knew it. They, and others from the older settlements, were busy expanding into Iowa, and then Minnesota. Meanwhile, a new wave had come at the start of the new decade, in 1860–61: the largest wave of immigrants yet. These newest arrivals were in for a double shock. They found themselves not only in a new country, but one plunging into civil war.

They didn't know it yet, but the Viking heart in America was about to undergo its greatest test thus far.

10

"We Are Coming, Father Abraham"

Scandinavians in the American Civil War

> That which we learned to love as freemen in our old
> Fatherland — our freedom — our government — our
> independence — is threatened with destruction.
>
> — Colonel Hans Christian Heg, October 1861

THE SCANDINAVIANS' IMPACT on their new chosen homeland would first be felt in the Civil War. One could argue that the impact would be decisive both for the course of the war and the future of Scandinavians in America.

As Abraham Lincoln watched the weary lines of the wounded after the first battle of Bull Run in mid-July 1861, he realized this war with the rebellious South was going to be a long, hard struggle. The Union would need many more regiments of volunteers, ordinary men who would have to transition from civilian life to risk their lives for the sake of the Constitution and liberty. This would be especially true in the West, where the sprawling geography and multiple river valleys left many points to defend against a confident enemy — and many more to take away from that enemy too.

That would mean recruiting regiments in frontier states like Iowa, Minnesota, and Wisconsin. These were hard-core pro-Union, antislavery states — not least because of their sizable Scandinavian population. As early as January, months before any shot was fired at Fort Sumter, the state legislature of Minnesota had passed a resolution insisting that the South's act of secession the previous year was tantamount to revolution. It pledged that Minnesota would support "with men and money" whatever the federal government needed to assert its authority. Wisconsin's governor, Alexander Randall, warned his state legislature around the same time that it might have to vote the men and means necessary "to sustain the integrity of the Union and thwart the designs of men engaged in organized treason."

Then in August — a month after Bull Run — Randall issued a call for Wisconsinites to organize five new regiments for the fight. One, the Wisconsin Ninth, would be raised specifically from among Wisconsin's recent German immigrants. Another, the Eleventh, would be largely Irish. This inspired J. A. Johnson, a Norwegian merchant from the state capital of Madison, to wonder: why not raise a regiment of Norwegian men, drawn from communities like Koshkonong and Muskego? He issued the call at the end of August, and in September he and five other Wisconsin citizens of Norwegian birth sent a letter to the governor, asking for permission to recruit Norwegian immigrants to help defend the Union. The letter contained one other recommendation: that one of their number, Hans Christian Heg, be appointed as the regiment's colonel.

Heg had been involved in organizing a Norwegian or Scandinavian army unit from the beginning, when Johnson was still wondering whether they would find enough Norwegian volunteers to fill a company, let alone an entire regiment. Born in 1829 in a small town outside Kristiania, Norway, Hans was the son of Ever Heg, who had immigrated to the United States in the spring of 1840 and settled in Muskego. There Ever became the successful publisher of a Norwegian-language newspaper, and something of a community celebrity.

This was because the use of Norwegian in print had consequences reaching beyond America. Norwegian was still emerging as a separate language as late as the 1840s, as far as political authorities back home were concerned. A key figure in this development was Henrik Wergeland, poet and publicist, who combined the historical researches of P. A. Munch, who had worked to separate a history of Norway out from under the shadow of Danish history, and the traditional stories collected by the folklorists P. C. Asbjørnsen and J. E. Moe. Wergeland's goal was to reshape the Norwegian dialect that had been accepted by Danish authorities, "the language of the realm" (*riksmal*), into a language that ordinary Norwegians spoke as part of their daily lives, or "the language of the land" (*landsmal*).

Then in 1836 a farm laborer's son, Ivar Aasen, announced that he was leading the effort to create a truly national language of Norway, which would combine the dialects of the most populous parts of the country (western Norway, where Aasen himself was born) with their original Old Norse roots. It was not until 1858 that the grammar Aasen had published finally received wide acceptance and Norwegian really did exist as a discrete national language.

Publishing a newspaper in Norwegian made Ever Heg a bold man. His son Hans proved even more adventurous. He had set out at age twenty to join the gold rush in California, making stops at Fort Laramie and Salt Lake City, and spent two years trying to make a fortune for himself in the gold fields when news of his father's death, in 1851, brought him back to Wisconsin.

Instead of farming, Hans Christian Heg turned to politics and the brand-new Republican Party. When war broke out, he was serving as Wisconsin's prison commissioner. Heg was no bureaucrat or place server. A fierce enemy of slavery and passionate about preserving the Union, he had signed up in answer to Lincoln's call for volunteers as early as April 1861, in Waupun. The opportunity to raise, and possibly command, a regiment in the Union cause consumed his every thought and all his energy.

His commitment to saving the Union had plenty of company among Norwegians in Wisconsin. In a conflict that was splitting the nation and its communities, even its families, into rival camps, Scandinavians were overwhelmingly pro-Union. The specter of armed rebellion against the US government seemed positively repellent: Lutheranism taught a strong respect for established political authority, whether in the new country or the old. And they tended to support antislavery and pro-equality causes too.

There were those who signed up with the South, to be sure, some of whom served at a relatively high level. The commander of the Confederate artillery at the Battle of Shiloh, in April 1862, for example, was Major J. H. Hallonquist, the son of Swedish immigrants; born in South Carolina, he was a graduate of West Point. Roger Hanson from Maryland commanded the Confederate right wing at Fort Donelson in February 1862, a defeat for the Confederates and the battle that made Ulysses S. Grant famous as "unconditional surrender" Grant. Other immigrants from Texas sided with the South as part of their identification with their new homes.

But other Scandinavian Texans did what they could to avoid serving on the secessionist side. For example, S. M. Swenson, owner of a highly successful cotton business based in Austin and a major figure in Texas's Swedish community, was well known for his antislavery views. When Texas seceded, Swenson chose to leave the state rather than support the Confederate cause. Others looked to the local Swedish consulate to help them evade military service.

In the case of Wisconsinites, the summons to rally to the Union proposed in the letter to Governor Randall got a passionate response.

"The government of our adopted country is in danger," Heg declared in an appeal in the fall of 1861. "That which we learned to love as freemen in our old Fatherland — our freedom — our government — our independence — is threatened with destruction. Is it not our duty as brave and intelligent citizens to extend our hands in defense of the cause of our country and of our own homes?"

Heg saw his proposed regiment as made up of not only Norwegians but all Scandinavians, including Swedish and Danish volunteers. "Shall we Scandinavians sit still and watch our American, German, and English-born fellow citizens fight for us without going to their aid?" he asked. "Come then, young Norsemen, and take part in defending our country's cause ... Let us band together and deliver untarnished to posterity the old honorable name of Norsemen."

The comparison with the Norsemen of history is striking, and fairly novel. Scandinavians back in the old country had only recently rediscovered their Viking heritage.* The feats of Nordic warriors had taken on a new romantic

---

* See Chapter 11.

glamour among their descendants, but particularly among Norwegians. Having only recently gained respect for their own national language, and lacking a nation of their own, Norwegians eagerly reached back to the world of longships and intrepid warriors as a source of pride and identity. For a man as conscious of his Norwegian cultural identity as Heg, the Vikings would have seemed fitting role models.

He was not alone. By the time Heg had penned this appeal in the Norwegian-language newspaper *Emigranten* on November 18, 1861, he already had more than six hundred men signed up to serve in the regiment. Heg, however, wanted at least a thousand. In October he made a swing across the upper Midwest that took him to Chicago; to Decorah, Iowa; and to Fillmore and Houston Counties in Minnesota. It must have been on this swing upcountry that he recruited my great-great-grandfather.

He was born Iver Jacobsen Sorlie on July 25, 1835, in Hadeland, Oppland, Norway. He had dropped the name Sorlie, which was the name of the farm his father had owned, when he immigrated to America in 1853, at age eighteen. Like so many of his countrymen, Iver Jacobsen made his way first to Wisconsin and Dane County, where he worked in the pineries, floating logs down the Wisconsin River to St. Louis, a leading market for white pine. He then moved to Decorah, Iowa, where he married, and then he and his bride set out for Freeborn County, Minnesota, in October 1859.

Their first home was a typical dugout in the side of a hill, with a front wall made of logs and a small window cut out on either side. The Sorlie bride and groom had brought with them a stove and a bedstead with woven rope tied across the frame to support a mattress stuffed with straw and cow hair. Two chests served as table and chair. Of her father's tools, his daughter remembered the broadax, "perhaps the most versatile tool ever created" — and a direct descendant of the Vikings' most characteristic weapon of war.

A little more than two years after arriving in Freeborn County, Iver enlisted in the Union army, on November 24, 1861; he was formally inducted on February 11, 1862. With him was a neighbor, Ellend Erickson, and the man who recruited them both, Mons Grainger, became captain of their company. For a married man, leaving his responsibilities to his family and the farm must have been hard. Certainly the $300 bonus he was paid for signing up assisted in easing any second thoughts — and would help support his wife and two small children while he was away.

The regiment he joined had assembled earlier, in December 1861, and was numbered as the Fifteenth Wisconsin. The regimental depot was Camp Randall, where some three thousand men were under canvas when Iver Jacobsen (as he was now calling himself) arrived. Eventually that number was winnowed down to nine hundred, with my great-great-grandfather joining Company K, most of whose men were from either Minnesota or Iowa.*

But either way, it was a solidly Norwegian regiment, with barely a smattering of Swedes and Danes, plus a few Germans and Anglo-Saxon Americans. Their names must have posed some challenges for the officers. There were, for example, five Ole Olsens in Company F alone. Company B had three Ole Andersens. In all, out of 900 men, no fewer than 128 had the first name Ole. There was a large contingent of recruits from Illinois, including seventy-two from Chicago, a fast-growing Scandinavian enclave. Two of the men from Chicago were father and son, Gabriel Somme Senior and Gabriel Somme Junior. The father would survive the war and a Confederate prison. The son would not.

Some recruits were virtually fresh off the boat. Bersven Nelson, for example, had arrived in La Crosse from Norway on July 16, 1861. Four months later he found himself a private in the Fifteenth Wisconsin.

Most men in the regiment spoke only a little English. It was understood from the beginning that their officers would be issuing commands in Norwegian (what the Swedes and Danes in the Fifteenth Wisconsin thought of this is not recorded). Iver and his comrades gave their companies names that resonated with traditions of the homeland. There were the St. Olaf's Rifles, commanded by a former Chicago police officer named Andrew Torkelson. There were also Odin's Rifles, the Norwegian Bear Hunters, Heg's Rifles, and Clausen's Guards. This last one was my great-great-grandfather's Company K; Captain Clausen was also the regimental chaplain.

Just because they were mostly Norwegians, of course, still didn't mean they all spoke the same language. They were more or less eight hundred men from

---

* Interestingly, officials in Minnesota, which had just become a state in 1862, were furious that Heg and other Wisconsin men were poaching on their turf to find recruits.

different, even remote parts of Norway; they found that often they couldn't understand one another, let alone the Swedes in their midst.

"God knows what kind of folks we've got in with," says a character in a novel based on the real-life experience of life in the Fifteenth Wisconsin. "They claim they're Norwegian, and they cuss in Norwegian, but I can't make head nor tail of what they say." The irony was that in this Nordic Tower of Babel, with its confusion of tongues, most recruits found that using their pidgin English, however imperfect, was the only way they could communicate.

The Fifteenth Wisconsin set out with great fanfare for St. Louis on March 2, 1862, from the Madison railroad station. When they reached Chicago, a Norwegian social club presented them with a regimental flag to accompany the Stars and Stripes, with the arms of America and Norway united, and the picture of a lion with an ax on a red field. The motto read FUR GOD OG VORT LAND (For God and Our Country).

They also had a regimental song, with English words but set to a Danish patriotic tune, of all things, called "Den Gang Jed Drog Afsted" ("The Brave Country Soldier"):

> I shall never forget that day
> When first I went away —
> Me lassie, dear, she would not stay!
> Of course she would not stay!
> You cannot go along,
> Through warfare, strife and throng,
> But if they don't kill me, dear, I shall return with song;
> I would, was there no danger, Sis, as life remain with thee,
> But all the girls of North, you see, rely just now on me,
> And therefore I will fight
> The rebels left and right. Hurrah! Hurrah! Hurrah!

The men of the Fifteenth Wisconsin were heading for three years in harm's way; they would serve across Mississippi, Kentucky, Tennessee, and Georgia, participating in most of the bloodiest battles of the western campaign. In fact, one out of every three men who left for St. Louis that day would be dead or disabled before it was over.

Like their other Norse neighbors, Swedish Americans enthusiastically supported the Union cause. One of the first communities to raise a volunteer unit was none other than Bishop Hill, and the first commissioned officer was the late Erik Jansson's own son, Eric. At age twenty-three he became a lieutenant in the Illinois Volunteers and would go on to fight at Shiloh and Pittsburgh Landing. It was during the siege of Corinth, in the spring of 1862, that he developed typhoid fever and had to be invalided out of the service.

Other Bishop Hill residents stepped up to take his place, men like Lieutenants Eric Forsse, Eric Bergland, and Andrew Warner: all three would serve together at the Battle of Shiloh. Other Illinois units had their share of Swedish heroes, while Illinois's famed "Western Sharpshooters," a multi-state militia regiment that served widely in the Civil War's western theater, was commanded by a Swedish immigrant, Colonel John W. Birge.

But the Swede who did the most for the Union cause was not a typical immigrant at all. The war found him in the United States almost by accident when his services were most needed — and the service he rendered changed the course of the war.

John Ericsson was an engineer. He was irascible, arrogant, imperious, and supremely gifted. Everyone who met him recognized that gift, even though working with him ran powerfully against the grain. No one has met a Swede yet who will back down when he or she knows the cause is right, and Ericsson was no exception. The cause, in this case, was not just the Union, but his own design of a ship like no other one afloat.

Ericsson was born in Värmland province, in a tiny village called Langbahnshyttan, the son of a mining engineer. John himself proved to be a natural engineer: at the age of five he devised a working windmill made from scraps from an old clock. When his father went to supervise work on the Gota Canal, which was being built to cross the width of Sweden, John went with him and soon absorbed an extensive knowledge of engineering and surveying. At the age of sixteen, he was leading a team of six hundred men and was responsible for drawing up the plans for the entire canal, as well as the machinery to run and maintain it.

Gifts like these were not going to go unnoticed. In 1820, John Ericsson found himself in the Swedish army and above the Arctic Circle, doing topographical surveys that were instantly recognized as masterpieces and stored safely away in the Royal Archives. But it was in the army that Ericsson discovered his true calling: working with steam engines. He was anxious to prove his theory that he could create a "dry" hot-air engine that would be more efficient than the current "wet" engines, which relied on steam as their source of power. His work on developing what he called the flame engine earned him the attention of a syndicate of London bankers, who invited him to leave Sweden for more prosperous shores. He quickly packed and set off for England. He would never see his native country again.

His plans for the dry engine proved fruitless in the original housing for the steam engine. He was frustrated by the fact that coal-fueled fires couldn't heat up his invention sufficiently to give it the power of a regular steam engine. But then John Ericsson's attention shifted once again, this time to shipbuilding. The British navy, and navies around the world, were undergoing a technological revolution; sails and wooden walls were giving way to steam-powered ships of iron. Ericsson decided he was just the man to take the lead in developing the two technologies — steam power and iron plating. They had come together perfectly to transform naval warfare in mid-century, just as the Nordic longship and the square sail had come together to turn the Vikings into the invincible lords of the seas in the Dark Ages. Iron-plated warships would have been ungainly and unmaneuverably slow without the power of steam. Likewise a ship's steam-power plant would have been a lethal fire hazard, especially in battle, without the protection of layers of iron plate.

The world's first iron-hulled battleship was the HMS *Warrior,* launched in 1860. Yet almost two and a half decades before, in 1837, Ericsson had designed a warship driven by steam power, armed with shell guns, and protected by iron plating. Ericsson's problem, then and later, was that he was a little too much ahead of his time. His plans ran afoul of the tradition-bound skeptics who still ran the Royal Navy. Even after his working prototype, the *Francis Ogden,* did a successful test run on the Thames using the world's first screw propeller —

the model for every screw propeller since — the navy brass ignored it. So he packed his bags once again and headed to the country where more and more of his fellow Swedes were likewise heading: the United States.

Ericsson's goal was not to settle there but to sell his innovative design. He did find a more receptive audience, especially in the federal government.* He joined forces with an American engineer, Robert Stockton, to build a prototype they dubbed the *Princeton,* in 1842. It truly represented a revolution in naval technology. Entirely built around the principle of the screw propeller, it incorporated a radical new steam-engine design that fit belowdecks, giving the *Princeton* a low silhouette in the water. It was also armed with a twelve-inch gun of Ericsson's own devising. Unfortunately, during a test the gun was carelessly loaded and blew up, killing eight. Stockton put the blame squarely on Ericsson, and the project died.

Failure again. Undeterred, Ericsson reached out to the French emperor, Napoleon III, with a completely new but fully developed design he dubbed the "sub-aquatic system of naval warfare." This was an entirely iron-clad vessel (the *Princeton* had been made of wood, complete with a set of sails) that rode low in the water and mounted a gun in a rotating turret: "a semi-globular turret of plate 6 inches thick revolving on a vertical column by means of steam power and appropriate gear work." It was, in fact, the exact ancestor of the USS *Monitor.*

The year was 1854, fully six years before the Royal Navy's *Warrior* came to define the state-of-the-art ironclad warship. Had Napoleon III been as bold and visionary as his prospective Swedish ship designer, it might have been the French, not the British, who "ruled the waves" for the rest of the nineteenth century.

Unfortunately for Ericsson, the French emperor's response was tepid; likewise the French naval experts were not enthused. It has to be said: Ericsson didn't help his cause. No one knows how much the serial rejection of Ericsson's designs had to do with sincere doubts about their overall soundness and how much it concerned the man's personality. Accepting his design would mean

---

* Ironically, one of his biggest champions would be the Alabama senator Stephen Mallory, later the secretary of the navy for the Confederacy.

months, even years, of working with someone who could be irascible and de-manding toward his admirers and obnoxious and dismissive toward any and all critics. Few had the courage to face that fate.

In any case, his "sub-aquatic system of naval warfare" went on the shelf, like Ericsson's other projects. Undaunted, he got on with other engineering work from his home and office on Beech Street in New York City (he had become a naturalized US citizen in 1848). Then one day in the summer of 1861, the Navy Department woke up to the news that the newly seceded Confederacy was working on a design for an ironclad warship using the hulk left by the USS *Merrimac,* which had been set afire when Rebels occupied the Norfolk ship-yards. The man pushing the Confederate project was none other than Erics-son's old advocate for the *Princeton* project, then a senator from Alabama but now the Confederacy's secretary of the navy, Stephen Mallory.

Fortunately, the Union's secretary of the navy was Ericsson's *other* cham-pion, Gideon Welles. Ericsson offered the department his radical new design, the all-armored sub-aquatic vessel. Welles had to tell his protégé that the navy board was inclined to reject it because they feared it might be unstable. "Un-stable?" Ericsson bellowed. "No craft that ever floated was more stable than she would be. That is one of her great merits!"

Whatever doubts lingered as to the ironclad's unorthodox design, Amer-ica's back was to the wall. Welles and President Lincoln had no options left. This was the first great arms race of the mechanical age, and the Swedish expa-triate John Ericsson was right in the middle of it.

Building the USS *Monitor* was the single most difficult project that American industry had ever undertaken. Almost all the contractors involved were based in New York City or elsewhere in New York State. Albany Iron Works, Rens-selaer Iron Works in Troy, Continental Iron Works in New York City, and Novelty Iron Works in Brooklyn, across the river from Continental, would be building the turret; Delamater Iron Works, a company owned by Ericsson's closest friend (probably his *only* friend), Cornelius Delamater, had the job of building the boilers and machinery for the main engine. The revolving tur-ret would hold two massive smoothbore guns, which had been designed by

Commander John Dahlgren, the son of the Swedish merchant Ulrick Dahlgren and Sweden's counsel in New York City.

After enlisting in the navy in 1826 as a midshipman, John Dahlgren grew steadily more fascinated with guns and cannons. By 1847 he had arrived at the Washington Navy Yard as an assistant to the master of naval ordnance. His moment of revelation came two years later, when a thirty-two-pounder gun exploded while being tested for accuracy, killing a gunner. Dahlgren realized it was time to develop a safer, more powerful naval cannon that could do the heavy fighting necessary for modern maritime warfare without posing a threat to its ship or its crew.

Guns were still loaded the way they had been since the Middle Ages, from the front end, or muzzle. There was always a risk that the extra gunpowder needed to hurl a large projectile farther and more accurately might also cause the gun's base, or breech, to explode: witness the tragic accident in the Navy Yard in 1849.

The answer, Dahlgren believed, was redesigning the gun with a smoother, more curved shape, to equalize the strain of the initial explosion needed to launch a shell by concentrating more of the weight of metal in the gun breech itself. By containing the expanding propellant gases safely, it would be possible to keep the gun from blowing apart, even with a massive powder charge. Because of their rounded contours and distinctive shape, Dahlgren guns were nicknamed "soda bottles."

This new way of thinking about ballistic science would revolutionize naval gunnery almost as thoroughly as Ericsson's ironclad revolutionized ship design. Dahlgren's design became standard issue in the US Navy just before the Civil War, and when Dahlgren's superior resigned from the Washington Navy Yard, President Lincoln wanted him named as successor. But since Dahlgren was only a commander, and command of the Navy Yard required the rank of captain or flag officer, Dahlgren was passed over.

But artillery based on his principles would dominate the war. Both at sea and on land, Dahlgren guns emerged as super-powerful siege artillery. Although John Dahlgren and his fellow Swedish American John Ericsson never had the chance to meet, Ericsson was counting on having two of Dahlgren's eleven-inch-diameter guns mounted in the turret of the *Monitor* (eight similar Dahlgren guns served on the Confederate ironclad *Merrimac,* which Ericsson's *Monitor* was destined to meet in combat).

The course not only of the Civil War, but of naval warfare in general, was beginning to turn, all because of two Swedish American engineers.

Incredibly, despite the difficulties of design (and the fact that no one could stand working with the designer), by New Year's Day, 1862, the *Monitor* was nearly finished. January 30 saw its official launch, as an enormous crowd gathered to stare — and not a few to guffaw.

Every Civil War buff knows about this vessel's appearance, eloquently described as a cheese box on a raft. The *Monitor* was so unlike any other large craft on the water that it was quickly dubbed Ericsson's Folly. Built with five-inch-thick armor plating wrapped around twenty-four-inch-thick wooden timbers, it had no masts, no sails, and no rigging. Ericsson had blithely ignored the navy's requirement that the *Monitor* be outfitted with all three. The ironclad ship had an absurdly low waterline, with less than a two-foot clearance. The crowd in Brooklyn Navy Yard fully expected it to sink the moment it left the slips. They were almost disappointed when this didn't occur, as the ship and its crew of forty-nine officers and enlisted men unceremoniously sailed from the mouth of the East River and headed out to sea.

What these observers couldn't see was all that was taking place below the waterline. There were no windows or portals, though curtains and drapes had been installed in the officers' cabins as if there were (Ericsson insisted on this detail). Captain John Worden's cabin had a private washstand and toilet. But how could the latter be flushed, positioned as it was beneath the waterline? Ericsson had an answer for that. The toilet emptied into a tube that ran to a portal in the lower hull. There, the interior end of the tube could be sealed as the exterior end was opened, so that the contents could be pumped into the sea. It was the first system for underwater toilets, and it was still in use on submarines as late as World War II. In fact, the *Monitor* contained no fewer than forty-seven patentable inventions. Ericsson's ironclad was a floating science lab, the equivalent of the Manhattan Project and the moon shot inside a single vessel. Through Ericsson's expertise, the Viking heart had found a new outlet in the science of engineering and mechanical design.

When the *Monitor* reached open sea, its chief engineer, Alban Stimers, had the men check everywhere for leaks. Apart from a couple minor ones on the deck and at the forward main hatch, the vessel was as dry as a bone. Captain Worden and the other officers sat down to a celebratory dinner that night, and Stimers wrote to Ericsson, "I never saw a vessel more buoyant or less shocked, than she was yesterday."

That was good because there was no time to waste. Rumors that the Confederate version of the ironclad warship was ready to go into action had proved true. As for the *Monitor*'s watertightness, Stimers's optimism was premature. The next day, the weather turned so bad and the seas so rough, even Captain Worden and the ship's surgeon became violently seasick. So much water poured in from around the turret that the ship was in danger of foundering. Seawater ran into the engine room, and the ship's twin steam engines sputtered and died. Only a bucket brigade involving most of the crew, and a discreet turn into calmer waters, managed to keep the *Monitor* from going under. The second night it nearly sank again, as rough water poured in from the anchor chain this time and threatened to again extinguish the engines.

But then calmer weather arrived, putting an end to the crew's troubles, and on Saturday morning they passed Maryland's eastern shore and headed for Cape Henry in Virginia. As they passed Fort Monroe, the last federal outpost, they could hear gunfire in the distance. What had been the *Merrimac,* now known as the CSS *Virginia,* was wreaking havoc with the wooden ships guarding Hampton Roads. When the *Monitor* arrived on the scene that night, the destruction of the US Navy was almost complete.

The most powerful warships in the fleet, the USS *Cumberland* and USS *Chesapeake,* had both been sunk. The USS *Congress* was ablaze, lighting up the night sky. The *Minnesota* had run aground, the *Roanoke* was immobilized, and the frigate USS *St. Lawrence* was also aground. The Confederate ship *Virginia* had taken a battering in the fight too but was clearly the master of the situation. It would be back in the morning to complete the devastation.

The *Monitor* tied up for the night, as flames from the *Congress* cast a red glow on the night sky. At midnight the fire reached the *Congress*'s magazine, and it blew up in a terrible roar.

In Washington, panic set in. There were frantic calls for the *Monitor* to come to Washington to protect the capital from the marauding *Virginia*. Secretary of War Edwin Stanton gloomily stared out his office window, expecting to see the Confederate ironclad steaming up the Potomac at any moment. But the *Monitor* stayed put and prepared for battle. Dawn on March 8 brought a thick fog, which dissipated at eight o'clock as the *Virginia* hove into view, looking like "a huge, half-submerged crocodile," according to one awed observer. Without a glance at the *Monitor,* it made straight for the stranded *Minnesota.*

Captain Worden had his men called to battle stations and set out to meet his Confederate counterpart, Captain Franklin Buchanan, in the naval duel of the century. For two hours, their Dahlgrens blasted away at one another, shots bouncing off iron plate and ricocheting far across the bay. Men inside the two ironclads learned not to lean against the bulkheads — even touching the iron plate when a shell hit could be fatal.

Captain Worden and quartermaster Peter Williams were at the wheel in the pilothouse. When the *Virginia* tried to ram its opponent, Williams was quick at the helm and maneuvered away. "He saw more of the *Virginia* than any of us," another sailor recalled; the Confederate ironclad sometimes slid by just a few feet away.

Then, after another pass, Williams found himself staring straight into the *Virginia*'s guns. "Captain, that is for us," he warned, just before the salvo came.

It hit the pilothouse with uncanny accuracy. Flying shards of metal severely wounded Worden. He slumped to the floor of the wheelhouse, bleeding and stunned. Williams coolly stayed at the wheel and managed to avoid another attempted ramming until, at last, the *Monitor*'s second-in-command reached the pilothouse and had his men take the unconscious captain below.

The two vessels continued to blast away without serious damage to either. At one point the *Virginia* ran aground but was able to sheer off. Largely unscathed but almost out of fuel and ammunition, the *Virginia* soon enough headed back to Hampton. As it steamed away, the *Monitor*'s crew raised a tremendous cheer. Although they did not know it then, they had just won one of the decisive battles of the Civil War.

The *Virginia* never saw action again. When federal troops later retook the Virginia peninsula and closed on the Norfolk docks, the ship's keepers had it destroyed. The *Monitor* didn't see action again either. Less than a year after the historic battle of the ironclads, it sank in a storm. But over the course of that year, a Swedish engineer had built the ship that saved the US Navy and its blockade of the Confederacy, doomed the South, and transformed naval warfare — all in the course of a morning and afternoon. And a Norwegian-born sailor had piloted the *Monitor* to victory and won the Congressional Medal of Honor.

The ship's quartermaster, Peter Williams, had been born in Norway in 1831. He had come to California to work as a civilian sailor before joining the US Navy for a three-year stint that ultimately took him aboard the *Monitor.* Beyond the fact that he won the Medal of Honor for his actions on March 9, we don't know much about him. A photograph after the battle shows him on deck, sitting apart from the other sailors and quietly reading the paper.

Strangely, he was not the only sailor from Norway with the name Williams to win the Medal of Honor during the War Between the States. So did Augustus Williams, born in 1842, for his actions during the assault on Fort Fisher in 1864. In fact, six of the eight Norwegian-born men who won the medal in that war were sailors: proof (if proof was needed) that no one knows how to wage a war at sea quite like a Norwegian.

Meanwhile, as the *Monitor* and Peter Williams were recovering from their ordeal, other Norwegians were on the move.

The Fifteenth Wisconsin's first active posting was a tiny island in the Mississippi River on Illinois's southern tip, some fifty miles south of Cairo. Designated Island No. 10, it was barely two hundred acres in size, but Confederate guns on the island had a commanding position from which to block river traffic on the Mississippi. Shortly after Union troops laid siege to the island in early April, however, the Confederates pulled out. What the Wisconsinites discovered when they overran the former Rebel camp, and rounded up some Confederate stragglers, was that Island No. 10 was a morass of disease.

It is estimated that two-thirds of the 600,000 Americans who perished in the Civil War died from disease rather than a cannonball or a bullet. On Island No. 10 the Fifteenth Wisconsin lost exactly one man through enemy action, whereas forty-two died of one illness or another — typhus, typhoid fever, chronic diarrhea, tuberculosis, or streptococcal infections, to mention a few. Typhoid and measles were particularly deadly. When the regiment was ordered to leave the island and cross over to Kentucky at the beginning of June, it had to leave nearly seventy-five men behind in one state of ill-health or another.

Somehow, Colonel Heg had managed to stay healthy during their stay on Island No. 10. His second-in-command, Major Reese, had fallen ill and was sent home. Heg and the Fifteenth Wisconsin advanced steadily through Kentucky toward Nashville, the main junction of Confederate forces in that theater. At Bowling Green, Colonel Heg met with their new commanding officer, General Rosecrans: "He always calls me Heck," the colonel confided to his wife in a letter. This time he did get struck down with fever, and it was several weeks before he was fit to travel. He rejoined his campaign at the camp near Nashville in the first days of December 1862. On the eleventh he was in a reflective mood as he wrote a letter to his wife back in Wisconsin. It was the day after their wedding anniversary.

"Eleven years ago," he wrote, "in the old log house — it does not seem so very long to me — how many changes since then. I think we have spent those eleven years as happily as most people — 14 years more, and we can have our silver wedding."

He sent another letter on Christmas Eve. His men were advancing on Confederate positions at Nolensville. At Knob Gap there was a sharp battle, as Heg put it. He had personally led the Fifteenth Wisconsin in an uphill charge on a Rebel battery, seizing a cannon, a caisson, and a slew of prisoners and horses — all without losing a single man. "I hope you will not feel uneasy if you do not hear from me for a few days," he wrote. He had a premonition that a serious battle was very close.

He was right. Less than a week later, on the morning of December 30, the regiment advanced on Rebel positions near Murfreesboro, Tennessee, at a stream known as Stones River. Heg sent Company E forward as skirmishers; at around noon they ran into the enemy.

When the rest of the Fifteenth caught up, Colonel Heg found that Company E's commander, Captain Ingmundson, had been killed, and one of his men wounded. The regiment pressed forward through a dense cedar thicket.

Under a severe fire of grapeshot and shell, Colonel Heg found the enemy in heavy force behind a rail fence near the house of Mrs. William Smith.

At first Heg's men had stood and fought "under the heaviest fire I ever saw," Heg later wrote. But when the regiment to their right panicked and fled, the Norwegians had no choice but to fall back. In addition to the death of Captain Ingmundson, two other captains had been wounded; Heg's horse had been shot out from under him.

These Norsemen were meeting the enemy in a life-or-death struggle, just as Norsemen had in the ancient past, only this time fighting not with sword and battle-ax but with rifles and cannon and minié balls. It would be fascinating to know whether the parallel crossed their minds. It was a moment of supreme testing for the Viking heart in America. To Heg's lasting pride, his men passed it.

They gave "two solid volleys as we retreated," Heg later informed his wife, even as officers and comrades were falling all around them. One of those who fell was "Gunder Hanson of [Company] C, son of the old man at Oles Store"; another was one of their neighbors from Waterford. But "our dead and wounded," he reassured her, "we got off to a House nearby, and they were well taken care of."

That night the survivors of the Fifteenth Wisconsin had to make camp on the battlefield, with no fires, and surrounded by the cries of the wounded. Heg and his men lay awake, wondering what would happen the next day. "It was a cold, frosty night," he wrote, "and as I walked along my little regiment, I could not help but think how little the people at home know of the suffering of the soldier."

One of those sufferers, as it happens, was my great-great-grandfather Oscar Jacobsen, who was lying wounded several hundred yards away. He had been hit in the leg during the retreat, and though Confederates took many of the wounded as prisoners, he had managed to avoid capture. Instead he lay on the field for three days while the battle raged back and forth around him. At one point he stopped some passing Rebel soldiers to beg for food. "Don't you know we have nothing to eat ourselves?" they angrily told him. They did give him some water and then went back to the fighting.

The battle was just getting started. On the last day of 1862, the dawn came up after a wet night of wind and rain. Heg and his men were just making coffee when they began to hear the staccato sound of gunfire from the southwest. Then came the sound of cannon fire, followed by the high-pitched bark known as the Rebel yell. The Confederate army under General Braxton Bragg was launching a surprise attack. Within minutes the Union general Alexander McCook's entire corps collapsed, as troops, wagons, and horses streamed toward the rear.

It was for the men of the Fifteenth Wisconsin to join a fight even fiercer than that of the previous day. "Lt. Col. McKee fell here — shot through the head — Lt. Tanberg was wounded, Lt. Brown of Co. E. also, and both taken prisoner." At one point Heg's Norsemen had to retreat across an open field "while the rebels poured into us an awful volley of musket balls." In the end "what men I had left, about 100 — I again rallied on the other side of the field, and in company with the rest of the Brigade, retreated toward the Murfreesboro Turnpike where we knew old Rosy [General Rosecrans] was waiting with the rest of the Army."

There the Army of the Cumberland managed to make a stand while "the Rebels came pouring along shouting like Indians . . . It is impossible for me to describe the slaughter they met." The Union troops finally held, at the crucial point known as Round Forest. They beat back one desperate Confederate attack after another until nightfall. Heg had stood behind a small tree, giving orders to his men, as bullets smacked time after time into the tree trunk. In the morning he counted no fewer than five minié balls wedged into the tree, in addition to the one that had passed through his coat without striking him.

The next day both sides were too exhausted to renew the fight. Over the next couple of days, January 2 and 3, there were sporadic clashes. It was not until January 4 that Rosecrans, Heg, and his men finally drove the Rebels back — they had won the Battle of Stones River, the largest the Army of the Cumberland had ever fought. But the losses were heavy for all units, including the Fifteenth Wisconsin: eighty-five killed or wounded and thirty-four missing. Heg's second-in-command was dead. Three of his company commanders were wounded.

As for Iver Jacobsen, friendly troops had found him at last and sent to the

A reunion of the Fifteenth Wisconsin Regiment, 1880. Note the Norwegian flag, far right. Wisconsin Historical Society

hospital in Nashville. Doctors debated whether to amputate his leg. Someone in the next cot cried out, "Die with your leg on!" So my great-great-grandfather refused the operation. After three months recovering in Nashville, and another three months in New Albany, he was invalided out of the army in May 1863. He had done his duty to his new country. The future would ultimately take him from Minnesota to the Dakota Territory, where other Scandinavians would make new lives for themselves when the guns fell silent.

• • •

Iver Jacobsen Sorlie was mustered out on May 13, 1863. Two weeks earlier his former commanding officer, Hans Christian Heg, was promoted to the command of the Third Brigade of the First Division of the Army of the Cumberland: the Wisconsin Fifteenth transferred over with him. That summer was one of constant maneuvering farther south (in August Heg had the honor of leading the first federal troops to cross the Tennessee River) until Union and Confederate forces met along a sluggish stream in northern Georgia called the Chickamauga in the third week of September.

"The rebels are in our front and we may have to fight him a Battle," he wrote to his wife, in his last letter. "If we do it will apt to be a big one." He added, to reassure her, "I shall use all the caution and courage I am capable of and leave the rest to take care of itself."

He was right about the battle. In human lives, Chickamauga was the second-costliest battle in a very costly civil war: only Gettysburg saw more dead and wounded. Sadly, one of those sixteen thousand Union casualties was Colonel Hans Christian Heg. The hero of the Fifteenth Wisconsin was struck down by a sniper's bullet on the first day of the two-day battle, not far from where his old regiment was fighting for its life. That night, some of his former officers visited him at the field hospital, where he was slowly dying.

"I was glad the Fifteenth held their places like men and did their duty to the last," he told his old regiment's new commanding officer, Lieutenant Colonel Ole Johnson. "Tell my boys of the Fifteenth that I kept myself where I was needed and that I knew they didn't need me." He died shortly before noon on September 20, as the battle was still raging on. His last words: "I have given my life in a just cause."

Thousands of Norwegian, Swedish, and Danish volunteers on the Union side, and their families, would have agreed. In the War Between the States, their newly adopted country demanded they give their "last full measure" in devotion to the cause of freedom. Like Hans Heg and my great-great-grandfather, they had met the test with full honors.

Heg's leadership and heroism earned him a statue on the grounds of Wisconsin's state capitol and fame among Norwegian Americans to this day. All the same, it may have been a Swede who had the most extraordinary career for a Scandinavian American soldier in the Civil War. He was Charles John Stolbrand, born in Kristianstad in southern Sweden in 1821. His original surname was Stalbrand, meaning "fiery steel." It turned out to be appropriate.

He had originally served in the Swedish artillery, rising quickly from private to sergeant. He immigrated to America in 1851 with his wife, Carolina Pettersson, the daughter of another sergeant in the same Swedish regiment. After reaching Chicago and landing a job in the Cook County Recorder's Office, he became an enthusiastic Lincoln supporter during the 1860 presidential campaign. When war with the South broke out, he immediately volunteered and became one of the most sought-after and prized artillery officers in the Union army. He fought at Vicksburg and later was captured by the Confederates, in May 1864. As a POW, Stolbrand found himself imprisoned in the infamous Andersonville Prison in Georgia — a certain death sentence for thousands of federal prisoners, including forty-nine soldiers from my great-great-grandfather's Fifteenth Wisconsin.

Incredibly, after two unsuccessful attempts at escape, Stolbrand managed to break out of Andersonville and found his way back to his unit. He served the remainder of the war in Beaufort, South Carolina — "a braver man than General Stolbrand could not be found in the entire army," General William T. Sherman once declared. After the war Stolbrand purchased a plantation, formerly worked by slaves, outside Beaufort and became one of South Carolina's most prominent politicians of the Reconstruction era. He helped draft the state constitution that gave the vote to former slaves, and he was a delegate to the Republican National Convention in Chicago that nominated his former commander, Ulysses S. Grant, for the presidential ticket in 1868.

Stolbrand, Hans Heg, Medal of Honor winner able-bodied seaman Williams, and thousands of other Scandinavian Americans had helped save their adopted country from being permanently torn asunder. At least two, John Ericsson and John Dahlgren, provided essential tools that enabled the US government to win the war. In Stolbrand's case, we can safely say that he helped put South Carolina, and America, back together, on the basis of freedom and justice.

But what kind of America would emerge in the war's aftermath? This question had haunted Abraham Lincoln from almost the first day of the conflict. When it was finally over and the South was defeated, Lincoln had a meeting with his cabinet. He told them about a dream he had just had — the same one he had experienced just before the most important events of the war, from the firing on Fort Sumter and Stones River to the Battle of Gettysburg and the capture of Atlanta. As the president described the details, Navy Secretary Gideon Welles, the man who had brought on John Ericsson to build the *Monitor*, wrote it down:

"Lincoln said the dream had to do with my department," Welles wrote, meaning "it related to the water; he seemed to be in a singular, indescribable vessel . . . and that he was moving rapidly toward a dark and indefinite shore." The other cabinet members expressed puzzlement; no one seemed to have a clue about what the dream meant. If Lincoln did, he never told anyone. That night, in fact, he attended the performance of *The American Cousin* at Ford's theater and was shot dead.

What kind of vessel did Lincoln see in his dream? He wouldn't, or couldn't, say. Ericsson's *Monitor*, perhaps? Perhaps the ships that would bring floods of European immigrants to the United States in the decades after the Civil War, including Scandinavians?

Perhaps even the Viking longship that made that first journey "to a dark and indefinite shore" in America many centuries before?

We do not know what the reconstructed United States might have looked like if Lincoln had lived. What we *do* know — and what the Scandinavian veterans of the war could not begin to guess — was that a multitude of vessels from their "old countries" would soon be coming to American shores, to the rededicated Land of Liberty.

11

"More Wonderful Than Riches"

American Fever and the Great Migration

Farewell, O Mother Svea, now must I sail the sea.
Thank you from my heart because you fostered me.
Of bread you gave so little, it could not life uphold
— although to many others you gave wealth manifold.

— Swedish emigrant ballad, about 1900

THE 1850S HAD been the great decade of Norwegian immigration to America. Then in 1867 and again in 1869, tens of thousands of Swedes sailed across the Atlantic with the same destination — over 32,000 in 1869 alone. A decade or so later a wave of cheap grain from America — ironically, much of it from farms run by Norwegian immigrants — placed still more pressure on a Swedish agriculture that could no longer feed its own people. This detonated an explosion of immigration that would continue almost without interruption from the late 1860s to the eve of World War I. Floods of Norwegians and Danes expanded the influx. After peaking at 88,000 in 1881–90, the Swedish Great Migration swelled again to 65,000 in 1900–1910.

In terms of numbers, the Norwegian Great Migration was the largest. Between 1866 and 1879 Norwegian immigration to America amounted to

137,954 people. That number more than doubled over the next sixteen years, 1880–96, to 279,920 people. In 1882 alone, almost 30,000 Norwegians left home for America — a number never equaled before or since. This surge dwindled over the next three years, to a total of only 15,919. But the numbers rose again in 1900 to 10,786. Until the outbreak of World War I, the annual total averaged 14,332 people. The second peak year came in 1903, with over 25,000 Norwegians heading for the far Atlantic shore. By 1910 America was home to more than 400,000 Norwegian immigrants.

Danish immigration surged as well, from 31,770 in 1871–80 to almost triple that number over the next decade: 88,132 people between 1881 and 1890. The next two decades would bring another 115,516 Danes to American shores.

After the Great War, Norwegian immigration continued unabated until the 1920s, reaching a grand total of 888,520 people. In sheer numbers, their demographic impact doesn't compare to that of Ireland or Italy or eastern Europe. But in terms of cultural impact, Norwegians and other Scandinavians were hitting well above their weight. They were, in many ways, the model immigrant population, prime ingredients for the great American melting pot, yet they did not completely lose their ethnic character or their loyalties to the world that had made them.

The Great Migration also changed the Scandinavian profile in the American population. These new immigrants tended to be younger, for starters. Of the 172,000 Danes who arrived between 1865 and 1900, 55 percent were between fifteen and twenty-five years of age. They tended to be single rather than unmarried, and more urban in their orientation than their predecessors had been. In 1865, for example, less than one-fifth of Norwegian immigrants were settled in towns. In 1900, that percentage grew to more than a third.

On arrival, the newcomers found that a welcome had been prepared for them by the hardy, even heroic, Scandinavians who had come before them. In Iowa (where, after leaving Norway, my grandmother stopped to live with cousins in the town of Lansing), Minnesota, Wisconsin, northern Illinois and southern Michigan, and across the Dakotas; in Chicago, Minneapolis, Detroit, and Milwaukee — they found communities structured around familiar churches and religious creeds, with schools and colleges founded by Scandinavians and catering to their particular educational needs, with newspapers in their national languages (Scandinavia's boom in elementary education in the later nineteenth century meant that nearly every new immigrant was able to read and write), and a growing network of fellow immigrants who had carved out reasonably successful lives for themselves and their families in America.

Why did they come in such numbers in those years? The search for economic opportunity was a driving force, of course. But there was also a thirst to escape from entrenched social systems back home that increasingly seemed stagnant and stultifying, especially compared to the freedom of the wide-open spaces of America.

For Danes, in particular, there were also the traumas of the 1864 war over Slesvig and Holstein, and its brutal aftermath that had cost the country no less than 40 percent of its population.* Tens of thousands of Danes fled to escape domination by Prussia and Germany, and many of them chose a transatlantic exit in the direction of America. According to one estimate, some fifty thousand left Slesvig in those years. The majority headed to the New World.

For Swedes and Norwegians, but also for many Danes, it was also hard to resist the pull of the United States they had heard about in letters from family and friends, and ruminated about and romanticized in their imagination over long winter evenings. "All through the winter I helped mother with the preparations," one Norwegian woman remembered. "In the evening darkness my brother and I often sat and built air castles, dreaming of what we should do when we got to America."

America came to represent a shining city on a hill, the home of new kinds of freedoms, not just religious but also political and social. On January 6, 1845, a group of eighty Norwegians had written an open letter to the Norwegian-language newspaper *Morgenbladet,* which became famous as the "Muskego Manifesto." It explained why they had moved to America, despite the difficulties and "lack of the most essential necessities of life." It read:

> We harbor no hopes of acquiring wealth, but we live under a liberal government in a fertile land, where freedom and equality prevail in religious as well as civil affairs, and without any special permission we

---

* See Chapter 14.

can enter almost any profession and make an honest living; this we consider to be more wonderful than riches, for by diligence and industry we can look forward to an adequate income, *and we thus have no reason to regret our decision to move here.*

That feeling of freedom had intensified after the Civil War put a seal on that promise by ending the hateful institution of slavery. But on both sides of the Atlantic, there was also a new awareness of a special relationship between America and Scandinavia going back to the very first Scandinavian who had come to North America's shore nine centuries earlier: Leif Erikson.

This revelation was sparked by, of all things, an unassuming book: Rasmus Björn Anderson's *America Not Discovered by Columbus.* Anderson was a less than outstanding writer and historian, and large parts of the book itself were deeply misleading. But with one simple thesis, Anderson had spun a historical thread that directly connected the world of Scandinavian American immigrants to their glorious Viking past.

Anderson was born in 1846 on a farm in the Norwegian settlement of Koshkonong in southern Wisconsin. His father and mother had immigrated to America during the heroic years of the 1830s, settling first in the Fox River Valley, which had attracted many Norwegian immigrants, before building a farm on the prairie at Koshkonong — soon to become the biggest and most prosperous Norwegian settlement in the pre–Civil War era.

The family managed to scrape together enough funds to send their son to brand-new Luther College, founded by Norwegians in Decorah, Iowa; it had been created in 1863, in the shadow of the War Between the States. Anderson proved to be a handful, intellectually speaking. Constantly quarreling with his professors, he was finally expelled from the college. He also took up the cause of the breakaway Norwegian Evangelical Lutheran Church, or Norwegian Synod, which had separated from the prevailing Lutheran Synod in 1853 over the issue of slavery (as it happened, the presiding firebrand in the Norwegian Synod was Pastor C. L. Clausen, later the chaplain of the Fifteenth Wisconsin and my great-great-grandfather's company commander).

None of this, however, caused Anderson to swerve from his intellectual track; he was determined to understand the deep Nordic roots of American freedom. He was nineteen and still in college when the Civil War ended. Although he was not able to complete his last year, he pushed on to the University of Wisconsin after a stint of teaching at Albion College. It was in Wisconsin that his fierce energy and persistence finally forced the faculty to concede to his demand for a Scandinavian studies curriculum, including Norwegian, Icelandic, and other Norse languages as well as Scandinavian culture and history, including the history of the Vikings.

Out of this effort came Anderson's first significant work, *Norse Mythology*. Published under Anderson's name as author in 1875, *Norse Mythology* was virtually a textbook (or lawsuit) exercise in plagiarism. Fully 80 percent of the text was a direct translation of a work in Danish by a professor at the University of Copenhagen, N. M. Peterson. The plagiarism revealed Anderson's methods as a scholar, which left something to be desired, but as a publicist for Nordic myth and its superiority over its Greek and Roman counterparts, he was without equal. He asserted that "the myth is the oldest form of truth" and that the Nordic people "have been forever a chaste race we abhor the loathsome nudity of Greek art." These claims were as much Peterson's in Danish as Anderson's in English—and just as wide of the historical mark. But Anderson's book made its point to English-reading audiences: the world of the Vikings was richer and more profound in its understanding of the cosmos and the human condition than most people had hitherto realized.

Anderson took over as editor of a Norwegian-language newspaper, *Amerika,* which he published for twenty-two years. President Grover Cleveland later appointed him ambassador to Denmark. But nothing Rasmus Björn Anderson wrote or did compared with the impact of his 1874 tract, *America Not Discovered by Columbus.*

Originally this work was meant to raise funds for a statue of Leif Erikson, a scheme concocted by Anderson and another master publicist and impresario —and supremely gifted violinist—Norway's favorite musical son, Ole Bull. The two had met in the late 1860s when Anderson was still at Albion College; Bull had written an invocation to the Norwegian students studying at Albion College that had concluded with these words: "Live for truth and freedom!" Anderson and Bull got together again on Anderson's second trip to Norway, in 1873, where they conceived the idea of erecting a statue of Erikson on the campus of the University of Wisconsin in Madison.

Interest in the Vikings in Norway was exploding, and the discovery of the Gokstad boat in 1880 would further intensify it. Norwegians were coming to realize that the Norsemen weren't just remote ancestors, shrouded in myth and legend; they endured as a tangible presence, shedding a glorious light on Norway's present and future. Anderson made it his mission to beam that light on Norwegians in America.

At the first fundraising concert, in Bergen, Edvard Grieg was present while Bull performed. Bull's tour made headlines, but it raised little money. In the end, the plan to erect a statue in Wisconsin sputtered and died, to Anderson's profound disappointment. Bull didn't give up, though. In 1876 he founded a committee based in Boston to take up a similar project. Made up of luminaries such as James Russell Lowell, Oliver Wendell Holmes, and Henry Wadsworth Longfellow, the committee soon found the funds to raise a statue to the Viking hero on Commonwealth Avenue.

But out of the ashes of Anderson's failed statue project in Wisconsin came the work that would make him, and Leif Erikson, famous. *America Not Discovered by Columbus* began by explaining its objective: "to present the reader with a brief account of the discovery of early voyages to and settlements in the Western Continent by the Norsemen, and to prove that Columbus must have had knowledge of this discovery by the Norsemen before he started to find America . . ." The text then recited the evidence of the Viking voyages not only from the Norse sagas, which were undergoing a renaissance of their own back home,* but also from medieval chroniclers like Adam of Bremen. It also presented what Anderson insisted was hard physical evidence of the Norse discovery of America, proof that Leif Erikson ought to be celebrated as "the first white man who turned the bow of his ship to the west for the purpose of finding America." Anderson added:

Let us remember his brother, THORVALD ERIKSON, the first European and the first Christian who was buried beneath Ameri-

---

* See Chapter 14.

can soil! Let us not forget THORFINN and GUDRID, who established the first European colony in New England! Nor their little son, SNORRE, the first man of European blood whose birthplace was in the New World!

The names and attributions were, of course, drawn from *The Saga of the Greenlanders* and *The Saga of Erik the Red;* they were by no means original to Rasmus Anderson. In fact, several authors, including American scholars, had written on the Norsemen in America based on what they found in the sagas. The number of editions of *The Discovery of America by the Northmen,* an 1839 lecture by the American writer Ashbel Davis, had grown in a single decade to as many as twenty-one.

Anderson, however, gave the story a specifically Norwegian focus and an expressly Norwegian hero in Erikson. Some of his claims regarding physical signs of the Viking presence in North America did get him into trouble. He cited as evidence, for example, the so-called Dighton Rock, a forty-ton boulder covered with strange petroglyphs that was found in a Massachusetts riverbed, and the Newport Tower, an old round tower built of stone in Newport, Rhode Island, which some supposed to have its origin in pre-Columbian times (in truth, it was the foundation of a seventeenth-century windmill built by the English). Then there were the human remains found at Fall River, Massachusetts, which some self-declared experts attributed to a Viking chieftain.

Anderson ignored the fact that all this so-called physical proof had been debunked decades earlier. He also further hurt his cause by trying to portray Christopher Columbus as a fraud, arguing that the Italian sailor had denied knowing what Anderson insisted must have been obvious: Norsemen had arrived in the New World nearly five centuries ahead of him — on the coast of Massachusetts no less, and almost within shouting distance of Plymouth Rock.

Despite its many faults, however, Anderson's account was convincing enough to enable Ole Bull to persuade intelligent Bostonians that a statue to Leif Erikson in the middle of their city was historically fitting and proper. Above all, *America Not Discovered by Columbus* presented the story to the audience that mattered most: the Norwegian immigrants. Among them, the book was a total sensation. When Anderson said (quoting Ashbel Davis), "Let us praise Leif Erikson for his courage, let us applaud him for his zeal, let us respect him for his motives, for he was anxious to enlarge the boundaries of knowledge, not to conquer or despoil other peoples," his readers were willing to believe it.

Anderson's scholarship was sloppy. His prose style was lamentable, and his personality vainglorious. But his book revealed to his fellow Norwegian Americans that their connection with their new home was far more intimate than previously imagined. Scandinavians and America were a natural fit, it seemed. The Viking past put the living present in a new light. No wonder my Norwegian grandfather kept a water-stained copy of *America Not Discovered by Columbus* by the fireplace at his house on Eagle Lake, Minnesota.

"The spirit of the Vikings," Anderson concluded, "still survives in the bosoms of Englishmen, Americans, and Norsemen, extending their commerce, taking bold positions against tyranny, and producing wonderful internal improvements in these countries." And when Anderson wrote (the words, characteristically, were Davis's, not his own) that Erikson had "reached the wished-for land," his fellow Norwegian immigrants had to feel that Erikson's voyage had been more than a little like their own: a journey into the unknown, toward a better life and a better understanding of the world and themselves:

> *Where now the western sun,*
> *O'er fields and floods,*
> *O'er every living soul*
> *Diffuseth glad repose.*

Vikings like Leif Erikson had made their voyages in longships, of course. The voyages of Norwegians, Swedes, and Danes in the 1840s and 1850s, before steamships took over the transatlantic crossing, were scarcely much safer. The long weeks, sometimes months, at sea; the miserable food, once whatever stores passengers had brought with them had run out; the unavoidable filth and disease; and then disembarkment into a strange land where people spoke a different language. If they could observe such moments, those Viking forebears certainly would have nodded in sympathy and said, "Eg skill pad!" ("I get it," in Icelandic).

Then, in the late 1860s, the first steamships began making regular trips from Europe to America, trimming weeks off the journey. By 1875 every ship carrying passengers from a Norwegian port was a steamship. The routes from Scandinavia were still not direct. Most Swedes and Norwegians wound up crossing the North Sea for ports in England, such as Southampton or Liverpool, from which ships bound for America regularly sailed. Danes had the option of leaving from German ports, particularly Hamburg, from which the Hamburg Line carried literally tens of thousands of immigrants, including Scandinavians, Polish and Russian Jews, and others from eastern Europe.

A major British or German steamship line would transport the would-be immigrant to America within two or three weeks — a trip that used to take sixteen. Prices fell, as well. As the journey became shorter and cheaper, young people, even single young girls, were willing to brave it on their own. My grandmother Anna Carlson was eighteen and living in Ulefoss, Norway, when her brother unexpectedly sent her a steamship ticket so that she could stay with cousins in Lansing, Iowa, before joining him further west. She hadn't planned to go to America. But, as she told me, she felt she had no choice. Besides, a transatlantic trip that would have been considered almost unimaginably dangerous two or three decades before now seemed within the bounds of reason.

Others would save up for a ticket, perhaps receiving an advance from an American employer against the next year's wages. But because of the higher wages in America, for those already there, it was less burdensome to purchase a ticket for someone in the old country. That was the case for Anna Carlson's brother.

By the 1890s a plethora of expert advice had been published on how to immigrate. Lists of do's and don'ts for the aspiring traveler were popular. A very early expert, the Norwegian author Ole Rynning, insisted that the best time to go was in early spring, so that immigrants would arrive in time to plant buckwheat (at the end of June), turnips (early July), and potatoes. According to the scholar Theodore Blegen, "The result was that the spring months of March, April, and May became the gala season for emigration" out of Norway.

One of the most popular Danish handbooks was Holger Rosenberg's *100 nyttige Raad for Udvandrere* (*100 Pieces of Advice for Emigrants*), published in Copenhagen in 1911. The advice started with three basics:

1. If you have decided to emigrate, don't wait a minute before learning a little English;
2. Choose your travel route with care and buy a ticket directly to your destination;
3. Purchase a ticket for the cheapest class of travel and order it in good time.

Then Rosenberg moved on to a review of current immigration laws:

The Americans have tightened up their immigration law [in 1907]. Make sure, therefore, that you fulfill the following requirements for even getting into the country. Admission is refused to:

i. Idiots and persons with mental and physical deficiencies;
ii. Persons suffering from serious or dangerously contagious diseases;
iii. Persons convicted of disreputable acts;
iv. Polygamists [by now Mormons had changed their laws];
v. Except for personal servants, persons who report upon disembarkation that they have a written or oral promise of work;
vi. Persons who are recipients of alms, who are unable to work, or deemed to become a burden to the government, especially those who are over 60, crippled, blind, deaf and dumb, unmarried pregnant women, mothers with illegitimate children, single women traveling along with minor children, and children traveling alone under the age of 16.

The author pointed out that the law did allow section v immigrants to enter the country if "they can show notarized documentary evidence from close relatives in the U.S. that these have the ability and desire to receive and support them." And the ban on people with oral or written promises of work makes sense because the 1907 immigrant law aimed to reduce contract labor arrangements, which flooded the job market with part-time foreign workers.

Rosenberg also had this homey tip for what to do just before the trip: "A Danish newspaper will be comforting over there; it will be a faithful connection with your home, and it can be sent to you everywhere. Subscribe to one before you leave."

His shrewdest advice concerned how to save money and avoid trouble once in America:

58. Time is expensive in the U.S. and the cities are far too large that it can pay to walk from one place to another. Use the streetcars.
59. Don't waste money on cabs and automobiles.
60. Even if you find an American street to be a hellaciously noisy place, don't lose your head. Take it easy, and learn to protect your nerves.
61. Police officers in general are your good friends. Turn to one if there is anything you are having trouble with.
62. Another American institution that is most helpful is the "drug-store." If you need something, go there. You can get headache powders, matches, stamps and writing paper, the latest sensational novel, and the most wondrous patent medicines.
63. If you need a toilet, go to the hotels. They are free.

Rosenberg offered a few points of etiquette to help newcomers fit into American society. These touched on the key feature of this new country, namely, its celebration of individual freedom:

In few places on earth does one have as much freedom as in the U.S. to do exactly what one wants to do. But even here there are certain rules of etiquette which should not be transgressed. Here are the most important ones: Don't stick your nose in other people's business; don't push between two people walking together on the street; when

walking with a lady, walk between her and the curb; take your hat off
indoors if a lady is present; otherwise, it can stay pasted to your head.

Rosenberg's last words concerned the homeland: "Travel home to old
Denmark when you have increased your knowledge and bank account, and let
all of this be useful to your motherland. Another young person can then travel
over the Atlantic in your place."

It was significant advice. No Scandinavian expected to be the last one to
leave for America. Although Swedish authorities began to worry about the
"emigration drain" to America as early as the 1880s,* none could imagine that
the tide would cease anytime soon, so long as conditions remained as harsh
as they were at home, and so long as America was willing to welcome all who
sought its shores.

Holger Rosenberg also had a recommendation for the voyage out: "Dress
warmly for your journey, even if it's mid-summer. On the ocean it is cold in
the evenings and even during the daytime." He added, "Make the ocean trip a
pleasure trip. You yourself are partly responsible for this." Such words would
have been wasted in the days of the "coffin ships," in the 1840s and '50s. But a
quarter of a century later, the Atlantic crossing offered a very different experience, even for a passenger in steerage. For the average Norwegian peasant leaving Liverpool for New York or Quebec, a liner could seem as fine as a palace.

The first thing the immigrants encountered on the ship to America was
a veritable Tower of Babel. Swedish, Norwegian, Danish, and Finnish, including the many country dialects of each, plus Russian, Polish, Yiddish, German, Gaelic, and English swirled together in third class and steerage, where
families silently ate and prayed together, children crawled and cried, and
men and women quarreled; even the occasional fistfight broke out. But also
in third class and steerage, compatriots bonded and the passengers enjoyed
music (Norwegian Hardanger fiddles and Danish and German accordions)
and games, endless games, to while away the days and weeks.

In the old days, immigrants climbed aboard with as much baggage as they

---

* See Chapter 14.

could manage, including trunks of tools and also food, the only sustenance they would have during the trip. Steamship passengers were free to travel with much less, since their ticket entitled them to meals and medical service if needed. The food provided by the liner was often monotonous, but it lasted for the entire voyage. For breakfast, there would be coffee with condensed milk, bread, and Danish butter. Dinner consisted of soup with boiled meat for the first day, then sailors' fare for the rest of the trip: salted fish or pork and dried peas and beans. There was cheese, sausage, and pickled herring for snacks.

For those traveling on the Hamburg Line with Jews coming from eastern Europe, there was a special treat. Many Jewish families equipped themselves with packets of ground beef, which they flattened into patties for quick frying on a small stove or fire, then consumed between two slices of bread. The Hamburg Line gave its name to this ready-made meal. Danish and Norwegian immigrants on shipboard were witnessing the birth of the hamburger.

Despite all of the steamboat's advances in comfort, sanitation remained a problem. Seasickness struck young and old alike, and the mess could accumulate in corners and on floors, making life miserable. The Swedish parents of the future nuclear scientist Glen Seaborg had immigrated in 1867 and remembered how their luggage slid around on a deck lubricated by vomit. All the same, though diseases were hardly unknown belowdecks, basic medicine had advanced, and epidemics no longer threatened to decimate entire ships, as in the old days. It was frustrating, however, that water supplied by the liner was to be used only for drinking. It was not available for bathing or cleaning. The presence of stale food, tobacco smoke, garbage, and mass body odor must have made the smell in steerage, after a week or two at sea, rather bracing.

Not until the last day, when land was almost in sight, were passengers allowed to use water for bathing. Then they could step onto the deck, fresh and cleansed, to catch a glimpse of the iconic Statue of Liberty.

Designed by Frédéric Auguste Bartholdi, gifted by the French government to the United States, and erected in 1886, the statue was not meant to be a symbol of America's beckoning to the "poor huddled masses" of immigrants, though it would later be understood as that. (Emma Lazarus's poem invoking those masses was emblazoned in brass on the interior wall of the pedestal at the bequest of the New York socialite Georgina Schuyler, a friend of Lazarus, in 1903.) Instead, the French benefactors had intended that the statue's lamp of liberty be seen not as beckoning *in*, but rather shining *out*: symbolizing how American ideals could inspire other nations and peoples.

It was the immigrants who gave the Statue of Liberty its new meaning as a powerful welcoming gesture to America's newcomers. "They saw it not as a beacon to other lands," writes the historian John Higham, "but as a redemptive salutation to themselves. The memory of that awesome moment and the unspoken greeting it contained was a thing to cherish, a thing to tell one's children about." So it was for Scandinavian immigrants. Upon seeing Lady Liberty for the first time, their sentiments echoed those of the traveler Edward Steiner, who saw the statue in 1906 as "this new divinity into whose keeping they now entrust themselves."

Those laying eyes on the Statue of Liberty were, of course, disembarking in New York City — at first at Castle Garden at the southern tip of Manhattan, and then, after 1892, at Ellis Island.* Many others (like my grandfather Carsten Flaaten) took the trip that brought them to Quebec, where they disembarked and then boarded steamers to take them up the Saint Lawrence River and through the Great Lakes to Milwaukee or Chicago, which by the 1870s was becoming a major Scandinavian colony. For many it was also the last stop — it was where their money ran out.

Routes from New York City also pointed the way west to Chicago, and then to Minneapolis and Duluth in northern Minnesota, via Buffalo (another typical stopover for enterprising Scandinavians, who might find work in its factories and industrial workshops). But for nearly everyone, the biggest trauma was dealing with New York City. "New York City itself," writes the scholar Dorothy Skardal, "made a consistently bad impression on Scandinavian immigrants."

---

* They were not exactly poor huddled masses, either. It is easy to forget that immigrants arriving at Ellis Island were required to have a certain amount of cash (forty dollars, not an inconsiderable sum at the time, and a ticket for a final destination in America).

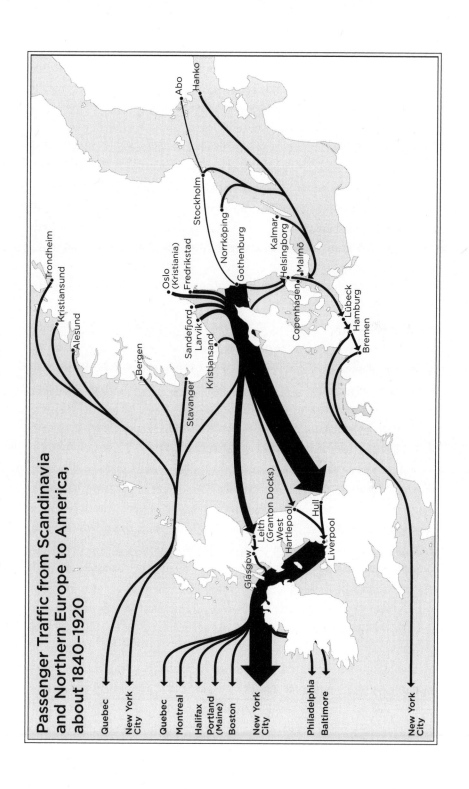

Passenger Traffic from Scandinavia and Northern Europe to America, about 1840-1920

Trondheim
Kristiansund
Alesund
Bergen
Stavanger
Sandefjord
Larvik
Kristiansand
Oslo (Kristiania)
Fredrikstad
Gothenburg
Norrköping
Stockholm
Abo
Hanko
Kalmar
Helsingborg
Malmö
Copenhagen
Lübeck
Hamburg
Bremen

Glasgow
Leith (Granton Docks)
West Hartlepool
Hull
Liverpool

Quebec
New York City
Quebec
Montreal
Halifax
Portland (Maine)
Boston
New York City
Philadelphia
Baltimore
New York City

The noise, the dense mass of people, the horse dung ankle-deep in the street, the big buildings: "In form how big, in character how small!" was the bitter reaction of a Copenhagen poet when he arrived in 1874. A Norwegian poet was likewise disillusioned by what he found, and saddened to see that the magnificent Statue of Liberty was actually covered in rust and mold — entry into the new promised land got off to a less than propitious start. As Holger Rosenberg would warn the Danish immigrants of the future, simply stepping onto an American street could be a traumatic experience. Many Scandinavian immigrants remembered that they had been glad to see the last of New York City. With a sense of expectation and relief, they set off for destinations in the American heartland.

The geographic extent of Scandinavian immigration had grown somewhat by then. Almost all newcomers took Rosenberg's two-word piece of advice encapsulated in number 77 of his *100 Pieces of Advice for Emigrants*: "Go west!" A couple of decades earlier, the open country had meant Illinois, Iowa, and Wisconsin, though some hardy souls did set off for more distant destinations such as Utah and California. Now Wisconsin and Iowa were simply stopping points for those headed for places like Minnesota and the Dakota and Montana Territories — regions that Scandinavians would shape according to their own vision of what America could and should be.

Whereas earlier immigrants had had to rely on canal boats and covered wagons, rail transport was now available. There were, in fact, specific immigrant trains, which moved people from major cities and railheads like New York and Quebec into the interior. The earliest of these trains, which began service in the 1850s, were poorly designed and completely unfurnished; those running between Quebec and Detroit accommodated passengers in cattle cars. A Norwegian American businessman, Halle Steensland, took this type of train from Quebec to Chicago in 1854, riding with immigrants in what were essentially freight cars fitted with rough planks to sit on, with no back supports.

Two decades later the conditions had improved, and the travelers moving along by train could take a moment to look at the land they traversed. It was very different from what they had left behind. Even the daylight had a different character: a Norwegian or Swede or Finn would be amazed to discover

that America had an early twilight in summer, though the weather stayed uncomfortably warm. The immigrants were equally shocked to see almost the
same balance of light and dark all year round.

They also noticed that in the farms and fields they passed, the cows and
horses appeared much larger than those of even the wealthiest estates back
home. One recent immigrant thought American cows as big as elephants.
These scenes whetted the newcomers' appetite for what lay ahead. Who
wouldn't, wrote Nicolay Grevstad, editor of the newspaper *Skandinaven,*
"make a beeline from the little plot of ground on a hillside in Norway to the
princely 160 acres waiting for him in the west?"

Upon arrival, the travelers discovered that this new land did have a familiar side: namely, other Scandinavians. It was fairly typical, upon disembarking in Wisconsin or Minnesota, to find other Swedes or other Norwegians,
including family, waiting to greet you. The churches seemed familiar; the services employed the language of home. The general store run by a Danish or
Swedish immigrant had delicacies just like those at home, as well.

There was also a support network of schools and colleges ready for those
who wanted an education. Coming from countries with a high degree of literacy, Nordic immigrants naturally expected and insisted on the same standards
in their own adopted home. "The loyalty of the Scandinavians to the public
school system has been of far-reaching consequence to the immigrants themselves as well as to American society," wrote one scholar, Kendric Babcock, in
1914. As for higher education, "they have founded numerous seminaries and
so-called colleges," all of which were originally tied to religious denomina-
tions and loyalties. Luther College in Decorah, Iowa, was probably the first.
But others joined the pack, such as Gustavus Adolphus College in Saint Peter,
Minnesota; Augustana College at Rock Island, Illinois; Bethany College at
Lindsborg, Kansas (a solidly Swedish enclave on the Kansas prairie); Red Wing
Seminary in Red Wing, Minnesota (founded in 1878); and Dana College, a
Danish educational enclave founded in Blair, Nebraska, in 1884. In 1896 Finn-
ish immigrants in Hancock, Michigan, created their own Suomi College (now
Finlandia University). By 1893 one student of Scandinavian higher education
in America estimated the total number of Scandinavian colleges, schools, and
seminaries at thirty-six, with an attendance of over five thousand.

Of those, sixteen, or almost half, were located in the state that had become the center of Scandinavian American life: Minnesota.

In the 1850s, the Minnesota territory began to attract the attention of Norwegian settlers like my great-great-grandfather Iver Jacobsen Sorlie, who put down roots in Freeborn County. By 1880 this county was one of a number that had become heavily "Norwegianized"; others included Houston, Dodge, Rice, Faribault, Steele, and Waseca. In fact, Spring Grove Township in Houston County was "one of the most densely settled Norwegian American colonies in the United States." Most of those settlers came from Hallingdal, and the farms they built looked a lot like the farms that Hallings were familiar with from back home, "a cluster of small buildings consisting of horse stable, cow barn, sheepfold, hog barn, doghouse, chicken house, wagon shed, granary, corncrib, hay sheds — merely a roof supported by four posts — even a smoke-

Swedish lumberjacks in Mora, Minnesota, in about 1890. Minnesota Historical Society

house for meats," plus the outdoor privy located close to the house for convenience in the long winter months.

But by the 1890s, the big draw for Norwegians was no longer the sprawling acres along the Mississippi River or the Fox River Valley, but rather the urban center of Minneapolis. By 1903, it was the second-largest Scandinavian city in the world, after Stockholm. Norwegians, Swedes, and Danes occupied large swaths of it, including the stretch from Washington Avenue to Cedar Avenue known as "Snoose Boulevard" after its Scandinavian residents' favorite vice, snuff, or *snoose*. The author Lincoln Steffens described Minneapolis as having "a round Puritan head, an open prairie heart, and a great, big Scandinavian body."

Cedar Avenue South was the business center of Norwegian Minneapolis, within easy walking distance of the Norwegian neighborhoods. In 1880 there had been only 3,315 Norwegian immigrants in Minneapolis. By 1890 there were over 16,000. Swedes came in smaller numbers, and Danes in the smallest of all. But all were finding work in an urban economy; steady farm work had been a previous generation's dream.

Writing in 1911, Holger Rosenberg had included urban-oriented skills that might be used in the range of occupations that Scandinavian immigrants were known to be good at. They worked as servants, cooks, railroad workers (the poet Carl Sandburg's Swedish father was known as a steady and reliable railway worker, as was my Norwegian grandfather Carsten Flaaten), artisans, factory workers, businessmen, and office workers. Scandinavians were proving to be the indispensable foot soldiers of the American industrial revolution as it spread out across the Midwest and the prairie states.

Living in an urban environment like Minneapolis or Chicago also meant that Norwegians were likely to bump up against non-Norwegians both as neighbors and employers. This often meant other Scandinavians, of course, especially the Swedes who were taking over neighborhoods and small towns almost as quickly as the men and women from Norway. In response to this trend, several civic organizations sprang up that specifically catered to Nordic immigrants, such as the Scandinavian Lutheran Temperance Society, the Scandinavian Old Settlers Society, and the Scandinavian Brass Band.

It also meant close encounters with non-Scandinavians, from Germans and Slavs to Scots, Irish, Hungarians, Jews, and Native Americans (particularly in a city like Minneapolis or Madison, Wisconsin). The exact ethnic distinctions were sometimes vaguely understood, or entirely misunderstood. One writer remembered that in the Norwegian Boys' Association, the members and their parents referred to all non-Scandinavian children as "the Irish" and let it go at that. Likewise, all the non-Scandinavians simply called him and his fellow Scandinavians "Swedes," and let it go at *that*.

Other Norwegians still preferred the farming life. When the Red River Valley on the Minnesota side seemed to fill up with settlements and farms, many turned their attention farther west, toward the Dakota Territory.

Scandinavian journalists at the time called it "Dakota fever." It first struck in the 1880s. "The Norwegian exploitation of what became North Dakota opened with a paean of praise and was carried forward with a wave of high hopes," wrote the historian Theodore Blegen. As a boy living near the edge of the Dakota Territory in 1882 remembered it,

> We watched the [prairie] schooners come up from the south, zig-zagging up the tortuous trail like ships beating up against the wind. Slowly they drew nearer — sometimes one, sometimes five or six in a fleet . . . Usually the woman was sitting at the front driving the team, and beside her or peeking out of the front opening were a flock of dirty, tousled, tow-headed children. Often she held a small baby in her arms.

The young child would note a small flock of cattle would follow, with the man of the household walking along behind. Then "slowly the wagons passed on, the children now peeking from the opening in the rear, the schooner receding into the distance . . . then disappearing below the horizon."

A beautiful image — which covers over the fact that much of this settlement of prairie lands was possible because of the often violent expropriation of these territories from Native American tribes. Although we can't ignore the ugly side of what used to be called "the winning of the West," we still have to bear in mind the mentality of Scandinavians who made the journey to America. Desperate for land, they were prepared to endure any hardship, including Native American resistance, to establish new lives for themselves and their families. The white authorities had told them that the land was theirs for the taking, and they made the best of a situation ultimately not of their making.

One of those, for example, was my great-grandfather Oscar Sorlie, the son of the Stones River veteran Iver Jacobsen Sorlie. After the Civil War (and the Sioux uprising that killed Custer, during which my great-great-grandmother fed some visiting Sioux from the family porch), he enrolled in Decorah Business School. His mother had hoped he would enter a Lutheran seminary, but he never did. Instead, he headed for North Dakota in 1886 to run a business in Hillsboro. In the end, however, the Norwegian obsession with land bit him as well, and he wound up farming in the Red River Valley. The only rule was "you had to be first in the field to secure the best land." By 1900, when Oscar Sorlie settled down, Norwegians had carved out of North Dakota an enclave of some twenty counties bounded to the east by Minnesota and to the north by the Canadian border. Fargo, its de facto capital, had a population that was half Norwegian by either birth or descent.

Either way, the land in Dakota was a shock, even for those now used to farming in America. The endlessly flat land stretching to a cloudless horizon, the rich black dirt that begged to be plowed and cultivated, and the vast sky overhead had to be seen to be believed.

"What a country, this Dakota!" one farm laborer from Norway wrote in the 1880s. The sunsets in Dakota were like nothing he had ever seen, "blood-red in hue and of an intensity almost defying description." The laborer's name was Knut Hamsun. Later, he would return to his native Norway and become one of its most famous authors, winning the Nobel Prize for Literature in 1920.

He returned, however, an angry man. His first important book, *Adventures in the New World,* was a diatribe against everything he found in America: its cultural pretensions (he felt that the Minneapolis public library was a joke), its religious hypocrisies (Minneapolis had more than 140 churches compared to Copenhagen's 29, which prompted Hamsun to ask sarcastically, "Is there more of God in Minneapolis?"), and above all its materialism, which he believed had come to infect the Norwegians and Scandinavians around him. He was not alone in his criticisms. There was trouble brewing in the Scandinavian American paradise.

"Don't expect people to give you a helping hand in the U.S. Rely on yourself."

That was the advice Holger Rosenberg gave to aspiring Danish emigrants before they set sail for America. It was good advice for Scandinavians in general. The "safety net" in those days consisted almost solely of family and close friends. For the lucky ones, it also meant a supportive community of fellow Danes or Swedes or Finns who could help new arrivals find their feet. What they were finding out about America, however, was that "the land of the free" was also the land where self-reliance came with a warning label: *caveat emptor*, or "buyer beware."

On the one hand, a resourceful worker could make more money in a month or two than he or she might earn in wages for a year in the old country. But prices were higher too. The carefully tended nest egg, brought over across the sea, went fast. A Danish settler in Dakota, for example, found that just putting up a rough shed to shelter his wife and family cost him more than $150. The price tag for those highly desirable cows and horses seen on the train ride from Chicago or Minneapolis also proved dear: too dear for some, who found themselves working someone else's land in order to make ends meet.

Then there was crime. There were plenty of warnings meant to protect gullible immigrants just off the boat: avoid telling strangers how much money you have on your person; don't trust someone who offers to buy you a ticket for the train or steamship to your next destination. Most distressing were fellow Swedes or Norwegians who turned out to be crooks. Some immigrants found themselves stranded in New York or Chicago because they put their faith (and their money) in someone who happened to speak the same language. It was part of the heartbreak that sometimes went with "Welcome to America."

Many, if not most, of the immigrants came to refer to the first stretch of time in the new country as "the dog years," when they struggled with the new language, customs, and culture while trying to make a living. Overall, the Danes seemed to suffer the least from culture shock and to assimilate the fastest. As we've seen, one reason for this might be that the Danes were already used to dealing with different cultures, and many, because of their close ties to Germany, were bilingual. Danes also came in their largest numbers in the late nineteenth and early twentieth centuries, and therefore had an easier passage than the Swedes and Norwegians who preceded them. Those earlier immigrants had to rely more heavily on family and community from the old country to integrate into American life. And perhaps Danish men made the effort to assimilate more quickly because there was a shortage of Danish women in America. Many of those hoping to marry would have to look outside their ethnic group to find a wife and raise a family.

Also, the Danes had witnessed the sad decline of their country after the traumatic events of 1864, when the Prussians occupied a large portion of Denmark. Why look back with nostalgia to an old country that was no longer there? A Danish American writer in 1896 noticed this sense of disillusionment among the Danes he met: "The sentiment of patriotism and national pride too is waning . . . and a feeling of national helplessness is becoming dominant." Perhaps a full-blown attachment to America came more naturally to those who felt they had nothing much to lose.

But above all, Danes made a fairly easy connection to the democratic egalitarian values of American urban life. More than other Scandinavians, they seem to have found a fast-paced, bustling city like Chicago congenial. "Half the store signs on North Avenue displayed Danish names," remarks a character in a Danish American novel about a recent immigrant stopping in Humboldt Park, the center of the Danish quarters: "There were more than half a dozen Danish bakers; there were banks which changes crowns; there were restaurants that served open-faced sandwiches; there were food stores which sold liverwurst and pork sausage and Danish cheese." Not to mention the bars, "where one could curse in his mother tongue and drink himself to a thumping great hangover in Aalborg Aquavit."

This is not to say that Swedes or Norwegians had a rough passage becoming Americanized, or the Finn or the occasional Icelander, for that matter. Of course, they all had certain advantages. They were white Protestants almost to a person, and they benefited from what some today would call white privilege. They (except for the Finns) also spoke a Germanic language that, despite the differences, made English easier to tackle than it was for the average Russian or Hungarian or Italian immigrant. The American public school system, in which Scandinavian immigrants, Kendric Babcock noted in 1914, put so much faith and which was "one of the best evidences of the desire of these people from the Northern lands to become Americanized," was a much easier proposition for speakers of Norwegian or Danish than it was for other immigrant groups, then or later. The ancient links between Old Norse and Anglo-Saxon, which predated the Viking invasions, paid off in the long term for the Scandinavian immigrants to America.

Add to this the undying sense that, for so many Scandinavian immigrants, America was the promised land of freedom and liberty that Cleng Peerson, Hans Christian Heg, and Rasmus Anderson had celebrated; Heg had even given his life for it. While immigrants from other parts of the world may have felt the same about their adopted land, for Norwegians, Swedes, Danes, Finns, and the occasional Icelander, the United States seemed to represent a very special preserve for the future of the Viking heart: we call it the American Dream.

And yet, weighing the values of the new country against those of the old might mean finding, from time to time, that the former were wanting. In her book *The Divided Heart,* the scholar Dorothy Burton Skardal traced three differing attitudes toward the new country in works of fiction by Scandinavian American writers in the wake of the Great Migration. The first were the accommodationists, who found everything in America better than in their homeland and were happy to ditch their native customs, including their language, in the scramble to become 100 percent American. Then there were the preservationists, who fought at every step to keep their old ways and lamented the loss of traditional Scandinavian identities and virtue in the onslaught of American culture. Probably the best-known of these critics was the novelist Ole Edvart Rølvaag, the Norwegian-born author of *Giants in the Earth.* His portrayal of the Norwegian immigrants making new lives for themselves on the Dakota prairie left an indelible picture of the Scandinavian experience in America.

This portrayal was not true to Rølvaag's own experience, though. He was a relative newcomer to America, leaving home when he was twenty years old in 1896 and taking up work as a farmer in South Dakota before becoming a teacher and eventually a professor at St. Olaf College in Northfield. His novels, written in Norwegian, actually look back to the homesteading way of life of the 1850s and '60s rather than turn-of-the-century Minnesota. Rølvaag portrays it as a series of grim battles against the elements, deprivation, and loneliness — battles that the protagonists often lose. For him, the constant daily assault of American values on the Scandinavian character was the grimmest of all. His writings were a cry of protest against the ideal of the melting pot: "If this process of leveling down, of making everyone alike by blotting out all racial traits, is allowed to continue, America is doomed to become the most impoverished land spiritually on the face of the earth; out of our highly praised melting-pot will come a dull . . . smug complacency, barren of all creative thought and effort. Soon we will have reached the perfect democracy of barrenness."

Other traditionalists were usually not willing to go as far down the dark path of cultural despair as Rølvaag — or endorse the harsh criticisms of Knut Hamsun. They wanted to keep what reminded them of the old country and the family and community connections they had there. But they also held fast to the American virtues that had drawn them in the first place. The sense of independence and free spirit that was part of their own Viking heritage had room to stretch in their new country — even if they had hardly any money to jingle in their pockets.

"There is a middle way," says a character in one of the novels by the Danish American writer M. Sorensen. "When we keep the best of our old Danish culture and at the same time understand how to assimilate the best of what is to be found here, then we will be able to carry out our role and exercise influence. Then we will have something to live on and to live for."

For better or worse, it was the middle way that most Scandinavian immigrants chose. As one Swedish immigrant put it, the goal was to love the old country like a mother and love the new country like a bride. It didn't always work that way, of course. But as time went on, some Scandinavians came to realize that the very traits in themselves that drew them to "the land of the free and the home of the brave" could help change America for the better.

Students at Dana College, the first Danish American institution of higher learning, spell out the letter D on campus grounds. Danish American Archive and Library

• • •

By now the Scandinavian experience had also become part of American literature. Ole Rølvaag would be the most famous, but authors like the Swedish-born Edwin Bjorkman, the Danish immigrant Carl Hansen, and the Norwegians Waldemar Ager and Dorothy Dahl were helping to shape the common understanding of the Scandinavian experience in America. Works by Lars Stenholt, whose books were published by Waldemar Kriedt in Minneapolis, were so popular that Stenholt was able to make a living as a writer — the only Scandinavian immigrant to do so at the time, even though his books were a thinly disguised attack on his fellow Norwegian Americans for their hypocrisy, greed, and adultery. Jews and the super-rich get a good working over as well.

By then, two Scandinavians were also documenting the intersection of old and new in original and contrasting ways. Both, although they were happy to be Americans, found that aspects of the American Dream were less than satisfactory. One was content to document those aspects, while the other would not rest without doing something to change them.

The latter was Jacob Riis. Born in Ribe, Denmark, in 1849, Riis immigrated to America in 1870, arriving in New York well before the beckoning Statue of Liberty had been erected. In fact, Riis found America to be very different from the Emerald City of his expectations. Instead, he wound up working a range of appalling jobs until he found himself penniless and homeless on the streets of Manhattan.

He slept in doorways and sorted through garbage cans for food. Like many of the homeless, he adopted a stray dog. When a police patrol gave him a hard time and the dog growled menacingly, a doorman at the building where he was taking shelter grabbed the dog by its back legs and beat its brains out on the pavement.

In 1873, Riis's fortunes suddenly turned. He found a job as a reporter for the New York News Association, eventually becoming editor of the *Brooklyn Daily News* and then its owner. After he sold the paper so he could return to Denmark and get married, he and his bride returned to New York, where Riis landed an odd job as a crime reporter for the *New York Tribune.* It was 1877. Riis set up his observation post at 301 Mulberry Street, which would be the center of his world for the next twenty-four years.

The biggest disappointment of all about America, in Riis's eyes, was the appalling poverty of New York City, the country's richest metropolis that was also a cesspool of crime, corruption, and grinding pauperism, especially for newly arrived immigrants. Crammed into tenements in the Lower East Side and Greenwich Village, most of them lived in destitution that endless work couldn't improve, and only drink and opium could alleviate. A life of crime seemed like the one rational choice, for many, in a world where one had to prey on others lest they be preyed upon.

Riis decided to use his journalistic platform to force reforms. In addition to the written word, he found a secret weapon in the photographic image. He was the first journalist to use indoor flash photography to document the appalling conditions in which so many of New York inhabitants lived, first in a series of magic lantern slides and lectures, then in his book *How the Other Half Lives,* first published in 1890.

Riis had to learn by trial and error to use the right amount of flash powder: enough to light up a darkened room or alleyway but not so much as to spark a veritable indoor explosion. In one incident he set fire to his residence on Richmond Hill. Another time he nearly blinded himself.

But once he got the mixture right and set out with his camera and tripod for places where even the police refused to go, a gallery of misery emerged — from homeless children sleeping in doorways to sweatshops and "penny hangs" (hotels for the poor where a penny bought you space on a rope on which to lean and sleep) and opium dens. Americans, even the New Yorkers, had never seen anything like it, and it stirred hearts and minds across the country. President Theodore Roosevelt himself wrote the introduction for a new edition.

Some of the writing in *How the Other Half Lives* makes for hard reading today. Riis weighed in mercilessly on the failure of some immigrant groups, especially Black and Chinese Americans, to improve their lives. He threw around racial stereotypes, including pernicious ones about Jews, which now make readers cringe. The single ethnic group that doesn't come under fire is Riis's fellow Scandinavians, in large part because they weren't present. New York just wasn't their kind of town. At times, though, Riis almost seems to imply that immigrants from other backgrounds shared one particularly severe misfortune — they weren't Danes (nor were they Swedes).

Racist rhetoric aside, Riis's larger point was that the true responsibility for immigrants' unhappy lives fell squarely on the shoulders of American society, not on those of the immigrants themselves. His book was a clarion call to change conditions in the inner city and to reform the urban landscape — the first of what would be many over the next century. By any measure, *How the Other Half Lives* was one of the most influential social tracts ever published.

Under the circumstances, his later autobiography, *The Making of an American,* had a somewhat ironic ring in its pessimism. Riis never regretted leaving the Danish homeland. Quite the opposite. Although he expresses great affection for Denmark as the home of his family, his belief that America had a great destiny was never shaken. But in the end, his life and work reflected a view that, for himself and the ever-increasing numbers of his fellow Scandinavians, this new country still left a good deal to be desired despite its promise.

In his own way, Thorstein Veblen came to much the same conclusion. Born in Cato, Wisconsin, he was the fourth of twelve children born to Thomas and

Kari Veblen, who had immigrated to America in 1847. Thomas, trained as a carpenter, had built his family a model farm outside Nerstrand, Minnesota.

Although his English was never very strong, Thomas could console himself with the fact that he had a very intellectually gifted family. All his children ended up going to college — no mean accomplishment in the late nineteenth century. Thorstein Veblen's older sister Emily was the first daughter of Norwegian immigrants to graduate from an American college, Carleton College (its Norwegian-funded sister school in Northfield, Minnesota, St. Olaf College, wasn't founded until 1874). Thorstein's brother Andrew became a physicist and taught at the University of Iowa. And Andrew's son Oswald grew up to be an outstanding mathematician and a colleague of Albert Einstein at Princeton.

But Thorstein, the family rebel, was the most gifted and famous of them all.

After graduating from Carleton in 1880, he had gone on to the Johns Hopkins University to study philosophy with C. S. Peirce, the father of American pragmatism and an expounder of the Scottish philosophy of common sense. He then moved on to Yale, where he attended classes with Professor William Graham Sumner, who introduced him to the doctrines of social Darwinism. Sumner's evolutionary theory of society appealed to Veblen, but the Norwegian American gave it his own characteristic twist. While orthodox social Darwinists tended to draw the conclusion that whatever is, is right, Veblen's invariable conclusion was the opposite: whatever is, is *wrong.*

This made him an intellectual outlier. Veblen's manifesto appeared in 1899, with the publication of *The Theory of the Leisure Class,* a pitiless and devastating portrait of the super-rich of the Gilded Age, the men and women who ran America's largest corporations and built the great mansions on Fifth Avenue and in Newport, Rhode Island. In it Veblen coined the phrase "conspicuous consumption," which alone, as one scholar has put it, made *The Theory of the Leisure Class* the most-quoted and least-read book in America.

From Veblen's perspective, however, the term was more than just a sound bite. It exposed the obverse side of the American Dream, that of a status-conscious materialism Veblen saw as a form of social entropy — a dysfunctional trend that, ironically, was unfolding at the same time as the horrors described in *How the Other Half Lives,* at the opposite end of America's social spectrum.

The Theory of the Leisure Class became an economic and sociological classic, and rightly so. But in the end what may have troubled Veblen most about the profligate Vanderbilts and Astors was something that flew in the face of his Norwegian soul, and offended centuries of the Lutheran work ethic. So it's not surprising that later Veblen would compose another, much less celebrated essay that is a kind of general meditation on the Scandinavian experience in America, and ultimately the Viking heart itself.

The Instinct of Workmanship drew upon the ideas of his teacher C. S. Peirce and Peirce's fellow pragmatist William James, who were both interested in the power of habit and instinct over reasoned patterns of behavior. Published in 1914, it deals with the phenomenon of attention to detail that the experienced craftsman and artisan — someone like his father, Thomas Veblen — brings to his or her labor, and the state of mind and habit that underlie it.

Veblen admits it may be difficult to define and analyze this instinct for good work, in part because it's been ignored. Thinkers have tended to take it for granted rather than lend it serious philosophical attention. Yet according to Veblen, "workmanship is none the less an object of attention and sentiment in its own right." It "denotes the conscious pursuit of an objective end which the instinct in question makes worthwhile."

The driving force behind this type of effort is not the desire for profit or self-improvement, as conventional economists might assume. Instead, Veblen decided, it is "a proclivity for taking pains" that is self-rewarding, even self-delighting, apart from any material or monetary reward. As Veblen put it, this impulse is "a disposition to do the next thing and do it as well as may be," when "there is work at hand and more of it in sight," whether it's building a longship or constructing a house, mending a net or plowing a furrow, forging a sword or painting a portrait, or, a little later, forging a bit of steel into a tool or an engine part for an automobile or a four-engine bomber.*

The workmanship instinct "shows at its best, both the individual workman's technological efficiency and in the growth of technological proficiency and insight in the community at large ..." It "proceeds on the accumulated knowledge so received and current, and turns it to account in dealing with the

---

* See Chapter 13.

material means of life." In fact, no real capacity for innovation or lasting improvement, no real material or monetary advance, is possible if this quality is missing. Instead, a society becomes stultified and stagnant, and succumbs to mere habit or, even worse, a self-regarding complacency disguised as sophistication.

"The instinct of workmanship," Veblen concludes, "brought the life of mankind from the brute to the human plane, and in all the later growth of culture it has never ceased to pervade the works of man." It is key to man's biological survival. The only other instinct that is remotely comparable with it is the parental instinct. "Indeed, the two have much in common."

In the end, the habit of doing good work, and looking forward to doing it, is fundamental to the well-being of the community and the human race at large, both materially *and* spiritually. Veblen sensed that when it is in decline, it's easily replaced by what he called salesmanship. While true workmanship "occupies the interest with practical expedients, ways and means, devices and contrivances of efficiency and economy, proficiency, creative work, and technological mastery of facts," salesmanship focuses on the label on the bottle, not what's inside. Salesmanship, and the prevalence of the salesperson's instincts, in society is a danger sign — and Veblen sensed it was already casting a shadow over the United States of his day.

That is, unless perhaps those Scandinavian immigrants and their offspring, for whom that instinct had been preserved and honed since they made those first Stone Age boats and for centuries had worked harmoniously with hands, minds, and hearts, could come to the rescue of the American Dream.

With the recognition of the instinct of workmanship, we come to a crucial landmark in the search for the Viking heart. The instinct for achieving perfection in what we shape by physical and mental craft shaped a Viking lord's longship or sword, or an Icelandic free man's farm. It's the instinct that shaped a skaldic saga and, ultimately, drove Scandinavia's greatest rulers, men and women alike, to strive for a political unity greater than the reality on the ground would allow, whether in the Union of Kalmar or on the battlefield at Breitenfeld. The "proclivity for taking pains" is a source of spiritual power; without it the Viking heart can become merely self-regarding or even destructive.

Veblen himself never put his thesis in precisely these terms. Nevertheless, according to Veblen's stepdaughter, he considered *The Instinct of Workmanship,* not *The Theory of the Leisure Class,* to be his best work and the key to all his thinking. It was certainly the one that pointed most perceptively to society's future, as well as its past and present.

Thorstein Veblen died on August 3, 1929. He could see where the instinct for salesmanship was heading in the booming Wall Street stock market — but he died before the crash, which occurred just two months later. His *Instinct of Workmanship* remains an intriguing signpost for a very different future, one that links Nordic heritage to a desire to make things as good as they can possibly be.

12

Land of Wonders

How Two Scandinavian Icons
Transformed Jazz Age America

> Choose any American at random, and he should be
> a man of burning desires, enterprising, adventurous,
> and, above all, an innovator.
>
> — Alexis de Tocqueville, *Democracy in America,* 1835

ON APRIL 6, 1917, America entered World War I. President Woodrow Wilson's address to Congress rebuking Germany had provided soaring rhetoric about how "the world must be made safe for democracy" and championed "the rights of mankind," ending with the declaration that "to such a task we can dedicate our lives and our fortunes, everything we are and everything we have . . ." After a century of avoiding entanglement in European conflicts, the United States emerged from the war, on November 11, 1918, as the most powerful nation on earth. Its new destiny as an economic, financial, and eventually military and cultural hegemon would transform America in profound ways. It would also transform the world.

At home, however, Wilson's soaring rhetoric fell flat as disillusioned and disgruntled doughboys returned from France to tell how their sacrifice (more than 100,000 dead) had not made the world safer for democracy, but rather weakened it. A postwar depression followed race riots and Prohibition, as well as a crushing defeat in Congress for America's hopes of joining the new League of Nations. President Wilson's promise that the bloody conflict would be "the war that ends all wars" was unceremoniously dashed. As the 1920s dawned, America was disillusioned, depressed, and dry. What's more, the debate over which immigrants to admit to America, and how, had come to divide American politics as never before.

The history of American immigration has many unexpected twists and ironies. Certainly today's debate is nothing new. In the past as in the present, debates over immigration have swirled around certain catchphrases: melting pot (first popularized in 1908) or multicolored tapestry; deportation or open borders; path to citizenship or paths to illegal crossings; separating children or stopping MS-13; putting up walls or rolling out welcome mats. Today the discussion has never seemed more emotional, or more confused.

In fact, the issue had become highly charged even before World War I, for Scandinavians as well as other newcomers. By 1910, 15 percent of America's population had been born outside the country. Some, like Randolph Bourne, believed the influx of the foreign-born, including those from Nordic countries, was a good thing. In July 1916 he published a landmark article in *The Atlantic Monthly*, which stated: "We have needed the new peoples — the order of the German and Scandinavian, the turbulence of the Slav and [Hungarian] — to save us from our own stagnation."

Cultural stereotypes aside, the US entry, less than a year later, into a world war would place Bourne and his views in a definite minority. German Americans, the largest non-English-speaking minority in America, became the target of suspicion, persecution, and even the occasional lynching. German-language classes were banned. In South Dakota, speaking German over the telephone was outlawed. Even performing music by German composers such as Beethoven was forbidden. German terms that had crept into English had to be replaced: *sauerkraut* became "Liberty cabbage," and *hamburger* became "Liberty steak."

Some of this hysterical suspicion spilled over to the German's Nordic brethren. In a conflict that the Allies were calling a "war for civilization," the

Scandinavian homelands remained neutral; it seemed a moral abdication.*
In any case, the end of the war, in 1918, found the United States at a cross-
roads as to immigration. Were foreign-born citizens a boon or a danger? There
were many in powerful places who were prepared to say that America's doors
needed to shut — or at least the aperture needed narrowing.

To modern eyes, the story of Scandinavian Americans seems to shed no
light on these issues. After all, by today's measure they would seem participants in what is described as white privilege. They were also overwhelmingly
Protestant and never suffered the discrimination that Catholics, like the Irish
or Italians or Hungarians, had to endure. As a group, they were also more lit-
erate than any other foreign immigrant group except perhaps the Scots (in
Norway, for example, illiteracy had been almost unknown since the mid-
eighteenth century).

But America had posed challenges to Scandinavians, all the same — especially their sense of tradition and identity. At stake were the cultural ties
that connected the Scandinavian immigrant to his or her original homeland;
America the melting pot seemed to require giving it up without supplying
any clear cultural identity in return. What it meant to be American remained
a mystery to many, compared to what it had meant being a Dane or a Swede
or a Norwegian. The novelist Ole Rølvaag summed up these cultural anxi-
eties in this way: "We are strangers to the people we left behind, and we are
strangers to the people we came to. We gave up the fatherland which was our
heritage of a thousand years, and we of the first generation can never find another . . ."

That might have been true in the early years of the Great Migration. But
for those of the next generation, and even for some who had come directly
from Scandinavia, America *was* their home. It was a home, however, where
the backlash against immigration included an effort to impose quotas on
new arrivals to America. Ethnic exclusiveness became the new crusade among
American progressives and intellectuals, while recent immigrants found themselves praised (like English and Germans and Scandinavians) or damned (like

---

* See Chapter 15.

Hungarians, Italians, and eastern Europeans) according to a constantly evolving scale of approval and prejudice.

"God damn the continent of Europe," the novelist F. Scott Fitzgerald wrote to his Princeton classmate Edmund Wilson in 1921. "Raise the bar of immigration and permit only Scandinavians, Teutons, Anglo-Saxons, and Celts to enter."

To some purists, even this was not enough. That same year, Scandinavian groups had to join with Irish American and German American associations to protest the new quota-based immigration law designating that immigrants from the British Isles would make up 57 percent of the total immigrant pool, with the other western European countries, including the Nordic nations, getting short-ended. The protesters earned the scorn of the law's supporters, who denounced the Scandinavian groups as among the "alien blocs" trying to gut America's protections against being overrun by undesirables.

Suddenly, Scandinavian Americans found themselves in a new homeland disillusioned by war, crippled by economic depression, embroiled in racism and anti-immigrant sentiment, undergoing the upheaval of Prohibition (which was also largely aimed at foreign-born immigrants), and prepared to lump immigrants from Norway, Sweden, Denmark, and Finland in with those they considered undesirable aliens.

And yet despite the odds, a legendary — and in some cases, infamous — group of Scandinavian Americans stepped up to give their country a new sense of optimism, hope, and a renewed belief in the American Dream — as well as a new heroic self-image, even as their own actions sometimes left a lasting stain.

The truth was, the Scandinavian American experience touched something deep in the American identity, and vice versa.

Ten years after the ship *Restauration* docked in New York Harbor with America's first Norwegian immigrants, Alexis de Tocqueville published his landmark work *Democracy in America,* a penetrating analysis of what made the new republic different from other nations, including its European forebears. By any measure, it remains a foundational essay concerning American exceptionalism. The America that Tocqueville* found had rewarded inventiveness,

---

* We can note in passing that Tocqueville's surname was itself of Viking (that is,

enterprise, and above all a sense of adventure. For Americans, the Frenchman wrote, "something which does not exist is just something that has not been tried."

At the same time, Tocqueville discovered that Americans respected the ties of church, family, community, and voluntary association. They were determined to make their own way and their own fortunes, but they also wanted to shape a good future for their families. For the average American, life was a game, a contest, virtually "a revolution." It was a supreme test of the human being's intellectual and moral qualities, which brought out something Tocqueville could only describe as heroic.

"America," Tocqueville wrote, "is a land of wonders." A century later, Scandinavian Americans gave back that sense of wonder to relieve America's postwar malaise — the sense of adventure, of pride in endless possibilities and in personal and national missions fulfilled. In short, the perfect breeding ground for the Viking heart.

The football coach Knut Rockne, the aviator Charles Lindbergh, the sculptor Gutzon Borglum, and the poet Carl Sandburg were the children of immigrants. The auto industry executives who became the architects of America's Arsenal of Democracy in World War II, William "Big Bill" Knudsen and Charles Sorensen, were immigrants themselves. But all of them would become living legends, if not always for the best of reasons. Charles Lindbergh and Gutzon Borglum, in particular, couldn't resist the tide of xenophobia that swept over certain corners of postwar America. Nevertheless, all left a mark on the United States — an imprint that, in its own way, made the Scandinavian American experience America's own.

Lars Rokne's family emigrated from their home in Voss, Norway, in 1893. Back in Norway, Lars Rokne (the letter *c* would be added to the surname once they arrived in America) had been a buggy maker to royalty. Known locally as the Master Fixer, he made hand-crafted vehicles that were so famous, the kaiser, Wilhelm II of Germany, ordered a batch for his personal stables. In 1891, Lars traveled to Chicago to the World's Fair, where he unveiled one

Norman) origin. See Chapter 4.

of his fabulous carriages and won the grand prize. After taking a look around the city, he sensed that he and his family had a future there. He wrote to his wife, Martha, asking her to ready herself and their three children to join him in a year.

When the family arrived, they settled into a small apartment near Logan Square, on the last stop of the elevated train. The city was already famous as a major hub for immigrants from foreign lands, but the Norwegians had virtually beaten everyone to the door. By 1836 a small Norwegian colony had grown up north of the Chicago River — which included a family from Voss — and fourteen years later it numbered more than 560. With its strong nuclear families and equal numbers of men and women working at jobs and running shops, Norway's Chicago enclave closely resembled agricultural settlements back home in its division of labor between the sexes and its passion for hard work — and, one might even say, an instinct for workmanship.

Industrial development moved the families south around the blocks of Kinzie Street and Milwaukee Avenue, where the 1,573 Norwegians living there by 1862 were active in Great Lakes shipping as sailors and craftworkers. Others put in their time digging the Illinois and Michigan Canal, which got underway in 1848.

The numbers only continued to swell. When the Rocknes arrived, an estimated 62,000 Norwegians, 35,000 Danes, and 100,000 Swedes were living in the city. In fact, Chicago was, after Copenhagen, Stockholm, and Kristiania (as Oslo was still known), the fourth-largest Scandinavian city in the world. At the time Minneapolis, by contrast, was only sixth or seventh. The Rocknes were happy to find that the nest of Norwegian businesses, restaurants, and saloons along North Avenue included many families from their small town. By the 1890s, in fact, Vossings had become an essential part of Chicago life, as well as part of Norwegian immigrant life in general.

For example, one family from Voss, the Nelsons, would produce a governor and a senator from Minnesota. Still another, the Nestos, a governor of North Dakota. The Vinges, also from Voss, would put one of their offspring on the Wisconsin Supreme Court. And another Vossing from Chicago, Victor Lawson, would become the publisher of the *Chicago Daily News*. But the most famous of all of the Vossings, Lars's son Knute, would transform the meaning of American sports.

Even when he was a boy, everyone who met him realized Knute was different from other kids. He could barely speak a word of English when he started school but quickly rose to the top of his class, with a proven gift for math and a memory for history. Like other immigrant children, Scandinavians and non-Scandinavians alike, he divided his time between school and work. When classes ended, there were odd jobs washing windows and picking beets and corn on farms north of the city. But from the beginning, his main passion was sports. All the local kids' heroes were athletes: the boxer Joe Gans or the Chicago White Sox manager and star player, Cap Anson. It was when Knute was playing sandlot ball in the neighborhood that a missed grounder broke his nose. The injury gave him that endearing pugilistic countenance that the columnist Westbrook Pegler once described as "the face of a battered oilcan." An oil can, he added, "giving off champagne."

And then there was football. This was rough-and-tumble sandlot football, without helmets or pads, with neighborhood teams pitting Scandinavians against the local Irish. Rockne later recalled that games regularly had five cops on hand to make sure the crowds watching didn't turn their kids' contest into an adults-only free-for-all.

At Northwest Division High School Knute played football — good football. His ultimate goal was to go to college, either the University of Chicago (which in those days had a stellar football team) or the University of Illinois in Urbana. But the days when students could earn athletic scholarships to attend the university were decades away. And especially once the family made him quit high school to take a job with the post office that paid six hundred dollars a year (for a shift from midnight to 8:30 in the morning), college seemed a remote dream.

He manned his postal job for three and a half years until two Irish friends, who were stars of track and field, told him they were headed for the College of Notre Dame in South Bend, Indiana, and convinced him to apply with them. Notre Dame was one of the few colleges in the country that would accept a high school equivalency exam for admission. He took the exam, passed with flying colors, and announced to his family in the spring of 1910 that he was headed for Notre Dame, which was run by a Catholic religious order.

The Rockne family was shocked, not to say horrified. As good Lutherans, and like most Norwegians (or Swedes or Danes), they took a dim view of the Catholic Church.* The possibility that their son might fall in with the wrong crowd there, or even perhaps convert, must have filled them with apprehension. But they had learned there was no standing between Knute and what he wanted, and so that September he arrived at the South Bend train station with a single suitcase containing two pairs of pants, a couple of shirts, and three neckties.

He was twenty-two years old, already balding, and didn't know a soul beyond his two friends at Notre Dame. In addition to dealing with the unfamiliarity of the school's Roman Catholic faith, he discovered that he was the sole Scandinavian in his class. Negotiating the religious differences required a delicate balancing act that he would maintain for the rest of his life. If the Catholic fathers who taught at and ran the school ever worried where his heart truly lay, Knute's aptitude for chemistry (for a time they considered hiring him while still an undergraduate to teach classes in chemistry) and above all for football kept him in their good graces.

College football then was still a brutal sport. It could be virtually lethal to players and was nearly banned until President Theodore Roosevelt intervened to impose a set of rules — including banning the flying wedge — and saved the competitive sport. But it was Knute Rockne who transformed it, starting at this tiny Catholic college no one had ever heard of, from an absorbing interest for some into a sustaining collegiate industry for all.

Above all, Rockne was an innovator. The 1913 game Notre Dame played against Army, in which a series of passes from Charles ("Gus") Dorais to Rockne led to an upset victory by Notre Dame, is generally credited with popularizing the forward pass. The rules had made it legal since 1906, but it still hadn't been widely adopted. Following his graduation in 1914, Rockne

---

* Not unlike my Norwegian grandmother, who, when she learned I was studying Latin in college, worried that I might have fallen in with the wrong crowd — that is, some Roman Catholics, or worse, the Jesuits.

was offered two jobs: one as an instructor in chemistry and the other as assistant football coach at Notre Dame, under Jess Harper. It was not until 1918, as World War I was ending and American soldiers were getting ready to come home from war, that he became head coach as well as athletic director.

The next thirteen years became legend. Under Rockne's leadership, from 1918 to 1931, the Notre Dame teams won 105 games while losing only 12 and tying for just 5. They were declared national champions in 1924, 1929, and 1930 (there was no official poll in those days). Rockne's most famous player was George Gipp, a makes-it-look-easy star at fullback and kicker who played only two seasons for Rockne (one of them, in 1919, brought a 9–0 unbeaten record) before illness cut him down midseason in 1920. Gipp's death that December, which plunged the entire college and its fans around the country into mourning, became part of the Rockne legend — just as Rockne's admonition to his players, "Win this one for the Gipper," passed into American idiom.

The other Notre Dame legends were the so-called Four Horsemen, Rockne's stellar backfield in Stuhldreher, Miller, Crowley, and Layden, who dominated the college football scene from their freshmen year in 1921 until 1924. The sports writer Grantland Rice dubbed them the Four Horsemen of the Apocalypse because their appearance on the field meant doom to their opponents. The name stuck. Rather than take offense, Rockne made sure the boys had their picture taken with each of them actually sitting on a horse on the football field — one of the most famous photos in American sports.

Rockne was a master publicist. He knew, for example, that the story of the little Catholic college with the Norwegian immigrant coach and the team that couldn't be beat made great press, and he made the most of it. Notre Dame gained national recognition not just through the excellence of its teams but also through Rockne's tireless promotion and his cultivation of prominent sportswriters. Rockne gave his name to a ghostwritten syndicated newspaper column and numerous magazine articles, was a celebrated off-season banquet speaker, and became a spokesman for several businesses and products, most conspicuously Studebaker automobiles.

Following Notre Dame's upset of Army in 1928, sportswriters spread the story that Rockne had inspired his players at halftime to "win one for the Gipper," but he knew the key to his success wasn't his fiery inspiring pep talks (although he was happy to let recording companies turn them into popular playing disks). Rather, it was his fierce attention to every detail of the game, his team, and his players.

"I try to make every player on my team feel he's the spark keeping our machine in motion," he once said. "On him depends our success and victories." Part of that was the attention Rockne paid to every aspect of their gear and their health. He usually packed all the team equipment, including medical supplies, himself. "I just know someone is going to forget something," he would mutter. "It could cost us a game."

He never bothered bringing a doctor on the road. Rockne was the team doctor. "He was his own doctor, trainer, and bruise and tape artist," according to his biographer Jerry Brondfield. Jimmy Crowley, one of the Four Horsemen, remembered Rockne preparing his own homemade soaking solution and, the morning before a game, spending an hour soaking and then taping Crowley's bum wrist. Another player, George Vergara, grew used to his coach doing all the taping of an injured knee or foot. "We knew he knew his stuff," Vergara later said. "We trusted him completely."

At one point a visiting orthopedist from the Mayo Clinic came to the campus to discuss the subject of athletic injuries. After a two-hour talk, the physician was impressed enough to ask one of Rockne's assistant coaches where Rockne had gone to medical school. He was flabbergasted to learn that Rockne had never so much as taken a pre-med course.

Rockne felt a deep sense of responsibility for his players, and he expected them to reciprocate. He was a fierce disciplinarian, but it was a discipline he also imposed on himself. He had to. For most of the years when he was America's winningest football coach, Rockne was also Notre Dame's most popular chemistry teacher, running two classes a day and two hours of lab per week. They were tough courses: "He had us on our mental toes all the time," remembered Roger Kiley, who was also one of his players, "just as he had us that way on the football field."

The university finally convinced Rockne, just before the 1925 season, that it needed him to devote all his time to the football team. Rockne reluctantly hung up his white lab coat and put away his test tubes and Bunsen burners for the last time. It wasn't giving up chemistry that upset him so much, he had to admit. It was that the university president made him give up coaching the track team as well.

Rockne's tenure marked Notre Dame's arrival at the pinnacle of intercollegiate football, where it would remain for years under Rockne's many successors. But there was another remarkable aspect to the man's success that doesn't get as much coverage.

Notre Dame's teams, as well as its student body, were decidedly Roman Catholic and non-Nordic in makeup, with plenty of Irish, Italian, and Polish players at a time when anti-Catholic feeling was still strong. The familiar name of the football team, the Fighting Irish, wasn't adopted until the late 1920s. The original sobriquets, the Ramblers and the Nomads, reflected the fact that the nearby Big Ten rivals declined to play the all-Catholic squad, so it had to play a national schedule out of necessity. Rockne's genius was to turn necessity into a virtue. By crisscrossing the country to play teams like Army, Georgia Tech, Southern California, Southern Methodist, and Nebraska—as well as fellow Catholic schools like Holy Cross—Notre Dame became known as a national team, with a national fan base to match. The university's administrators soon recognized the public relations advantages of being known as the representative school for Catholics and new immigrants throughout the country—including, of course, the Norwegian immigrant at the team's helm.

Thus, Knute Rockne became football's first celebrity coach. Under his guidance, Notre Dame developed the dominant football program in the country and the benchmark against which all others would be measured. He seemed indestructible, so it was with a sense of shock that America learned of Rockne's death, in a plane crash in a Kansas cornfield, in March 1931. His passing prompted tributes from across the nation. President Herbert Hoover pronounced the tragedy "a national loss," and King Haakon of Norway sent a special delegation from his embassy in Washington to attend the funeral.

More than 100,000 people stood along the route for Rockne's funeral train into South Bend. The Columbia Broadcasting System arranged for a coast-to-coast live radio hookup to carry the funeral services, followed by a one-hour memorial tribute by the sportscaster Ted Husing.

Knute Rockne was just forty-three years old.

After Rockne, for good or ill, the measure of a school's greatness was no longer its teachers or its library or its labs. Rather, a college was measured by its football team and its coach, the supreme commander and master strategist but also a father figure to his players and to the fans who revered him — or perhaps reviled him. To each and every coach who would follow him, Rockne left these words of wisdom: "Losing one game isn't bad for the team, but losing several games is bad for the coach," and "one man practicing sportsmanship is better than a hundred teaching it."

An airplane proved to be a death sentence for one prominent Scandinavian American. But for another, Charles Lindbergh, an airplane enshrined him in American history.

His father, Charles August Lindbergh, was born in Sweden in 1859. He was the illegitimate son of a man with a checkered past, August Mansson, who had been a member of the Swedish Riksdag and a prominent bank manager until he was charged with embezzlement. Mansson fled Sweden, along with his wife and seven children. Later, in the company of his nineteen-year-old mistress, Lovisa, and their baby son, Charles August, Mansson changed his name to Lindbergh and headed for America to start a new life.

He joined the first major wave of Swedish migration in the late 1850s and arrived in Minnesota in 1859. Having fled a tumultuous past in Sweden, he found himself in a tumultuous America. It was soon plunged into the Civil War and also the Sioux uprising of Chief Little Crow, when 350 settlers were killed and terror stalked every farm in Minnesota. August, Lovisa, and their growing family (eventually there would be eight children, including the eldest, Charles August) had to flee their farm. But they returned to find it intact. In 1867 August acquired 160 acres in Stearns County. The homestead proved a disaster. Grasshoppers devoured the crops three years running, and three of the Lindbergh children died of whooping cough. A horrendous accident with a buzz saw left August permanently crippled; doctors had to amputate his left arm at the shoulder. He asked doctors for the arm so he could give it a proper burial in his garden, and then August Lindbergh simply moved on. At harvest time, he rigged up a special belt so that he could continue to swing a scythe with one arm without losing a stride.

August Mansson Lindbergh had his share of hard breaks in his new country. But he was proud to become a naturalized American citizen in 1870, and especially proud of his intelligent and good-looking son Charles August. August Mansson Lindbergh would never get to meet his grandson. But Charles August would prove to be a key player in the life of his extraordinary son, Charles Lindbergh Jr. In fact, there's no understanding the son without understanding the father. Six feet tall, handsome, and charismatic, Charles August Lindbergh might well have become a Lutheran minister a quarter of a century earlier, with his booming voice, ready smile, and brooding eyes. He could have moved a congregation to laughter, tears, and devotion.

Instead, Charles August Lindbergh found his future in politics. After graduating from University of Michigan Law School and marrying the daughter of a wealthy doctor, he became prosecuting attorney in Morrison County, Minnesota. Then in 1906, a year after his son Charles Jr. was born, he was elected to the US House of Representatives. He was part of a rising tide of Scandinavian American politicians across the Midwest who would make progressivism an integral part of the bipartisan political landscape — and signaled the triumphant arrival of Scandinavian immigrants in the realm of political power.

The trend started in the 1890s with Nils Haugen, a Norwegian-born politician and congressman from Wisconsin who had come to America with his parents in 1854, when he was five. The village of Haugen, Wisconsin, is named after him.

In Minnesota there was John Johnson, the son of Swedish immigrants, who was elected governor of Minnesota in 1905 and would return to office three times. A Democrat, he became prominent enough to run for the presidential nomination in 1908 but lost to William Jennings Bryan. His sudden death in 1909 kept him from trying again in 1912 against Woodrow Wilson. Johnson was succeeded in 1909 by Adolph Eberhardt, a Republican who had been born in a village in Värmland in Sweden. He was followed by Joseph Burnquist, who was the child of Danish immigrants and governor of the state from 1915 to 1921. Later, in the 1930s, Floyd Olson, the son of what Minnesotans would call a mixed marriage — that is, a Norwegian father and a Swedish mother — sat as governor from 1931 to 1936, and Konrad Solberg was lieutenant governor of the state from 1933 to 1936. Konrad Solberg and Hjalmar

Petersen (the governor from 1936 to 1937) were both from a new voice on the political scene, the Farm Labor Party — the foundation of the later Democrat Farm Labor, a coalition of the kind that Social Democrats back in Scandinavia would have recognized.*

But probably the most influential of Minnesota's Scandinavian politicians was Andrew Volstead, born in Kenyon to Jon Vraalstad and educated at St. Olaf College. He served as mayor of Granite Falls before being elected to the Seventh District, where he served for twenty years. His name is linked forever to the bill that launched America's Noble Experiment of Prohibition, called the Volstead Act, although the bill itself was largely drafted by Wayne Wheeler of the Anti-Saloon League. Although the act was enough to put Volstead on the cover of *Time* magazine — the first Scandinavian American to be so honored — it is largely remembered as a disaster. It, and Volstead, would be swept into oblivion by Repeal in 1933.

Volstead, however, deserves better. His other legacy was the Carper-Volstead Act, which exempted those most Scandinavian of rural American institutions, the farmers' cooperatives, from the Sherman Antitrust Act. The exemption has lasted to this day.

During Prohibition in the 1920s, the man designated to prosecute the Volstead Act's violators was Minnesota's attorney general — another Swedish American, Aaron Youngquist; he had been born on a small farm near Gothenburg, Sweden. Youngquist could easily have been the Minnesota GOP's gubernatorial pick in 1929 but for the fact that he was drawn to Washington, DC, to become the US attorney general for the Hoover administration. Of the sixty to seventy cases he argued before the Supreme Court, the most famous case was his prosecution of Al Capone for income tax evasion, thus ending the bootlegger's crime spree in Chicago — which Volstead had inadvertently started.

Almost all these politicians and their fellow Scandinavian Americans in neighboring North and South Dakota (such as Governor Pete Norbeck of South Dakota) and Illinois (such as Congressman Fred Lundine) were progressives, reflecting a view of government as a benign force that could help

---

* On Social Democrats in Scandinavia, see Chapter 14.

raise all boats — an idea that was common back in the old country. The man who inspired much of the progressive wave in Wisconsin, and who would become its most famous presidential candidate, was the US senator Robert "Fighting Bob" La Follette. Though not of Scandinavian descent himself, he had grown up in a Norwegian neighborhood in Dane County, Wisconsin, and learned to shape his message to appeal to this important bloc of Wisconsin voters. It was even said that La Follette could converse with constituents in Sogn peasant dialect, which he had learned from his Norwegian playmates.

But perhaps the most extraordinary fate of any Scandinavian American politician in that age had to be the one that befell Wisconsin's Irvine Luther Lenroot, who was born to Swedish immigrant parents in Superior. He served in the US House of Representatives from 1909 to 1918 and in the US Senate from 1918 to 1928. Lenroot was Warren G. Harding's vice-presidential pick in 1920 and would have run with him on the Republican ticket but for the fact that doyens of the smoke-filled rooms at the national convention in Chicago decided they needed a New England man to balance the ticket. They chose Calvin Coolidge of Massachusetts, and Harding bowed to their wishes. If Harding had gotten his way, Lenroot would have been elected vice president that year. And upon Harding's death, in 1923, Lenroot, not Calvin Coolidge, would have become president — the first (and to this day the only) Scandinavian to hold the highest office in the land.[*]

When Fred Lundin was running for Congress in 1908, the *Svenska Amerikanaren* ran this paragraph: "If everything goes well in the next election, three Swedish-Americans will be elected to Congress, namely: Irvine Lenroot of Wisconsin, Charles A. Lindbergh of Minnesota, Frederick Lundin of Illinois. At the present time there seems no doubt that these three candidates will be elected with large majorities."

The newspaper was right, especially about Charles A. Lindbergh. Already known as the "brightest lawyer in Minnesota," he was determined to support

---

[*] Since then, the presidential nominees Hubert Humphrey (whose mother was Norwegian) and Walter Mondale also were unable to break fate's ban on Scandinavians in the White House.

the hardworking farmers of his state against what he called the speculative parasites of the big banks and trusts. Once elected to Congress, he became part of the progressive coalition that included the senators Bob La Follette of Wisconsin, Bill Borah of Idaho, and Albert Beveridge of Indiana, although according to one of their number, John Nelson of Wisconsin (who was himself of Norwegian parentage), Lindbergh was "perhaps the most radical and independent of the group." The muckraking journalist Ida Tarbell admiringly dubbed him "a Swede who dreams," as Lindbergh waged a relentless war on the big-money trusts' apparent stranglehold on the American economy — a war that sometimes won support from colleagues and at other times didn't.

His brooding over the power of Wall Street and perilous state of his country became an obsession. Ultimately it affected his marriage. His wife, Evangeline, left Washington to return to Minnesota, where she focused on raising her children, including Charles Junior. Eventually she sued for divorce, causing a major career setback for Charles Senior, who was already having his problems in Congress and back home.

Charles Senior's political ambitions finally came a cropper when he ran unsuccessfully for the US Senate in 1916, and then for governor, with the same result. Continuing as a member of Congress, he cast his vote against entering the war in Europe in 1917, one of fifty-six members who did. Like many Scandinavians, he was a firm believer in American neutrality (another vote against came from the North Dakota senator Asle Gronna, who was of Norwegian descent). Like German Americans, many Nordic Americans found President Woodrow Wilson's hostility to Germany and bias in favor of England and the Allies incomprehensible.

But Lindbergh's vote badly hurt him at home. With the onrush of American patriotism the war provoked, Charles August Lindbergh found himself surrounded by angry crowds everywhere he went. In Red Wing (ironically, the home of the Norwegian Americans' largest theological seminary) he was hanged in effigy. Once he was even dragged from the speaker's platform by a mob and nearly lynched. In another incident, he and his entourage were "driven from one town with a volley of shots." The printers' plates of his anti-Wilson book, *Why This Country Is at War*, were looted and smashed.

Despite his loss of the Senate race, Lindbergh was respected enough by

Wilson's war production czar, Bernard Baruch, to be invited to serve on the War Industries Board. The public outcry, however, forced Lindbergh out. In 1920, when the tide of American public opinion had shifted from support for the war to weariness and disillusionment with it, Lindbergh tried to resurrect his political career by running again for office, this time for his old House seat. But it was too late. He lost by a 2-to-1 margin.

Watching his father's unhappy political career, the younger Lindbergh learned a powerful lesson: the press could make or break a man's reputation almost overnight. He would also remember his father's bitter pronouncement: "If you are for America first, last, and all the time ... then you are classed as pro-German by the big press." Charles August also added this warning: "The trouble with war is that it kills off the best men a country has."

Trapped in a family with a deeply unhappy mother and a tortured father, Charles Lindbergh Jr. grew up a lonely boy whose only consolation was his love of gadgets. He saw his very first airplane in 1907. Years later he could recall every detail of the machine combing the sky overhead. It never left his imagination.

He joined the US Army with the sole intention of finding a place in its air service. After his discharge he went through a phase as a daring, barnstorming pilot touring the Midwest, taking anyone aloft who cared for a ride — for a modest fee. He was working as one of the pilots recruited to provide air mail service in the mid-1920s when he conceived the idea of making a solo flight across the Atlantic. That dream became an obsession. He only needed partners to finance the trip and the right airplane.

Twentysomething Charles Lindbergh was a quiet, unassuming young man, standing a rather awkward six foot three; he towered over most everyone. But he could inspire. In 1926 and 1927 his transatlantic dream caught the attention of two airplane designers, one in New York and the other in San Diego. Eventually Lindbergh chose the plane designed and built by Ryan Airlines in California. When he assembled his team on Long Island, on May 20, 1927, he was ready for the enterprise of the century.

Comparisons with Leif Erikson and other Vikings who made similar ventures into the unknown were inevitable. But it was Lindbergh, that Friday morning, who understood best the Viking spirit in its modern form: "I have felt the godlike power man derives from his machines," he wrote later, "the immortal viewpoint of higher air." It was a confidence in the ability of the individual to choose a destiny based on practiced skill — what Thorstein Veblen attributed to the instinct of craftsmanship — that Lindbergh set in motion that foggy morning in May. His solo flight would carry him three thousand miles in a little less than thirty-six hours — or so he hoped.

He described the flight itself in his memoir *We* (which I first read as a fourth-grader), other books, and even a movie. There were harrowing moments, when the wings iced over and when he nearly fell asleep, bringing his plane so close to the ocean below that spray from the waves slapped his face. And when he was nearing Paris, his switching of the gas tanks temporarily went wrong.

These became familiar episodes in accounts of the historic flight and were portrayed in the film *The Spirit of St. Louis.* Less famed, though, is what Lindbergh considered the most haunting moment of the entire trip. It occurred when he was still high over the vast Atlantic, twenty-four hours out from Long Island. Suddenly he found himself surrounded by spirits and visions: in his words, "vaguely outlined forms, transparent, moving, riding weightless, with me in the plane." The visions were human in shape but empty of form. They seemed to speak to him with human voices — ones he could not understand — then they vanished.

That's Lindbergh's story. There's no reason to doubt he saw and heard *something.* A fanciful person might speculate that they were the ghosts of Vikings past — Leif Erikson himself, perhaps, who had crossed over the same waters in a longship instead of an airplane? Might these spirits be watching over one of their own lineage, making the voyage alone, defying the storms, ice, and fog of the North Atlantic, which they too had faced? Perhaps they were hallucinations caused by a lack of sleep. The experience must have been disconcerting, enough to make Lindbergh leave the strange encounter out of the memoir *We* — might the mysterious title relate to this encounter? In any case, almost three decades would pass before he was ready to talk about the experience.

The Spirit of St. Louis touched down at La Bourget Airport on the evening of May 21, 1927. When Lindbergh woke up the next morning in a spare bedroom in the American embassy in Paris, with the international press gathered outside his door, he realized he was world famous. In addition, and to his mind more important, he had set in motion a new era, not just in air travel or the age of the machine, but in the ability of humanity to conceive and realize its most important dreams. It was a triumphant moment for the Viking heart.

"I was astonished at the effect my successful landing in France had on the nations of the world," he wrote. "To me, it was like a match lighting a bonfire."

America went wild. The outpouring of adulation extended from newspaper articles and telegrams of congratulations, including one from President Calvin Coolidge, to songs, dances, and musical pageants with titles like "Lucky Lindy," "The Lone Eagle," "Lindy, the Bird of the Clouds," and "Columbus of the Air." (No one, it seemed, published a song called "Leif Erikson of the Air.") At the high-brow end of the spectrum, the composer Kurt Weill and the playwright Berthold Brecht went so far as to create a cantata of fifteen scenes, for soloists, chorus, and orchestra, titled "Der Lindberghflug"; the tenor playing Lindbergh had to face symbolic foes such as Fog, Snowstorm, and Sleep.

Almost overnight, Lindbergh had become the most famous person in the world. Celebrity led to travel across Europe and Asia, and Lindbergh developed a restlessness and love of visiting distant places that never left him. He also married, and in February 1930 he and his wife, Anne Morrow Lindbergh, had a baby boy. If any man could be called happy, it was Charles Lindbergh.

Then it all came crashing down. First, in March 1932, came the kidnapping of the Lindbergh baby, which became the crime sensation of the decade. Suddenly, "for the second time in less than five years," writes his biographer A. Scott Berg, "the world revolved around Charles Lindbergh." There was a nationwide search for the missing child, and telegrams of sympathy poured in by the tens of thousands, sent by the likes of President Hoover and Will Rogers — even Al Capone. The first TV images ever broadcast were of the Lindbergh baby. Every family in America suddenly felt unsafe; the Lindbergh kidnapping changed the perception of children's vulnerability like no other event in American history.

After seventy-two agonizing days, during which the Lindberghs received more than forty thousand letters, the body of a baby was found in a field four miles away from the Lindberghs' home. An autopsy confirmed it was their lost child, killed with a blow to the head. National anxiety and sympathy turned to national mourning, then outrage, when a suspect, Bruno Hauptmann, was arrested. The Crime of the Century was followed by the Trial of the Century, then Hauptmann's execution, which was three times prepared but then twice postponed: an emotional cliff-hanger that almost seemed calculated to prolong the Lindberghs' ordeal.

Fortunately for his family, Charles Lindbergh had already decided to move on. He became absorbed in various scientific experiments, and the urge for air travel returned to him. In 1933 he contracted a flight over his father's homeland, Sweden, which enthralled him with its physical beauty. "I wonder why my folks ever left that place?" he declared later.

He was now also drawn into other national matters, particularly the state of American military aviation. He was saddened to see that America's former wartime ally, Great Britain, had all but given up on further technical advances in the field. Then came the invitation to Germany for the 1936 Olympics and a guided tour of the Luftwaffe's facilities with the *Reichsmarschall* himself, Hermann Göring.

That tour, and Lindbergh's subsequent remarks, would become his nemesis. He observed that "as much as I disagree with some of the things that have been done," Hitler "has done much for Germany" and that he saw "youth, hope and vigor in Germany today." These statements have passed into permanent notoriety. Lindbergh was also inclined to pass off the Nazi discrimination against the Jews as due in part to the support so many had supposedly given to Germany's Communists. His wife, Anne, was even more rapturous in her praise of the new Germany Hitler had built, and she blamed Jewish-owned newspapers for the bad publicity that their tour provoked.

Lindbergh was hardly alone in being impressed by Nazi Germany and taken in by its propaganda. In 1936–37 the future shadow of Auschwitz was visible only to a very few. But one thing about the tour left Lindbergh shaken: the steady advance of German air power. He returned for another tour in 1937, and what he saw deeply disturbed him. He saw the Luftwaffe's new fighter, the Messerschmitt Me 109, and its Dornier Do 17 bomber. At the factory works at Focke-Wulf he was shown the world's first working helicopter. He knew that neither the British nor the French, let alone the Americans, had anything that could remotely compete with those machines. When he returned home after a third tour of Europe in April 1939, he was determined to do something about it. He made a phone call to the head of the Army Air Corps, his friend Hap Arnold, and arranged a secret meeting at West Point, one that would have immense consequences.

At the time, Lindbergh's principal goal was not to get America ready to fight a war but rather to deter one. His deep conviction, shared by many, was that America and its former allies from the previous world war were simply not prepared to fight if conflict came to Europe. He remembered his father's words about how wars destroy a nation's best men. The idea of keeping America out of the next one became his guiding light. It led him to lend his name and prestige to the America First Committee.

When war actually did break out, in September 1939, millions of Americans shared Lindbergh's greatest fear: that the Anglophile Franklin Roosevelt would rally behind Britain, inevitably drawing America into the conflict, though, in their opinion, it had no geopolitical, economic, or even moral stake in it. Today, of course, with our knowledge of the Holocaust, we realize that the moral stakes were high. But for many Americans, ignorant of what was happening in Hitler's Europe, the moral scales seemed tipped the other way — especially after the disillusioning experience of World War I, which still hung in the air. As Fighting Bob La Follette's son, the Wisconsin senator Robert La Follette Jr., stated, "I will never give my vote to send American boys to fight and die on the battlefields of the Old World" — as Americans had done before. According to one of the big wheels of America First, Senator Burton K. Wheeler, "the preservation of our way of life here in America" was at stake.

As a military man, however, Lindbergh had another worry: Britain and France might lose this war, thanks to superior German air power. The precipitous fall of France in less than six weeks in May–June 1940 seemed to bear this prediction out. In an article that appeared in the *Atlantic Monthly,* Lindbergh asserted that the war in Europe was just "a continuation of the old struggle among western nations for the material benefits of the world." The United States needed to stay away from it, let alone side with the inevitable losers — Britain and France — in the struggle against Hitler. In fact, he added, a strong Germany was essential to Europe's security, "for she alone can either dam the Asiatic hordes or form the spearhead of their penetration into Europe": thus he raised the specter of a Germany permanently allied with the Soviet Union, thanks to their non-aggression pact signed in August 1939.

Through Lindbergh's increasingly strident speeches against involvement in the war in Europe, he essentially became the poster boy of the America First Committee, a coalition of antiwar politicians, intellectuals, and business and labor leaders that included the progressive Democrat senator Burton K. Wheeler of Montana, the Republican conservative senator Robert Taft of Ohio, and the Socialist leader Norman Thomas. Interestingly, most Scandinavian Americans — having seen their Danish and Norwegian homelands overrun by the Nazis — were less than impressed by the neutralist rhetoric of the America Firsters, Lindbergh included.

Lindbergh's words also earned him the permanent enmity of Franklin D. Roosevelt. Roosevelt denounced him as "a Copperhead," linking him to the pro-Confederate Northerners of the Civil War. Lindbergh felt his "loyalty, character, and motives" were being questioned, as well as his honor, and decided to resign his commission as colonel in the US Army Air Corps Reserve. It was a heartbreaking moment for Lindbergh. "The army meant so much to him," his wife, Anne Morrow Lindbergh, wrote in her diary. "It was the open world, his first chance; he blossomed there." Now he was consumed with preventing America from entering a war like the one that his father had opposed.

All spring and summer of 1941, Lindbergh spoke at rally after rally for the America First Committee while the war in Europe grew in intensity and, with Hitler's invasion of the Soviet Union in June, in scope. His critics slammed Lindbergh for speaking to audiences that included members of pro-Nazi groups like the German American Bund and the American Destiny Party. Libraries around the country yanked his books from their shelves, and cities stripped his name from streets and boulevards named in his honor. His hometown, Little Falls, Minnesota, repainted its water tower to blot out his name.

The criticism reached the peak of its crescendo on September 11, when Lindbergh gave a speech in Des Moines, Iowa, titled "Who Are the War Agitators?" In it he cast part of the blame for pro-war sentiment on American Jews: "their greatest danger to this country lies in their large ownership and influence in our motion pictures, our press, and our Government." Lindbergh concluded, "We cannot blame them for looking out for what they believe to be their own interests, but we must also look out for ours."

Lindbergh's remarks set off a firestorm. They prompted the *New York Times* to say, "The America First Committee had touched the pitch of anti-Semitism and its fingers were tarred," while *Liberty* magazine called Lindbergh "the most dangerous man in America." One pro-interventionist group even went so far as to title one of its pamphlets "Is Lindbergh a Nazi?"

What indeed was Lindbergh thinking? Was the man who had described Hitler as "a great man" and accepted an award from the German government (the Order of the Golden Eagle) a naive dupe, or something worse — what FDR's interior secretary, Harold Ickes, called "the No. 1 United States Nazi fellow traveler"? Ironically, the speech that brought Lindbergh so much notoriety and enmity was intended to compliment both Jews and the British people, the two groups (besides the Roosevelt administration) that he considered the chief advocates of America's entrance into the war.

"I am not attacking either the Jewish or the British people," Lindbergh had stated in the same speech. "It is not difficult to understand why Jewish people desire the overthrow of Nazi Germany. The persecution they suffered in Germany would be sufficient to make bitter enemies of any race." But that bitterness, Lindbergh went on, did not excuse what he saw as their effort "for reasons which are not American" to drag the United States into a war that would benefit just one country: Great Britain.

Certainly Lindbergh's reference to Jews as a "race" collides with our sensibilities today, although the phrasing was quite common at the time, even among Jews. Likewise, the implication that American Jews "are not American" was defamatory to say the least — and the attack on their supposed control of Hollywood and the media has powerful echoes of statements made by anti-Semites who say the same thing in their effort to fight the so-called Israel lobby.

In the end, as the biographer Winston Groom points out, Lindbergh was anti-Semitic "to the same extent that many if not most Americans of his era were anti-Semitic." Yet nothing in the historical record proves him to be pro-Nazi. Despite the flight of fiction in Philip Roth's portrayal of Lindbergh in

The Plot Against America, there is no evidence that the celebrated airman had fascist leanings. Long before war broke out in Europe in September 1939, and then afterward, he had no contact with anyone connected with Nazi Germany. The speech was, in fact, the one and only time Lindbergh ever mentioned Jews, favorably or unfavorably, in a public statement.

That of course does not excuse all his actions or expunge the historical record. His rhetorical embrace of a negative stereotype of Jews as manipulators of the media and political institutions bespeaks a lack of understanding, even humanity, that grates on the conscience — and stands at odds with the modern Viking heart. In many ways, his prominence as an American hero amplified his sins. In Winston Groom's words, his halo had become a noose. His reputation, which had stood so high, ultimately sank to unfathomable depths. It is difficult to reconcile the America First activist with the Lone Eagle who defied the odds over the Atlantic.

As usual, his staunchest defender was his wife, Anne. As vilification and vituperation descended on Lindbergh's head from all sides, she wrote in her diary that she herself would rather see America go to war than be "shaken by violent anti-Semitism" of the Nazi brand. She had urged him to include a sentence in that speech stating that he was not an anti-Semite and did not mean to attack Jews as un-American.

But he refused. For Charles, she wrote, the choice was simply "whether or not you are going to let your country go into a completely disastrous war for lack of courage to name the groups leading that country to war — at the risk of being called 'anti-Semitic' simply by *naming* them."

That explanation is grossly insufficient. We know (as Lindbergh didn't) the significance of America's eventual entry into World War II — just as we also know that Hitler's war against European Jewry had already grown to Holocaust proportions by the time Lindbergh spoke. History has judged Lindbergh harshly, and rightly so.

For a time, the enmity Lindbergh had earned was blown away when, three months later, on December 7, 1941, Japan attacked Pearl Harbor. The America First Committee vanished into history, and Lindbergh, almost overnight, went from antiwar activist to all-out supporter of American victory over its enemies. President Roosevelt refused him any reinstatement in the Army Air Corps, so

Lindbergh threw himself into the war effort on a purely voluntary basis. He became a human guinea pig at the Mayo Clinic for experiments related to the effect of high altitude on pilots' bodies. He helped fellow ex–America Firster Henry Ford build the factory at Willow Run to produce B-24 bombers, and later he flew on fifty combat missions in the Pacific Theater — a clear violation of the terms of his tour as a "technical representative" in the Pacific. He was supposed to demonstrate to army pilots how to get the most of their new twin-engine P-38 Lightning fighters — but he was not supposed to fight.

As a member of a similar technical mission, he flew to Germany shortly after the Nazi defeat. He visited the sites where he had witnessed the supposedly invincible German Luftwaffe. The Third Reich had been reduced to rubble by American bombers. Lindbergh set foot in the ruins of Hitler's inner sanctum at Berchtesgaden in the Bavarian mountains, "where the man Hitler, now the myth Hitler, contemplated and laid his plans," Lindbergh wrote in his journal, "the man who in a few years threw the human world into the greatest convulsion it has ever known and from which it will be recuperating for generations." Hitler, he wrote, "a man who controlled such power, who might have turned it to human good, who used it to such resulting evil . . ."

This is a strange epitaph from a man widely seen as a Hitler admirer and a Nazi sympathizer. If Lindbergh had been as insightful about the true character of the Nazi regime before the war as hindsight made him afterward, his reputation would stand higher today — and his place in the history of the Viking heart would not be so problematic.

History springs up ironies like mushrooms after a summer rain. The one that stalks Lindbergh the America Firster is that he can also lay claim to making one of the most substantial contributions to Hitler's defeat, and Japan's, even before the World War II started.

In March 1939, he had recently returned from Germany and called General Hap Arnold, chief of the Army Air Corps, for a secret meeting at West Point. When they met in the football field bleachers, Lindbergh spoke of his growing fear of Germany's air power, especially its bomber fleet, and the need for the Air Corps to build an advanced bomber of its own. That led Arnold to reach out to the Boeing company in Washington State, where an engineer of Norwegian descent named Claire Egtvedt was working on a design for a four-engine strategic bomber; it would become the B-17 Flying Fortress. Together with another Scandinavian American and the child of Swedish immigrants Philip Johnson, Egtvedt would go on to supervise construction of the most advanced strategic bomber in history, the B-29. On August 7, 1945, Egtvedt's massive, gleaming silver brainchild delivered the atomic bomb on Hiroshima, then four days later on Nagasaki, forcing Japan to surrender and bringing World War II to a close.

Could America and the Allies have won the war without the B-17 or the B-29? It's doubtful. Would engineers like Egtvedt have developed those tools of victory without Lindbergh's help? Almost certainly. Lindbergh's patriotism was never in question, any more than his personal courage or willingness to risk everything to fly into the unknown — all qualities of the Viking heart. But he was lacking some of its other qualities: the sense of compassion, of understanding the plight of others, and an openness to their pain and suffering. A heart with those qualities is immune to racism and prejudice.

In his autobiography Lindbergh asked, "Science, freedom, beauty, adventure: what more could you ask of life?" What indeed. A strong sense of moral and social responsibility, and better judgment as the world was being set ablaze, the Viking heart might answer. By December 1941, Lindbergh had woken up and seen what was happening in the world, and it was too late to save his reputation — but not too late to join in the effort to reverse the tide.

By then, in fact, two Danish Americans, both immigrants, were gearing up America's industrial might to produce victory in the greatest global conflict in history.

13

Men at Work

The Viking Heart and American Democracy

We can do anything if we do it together.

— William Knudsen

OF ALL AMERICA'S famous Scandinavian Americans, Charles Lindbergh remains the most controversial. Two of his sharpest critics were also Scandinavian Americans, although one of them undoubtedly deserves the same degree of scrutiny for his moral failings — perhaps more so.

His name was Gutzon Borglum. Born to Danish immigrant parents, he was in the 1930s the most famous sculptor in America, thanks to the masterpiece he had conceived and executed almost single-handedly: the ultimate monument to American exceptionalism, Mount Rushmore. During the great debate over whether America should enter World War II, Borglum had lashed out more than once at Lindbergh for his support for Nazi Germany: "No civilized man could condone such barbarities," Borglum told the press after the events of Kristallnacht, in 1938. Of Lindbergh himself he said, "The boy who flew the Atlantic is not the boy who accepts a gold medal from an S.O.B. and right-hand bower of the Hitler regime," meaning the Luftwaffe chief, Hermann Göring.

Borglum had earlier been a fan of Lindbergh. His daughter remembered how he had burst into their living room in San Antonio, Texas, waving the newspaper announcing Lindbergh's solo flight. Her father was shouting aloud with pleasure, with tears in his eyes. His attitude changed, however, as the situation in Europe deteriorated and the threat of Nazism and fascism grew — a threat that Lindbergh was unable to recognize; he even seemed to encourage the overreach.

For Borglum, that threat became personal. When the Nazis overran Poland in 1939, one of Borglum's own sculptures, his statue of President Woodrow Wilson in the central square of Poznań, Poland, fell victim to Hitler, who ordered it destroyed as an "artistic eyesore" — and as a reproach to the American president who had helped give Poland its freedom.

Yet Borglum himself had views about Jews that put Lindbergh's in a deep shade. His most recent biographers admit that "Gutzon believed the Jew was a parasite and Judaism a plague" — although that did not prevent him from including Supreme Court Justice Felix Frankfurter among his closest friends, or employing the Jewish banker Paul Warburg as his financial adviser, or including Jewish millionaires such as Samuel Colt and Eugene Meyer among his devoted patrons. Borglum's views on African Americans were nearly as contradictory. He was at the same time a friend of the Ku Klux Klan *and* a deep admirer of Abraham Lincoln. In fact, he named his eldest son after the sixteenth president.

Borglum's noxious racial views and his role in American art are likewise contradictory. This child of Scandinavia helped transform American art with his massive undertaking at Mount Rushmore. Indeed, in the 1930s, while the country was struggling with the Great Depression and participating in the New Deal, Gutzon Borglum was working on a truly gigantic scale to inspire his and future generations to take a fresh look at the founders of American liberty and greatness.

The monument stands unsurpassed in the annals of American public art. Whatever we think of the man, the deed remains a triumph of the instinct of workmanship.

The son of Danish Mormon parents, Borglum grew up in a household with two sister-mothers. In the 1890s his father moved the family to Los Angeles, where his five talented sons, including Gutzon, would find their way into successful careers. For Gutzon, painting was his first fascination, followed by sculpture. He turned out to be particularly talented at working with marble or bronze. The desire to unleash that talent boldly led him and his new wife, Lisa (née Putnam), to head to Europe, so he could exhibit his works and establish contacts with leading artists of the day, including the sculptor Auguste Rodin. It was in Paris that he exhibited his first important sculpture, a small bronze statue showing a pony bending over a fallen Native American warrior. Titled *Death of the Chief,* it won critical acclaim. The sculpture launched him on a career as the "American Rodin" — and praise and controversy followed him, as they did his famed mentor.

Borglum's skill flowed in multiple directions. He and his wife moved to London, where he enjoyed brilliant success as a portrait painter in the style of John Singer Sargent. He did not neglect his gift for sculpture, though. His bronze work *Apaches Pursued,* depicting three Apache boys mounted on wild horses, earned him critical respect as well as some serious money. He became a member of the Royal Society of British Artists. When he returned to America in April 1901, he was thirty-one years old and had garnered membership in three honorary artists' societies in three countries. More important, he had found his principal subject: the history of the country to which his father, Jens Borglum, had immigrated, having left Denmark in the spring of 1864.

Momentous events were sweeping across the American landscape at that time — the siege of Atlanta, the battles of the Wilderness and Spotsylvania. But Jens and his new bride (they were married on shipboard) were coming to create a new life as members of the Church of Latter-Day Saints, in a remote desert corner of a rugged, war-torn land.

When Borglum returned to the United States in 1901, however, the country was entering a different sort of new era. Industrialization had spread from the Eastern Seaboard to the Midwest; Wall Street wealth, rows of smokestacks, and shiploads of new immigrants were transforming the United States — and some argued that the change was for the worse. Borglum set for himself the ambition to remind his fellow Americans, immigrants and native-born alike, of their heroic roots and past struggles. He sought to invoke a time when the Viking heart had seemed instinctive, even among non-Vikings, and its values universal.

Borglum's message found an eager audience. His career exploded. From his New York City studio, he conceived a range of projects and was commissioned to do others; most of his subjects concerned heroic aspects of American history and Greek myth. In Washington, DC, he became a favorite for creating official portraiture that depicted, in marble or bronze, both the living and the dead. There were statues of General Philip Sheridan, a Lincoln bust completed in 1908 (it now lives in the US Capitol), and a seated Lincoln, finished in 1911. It was shortly after this that Borglum named his eldest son Lincoln.

There was a memorial to Henry Lawson Wyatt portraying the North Carolina state capitol; one for the former progressive mayor Henry Altgeld in Chicago; one for the author Robert Louis Stevenson in Saranac Lake, New York; and a work called *The Indian and the Puritan,* executed in 1916 for a park in Newark, New Jersey. In addition to the bust of Lincoln for the National Statuary Hall in the US Capitol, Borglum was commissioned to create three more sculptures for that honored setting — he has more works in the hall than any other sculptor.

Nonetheless, the American West, particularly the plains of Idaho and Nebraska where he grew up, attracted and inspired Borglum. His bronze works on western themes are recognized as artistic masterpieces. He might have gone down as the equal of Frederick Remington, or Augustus Saint-Gaudens, in the pantheon of immortal American sculptors had he not also been attracted and inspired by an organization that achieved a major resurgence just before, and just after, World War I: the Ku Klux Klan.

The white supremacist Klan had come a long way since its origin as a post-Confederacy terrorist group in the defeated South. Fueled by the success of the movie *Birth of a Nation,* it had achieved a superficial respectability as the defender of Americanism against what were seen as the hordes of foreign immigrants flooding America's shores. Even President Warren G. Harding, no enemy of America's Black population, became an honorary member. Borglum too felt the pull of the KKK's refurbished message — preserve America's racial heritage in order to protect its cultural and political freedoms — though he himself was a child of foreign immigrants himself (albeit acceptable Nordic ones).

While he embraced the KKK's racist message, Borglum (like many others) fused it with a politically progressive outlook. He was a profound admirer of Theodore Roosevelt, in fact. And one of his most celebrated statues of the 1920s depicted the iconic progressive martyrs to American injustice, Sacco and Vanzetti. Although he could be rabidly anti-Semitic in some of his public remarks and private letters, his circle of close friends, as we have noted, included many prominent Jews. In fact, Supreme Court Justice Felix Frankfurter said of his complicated and often tormented friend, "He was one of those artists who had delightful incapacities for running government, but knew exactly how to do it ... It was all clear, black and white, passionate, uncompromising ... People weren't wrong, they were crooked. People didn't disagree with him; they cheated him."

That point of view would characterize Borglum's next great project, and its unhappy outcome. Although a great admirer of Abraham Lincoln, he was also drawn to the "lost cause" of the Confederacy. When the opportunity arose to create an enormous frieze portraying the Confederate heroes Robert E. Lee and Stonewall Jackson, at the behest of the Daughters of the Confederacy, Borglum jumped at it. The scale of the project was breathtaking: the finished work was meant to command almost the entire width of the summit of Stone Mountain in Georgia. Borglum had never worked with such dimensions before. Nor had anyone else. In order to cast the original sketches onto the mountain, Borglum invented a new kind of light projector; it threw the image up onto the space where he would do the carving.

But Borglum's vision for the Stone Mountain monument conflicted with that of an important segment of patrons, the Ku Klux Klan. Borglum's progressive politics didn't square with the Klan's reactionary populism. It didn't help that the project had to be suspended because of the outbreak of World War I. Borglum also became entangled in a bitter battle for control with the Klan, whose members failed to raise the funds needed to get the project underway. It wasn't until June 23, 1923, that Borglum was able to start carving. In January 1924, the first section of the monument, Lee's head, was unveiled. But by then the project was doomed.

Finally fed up by the Klan's incompetence and malfeasance, in March 1925 Borglum smashed his clay and plaster models and left Georgia for good. A sheriff's warrant was issued for his arrest for "wilful destruction of association property," and Borglum led a car chase across the border into North Carolina.

The work he had done was blasted off the mountain's face to make way for that of his successor, Henry Augustus Lukeman. Almost ten years had been wasted —but not quite. Borglum had learned techniques for creating sculpture on a mammoth scale. All he needed was a suitable subject and a place to do it.

The opportunity came in a telegram from the state historian in South Dakota, Doane Robinson. It read: "Would it be possible for you to design and supervise a massive sculpture [here in South Dakota] . . . if it be possible . . . we could arrange to finance such an enterprise . . ."

Borglum received the telegram in the spring of 1924, while he was still struggling with the Stone Mountain project. Now this new idea consumed his imagination. It fit in with a plan "which I have had for years for great Northern Memorial in the center of the nation," he wrote after visiting South Dakota — a memorial to match, in size and scale, what he had wanted to execute at Stone Mountain. This work, however, was different in focus. It would celebrate "the principle of the Union itself" rather than just the soldiers and leaders of the South during the Civil War.

The novelist F. Scott Fitzgerald said that the measure of a first-rate intelligence was the ability to hold two opposing ideas at the same time, and still function. He might have been talking about Gutzon Borglum. The KKK collaborator who was also an admirer of Abraham Lincoln, the professed anti-Semite who counted Jews among his closest friends and patrons, the man who celebrated the men who won the West but also crafted in bronze a number of deeply sensitive tributes to Native Americans — in the end had a vision of America too big and too all-encompassing for a single ideology or political creed to hold. Borglum needed a place that could accommodate his epic vision in epic visual terms. He found it in the granite cliffs of Mount Rushmore, in South Dakota's Black Hills.

Borglum's obsessive drive and vision over fourteen years, from 1927 until 1941, made the conception and completion of Mount Rushmore possible. It was the Scandinavian instinct for workmanship on a titanic scale. But without the dedication and patient marshaling of resources, both financial and material, by South Dakota's governor, Peter Norbeck, himself the son of Swedish Norwegian immigrants, Borglum's vision could never have become reality.

The project was originally estimated to require fifty years of work. With Norbeck's help, Borglum managed to execute it in less than fifteen; his son Lincoln took over supervision of the project and its hundreds of workers while Borglum bounded off to Europe to fulfill other lucrative commissions, which helped to keep the big project afloat. He always returned as soon as he could to watch his greatest creation take shape.

Borglum himself selected the monument's subjects (observing one stricture — in 1927, President Calvin Coolidge insisted that at least two Republicans be represented). George Washington seemed an obvious choice. Abraham Lincoln, a particular hero of Borglum's and a president whose reputation as a national hero was on the rise, thanks to his Swedish American biographer, Carl Sandburg. Borglum selected Thomas Jefferson because he had instigated the Louisiana Purchase, which had more than doubled the size of the United States. Borglum even wanted the monument to include a carved representation of the purchase agreement, but the nature of the granite made it unfeasible, so Lincoln's head took its place. To complete the presidential quartet, he finally decided on Theodore Roosevelt — a progressive hero to Borglum and also the creator of the National Park Service. Mount Rushmore was to be its crown jewel.

The difficulty of the project was mind-boggling. Workers had to climb a five-hundred-step staircase carved into the rock face in order to reach the summit. Carvers had to dangle from safety harnesses hundreds of feet above the valley, just to wield their hammers and chisels to create the stone heads. Borglum originally wanted the portraits to be waist length, but there was barely enough funding to support the heads and faces.

Money, or more precisely the chronic lack of it, was a constant worry and source of tension and disagreement. It ultimately ruined Norbeck's health, and he died in 1937. Borglum had hoped that in the New Deal era of massive government-sponsored projects — Boulder Dam, the dams at Grand Coulee and Bonneville, the Tennessee Valley Authority — Mount Rushmore would be the object of similar Washington-directed largesse. In the end, however, appropriations by Congress were constantly trimmed, and only a steady trickle of dollars from private donors kept the project alive.

Still, Borglum used the unveiling of each head as it was completed as an opportunity for publicity. George Washington's head was dedicated first, on the Fourth of July, 1934. Lincoln's was ready for viewing on September 17, 1937, to coincide with the 150th anniversary of the signing of the US Constitution. Theodore Roosevelt's portrait was not finished until July 2, 1939, as war in Europe loomed.

The final cost was $1 million, a fraction of the total budget for the building of Boulder Dam; also, the sculpture was done in about a third of the time required by the construction of the dam. Amazingly, creating the mammoth monument had cost not a single human life — compared to Boulder Dam's death toll of ninety-six. As the project drew to an end, Borglum wrote a personal letter to FDR, pleading for $86,000 to complete the polishing of the granite for the presidential portraits. It was 1940. Borglum was seventy-four years old, and Europe was at war again. He also wrote to FDR: "Of course what Hitler et al., stands for cannot succeed. This world would never have reached its present position if the spirit that destroyed Czechoslovakia, destroyed Poland, robbed Denmark, lied its way into Norway, and is now destroying hundreds of thousands of unoffending people in the Netherlands and Belgium — if that spirit meant success . . . Excuse this but I am so wrought up over what's happening."

He wrote to another friend, the progressive Republican senator Burt Wheeler, "There is one single human obligation now before all decent fathers, mothers, governments — *Stop Hitler and his cutthroats.*"

Borglum died in March 1941, just months before Mount Rushmore was really and truly complete — and six months before Lindbergh's controversial speech in Des Moines, Iowa. Like Lindbergh's views on race, Gutzon's are alien to the modern Viking heart. Like their ancient forebears, both men strove to conquer the external world and to accomplish the impossible, one working in stone and the other alone in the air. But neither conquered the prejudice in his soul, any latitude allowed for the era in which he lived notwithstanding. We can look back with awe on the accomplishments of these men. But if we are looking for inspiring values, we have to search elsewhere.

America's industrial heartland offers a restorative contrast. In Detroit in 1940, just as the clouds of war sweeping over Europe were edging closer to America, two Danish immigrants were gathering resources to help their adopted country prevail in the coming conflict. Their contemporaries knew them as the Great Dane and Cast-Iron Charlie, twin dynamos of the two most important automobile companies in America, Ford and General Motors.

But Charles Sorensen and William Knudsen were far more than corporate executives. They had worked their way up from the assembly line to transform the American automotive industry in many more ways than their mentor, Henry Ford, had done. By 1940, they were ready to engage their own instinct of workmanship in a mammoth effort to save America and the whole world.

The pair of them lived and worked in the city where Charles Lindbergh had been born: Detroit, Michigan.

William Knudsen, eventually known as the Great Dane because of his height (six foot four) and extroverted personality, had immigrated to America in his early twenties. Born in Copenhagen, he was one of ten children of a government customs inspector who managed to make ends meet by putting his children to work almost as soon as they could walk. His son Bill started work at age six, pushing a cart of window glass for a glazier as he made his rounds in the city. William Knudsen was still a teenager when he landed a job at a bicycle import firm, and soon he and a friend were professional pacers for long-distance bicycle races across Denmark, Sweden, and Germany. They also built the first tandem bicycle seen in Denmark. In a country with more bicycles than people, Knudsen became a national hero.

Knudsen brought his bicycle-making skills with him to America. After a stint in the Brooklyn shipyards, where he also became an accomplished heavyweight boxer, he set his sights for Buffalo in 1902. The city was a common stop for Scandinavians looking for jobs in industry. Knudsen found his in a bicycle-making plant; this factory also made parts for a concern in Michigan that was manufacturing a "horseless carriage." Its proprietor was named Henry Ford. Early automobiles included a lot of parts similar to bicycle parts.

Ford was so impressed with Knudsen's skill in managing the manufacture of those automobile parts that, in 1911, Ford bought the Buffalo company lock, stock, and bicycle wheel, and forthwith moved Knudsen out to his own plant, on Piquette Avenue in Detroit.

But when he arrived, Knudsen discovered that another Dane had preceded him. His name was Karl Sorensen, generally known as Charles. He too was originally from Copenhagen. And after his family left Denmark, he grew up in Buffalo, not very far from the bicycle plant where Knudsen had worked. Sorensen was part of the core team who made Highland Park (the location of a new Ford factory) hum. The team members had been present when Walter Flanders, a veteran machinist with Singer Sewing Machine, explained to Ford the advantages of building his automobiles with as many interchangeable parts as possible.

Ford was convinced. It was just a question of how to achieve that goal for his machines. Fortunately, Sorensen, Carl Emde, and Peter Martin — Ford's core engineering team — were able to break down the assembly of the new Model T into eighty-four separate stages, then arrange them linearly to form a single process.

Later, in his memoirs, Sorensen liked to lay claim to having used this process to create the first true industrial assembly line. This wasn't entirely true. The first assembly line really got underway in 1913, more than eight years after the crucial conversation with Walter Flanders. But there is no doubt that Sorensen did rearrange the factory's machine tools for sequential machining production, a major step toward an assembly line flow. Sorensen had also figured out a way to make engine cylinders out of forged castings instead of machined metal — this earned him the nickname Cast-Iron Charlie.

Finally, Sorensen had also been essential to designing the new Ford plant at Highland Park, which was set up to accommodate the new industrial assembly line using interchangeable parts. There, in 1913, the first true realization of this concept was unveiled, a milestone in the manufacture of automobiles, and more broadly, a historic moment for industry in general.

Knudsen was there too, helping to transfer the assembly line concept to other Ford plants around the country. He had come up with another innovation: enabling the line to incorporate design changes directly into the production process, so that it wouldn't be necessary to shut down the assembly line and retool every time a new design feature popped up on the drawing board. Knudsen encouraged Ford to consider making this change as part of his transition from the Model T — by now the cheapest and most popular automobile in America, thanks to the principle of mass production — to the future Model A. Ford said no. Knudsen argued with the boss, and Ford, being the boss, fired him. It took a couple years for Knudsen to find a company where he could try out this new concept. The company was Chevrolet, and in the space of three years Knudsen turned General Motors' least profitable endeavor into a manufacturer ready to go head to head with Ford in producing the automobile of choice for customers who had to watch their wallet.

For Knudsen it was sweet revenge. For the automotive industry, it was a major breakthrough: the mass production method pioneered by Ford, Sorensen, and their team had now been superseded by *flexible* mass production, a process that allows for constant modification and change. It made possible the development of the annual model in the auto industry; it also allowed other industries to incorporate systematic innovation as part of their production process. In other words, the craftsman's eye for detail and drive toward improvement now became part of the history of the manufacturing. It made Chevrolet customers happy. It made Chevrolet's owner, General Motors, happy too, and it drove Henry Ford crazy. Because he rejected Knudsen's flexible model, Ford had to close his plant for almost a year and a half to retool in order to make Model A's, while the market share he lost was picked up by Chevrolet.

Knudsen became the new king of the American automotive business when he stepped into Alfred Sloan's shoes as CEO of General Motors in 1937. The name of the six foot four Danish immigrant was now a byword in the manufacturing world. This is why, when President Franklin Roosevelt needed someone to gear up America's industries to mobilize for war in the spring of 1940, his first phone call went to Bill Knudsen.

When Knudsen arrived at the White House on May 30, he made FDR a promise. If Roosevelt could give him a year and a half to organize the key players in American industry and outfit them with new machine tools and facilities for making tanks, rifles, trucks, and airplane parts instead of cars, radios, and refrigerators — and to reorganize the supplies of raw materials, from rubber and copper to aluminum and steel, to make the new products — he could guarantee Roosevelt that the United States would have more war matériel than any country on earth. It would be "coming out of their ears," Knudsen said. There was one stipulation: Roosevelt had to let Knudsen and his fellow captains of industry do it their way, not how the bureaucrats in Washington, or even FDR's New Deal team, thought it should be done. If Roosevelt said yes, Knudsen promised, not only America but the other democracies fighting Hitler would have all they needed to wage a modern war. In Knudsen's phrasing, America would become an "arsenal of democracy" — Roosevelt stole those words for his Fireside Chat in December 1940, as he described what Knudsen and his colleagues in industry were about to do.

And they did it. "I'm not a soldier or a sailor," Knudsen told the other members of the National Defense Advisory Committee at their first meeting in Washington, DC, on June 12, 1940. "I'm just a plain manufacturer. But I know if we get into war, the winning of it will be purely a question of material and production. If we know how to get out twice as much material as everyone else — know how to get it, how to get our hands on it, and use it — we are going to come out on top — and win."

Starting in the summer of 1940, Bill Knudsen guided the effort to convert America's manufacturing base to wartime production, using free-market principles and incentives instead of command economy–style diktats and controls. Although Knudsen eventually dropped out of the leadership of the government's Office of Production Management, as it was later called, the process he put in place transformed American industry and the war. When bombs dropped on Pearl Harbor, in December 1941, America was ready to fight not just Nazi Germany but imperial Japan as well.

The numbers Knudsen and his colleagues achieved were staggering. From July 1940 until August 1945, the United States produced war matériel worth $183 billion — almost two-thirds of the equipment used by all the Allies put together in World War II. That included 141 aircraft carriers, 8 battleships, 807 cruisers and destroyers and destroyer escorts, and 203 submarines, as well as 88,410 tanks, 257,000 artillery pieces, 2.6 million machine guns, and 324,750 aircraft of all kinds. The United States remained the war's single combatant with a growing civilian economy.

Knudsen's fellow Dane known as Cast-Iron Charlie Sorensen was not willing to be outdone in wartime production. When Knudsen approached him to see if Ford could help with making parts for warplanes, Sorensen angrily replied that Ford wasn't just going to make parts and engines. His company was going to make entire airplanes.

The plane Sorensen chose to make was Consolidated Aircraft's B-24 four-engine bomber, the rival to Claire Egtvedt's B-17 Flying Fortress. The current Model A consisted of 15,000 parts. The B-24 was made up of almost half a million parts, including 300,000 rivets in five hundred different sizes. Building B-24s demanded the construction of a brand-new Ford plant, at Willow Run out by Ypsilanti, Michigan; it had the longest assembly line ever created. Sorensen had to hire an entirely new workforce at a time when every company was screaming for manpower for wartime production, and then convert the Consolidated blueprints into ones that could be used for Ford-style mass production.

The story of Willow Run became an industrial saga of epic dimensions, with Charles Sorensen as the harassed hero. In the end, the bombers were built, though never as many or as soon as Sorensen had promised or hoped. But they were enough to help bring the war effort to a successful conclusion. Without the long-range B-24s built according to Sorensen's specifications at Willow Run and at the Consolidated plant in San Diego, the German submarine campaign might have crippled Britain's wartime economy.

His triumph at Willow Run made Sorensen a stellar member of the circle of Scandinavian Americans who contributed to the war effort, alongside Bill Knudsen, Claire Egtvedt, and Philip Johnson. They had made it possible to win the world's biggest and most destructive conflict, and they paved the way for America's emergence as a global superpower, and for the future military-industrial complex. It was a triumph for the instinct of workmanship, heightened to the level of modern engineering genius.

Those other Scandinavian Americans were crucial to the cause. But Knudsen had been the key figure all along. His favorite saying was "We can do anything, if we do it together." Another favorite was "My business is making things." It might be the motto of Veblen's instinct for workmanship. Both Knudsen and Sorensen had proved that Americans could win an immense, complex war so long as they did what they did best. It was a lesson that American politicians would try again and again to relearn, though with not much success. Most recently, it was put to the test when America went to work to combat the lethal COVID-19 contagion. I was proud to be involved in helping companies like Ford, GM, GE, and Northrop Grumman, mainstays of the World War II effort, become mainstays of the effort to get America producing enough ventilators, respirators, testing kits, and other health-care products to defeat death — and also proud that my earlier book on the Knudsen miracle, *Freedom's Forge,* inspired Operation Warp Speed, the race to create a coronavirus vaccine. It's no coincidence that the hero whom I and others invoked in this effort was Big Bill Knudsen.

The master formula for engineering victory in a crisis, which two Danish American engineers developed, can still work, but only if a leader is bold enough to unleash its power, as FDR and his team of crack engineers had done.

In the spring of 1941, as Gutzon Borglum was still brooding over the rise of Adolf Hitler, the winners of the Pulitzer Prizes for 1940 were announced. The prize for biography came as a surprise to no one. It went to Carl Sandburg, for his biography of Abraham Lincoln. It was a tribute to the six-volume work whose true value was not so much as a work of history but one of literature — one could even say poetry. Sandburg's mastery of writing was no surprise either. He was, after all, one of America's most popular and beloved poets, well known for his celebration of his Swedish American background. And within his biography of Lincoln lay the physical setting for much of the Scandinavian saga in America: the endless prairies of the Midwest heartland.

Sandburg's father had immigrated to the United States as part of the big wave that hit in 1869, about ten years after the one that had brought over Charles Lindbergh's grandfather, with whom he shared the same Christian name. August Sandburg met and married Clara Anderson, a hotel maid in Bushnell, Illinois, and then moved to a three-room cottage in Galesburg to work for the Chicago, Burlington, and Quincy Railroad.

By the 1860s there were so many Swedes in Galesburg that they made up one-sixth of the population. They formed a Swedish village within the village, as it were, with their own newspaper, *Hemlandet,* published in Chicago but edited by their local minister. It was in fact the first Swedish newspaper in the United States, and one that August Sandburg faithfully read every day, alongside his Swedish Bible.

August worked a ten-hour day, six days a week, as a blacksmith's helper for the railroad, which was Galesburg's connection to the outside world, including Chicago, 110 miles away to the east. August never visited Chicago, not even for the World's Fair that drew Knute Rockne's father. His was a quiet, abstemious life, with a built-in routine and plenty of time for his daily chores. "Hard work never killed anyone" was the Scandinavian credo he passed on to his children.

There were seven of them in all. Each child was born in the three-room house, and afterward slept on a tiny corn-husk mattress in a cradle at the foot of the parents' bed. On January 6, 1878, the Sandburgs were blessed with their second child. "De tar en poijke" (it's a boy), declared the Swedish midwife. His parents named him Carl August, after his father.

Later on, Sandburg would have vivid memories of life in the tiny house, with its nine-by-ten-foot kitchen, the center of life for nine people, seven days a week and twelve months of the year. He remembered his mother rising at six every day to make breakfast for his father; then breakfast for the children, the youngest first and then on to the oldest. "She did the cooking, washing, sewing, bed-making, and housecleaning," only to cook dinner for everyone at night.

Sandburg's blacksmith father resembled a figure out of Norse legend, whose tireless forge raised the instinct for workmanship to an almost epic level. Above all Sandburg remembered his father's hands: "the calluses inside his hands were intricate with hollows and fissures." He watched his father wash the black soot out of the crevices at the end of each day, which took longer than any other part of washing up. After his ten-hour day and after dinner, August Sandburg would head out to the garden in the back, "picking tomatoes and digging up potatoes by the light of the moon." But August was never bitter about his hard life. On the contrary, he would remind all his children that "in the old country we had white bread only at Easter and Christmas. Here in America we have white bread every day of the year!"

Carl Sandburg turned out to be the trickster of the family. Although he learned to speak Swedish before he spoke English, he became a bright and eager paperboy while enjoying, together with his friends, playing pranks on neighbors. One of their favorites was setting up strings of firecrackers on someone's doorstep, scaring the daylights out of everyone inside. At one house the trick failed to get a response. No one came to the door, and no one's head burst out the window to see what was going on. Then Sandburg and the boy he was with realized the family was deaf and mute. Thoroughly ashamed of themselves, the two literally took turns kicking each other's behinds all the way home.

One aspect of Galesburg would be forever etched on his mind: the endless prairie that surrounded the town. As one biographer described it: "The trees stood out in bold relief, stark and bare against the winter sky, lush and green in spring and summer days . . . leaving a kind of Gothic etching in his mind that later was to appear in the vivid images of both his poetry and prose."

Sandburg would one day include this landscape as the background for the first volumes of his biography of Lincoln, *The Prairie Years*. The sense of homesteading on the edge of the vast unknown — of creating a home where one would be utterly alone but also left alone — connected the writer with his hero and the subject of his greatest work.

One other aspect of life that the two shared was an intimate connection with the Civil War, which had ended barely thirteen years before Sandburg was born. Galesburg's veterans lived all around him. So did constant reminders of the reason why the war was fought. Because Galesburg had been a sanctuary on the Underground Railroad, it had a sizable Black population. An assortment of immigrants lived there too, including Irish, Italians, Chinese, and even the occasional Japanese student studying at the tiny Universalist college in town. Sandburg remembered that the one time he heard his father speak of the war, it was to say, "The Civil War was a fight so that they could put it in the Constitution no man could have slaves."

Galesburg had also been one of the sites of the Lincoln-Douglas debates, at the east front of the Old Main building of nearby Knox College. On the north front of the building was a bronze plaque with a quotation from Lincoln: "He is blowing out the moral lights around us, when he contends that whoever wants slaves has a right to hold them." Sandburg reflected: "I read [those words] in winter sunrise, in broad summer daylight, in falling snow or rain, in all the weathers of a year" — and he never forgot them.

A love of delivering newspapers evolved into a love of newspapers themselves. After attending school at Lombard College, the Universalist school, and after a wandering tour of the East Coast, the teenage Carl Sandburg set off for Chicago, looking for work in the newspaper business. He found it first with the *Chicago Daily News,* then in Milwaukee with the *Milwaukee Sentinel,* where he also became involved in the politics of the local Social-Democratic Party. Progressive politics dies a hard death among Scandinavians and Scandinavian Americans alike. These were the years of Bob La Follette entering the US Senate, of Burton Wheeler and William Borah raising the progressive banner in the far west, and Theodore Roosevelt raising it on the presidential stage, with the creation of the Progressive Party, or Bull Moose Party, in the 1912 election. Wisconsin politics seemed to be part of a rising trend around the country.

But Sandburg's most primal fascination was always the city of Chicago. It was home to tens of thousands of immigrants, from Swedes, Danes, and Norwegians to Italians, Irish, Hungarians, and Slovaks, and every nation in between, and to Sandburg there seemed to be a particular kind of magic to its cacophony of industries and its Tower of Babel of foreign tongues. When *Poetry* magazine launched a poetry contest in 1914, Sandburg saw his chance. He penned a poem called "Chicago." Anyone reading the first stanza knew at once it was destined to be a classic:

> *Hog Butcher of the World,*
> *Tool Maker, Stacker of Wheat,*
> *Player with Railroads and the Nation's Freight Handler;*
> *Stormy, husky, brawling,*
> *City of the Big Shoulders.*

The poem not only won the prize but also changed Sandburg's life. Some were horrified by its critical tone and brash language. Confronted by critics, Sandburg wrote to a friend, using a metaphor that Thorstein Veblen, or even St. Brigitte, would have identified with: "A man was building a house. A woodchuck came and sat down and watched the man building the house."

Sandburg would soon build many more houses, so to speak, not only in *Chicago Poems* but also *Cornhuskers; Good Morning, America;* and a collection of fiction titled *Rootabaga Stories,* which appeared in 1922. He also became interested in American folk and popular songs, and his *American Song*

Bag began a national fascination with collecting folk songs. Sandburg himself enjoyed touring and performing the songs on his guitar, especially those with a distinctive Scandinavian immigrant flavor:

> *My name is Jon Jonson, I come from Wisconsin,*
> *I work in the lumber camps there;*
> *When I go down the street, the people I meet,*
> *Say, "Hey, what is your name?"*
> *I say, My name is Jon Jonson, I come from Wisconsin,*
> *I work in a lumber yard there;*
> *When I go down the street, the people I meet,*
> *They say, "Hey, what is your name?"....*

By doing this, Sandburg set a trend for American minstrelsy that would be followed by the likes of Woody Guthrie and Pete Seeger, and eventually spawn a genre of popular music that would flourish with Bob Dylan and Bruce Springsteen.

But his serious work on Abraham Lincoln had begun before that. One of the earliest published pieces dated from 1909, when the United States Mint replaced the old Indian Head pennies with ones bearing Lincoln's profile. "The face of Abraham Lincoln on the copper cent seems well and proper," Sandburg wrote for the *Milwaukee Daily News*. "If it were possible to talk to that great, good man, he would probably say that he is perfectly willing that his face is to be placed on the cheapest and most common coin in the country."

Sandburg added: "Follow the travels of the penny and you find it stops at many cottages and few mansions. The common, homely face of 'Honest Abe' will look good on the penny, the coin of the common folk from whom he came and to whom he belongs."

Sandburg began collecting books about Lincoln and newspapers with stories about him; then he took up interviewing people who had known or seen Lincoln. The various papers and memorabilia soon overflowed his office, then his home. Much of it was material no one had seen before, and Sandburg obtained personal interviews with people who would soon pass from the scene, leaving him as the last biographer to speak with them. In 1923 he paid a visit to New York City and had lunch with the publisher Alfred Harcourt at the Chatham Hotel. At first he proposed writing a boy's life of Lincoln. Then the project spilled from one to two volumes; then came others. When it was finally done, in 1926, Sandburg had filled four thick volumes and still had not gotten past Lincoln's presidential inauguration in 1860.

These two volumes became known as *The Prairie Years,* covering the period in which life on the prairie had shaped the man and future president, not to mention the people Lincoln came to represent, first in Congress, then as president. It was in many ways a Lincoln no one had written about before; also, his constituency was likewise portrayed in a sympathetic and insightful way that was new and fresh.

Here is Sandburg's description of the local people coming to hear Lincoln in his first debate with Stephen A. Douglas, in early October 1858:

The damp air chilled the bones of those who forgot their overcoats. For three hours the two debaters spoke to people who buttoned their coats tighter and listened. They had come from the banks of the Cedar Fork Creek, the Spoon River, the Illinois, Rock, and Mississippi Rivers, many with hands toughened on the plow handles, legs with hard, bunched muscles from tramping the clods behind a plow team. With ruddy and wind-bitten faces they were of the earth; they could stand the raw winds when there was something worth hearing and remembering.

They were the people Sandburg grew up with. Indeed, the parallels between his life and Lincoln's seemed inescapable. This, despite the fact that Sandburg was the son of a Swedish immigrant who never learned to write Swedish or read English, whereas Lincoln's family background was classic WASP. But both were part of pioneering American families and communities. The experience of being in America, and working and making a life there, united the two men — just as they united the nation as a whole, whatever differences in class or ethnicity or religion or national origin might exist.

The Prairie Years shows that the Scandinavian experience in America had become an American experience, and was of universal value as such. A marker had been placed, and other immigrant groups could follow and chart a similar course in the new country if they wanted to. But *The Prairie Years* also told another story. By the end of the last volume, in which Lincoln's time in Illinois comes to an end, it becomes apparent that his experiences there had quietly readied him for greatness.

Sandburg's writing of *The War Years* took a little longer. By the time the publication date rolled around, in the fall of 1939, the original idea of a boy's life of Lincoln, which was supposed to total about 400 pages, had grown to six volumes of 650 pages each. The timing of the publication turned out to be ominous. War had come again to Europe, and again America might be drawn into it. The country needed a president who could guide it through its fiery trials, as Lincoln himself would have said.

Sandburg's confrontation with the perils of war dramatically departs from that of Charles Lindbergh and other Scandinavian Americans who gave in to the temptations of xenophobia. Sandburg became a committed supporter of Knudsen and Roosevelt's effort to help the Allies fight Nazi Germany. He offered to write the soundtrack narration of the documentary *Bombers for Britain* — its title epitomized everything Lindbergh was fighting against. In a speech Sandburg gave in Chicago, for a national rally in support of Britain, he spoke directly of the "famous flyer who has quit flying and taken to talking," who was attacking the opponents of America First as hysterical; Sandburg's ire was obvious. He added that Lindbergh "doesn't know that the hysteria he mentions is in part the same anxiety, the identical deep fear that men politically free have always had when there were forces on the horizon threatening to take away their political freedom."

Later Sandburg said, "fools and idiots want war." But sometimes "the issue comes before a nation of people: Will you fight a war now, or would you deliberately choose another later inevitable war" — against an antagonist that may have become stronger and more confident of victory because of the refusal to fight earlier?

Lindbergh and Sandburg had actually met a year earlier and liked each other well enough. Afterward, Lindbergh's wife described Sandburg as "so sound, so rooted, so American. As American as Charles." That was part of the problem. Their common Swedish descent could not resolve the clash of their

Carl Sandburg posing with a bust of Abraham Lincoln. Courtesy of the Rare Book & Manuscript Library, University of Illinois at Urbana-Champaign

visions for America. The bombs that fell on December 7, 1941, fortuitously swept aside the issues that had divided these two men. But for the country as a whole, those clashing worldviews were never truly resolved. They would re-surface again several times, whenever America faced the possibility of war, its people left wondering if the finger pulling a trigger came too soon — or per-haps too late. These issues would continue to arise as Americans came to real-ize their power and feared its unintended consequences.

They split Scandinavian Americans along political and philosophical lines then, as they do now. But Sandburg and Lindbergh proved that, regardless of which side they stood on, no Scandinavian American carried the burden of war with an easy conscience.

The War Years, and the Pulitzer Prize, became the spark plug for Carl Sandburg's personal fame. He attended a warm meeting with Franklin Roosevelt, and he was asked to read the Gettysburg Address to a joint session of Congress, an event that made the address part of modern American political culture. Sandburg's deep voice, with its singsong Swedish cadence and broad Midwest vowels, became ubiquitous on radio, in personal appearances, and eventually on the earliest TV broadcasts. By the 1950s Sandburg was ready to climb what was then the ultimate summit for an American writer: Hollywood. He took on Twentieth-Century Fox's script for a life of Jesus titled *The Greatest Story Ever Told.*

But in fact the greatest story may actually have been Sandburg's biographical epic, an American version of a Norse saga and certainly the greatest study of an American by a fellow countryman.

Professional historians became frustrated by the biography's loose use of sources and rambling poeticizing. One review of *The Prairie Years* in the *Mississippi Valley Historical Review* purported to find nine historical errors in the four pages Sandburg wrote on the Black Hawk War. Others called it a literary grab bag. Sandburg himself wondered if what he had written was a kind of "history and Old Testament of America," rather than a biography of Lincoln as such.

A more apt comparison could be made to the *Heimskringla* and the other Icelandic historical sagas, which were part fact, part fable, and entirely inspiration for the imagination.

Much had been written on Lincoln before Sandburg's volumes appeared, and there would be much more written after. But Sandburg gets credit for putting Lincoln at the center of the American pantheon, where he has remained. Thanks to Carl Sandburg, Lincoln became the figure who unlocked the secret of the American experience and revealed the true nature of its exceptionalism. The critic Alfred Kazin characterized Sandburg's achievement this way: "Lincoln arose before the reader like a massive shadow of the racked civilization he had held together, a stupendous aggregation of all those American traits that were to find so ambiguous and moving an expression in him . . . More than a symbol of a distinct American experience, he had become the propulsion of a great symphonic poem; more than a leader, the people's legend of him now seemed the greatest of all American works of art." A great work of art by a consummate, if consistently underrated, artist.

"Life is a river on which we drift down thru [*sic*] an unexplored country," Sandburg once wrote to his wife, Paula, during their courtship. Venturing into unexplored country was what the Viking experience, and the Scandinavian experience in America, has been all about. Carl Sandburg may never have gotten to the end of that journey, but in his own way he had pointed the way for the rest of us.

The last of our sextet, Norman Borlaug, was younger than the rest. But he came out of the same prairie setting that shaped Carl Sandburg. Borlaug would transform this setting, as he would transform agriculture around the world.

He was born in 1914 and grew up in rural Iowa, the child of Norwegian immigrants who found in their tiny town of Saude, in the words of one of Borlaug's biographers, "a landscape at once chillingly vacant and full of promise."

His great-grandparents Ole and Solveig Borlaug had emigrated from Sogne Fjord in Norway in the 1850s when the potato crop they lived on was devastated by a terrible blight — the same one that had set off the Irish Potato Famine ten years earlier. Like many of the Irish, Norwegians like the Borlaugs had fled to America to find food.

And like so many Norwegian immigrants, the Borlaugs originally farmed in Wisconsin near Green Bay before heading for the Dakota Territory, where they and other families ran afoul of the Chief Little Crow Dakota uprising in 1862. The conflict sent them back east again, until they settled in northeastern Iowa.

Borlaug's biographer Charles Mann described the world into which Borlaug was born in 1914: "The new arrivals built cabins from logs chinked with mud; grew clover, wheat, maize, and oats; pastured a few milk cows; let their dogs run free. Half the area's inhabitants were Norwegian; most of the rest were Czech — Bohemian, as people said then." It was a world still steeped in the ways of the old country. Lutheran Norwegian parents told their children not to date the Bohemians, who were Roman Catholics; and "in the

Norwegian church, men sat on one side, women on the other. Ministers wore white ruffs and black satin stoles. Services were in Norwegian until the early 1920s. At Christmas the congregation placed a tree in the church entrance, lighted candles tied to the branches. After the service everyone unwrapped presents together."

The center of life, for adults and children alike, was working the farm for their daily food. Most of the farm work was still done with horses, which seems picturesque in retrospect. But at least half of the Borlaugs' acreage had to be set aside to make hay to feed the farm's three horses and twenty or so more acres for their cattle — an enormous burden on the available arable land.

What remained was set aside for one crop: corn. Earlier, that acreage had been wheatland. But in 1916, when Borlaug was two years old, the strain of wheat known as Marquis was hit with a fungus known as black stem rust. From Missouri to Montana and up into Canada, the North American wheat harvest failed for two years running. Community after community had to switch to another staple in order to survive. Some chose potatoes. Communities in northeastern Iowa chose corn.

This disaster and its aftermath haunted the adult Norman Borlaug, as did the struggles of his Norwegian great-grandparents. "I was born in that era when crop disease often forced people to flee," he would say later. "Despite almost seven decades trying to find enough to eat, my family had yet to escape famine's clutch." Finding ways to bring wheat back from the dead, literally, would be one of the great tasks of agricultural experts over the next two decades. Norman Borlaug would become increasingly obsessed with it.

As for the Borlaug farm, the forty or so acres of corn produced no more than twenty-five or thirty bushels an acre. This entire crop had to be harvested by hand, which on a farm like the Borlaugs' meant picking twelve thousand plants and husking a million ears of corn. Norman Borlaug would later remember the work with a shudder: "That was true hell. Although we wore cotton gloves and covered our forearms with sleeves torn from old sweaters, the husks still managed to cut and scrape until our hands and arms were raw and bleeding."

There was a premium on proficiency in this hard work: thousands of Iowans would show up every fall for the World Series of Corn, a corn-husking competition that pitted contestants against each other to see who could pick the most ears of corn in a single eighty-minute period. The champions could manage up to 4,000 ears — more than one per second. Sometimes as many as 150,000 spectators would show up to watch. The Goodyear Blimp would pass over what, in the 1920s, was by far America's single biggest sporting event. Its popularity may be reflected in the title of one of Carl Sandburg's collections of poems, *Cornhuskers;* the University of Nebraska gave the same name to its sports teams. Both pay tribute to one of the most arduous tasks any farm worker, Scandinavian or not, could undertake.

The teenage Norm Borlaug did not attend the University of Nebraska. He went to the University of Minnesota, in the heart of Scandinavian America, and specifically Norwegian America. At first he was interested in forestry and varsity wrestling. But then he met Professor Charles Stakman, who was devoted to gaining an understanding of black stem rust fungus, which had wiped out half the grain crop in North America when Borlaug was a toddler. Soon Norman was waging war on the fungus with the focused attention he had brought to plowing a straight furrow or building a pig brooder on the Borlaug farm. His instinct for workmanship had found its vocation in the agricultural research lab.

Borlaug became an expert in developing hybrid strains of plants that could outperform their parent strains. His painstaking work won the attention of the Rockefeller Foundation, which had an abiding interest in addressing the poverty in Latin America. When Borlaug arrived in Mexico for the first time, in 1944, to help boost crop yields, he launched a career that would ultimately transform agriculture in the third world. The subsistence farming that was so easily, and regularly, destroyed by natural disaster, resulting in millions of deaths due to malnutrition and hunger, came to be replaced with an agricultural ecosystem by which Mexicans, Indians, Indonesians, and millions of others could enjoy the unprecedented experience of being able to feed themselves on a regular basis. This development was called the Green Revolution, and its mastermind was Norman Borlaug.

The key to Borlaug's success was the strains of wheat he labored to develop. They had high yields and were resistant to disease. Borlaug taught farmers around the world to think of these high-yield varieties as a part of a triad of resources, together with nutrients, such as fertilizer both chemical and organic, and water management, meaning efficient irrigation. Once the triad came together, farmers didn't have to worry about the quality of the land they happened to have or whether enough rain would fall to keep their crops growing.

When Borlaug and his team arrived in Mexico, for example, the average farmer's acre yielded 760 pounds of wheat. By 1968 it was yielding 2,500 pounds: almost triple the harvest. A similar transformation was happening in India, and soon would occur in Indonesia. Meanwhile, improvements in rice crops were underway through the same means — hybrid strains of rice combined with fertilizer and more efficient irrigation systems. Again, the results were spectacular.

It seemed Borlaug's work was banishing natural famines from the human landscape (famines engineered by dictators or caused by war were another matter). That same year, 1968, Borlaug gave a speech in Australia describing what he and his team had accomplished. "Ours is the first civilization based on science and technology," he told his audience. "In order to assure continued progress we scientists . . . must recognize and meet the changing needs and demands of our fellow men." Two years later he won the Nobel Peace Prize, both for his scientific achievement and for the hope he had brought to tens of millions of human beings around the world by freeing them from the tyranny of lousy land and unpredictable weather. Just such a tyranny had driven his ancestors, and the Vikings, from their homes. He had embraced this mission as both an intellectual adventure and a contribution to his fellow humans.

Naturally, Borlaug's success drew criticism, especially from the Left. Many believed that only social revolution could truly change lives in the third world for the better. Cultural activists blamed him for destroying traditional ways. Green activists condemned the environmental impact that high-nitrogen fertilizers and heavy water consumption had on local ecosystems. Sociologists held him responsible for driving millions of peasants off their land, as rich farmers used the Green Revolution to prosper and expand their holdings while enabling those holdings to feed others — whether they stayed on the land or moved to the cities. One Marxist critic, the journalist Alexander Cockburn, even accused Borlaug of mass murder.

Yet the numbers don't lie. Between 1960 and 2000, wheat harvests in the developing world tripled. Rice harvests doubled, and corn harvests more than doubled. Across huge stretches of the planet, famine ceased to be the inevitable fate of masses of people.

Speaking to his biographer Charles Mann shortly before his death, in 2009, Borlaug answered his critics in this way: Where would we be today if the planet had witnessed the same growth in population that the recession of epidemic diseases and lower child mortality had brought, but we didn't have the crop-yield increases his research helped set in motion?

Borlaug finally asked Mann if he had ever visited a place where the majority of people don't have enough to eat: "Not just poor, but actually hungry all the time." Mann had to answer no, he had never seen places like that.

"That's the point," Borlaug said. "When I was getting started, you couldn't avoid them."

Places, in fact, like the Norway that his great-grandparents had escaped from to head for America. And ironically, the Norway that had sustained some of the Vikings who had robbed and enslaved the poorest of the world. This same place could now be seen as the ancestral home of the Scandinavian who kept the poorest fed. Borlaug, like many Vikings, had pushed the physical limits of what humans can do, but he did so in the name of peace and progress, not war and pillage.

Borlaug, like many other Scandinavian American pioneers, believed in American democracy. Carl Sandburg likewise had said that democracy "gives more people more chances to think, to speak, to decide their way of life . . . than any other system." Norman Borlaug would have agreed. But he would add that it's also important to have enough to eat. He had secured this reality for vast numbers of people.

Charlie Sorensen and Bill Knudsen had turned the Viking heart's "instinct for workmanship" into an arsenal of democracy. Norman Borlaug had figured out how to feed the postwar world in a supreme gesture of the Lutheran work ethic — labor as a gift of love to fellow human beings.

14

The Viking Heart Comes Home

Yes, you sons of a giant race!
We are each made according to our last,
And freedom is what serves us best . . .

— N.F.S. Grundtvig, 1832

IN NOVEMBER 1863 — the year that Americans were fighting at Gettysburg and Colonel Hans Heg breathed his last on the banks of the Chickamauga River — Denmark single-handedly managed to plunge Europe into a war that would change the future of western Europe, including Scandinavia, down to this day.

For a power that had plummeted to second- or even third-rate status, it was an extraordinary moment — the last time a Nordic nation would make a decision of this kind. With its honor at stake, Denmark emitted one last gasp of nationalism, declaring war and calling on the God of Battles to help Denmark exert its will over its neighbors. It was a graphic example of how life's hardest lessons sometimes don't sink in until they have triggered catastrophe.

At the center of the conflict was the fate of Denmark's two southernmost duchies: Slesvig and Holstein. Slesvig was the original home of many of the German tribes who had swept over the Roman Empire fifteen hundred years earlier. Over the centuries it had become increasingly Germanized, especially its southern half, where German speakers outnumbered Danish speakers by a considerable margin. Although its capital, Lübeck, was originally a Viking settlement, the duchy of Holstein was still more solidly German. It was even formally a member of the German Confederation. The official language in Holstein's churches was German, the language in its schools was German, and even the language of government was German.

Danish nationalists, however, saw both duchies as historically and inseparably part of Denmark. Since 1773 they had belonged to the Danish crown, although neither was officially incorporated into the kingdom itself—a discrepancy the Danish nationalists in 1863 decided to correct.

The Danish Estates, backed by the Copenhagen press, convinced their new king, Christian IX, to declare Slesvig and Holstein fully and completely part of Denmark. This, despite the fact that Christian himself was a native German speaker and Denmark had signed an agreement eleven years before declaring it would never do any such thing. Christian IX's decision thrust Denmark into an international crisis — and it would never fully recover.

Prussia's new chancellor, Otto von Bismarck, was the first to jump into the fray. He saw this development as a brilliant opportunity to make Prussia a major player on the international stage — and to win the hearts of German nationalists by protecting Slesvig and Holstein's German residents from Danish aggression. Prussia had made a similar bid back in 1848, when the Germans in Holstein had revolted against the Danish crown. In 1848, Prussia had the worst of the fight when its troops ran up against the Danes. Now it was Bismarck's chance to set the record straight.* Prussia and Austria signed a formal alliance on January 16, 1864. Shortly after, the war was on, with Denmark facing not one but two great powers at once. No other country, not even Sweden, was willing to substantially support Denmark.

It was a grossly unequal struggle. Some fifty-seven thousand Prussian

---

* That conflict had ended with an international conference in London, which gave the rebellious province back to the Danish crown but forbade the Danes from making either Slesvig or Holstein legally part of Denmark — a treaty Copenhagen and Christian IX had now violated. Hence, Bismarck was not only protecting fellow Germans but upholding international law — an irresistible combination for the Iron Chancellor.

and Austrian troops stormed up to the Danish border, where fewer than thirty-eight thousand Danish troops were strung out along the Danevirke — ironically, the barrier built by Viking kings to halt invasion by their Carolingian foes. A thousand years later, the Danes were facing new German enemies — and ones who were far better armed. The Prussians deployed the world's first breech-loading rifles; Danish troops were armed with muzzle-loading muskets. Somehow the Danes managed to repulse a powerful Prussian attack on February 2, 1864, at Mysunde (from the Old Norse *Mjósund,* meaning "narrow strait") and to fight the Austrians to a standstill the next day.

On April 17, the inevitable happened. After a weeks-long bombardment, the Prussians overran the Danish positions at Dybbøl. Four and a half hours of savage fighting ensued. Prussian losses came to more than twelve hundred killed and wounded, while the Danes lost more than five thousand men — incredibly, almost 50 percent of their forces had become casualties. Compared to the losses at Gettysburg or at Chickamauga, the numbers seem minimal. But the percentage of losses would have horrified any American Civil War general, and his modern counterparts.

The war dragged on hopelessly for another five months, with Prussians and Austrians occupying virtually the entire kingdom except Copenhagen. Then, in October, a chastened Charles IX signed a peace treaty, and Slesvig and Holstein were lost to Prussia and Austria.

For the 200,000 ethnic Danes living in the two provinces, the treaty was bitter — but it was good news for the United States. The Danes in the two ceded duchies now faced the choice of living under foreign rule or abandoning their homes. More than 60,000 chose to leave, most of them heading across the border to Denmark. But many took passage farther west, to America.

For Denmark itself, the war had been a disaster of the highest order. The country had lost a large chunk of its territory and nearly 40 percent of its population to the German annexation, and had suffered a blatant humiliation on the international stage. And another kind of damage had been done. Both Sweden and Norway (which under Swedish rule had its own parliament and its own prime minister) had stood aloof from Denmark in its time of agony. The Swedish government had sent a telegram promising twenty-two thousand soldiers when war broke out, but then the Riksdag put up only a fraction of the money needed to send a force of that size. Norway's prime minister (under the union with Sweden, Norway had its own premier) advised everyone to stay out of the fray altogether.

The failure of Norwegians and Swedes to rally to their Danish brethren embittered many a Scandinavian intellectual, and not only the Danes. The aspiring Norwegian dramatist Henrik Ibsen, for example, had written stirring pamphlets calling for war in support of Denmark, then was devastated to see Sweden-Norway let the Prussian juggernaut crush the Danes. These events fueled Ibsen's pessimism about his fellow citizens, and about the human condition in general. In fact, the Scandinavian modernist movement, led by figures like Ibsen, August Strindberg, Georg Brandes, and Edvard Munch, took root in the disillusionment and sense of betrayal that the war left in its wake; this mood would characterize Scandinavian arts and letters right down to the twentieth century.

But in the long view, the events of 1864 formed a watershed in the making of modern Scandinavia. They convinced future generations in the North that for them, at least, war would never again be the answer. They were embarking on an arduous transition: a people to be feared in the age of the Vikings and Gustavus Adolphus were becoming a people to be envied — much, in fact, as they are today.

And they were heading in growing numbers to America. Yet at the same time, astonishingly, other Scandinavians were rediscovering the Viking heart, its spirit and its energies, literally on their own turf.

Improbably enough, this process began with a museum heist in Denmark's Christiansborg Palace, in 1802.

In those days the kongelige Kunstkammer, or Royal Art Museum, was in the building that today houses the Public Record Office. The thief in this case was one Niels Heidenreich, a notorious coin forger, watchmaker, and sometime goldsmith whose business was languishing. Heidenreich had decided to turn things around by breaking into the museum and stealing two of the most valuable objects in the collection. By doing so he set in motion a cultural revolution.

The objects in question were two ceremonial drinking horns made of pure gold. They had been unearthed by accident in a field in Slesvig in previous centuries: the first horn had been found in 1639, the second in 1734. Both were enormous, more than seventy centimeters long (roughly two and a half feet). They were known to be of great antiquity. At the time it was presumed that they originated in Denmark's Viking Age, a time that was still shrouded in myth and obscurity. (Modern experts think they were probably made even earlier, in the early fifth century.)

Heidenreich made a copy of the key of the front door of the museum. Then, on the evening of May 4–5, he crept in and stole both the horns and took them to his house, on the corner of Larsbjørnsstræde and Studiestræde. There he did something that to this day gives historians and archaeologists cardiac failure. He melted down the two golden horns to recycle the gold. Meanwhile, the theft caused a national outcry. A reward of a thousand rigsdaler was offered for information about the crime and was advertised in Copenhagen's newspapers.

But the grandmaster of the goldsmiths' guild, Andreas Holm, figured he didn't have far to look for the culprit. He suspected Heidenreich had been involved: the watchmaker had once tried to sell Holm forged Indian coins, with various Hindu deities as decoration; he had made them from subpar gold mixed with brass. Holm hadn't been fooled then, and he wasn't fooled now. He and his colleagues put a tail on Heidenreich as part of the investigation, which lasted for months. One night they spotted him dumping used coin stamps into the city moat. Heidenreich was arrested at last on April 27, 1803, and confessed on April 30. His buyers, meanwhile, returned the recycled gold, though it was too late to save any trace of the horns. As the saying goes, you don't know what you have until it's gone.

The Danes realized they had lost two priceless pieces of their history, which had been found entirely by accident.* And the timing couldn't have been worse,

---

* The first horn had been discovered by a young peasant girl from the village of Gallehus, near Møgeltønder in Slesvig. When she was digging, she unearthed the large horn, which was clearly made of gold. The second horn had been found about one hundred years later, on April 21, 1734, by one Erich Lassen, not far from the first

smack in those dark days when Denmark was reeling from its defeat by Admiral Horatio Nelson at the battle of Copenhagen. To that national humiliation was now added the irreparable loss of these relics from a vanished age, when Danish greatness was never in question — a heritage that many had taken for granted but that now seemed redolent, like the iconography of the lost horns, with their symbols of Thor and Odin, with virtues the modern age had lost.

When most people look to the past, they actually see the future: it happens more than historians like to admit. What Denmark's intellectual class saw in the story of the lost horns was projected onto an ideal modern future of Denmark when the Viking virtues reflected in the iconography of the golden horns would flourish once again. Once Danes and the occasional Norwegian got started on this theme, Swedish historians and writers soon followed.

The man who launched the rediscovery of the Viking past was, however, not a Scandinavian but Paul-Henri Mallet, a Frenchman born in Geneva in 1730, who taught French at the University of Copenhagen. He was one of the first to see the earliest manuscripts of the Icelandic sagas and recognize them for what they were: a record of a people from a vanished past who had left behind a rich and powerful literature, backed by a splendid mythology. Mallet also connected the Icelandic sagas with Europe's fascination with the supposed Dark Age Gaelic poet Ossian, whose works had been brought to light by the Scotsman James Macpherson in 1760. Ossian's epic poem *Fingal*, with its bards, sages, warriors, and damsels in distress, had enthralled the most sophisticated minds of the age, from Diderot and Thomas Jefferson (who deemed Ossian "the greatest poet in existence") to Lord Byron and Felix Mendelssohn. Napoleon himself had his bedroom at Malmaison decorated with scenes from the works of Ossian. They were a direct inspiration for Sir Walter Scott's hugely popular poetry and fiction, and they set off a European craze for the Dark Ages, particularly pre-Christian culture.

The works of Ossian, however, were eventually exposed as a forgery and a fake. With Snorri Sturluson and the Icelandic sagas, the Scandinavians proved to have the real thing. The Old Norse poetry of the *Edda*s, as well as the prose

---

horn. He gave it to the count of Schackenborg, who in turn delivered it to Christian VI of Denmark and received two hundred rigsdaler in return.

sagas, revealed a world rich in expressive power and human sensibility — an imaginative world the Vikings had made and left to their descendants.

One of the earliest Danish writers to realize the import of this connection was Adam Oehlenschlager, Denmark's best-known poet and playwright of the age. The theft of the golden horns, and their subsequent destruction, inspired a poem he later said he composed at a single sitting: "The Golden Horns."

> *Ye days long past,*
> *When the North was uplighted,*
> *And with earth heav'n united,*
> *A glimpse back cast . . .*
> *"Ye who are blind are straying,*
> *And praying,*
> *Shall an ag'd relic meet . . .*
> *That shall give ye a notion*
> *To hold in devotion*
> *Our gift, is your duty!" . . .*

But then the gift of the horns is lost forever:

> *Storm-winds bellow,*
> *Blackens heaven!*
> *Comes the hour of melancholy;*
> *Back is taken what was given, —*
> *Vanished is the relic holy.*

These words, with their vision of a new world born from the pain and destruction of the old, must have resonated deeply with the Danes after the humiliation of defeat in the Napoleonic wars. "The Golden Horns" proclaimed that a new Denmark — a new Scandinavia — would be born from the old, but only if the people rediscovered their ancient roots in the Norse past. "Ye days long past," as Oehlenschlager explained, "When the North was uplighted / And with earth heav'n united." What we were, the poet was telling his countrymen, we can be again.

The theme inspired not only the Danes but also their old rivals the Swedes. What can only be described as Viking mania took off, especially among Scandinavia's educated elite. The poet and historian Erik Geijer represented the Swedish arm of Viking mania with his founding of the Geatish (or Gothic, in English) Society in 1811. Swedes had been proclaiming their links to the ancient Goths, conquerors of Rome, since the days of Gustavus Adolphus. In the context of the Reformation and the religious wars, it had made sense for a champion of Protestantism taking on the forces of Rome once again to sense a historical continuity with Scandinavia's past. But now, stressing the Viking connection through the Goths who stayed home — the Geats — was not only more romantic but also safer. The Geatish Society became Stockholm's chief repository for research into the history of the Vikings and the rediscovery of their art and mythology. In 1818 it sponsored a contest to commission statues of Odin, Thor, and Freya — the first effort in Swedish art to represent the Nordic gods in sculpture since before the coming of Christianity.

The contest rules ran in the Geatish Society's periodical, *Iduna,* named after the Norse goddess Idunn, whom *The Prose Edda* describes as a granter of eternal youth. It was in *Iduna's* first issue that Geijer's poem "Vikingen" ("The Viking") appeared, making popular the Norse word for "traveler" or "wanderer" in its association with the heroic seafarers and warriors of the Viking Age.

The man who most powerfully fueled Viking mania in modern Scandinavian culture was the Danish writer, historian, and public intellectual Nikolaj Frederik Severin Grundtvig. For forty years he was Denmark's leading apostle of the classical liberalism then sweeping western Europe. An ideological ally of men like John Stuart Mill, Alexis de Tocqueville, and François Guizot, Grundtvig decisively shaped the future of his native country in more ways than one. He is the father of Denmark's national institution of folk high schools, the first of which opened in 1844 and soon spread from Denmark to Sweden and Norway. An entire suburban district of Copenhagen was eventually designed and named in his honor.

Grundtvig's chief contribution was to trigger the idea that Scandinavians, whether Danes, Norwegians, or Swedes, should think of themselves as a distinct people, thanks to their shared Viking past. His "matchless discovery," as he called it in his multivolume *World History,* penned in 1834–35, argued that Scandinavia, and Denmark in particular, was destined to lead the world once again, as it had in the Viking age, and this time to a new age of democracy and renewed Christian faith.

But the Viking sagas, and Denmark's Viking legacy, formed part of that mission as well. For Grundtvig, the sagas of the Norse gods expressed human dilemmas and allegories still highly relevant to the average Christian Dane. This was particularly true, he believed, because they were expressed in the idiom of a pure Norse language, which, by the time Icelanders wrote it down, had not been corrupted by the influence of Latin, the idiom of the corrupt Catholic Church and its alien culture. Like the good Lutheran he was, Grundtvig was the determined enemy of papal Rome and all its works. The Danish Protestant churches of his day, and the pagan Vikings of the past, would sail off together on a voyage to a new and brighter future for Denmark—and all of Scandinavia.

In retrospect, it is easy to see Grundtvig's message as a lost cause, especially as thousands of Scandinavians were beginning to gather up their possessions to head for America rather than stick around to lead the world from their homeland. But Grundtvig had established a crucial link between the Vikings of the past and the future of freedom. As he wrote in 1832, "It is freedom that serves us best," whether in Scandinavia or in America.

Grundtvig's other legacy was the movement known as pan-Scandinavianism, which swept over the intellectual classes and among university students across the Nordic countries in the 1830s and '40s. Inspired by their shared Viking past, the pan-Scandinavians saw themselves as a liberal nationalist movement akin to those sweeping across Germany and Italy at roughly the same time. Its most important literary monument would be the poem "Jeg er en Skandinav" ("I am a Scandinavian"), written by none other than Denmark's most famous and popular writer, Hans Christian Andersen.

> *We are one people, we are called Scandinavians,*
> *In three realms our homeland is divided;*
> *But between the great heavenly gifts*
> *It lies: our heart grows into one*

Let it be forgotten, if wrong was done unto us;
The spirit of time, like a cleansed Margarethe,
Unites us, it gives thrice the power,
Even the language unites us
On mountains, in woods and by the night-blue sea,
I shout with joy: I am a Scandinavian!

The hopes of pan-Scandinavianism would be dashed a few years later in the events of 1864. Part of the disillusionment sprang from the failure of Norwegians and Swedes to unite with the Danes. At its first crisis, Scandinavian solidarity had received a blow from which it would never fully recover. On another note, the experience also turned many Scandinavians permanently and fiercely anti-German. "The German language and German books have done us much more harm than German weapons or soldiers," Nikolaj Grundtvig wrote bitterly. That sentiment would stand many Danes, Norwegians, and Swedes in good stead in the twentieth century.

Nonetheless, Grundtvig, Geijer, and their colleagues had laid the foundation for future generations of scholarship on the Viking Age and its literary legacy in the sagas — a foundation on which R. B. Anderson would build the thesis of *America Not Discovered by Columbus*. They also set in motion a fascination with the Vikings in Scandinavia that would grow with the first spectacular archaeological discoveries, first the Gokstad Viking ship in 1880 and then the Oseberg find in 1903–4, both located in Norway. This went a long way in stimulating pro-Viking sentiment among Norwegians. The twin discoveries also took place against the background of the Norwegian push for independence from Sweden, which was achieved just a year after the Oseberg find, in 1905.

By then, however, the fascination with the Viking past had taken a deeply sinister turn, and in the very country that had drawn so much scorn and resentment from Nikolaj Grundtvig and other Nordic thinkers. That country was Germany, where Viking myth and legend eventually took on a monstrous shape. As before, this rekindling of Viking obsession began with the arts — not through poetry or sculpture or even archaeology, but rather music.

· · ·

"Already in Dresden I had all imaginable trouble buying a book that no longer was found in any of the book shops. At last I found it in the Royal Library. It ... is called the *Volsung Saga*—translated from Old Norse by H. von der Hagen ... This book I now need for repeated perusal."

The quotation comes from a letter written in 1851 by the young aspiring composer Richard Wagner. What he had discovered in the royal library at Dresden became a source book for Wagner's complete reinvention of musical drama and opera. Thanks to him, the legacy of the Norse saga was about to take a momentous turn.

Wagner had found an 1815 German translation of the thirteenth-century Icelandic work *The Saga of the Volsungs,* the story of the Norse hero Sigurd and his search for a treasure and a magic ring. This sweeping tale involves men, gods, dragons, and the female guardians of Valhalla, the Valkyries, as well as the most famous Valkyrie of them all, Brunhild, or Brunhilde. Wagner had been fascinated by the figure of Sigurd, or Sigfried, as he is known in German, ever since he had read the German medieval epic *Nibelungenlied.* But what he found in von der Hagen's translation of the Old Norse original was something far greater than the German version, and more profound.

"Although the glorious figure of Siegfried had attracted me for some long time," he later wrote, "it enchanted me fully only when I had succeeded in seeing it in its purest human manifestation" in the Icelandic version. Here was the heroic Siegfried "freed from all human disguises," with a meaning beyond a particular time or place. "Only now did I realize the possibility of making him the hero of a drama ... I had entered a new and decisive period of my artistic and human development..."

Wagner soon added *The Prose Edda* and *The Poetic Edda* to his Viking literature reading list. Their stories of the birth of the world and the gods; the building of their home at Valhalla; the exploits of Odin, Thor, and other Norse deities; and the final clash between the gods and giants for world mastery, culminating in the day of Ragnarok, the end of the rule of the gods, filled in the corners of his vision. All these Norse tales he proceeded to weave into a single narrative, *The Ring of the Nibelungen* (borrowing the title from the German epic poem), which he stretched over four full-length operas: seventeen solid hours of music, drama, and visual spectacle that evolved into an annual pagan-style ritual at Wagner's temple for his *Gesamtkunstwerk* at Bayreuth, in southern Germany.

The action of the cycle of operas springs from the competition for possession of a gold ring. It holds the secret to power over the world. Its makers are subterranean beings who inhabit Nibelheim, a realm of caves and caverns, who "with restless activity . . . heat, purify, and forge the hard metals." On the one side stand the gods, led by Odin. On the other are the giants whom Odin commanded to build his great palace at Valhalla, and who demand the ring as payment. In between are the humans, whom Odin needs to trick and coerce into securing the ring, because the Norns (the fates of Norse mythology) have decreed that only a human hero can save the gods from final destruction — Wagner's version of Ragnarok.

When Odin's chosen half-human hero, Siegfried, finally takes possession of the ring from the giant-turned-dragon Fafner (another spelling of Fafnir) and is about to realize its full powers, he is treacherously murdered (this follows the plot of the German medieval version). Siegfried's death and defeat lead to the downfall of Odin and other gods in a spectacular apocalyptic scene, as Valhalla catches fire from a Viking-style funeral pyre laid out for Siegfried by his lover, the Valkyrie Brunhilde. Nonetheless, Wagner's last opera in the cycle, *Götterdämmerung* (*Twilight of the Gods*) ends on a hopeful note that Wagner borrowed from Nordic sources. From the ashes of the old will arise a bright new world, where a future human race will grasp forever the power that was Siegfried's for a few fleeting moments.

Wagner saw his operatic sagas in more than just mythic terms. For him, the Norse legends offered a parable for modern society — one that bears a striking resemblance to the political views of his contemporaries and fellow revolutionaries during the Europe-wide upheavals of 1848 — Karl Marx and Friedrich Engels. Marx had seen the struggle between Europe's greedy bourgeoisie (whom Wagner portrayed as the giants in the *Ring* cycle) and an oppressed working-class proletariat (embodied in Wagner's hardworking dwarves, or Nibelungen) as one that must end in the victory of the working class. Instead of a working-class revolution, however, Wagner foretold a struggle against a soulless capitalism as heralding the arrival of a new race of heroes, a race of Siegfrieds and Brunhildes, who would be imbued with a godlike power to create

their own destiny — truly the Viking heart in the vanguard of world revolution. It would be a serious reach to call Wagner a Communist. But it is true
that the ideology underlying the *Ring* cycle couldn't have been further from
the liberal democratic ideals of the Norse saga's Scandinavian admirers like
Grundtvig.

Who attended these performances at Bayreuth? In the audience of the first
performance was the German emperor Wilhelm I himself. Also in attendance
was Wagner's disciple Friedrich Nietzsche, whose entire philosophic outlook
was shaped by his relationship with Wagner and the *Ring* cycle (although he
would later turn against his former mentor for not being radical enough). More
important, Wagner's operas helped detonate an explosive fascination with Germany's links to its Nordic past. For the first time, fantasies of the ancient German tribes and Vikings merging into a single "Aryan" race, whose purity and
power would be the key to renewing Western civilization, crept into German
intellectual and cultural life. Where German scholars were prepared to go in
devising a race-based history of the West, others were tempted to follow.

"Any attempt to tell the story of the Aryan race," wrote the classical scholar
Charles Morris in 1888, "would be equivalent to an attempt to write the history of civilization." For a linguist and scholar like Morris, the term *Aryan* also
embraced the Indo-European peoples who had conquered ancient Persia and
the subcontinent of India: the *arya* proper. But the identification of Aryan
excellence with Vikings and Germans, and a particular blond, blue-eyed, and
white-skinned physical type that "found its purest expression in Iceland, Scandinavia, and Denmark" as well as northern Germany and England, proved
irresistible.

Likewise, Morris argued that this Aryan excellence seemed to find its purest expression in Norse religion and myth, which encapsulated "the Scandinavian scheme of the universe — a rude and fierce one, yet instinct with a vigor of
imagination shown nowhere by men of non-Aryan blood."

However, the complete merger of Wagner's redemptive message borrowed
from the Norse sagas and Aryan racial ideology would have to wait for the
writings of Wagner's son-in-law, the English race theorist Houston Stuart
Chamberlain. His *Foundations of the Nineteenth Century,* published in 1899,
posited a pure Aryan race stemming from Scandinavia. Its people purport-

edly founded European civilization; modern Germans were its racial as well as cultural heirs. Aryan dominance, he argued, had been threatened throughout history by representatives of lesser races, especially the half-Asiatic Jews, who, in Chamberlain's warped historical narrative, continually worked feverishly to pollute the civilization the Aryans had built. "Their existence is a crime against the holy laws of life," Chamberlain thundered, referring to the Jews. The restoration of Aryan-Nordic purity, in his view, urgently required the destruction of the Jews.

This virulent anti-Jewish Aryan ideology did not take full flight in Germany until after World War I, with the founding of the Thule Society, in Munich in 1919. Originally calling itself the Study Group for Germanic Antiquity, the society was founded by a half-mad German nobleman named von Sebottendorff. The cult organization's name was taken from Thule, the ancient Greco-Roman name for Scandinavia. Its emblem was the Viking sun-disk symbol, or swastika. Sebottendorff's vision was a semimystical dream of re-creating the supposed racial dominance of Aryans through an all-out war against Jews and Communists, and against middle-class liberals. His ultimate goal was creating a racist political message that would appeal to Germany's working class.

That same year, he created the Thule Society's political wing in the form of the German Worker's Party. One of its original members was a disgruntled war veteran and failed artist named Adolf Hitler. In fact, virtually all of Hitler's earliest associates and future Nazi thugs had cycled through the Thule Society and its meetings. Eventually, Hitler would take over the German Worker's Party and give it a new name: the National Socialist German Worker's Party, or Nazi Party for short.

In German hands, the Viking legacy and the Viking heart took a deeply sinister turn. Although no one realized it, the stage was being set for a Ragnarok-scale disaster for Europe. What remained to be seen was whether Scandinavia, the original home of the Vikings, could hold out against the forces purloining the North's heritage in order to do evil.

The first step in reconstituting the future of Scandinavia, and saving the true Viking legacy at home, was stopping the hemorrhage of immigrants to America.

Sweden was the first to act. In 1907 it launched the Parliamentary Emigration Commission, which completed a study and published its results in twenty-one volumes detailing the steps needed to keep Swedes from leaving for America. More than two hundred testimonials told the same story: of rural poverty and urban hopelessness, of lives ruined and dreams thwarted — that is, until the opportunity to leave for America changed those fortunes. One woman described how, in her native Värmland, she was forced to start work at age eight, rising every morning at four and subsisting on a diet of dried herring and spoiled potatoes. Then, one day when she was seventeen, her brother in America sent her a steamship ticket so she could join him. "The hour of freedom struck," she gleefully told the commission, and she had never looked back.

The commission's recommendations were far-ranging and ultimately decisive for the future of Sweden. They included a wider franchise, with universal male suffrage not restricted by property qualification, and a devotion of national resources to support public education and economic development through industries such as forestry, steel making, and fisheries.

While the reform program grabbed public attention, Sweden's economy was already on the upswing, thanks to a loosening of traditional restrictions and regulations and the spread of railroad construction and hydro-electric power. What the reforms accelerated for Sweden, World War I completed for all of Scandinavia. While the rest of northern Europe, including Germany and Russia, were slaughtering their young men and tearing themselves to pieces on the battlefield and in the trenches, neutral Sweden, Norway, and Denmark experienced unprecedented economic growth. Even the Great Depression barely made a dent in the success story.

Between 1870 and 1936, for example, Sweden enjoyed the highest growth rate in the industrialized world. Between 1870 and 1924, Denmark had the sixth highest. After winning full independence in 1905, Norway followed a similar economic upturn as its government pursued what can be accurately described as free-market policies. It also became the first European country to give women the vote (Denmark followed suit in 1915, while Sweden's women had to wait until 1919).*

---

*Finnish women got the vote in 1906, a year earlier than their Norwegian sisters. But

Taken together, Sweden, Norway, Finland, and Denmark experienced faster growth than Germany, France, Britain, or Italy. They were the equivalent of the BRICS in the 1990s, the newly emerging players on the world's economic stage.

The rise of affluence diminished the incentive to find a better life in America; betterment was starting to happen at home. This development also gave birth to a new cultural archetype, the Scandinavian philanthropist — men (and in some cases women) who gave the Lutheran work ethic a new relevance in a globalizing age and defined a new mission for the Nordic countries. Having abandoned war as a matter of policy, Swedes, Danes, and Norwegians now adopted relieving the impact of war on others as a matter of humanity.

Of these philanthropic Scandinavians, certainly the best known is Alfred Nobel, the inventor of dynamite and creator of a massive fortune from his often-controversial explosive products. Curiously, it was the death of Nobel's brother Ludvig, a titan in the emerging petroleum business and a very wealthy man in his own right, that changed Nobel's life.

He and his brothers Ludvig and Robert, and four other siblings, were born and raised in Stockholm, where their father, Immanuel Nobel, earned a marginal living as an engineer. Only half of the eight Nobel children survived childhood — an interesting measure of the quality of life in Sweden at the time. It certainly made the perils of a voyage to America look relatively attractive to many.

In 1837, when Alfred was not yet four, the family got a break. Immanuel left for work in Saint Petersburg, Russia, where he became a very successful manufacturer of tools and explosives; he worked on an early version of the torpedo. By the time he summoned the family to join him in 1842, Immanuel Nobel was affluent enough to provide his brightest boy, Alfred, with private tutors. He became fluent in English, French, German, and Russian, in addition to Swedish.

But the youngest Nobel boy really excelled in chemistry. In 1850 he traveled to France to deepen his studies. There he met the Italian chemist Ascanio Sobrero, who had just discovered a powerful explosive called nitroglycerine.

---

historians note that Finland was then an autonomous zone of the Russian Empire, not an independent nation.

The compound was so volatile that Sobrero kept his discovery a secret for a year. Alfred became obsessed with making the volatile fluid safe to handle. He spent two years developing the techniques, then carried his experiments back to Sweden. There, at age thirty-one, he created a new, more efficient detonator, and invented the blasting cap. It was Alfred's — and nitroglycerine's — first venture outside the laboratory, and it did not come easy.

Accidents with the treacherous compound were common. One killed five people, including Alfred's own brother Emil. The family tragedy left the obsessive Alfred undeterred. Three more years of experiments and trial and error, sometimes catastrophic error, followed until he found a way to introduce sorbents and chemical stabilizers into the nitroglycerine, which made it relatively safe to handle but also didn't stifle its explosiveness.

He dubbed the result of this perfect formula dynamite. The year was 1867, and the place was his factory in Geesthacht, thirty-four miles southeast of Hamburg on the Slesvig-Holstein border. Geesthacht had become Prussian territory just three years earlier. Had Alfred been able to unveil his deadly invention in 1863, or even 1864, instead of 1867, it might have come into the hands of the Danish military in time for the crisis over the two duchies. The battle of Dybbøl, and the fate of Germany itself, might have looked very different if Danish generals could have deployed the most destructive compound known to humanity against their enemy's superior numbers.

But instead, nitroglycerine became the property of Alfred Nobel and no one else, and quickly became the making of his fortune. Nor did he stop there. In 1875 he invented gelignite, which was even more stable and more potent than dynamite. Then came ballistite, which was 10 percent camphor and equal parts nitro and collodion. It was the predecessor of smokeless gunpowder, or cordite, which virtually every army on the planet was using by the time World War I started.

Almost as famous (and much richer) were Alfred's older brothers Ludvig Nobel and Robert Nobel. In 1876 they had bought an oil refinery in Azerbaijan, which was then part of the Russian Empire. Virtually by themselves, the Nobel brothers turned the petroleum business into a global enterprise. At one point they were producing 50 percent of the world's oil. Rockefeller, Gulbenkian, and all the rest were merely their business disciples, following in their very Swedish footsteps.

In fact, Ludvig Nobel proved as handy as his brother the chemist when it came to inventing things. He designed and built the world's first oil tanker, which was able to adjust the liquid cargo it carried to changes in temperature, and was equipped with a special ventilating system. Dubbed the *Zoroaster,* it was built in Lindholmen-Matala in Sweden and launched in 1878. It made its first run from Baku to Astrakhan. Ludvig Nobel refused to patent his inventions, so that the technology was available to all. He also worked to improve the safety and efficiency standards for oil refineries and pipelines — the essential hardware of the modern petroleum business.

Then, in 1888, while vacationing in Cannes, Ludvig Nobel had a sudden heart attack and died. A Paris newspaper published an obituary of the Swedish multimillionaire but mistakenly ran Alfred's biography instead of his brother's. Alfred had the unpleasant surprise of opening the morning paper and reading his own obituary. He was even more appalled at the first line: "the merchant of death is dead." The paper went on to say, "Dr. Alfred Nobel, who became rich by finding ways to kill people faster than ever before, died yesterday..."

Alfred Nobel threw down the newspaper in disgust. Is that what people really thought of him, as a merchant of death? He was fifty-five, unmarried with no children, and rich many times over, thanks to not only his own enterprise but his share in his brothers' oil business. Before he really did die, he decided, he was going to leave a legacy very different from the one the newspaper had printed.

After consulting with lawyers and drawing up multiple drafts of trusts and wills, Alfred announced the final result at the Swedish-Norwegian Club in Paris, in November 1895. He would be leaving a large portion of his wealth to philanthropic causes, he told the audience. He hoped to help make the world a better place.

In this almost accidental way, Alfred Nobel founded the Nobel Prizes as the ultimate reward for intellectual and scientific achievement, including a prize for whoever "has done the most and best work for the brotherhood of nations and the abolishment or reduction of standing armies as well as for the establishment and spread of peace congresses." The Nobel Peace Prize still symbolizes an ideal of human progress and peaceful community, certainly the highest yearnings of the modern Viking heart. As for Nobel himself, "A more humane way of thinking is taking shape everywhere," he wrote hopefully, just before his death in 1898. "The thought lends its wonderful aura to a seduced and broken-hearted world."

His words may have been true for his fellow Scandinavians, but not for the rest of the world. It would take another philanthropist, a Norwegian this time, to stake his considerable reputation on healing the wounds of that broken-hearted world, one refugee at a time.

His name was Fridtjof Nansen. Though not as well-known today as Nobel, he combined more of the adventurous daring of his Viking ancestors with the modern Lutheran work ethic than most people could hope to accomplish.

Born in 1861 to a well-known seafaring family, Fridtjof had been largely a failure at the books in school. The outdoor life was his first love: hiking, skating, and above all, skiing; ski racing at Telemark had raised it to a new art. Fridtjof loved exploring the woods on skis, often spending weeks at a time outdoors "like Robinson Crusoe," as he later confessed in his memoirs, living off the land regardless of the weather.

When his mother died, the family moved to Kristiania. By then Fridtjof was an accomplished skater as well, setting the world's record in the one-mile race, as well as becoming a national cross-country-skiing champion.

Still, family pride demanded that he complete enough schooling to get into the Royal Frederick University (now the University of Oslo), which he entered in 1880. He decided he would study zoology because it would allow him to legitimately spend all his time in the outdoors and the wilderness. Sensing his adventurous spirit, a professor encouraged him to take a sea voyage to the Arctic. It was a life-changing event. Fridtjof, now twenty years old, discovered an intense passion for polar exploration that would be matched by other Scandinavians like Roald Amundsen; for them, the Arctic was simply an extension of the forbidding landscape of their homeland. (Incidentally, Alfred

Nobel shared this enthusiasm. He spent millions sponsoring various Arctic expeditions.)

"Our ancestors, the old Vikings, were the first Arctic voyagers," Nansen wrote in his account of his polar adventures, published in 1892. "As they were the first ocean navigators, so also were they the first to combat with the ice. Long before other seafaring nations had ever ventured to do more than hug the coast lines, our ancestors had traversed the open seas in all directions," discovering first Iceland and Greenland, and eventually America. It was in conscious emulation of Erik the Red, Leif Erikson, and the intrepid Norse voyagers that Nansen now decided exploring the Arctic region would be the center of his life.

When he returned to Norway in August 1882, he had taken up another interest: the neuroanatomy of marine creatures, such as the walruses and seals he had encountered in his travels. The books and study beckoned once again. But his real dream had to wait until 1887, when he put together an expedition to Greenland to test his theory that its enormous ice pack could be crossed on skis.

His fellow Norwegians thought it madness. But thanks to a Danish businessman, Augustin Garmel, and a Kickstarter-type fundraising effort by some university students, Nansen was able to set out with seven companions on June 2, 1888, on the seal-hunting ship *Jason*.

After negotiating the ice floes barring their way, the Nansen party reached Umivik Bay on August 11. They had hoped to reach Christianhaab (now Qasigiannguit) on Disko Bay, 371 miles away, by mid-September. Not until October 12 did they arrive at Godthaab (now Nuuk, Greenland's capital), after crossing ice ranges more than eight thousand feet in height, with snow, rain, and sleet descending at regular intervals. Not a man had been lost, nor had anyone been injured or gotten sick. It was the most successful Arctic expedition of all time. Although they had to wait out the Greenland winter, and it was not until April 1889 that they finally set sail for home, they reached Copenhagen on May 21 to a rapturous reception.

The next twenty-five years of Nansen's life would be mainly devoted to polar expeditions, usually on board his exploration ship, *Fram* (now preserved

at the museum at Bygdøy, where as a boy I was able to tramp along its decks).
In 1895–96 Nansen and the *Fram* sailed farther north than anyone had ventured before — 83 degrees 13.6 North, almost spitting distance from the North
Pole. Nansen also taught zoology at the Royal Frederick University and was
very active in the Norwegian independence movement. After independence
in 1905, he was appointed Norway's first minister to Britain. During his stay in
London, he developed yet another new interest, oceanography, and willingly
passed on his wisdom concerning polar exploration to a new generation of adventurers, including his fellow countryman Roald Amundsen.

Fridtjof Nansen was fifty-three years old, an established national figure and
leading scholar, when the World War I broke out. Although all three Scandinavian nations remained neutral, Nansen took a keen if saddened interest in
the bloody proceedings and the Great War's almost equally bloody aftermath.
The years of pandemic (the Spanish flu outbreak of 1918–20 would kill more
than fifty million people worldwide) and refugee crises in one country after
another presented Fridtjof Nansen with his next and final mission, also his
most daunting: helping Europe recover from years of conflict and misery. He
focused on the tens of millions who had endured catastrophic upheaval because of the war between Russia and Germany. Starvation and homelessness
had devastated central and southern Europe.

To bring about change, Nansen seized upon the newly created League of
Nations. He threw himself into the cause with the passion and discipline he
had used to plan and execute a polar expedition. He became president of the
League of Nations Society in Norway, and he campaigned heavily for Norway
to join the organization, which it did in 1920. He was one of Norway's three
delegates to its first General Assembly.

But Nansen's energies couldn't be confined to the League. He also devoted
himself to the repatriation of prisoners of war. The conflict in the east had, in
some cases, thrown these men thousands of miles from home. "Never in my
life," he said, "have I been brought into touch with so formidable an amount
of suffering." By 1922 he could report that he had helped to repatriate nearly
half a million former prisoners, most of them from Russia, where the Bolshe-
vik revolution had left them stranded.

From helping these prisoners, it was an easy step to help improve the lot of the nearly two million civilian Russian refugees whose lives had been turned upside down by revolution and civil war. As high commissioner for refugees in the League of Nations, Nansen tackled the human misery in the wake of the Russian famine of 1921–22 by organizing emergency food and other supplies for the famine's victims. Together with an American, soon-to-be president Herbert Hoover, Nansen probably saved Russian society from complete collapse.

Nansen also took up the challenge posed by the tens of thousands of refugees roaming Europe with no identity papers or proof of citizenship; some carried papers for countries that no longer existed. Nansen created a temporary document that became famous as the "Nansen passport," which allowed stateless persons, or those deprived of their national passports, to enter and travel through other countries. These passports would be used until 1938. By one estimate they saved more than 450,000 people from various forms of forcible deportation, concentration camps, or worse. The Nansen passport came to be officially recognized by more than fifty governments. More than any single document, it helped eastern and central Europe return to some level of normality. It came in handy when Nansen pitched in to help refugees in the wake of the Greek-Turkish war of 1921–22.

By now Nansen had turned sixty. His photographs show a man as lean and active as the polar explorer of a quarter century before, his walrus mustache and piercing blue eyes reminiscent of a Viking chieftain's. While attending the Conference of Lausanne in November 1922, Nansen learned that he had been awarded the Nobel Peace Prize. The committee chairman and presenter, Nansen's friend Frederick Stang, summed up Nansen's superhuman accomplishments in this way:

"The human mind cannot visualize this enormous activity any more than it can grasp astronomical figures . . . A program whose aim is to rescue a continent's millions from misery and death — this presents proportions so immense and involves such a myriad of jumbled details that we give up and allow our minds to rest." Stang added, "It will be the task of future generations to give this work its proper place in world history." Stang described Nansen's particular ability to lead others: "Perhaps what has most impressed all of us is his ability to stake his life time and time again on a single idea, on one thought, and to inspire others to follow him," whether it was crossing the Greenland ice pack or housing and feeding millions of Russian refugees.

Nor was he finished. Three years after receiving his prize, Nansen was organizing a massive rescue operation for Armenian refugees fleeing the genocide in their native country. By the time he died, in 1930, he had established a track record of effective humanitarian efforts that remains a model worth aspiring to.

Viscount Robert Cecil, one of the progenitors of the League of Nations and a recipient of the Nobel Peace Prize himself, summed up Nansen this way: "Every good cause had his support. He was a fearless peacemaker, a friend of justice, an advocate always for the weak and suffering." Cecil added, "He was almost the only man I have ever met who deserves to be called heroic ... He was in a class by himself."

Fridtjof Nansen is usually credited with being the first to say, "The difficult is what takes a little time; the impossible takes a little longer."

It might be the motto of the Viking heart.

World War I proved to be a watershed for Scandinavia, but not in the way it was for other nations, including the United States.

After a long and disastrous history of involvement in armed conflict in Europe, Sweden, Denmark, and newly independent Norway decided to sit this one out. Of course, neither the warring Central Powers (Germany and Austria-Hungary) or the Entente Powers (Britain, France, and Russia) considered them worth including. Nonetheless, the choice to remain on the sidelines was momentous. With the possible exception of the coming of independence for Norway in 1905, the decision to remain neutral in the midst of what, up to that point, was the greatest conflict in European history would be the single most important event in Scandinavian history in the twentieth century.

For one thing, the pre-war affluence and economic growth the Nordic countries were enjoying could continue unabated. In fact, they grew without interruption relative to the rest of Europe, where postwar depression and unemployment were virtually the norm.

For another, they found themselves joined by a new Nordic nation, Finland. The Finns had won their independence from Russia in 1917, then had to fight a hard and bitter war with the Soviet Union's Red Army to keep it. Despite this war and the hardship it caused for their fledgling country, the Finns fit in well with their Scandinavian neighbors, including their old Swedish colonial masters. In a few years they were experiencing the same economic boom as the rest of the region.

What's more, World War I and its interruption of transatlantic travel brought the Great Migration to an end. Admittedly, there would be a brief resurgence of the flight to America after the war. The numbers even hit a new peak in 1923, when twenty-five thousand more Swedes arrived, just before the restrictions of the new immigration laws passed by Congress in 1923–24 kicked in.

In fact, the 1923–24 immigration restrictions, which many in the United States condemned as unfair and ethnically biased, proved to be a windfall for Scandinavia. Instead of their best and brightest and boldest setting off for America, successive Norwegian, Danish, Swedish, and Finnish governments were able to focus on making the lives of ordinary Scandinavians better, so that no one would feel the need to leave again.

The chosen vessel, politically speaking, for this policy of amelioration was the Social Democrats. Former Marxists, the Social Democrats in all four countries became reconciled to the capitalist economies that were surging their own economy forward, as a generation of brilliant and charismatic political leaders came to the fore. Karl H. Branting in Sweden, Thorvald Stauning in Denmark, Chris Hornsrud in Norway, and Väinö Tanner in Finland: together they set the stage for Social Democrat parties to become the natural majority in Scandinavian politics — if not in terms of actual seats in legislative bodies, then certainly in terms of determining policy — right down to the present day.

That growth and prosperity not only took care of the emigration problem but also built up a tax base that allowed these countries to look after citizens' most basic needs: workers' compensation and retirement pensions, child labor laws and unemployment insurance, subsidies for agriculture and support for workers' and farmers' cooperatives, along with government-provided social services at low cost or no cost to users. These provisions, the bedrock of the Scandinavian welfare state, had by the 1930s become the envy of the world. Books like Marquis Childs's *Sweden: The Middle Way* celebrated the success of Nordic social democracy — without dwelling very much on its pro-capitalist, pro-growth fiscal foundations.

Sweden in particular fascinated journalists and politicians. They gazed with bewildered admiration at a country where a royal crown prince felt free to join a local consumers' cooperative (by 1925 one-fifth of all Swedes belonged to one kind of cooperative or another) and where reforms, such as workers' pensions and limits on the right to strike, were accepted almost without serious opposition. In other European countries those measures might have led to major political crises — possibly even civil war. But in Sweden, Norway, Denmark, and (belatedly but just as impressively) Finland, politicians like Karl Branting seemed to discover the secret of liberal democratic success, one that avoided the excesses of the Right or the Left while keeping a society united and intact — and prospering.

"If the test of the good life is the greatest good for the greatest number, now, here in the immediate present," wrote Childs in his 1936 book, "and not in some distant and debatable tomorrow, then one may well consider what has happened in these small countries . . . For they have achieved a measure of peace and decent living that will serve, and for a long time to come perhaps, as a standard for larger nations."

It was an impressive achievement, at a time when much of Europe was in deep turmoil: the Spanish Civil War, Mussolini's invasion of Ethiopia, Hitler's Nürnberg laws, and Stalin's show trials. But, as another admirer of the Scandinavian way, the English Labour Party activist and social scientist E. D. Simon, wrote in his book *The Smaller Democracies* in 1939, "A European war might well shatter all these splendid attempts to build a better social order."

Simon's words were prophetic. Scandinavia was about to undergo its severest trial in modern history, and the Viking heart its severest test since the days of the longships and the broadaxes.

15

The Viking Heart in War and Peace

A people who submissively gives in to a
violator, does not deserve to live.

— Adolf Hitler

IN SEPTEMBER 1939, Europe exploded into war for the second time in less than a quarter of a century. Once again, the Scandinavian countries hoped and planned to stay neutral, but this time in vain. None of them — not Sweden, or Norway, or Denmark, or Finland — could escape this global conflict. In the end, the traditionally neutral country to which hundreds of thousands of their former citizens had immigrated, the United States, wasn't able to escape it, either.

Scandinavian Americans played a major part in getting their country ready for war. Without the efforts of William Knudsen, Charles Sorensen, Charles Lindbergh, Claire Egtvedt, and others, it's difficult to see how the Allies could have prevailed in the largest armed conflict in history.

One could say the same about certain Scandinavians back at home — especially certain Norwegian commandos. But on the whole, the Nordic countries found themselves caught in the turmoil of a war in which they had no strategic or economic stake. As the Indian saying goes, when elephants fight, the grass gets trampled. Between 1940 and 1944, Denmark, Norway, Finland,

and to a degree Sweden proved to be grass under the feet of Nazi Germany, Soviet Russia, Great Britain, and the United States.

It wouldn't have been surprising if most Scandinavians had chosen the route of submission and collaboration, like many residents in other European countries in those years who found themselves ground under by far more powerful neighbors.

Instead, many Scandinavians chose the route of resistance: sometimes quiet, sometimes violent, but always with the aim of remaining true to their national and personal honor, a choice dictated by the imperatives of the Viking heart. And, with a few exceptions, they succeeded.

Finland was the first to rise up. For centuries Finns had served side by side with Swedes in Viking raids, in trade with Russia, and in Gustavus Adolphus's army. Handed over to Russia in 1814, Finns had enjoyed a special status under the Romanov empire, with more freedom and autonomy than most of its other possessions. For example, Finnish, not Russian, was the official language in Finland's schools and government.

But the Russian Revolution in 1917 triggered Finland's grab for complete independence, which came at a heavy cost. Twenty years later, it was the Finns who had the most to fear from a major European conflict, specifically one involving their powerful neighbor, Joseph Stalin's Soviet Union. Finland's entire eastern border faced onto what could easily become hostile territory. As early as 1931, Finnish politicians started reassessing their military options as war with the Soviets loomed on the horizon.

As for the Soviets, they feared that if Nazi Germany made a move into the Baltic region, Finland might serve as a jumping-off point for invasion. Finland's Karelian peninsula had served as the corridor for invading armies for centuries: for Russians and Mongols moving west, for Swedes, Poles, Teutonic Knights, and once, long ago, for Viking raiders moving east. Why not the Germans? An army crossing the Finnish border could surround Leningrad, the former Saint Petersburg, in a matter of hours.

When a Soviet emissary reached the Finnish capital in Helsinki in August 1939, he demanded that Finland submit to being in the Soviet Union's sphere of influence, just as the other Baltic republics — Latvia, Lithuania, and Estonia — had done. The answer was a stout no. Finland would not submit, not now, not ever. Stalin's response was a declaration of war, and on November 30, 1939, Soviet bombers swept over Helsinki as the war for Finland's future, even its existence, began.

The Russians threw everything they had at the Finns. Hundreds of tanks rumbled across the Karelian isthmus, where the intrepid Finns responded with lit bottles filled with a viscous mixture of gasoline, kerosene, tar, and potassium chlorate. The gasoline bomb, which the Finns called *polttopullo,* proved wickedly effective. The world, however, would come to know it by another Finnish name, *Molotovin koktaili,* or Molotov cocktail, named after Stalin's hated foreign minister, Vjacheslav Molotov.* All the same, columns of Soviet troops and trucks continued to trundle along the icy single-track roads leading into Finland. The outnumbered Finns had little more than their gas bombs, outdated rifles and machine guns, their skis, and their resolution to defend their country to the end.

The man in charge of Finland's defense was General Carl Gustav Mannerheim, Finland's leading soldier and the hero of the war against Russia by which Finland won its independence. Mannerheim had an edge too. He had served with the Russian army and knew their tactics better than they did. His plan of defense consisted of deploying his troops along the Russian army's flanks, slicing up the advancing columns like cords of wood, then breaking down each cut-off segment with savage, often hand-to-hand fighting, until the isolated, starved, and half-frozen Russians surrendered — or fought to the last man.

The Finns called the tactics *motti,* the Finnish word for "pile of logs." Except instead of producing piles of logs, there were piles of dead Russians, dying

---

* A similar weapon had been used sporadically by Republican troops against the Fascists in Spain, and by the Japanese against the Russians in Manchuria in 1939. The Finns, however, were the first to mass-produce it — the Rajamäki distillery, owned by the Alko corporation, produced thousands of them, each bundled with matches. Total production came to 450,000 during the Winter War.

in temperatures so cold that men who were shot froze solid almost at once, lying with arms outstretched or knees bent in a grotesque death agony.

The culmination of the Finnish humiliation of its Russian attackers came with the battle of Suomussalmi in December; it is still taught in military textbooks. The Russian motorized columns often had to advance along a single-track road through dense forest, where the *motti* tactics worked to perfection.

While an assault team swept in on skis and spread out on either side of the road, a sudden hail of mortar and machine-gun fire would rain down on the approaching Russians, cutting them off from the rest of the column. Then Finnish assault troops would storm in, spraying submachine-gun fire and hand grenades before vanishing into the woods. Once a gap had been blown through the Russian column, more Finnish troops would pour in and fortify the position on either side of the road-cut, sometimes three to four hundred meters wide — too strong and well-armed for the Russians inside to break out from, or for the Russians outside to break into.

Then the bloody business of reducing each isolated Russian position would begin, often degenerating into a vicious hand-to-hand contest in the snow, as cries of "No quarter" reverberated through the smoke-smudged forest. One of the last to fall was Suomussalmi village, where desperate Russian machine gunners barricaded themselves in cellars and had to be rousted out and killed one by one.

The last pocket of Russians fell on December 29. The elite Forty-Fourth Ukrainian Division had gone into the battle in mid-December with 30,000 men. By the time the fighting was over, fewer than 5,000 were left. By then the Russian 163rd Division was all but annihilated. The Finnish victors marched along the road that the 163rd had defended and passed 47 broken tanks, 270 abandoned vehicles, and more than 27,000 frozen Russian corpses. The Finns had lost only 900 soldiers, with 1,770 wounded, in the entire campaign.

The stunning Finnish victory at Suomussalmi made headlines around the world — and made *motti* as much a byword in popular military jargon as *blitzkrieg* would be in little more than a year. The unexpected success of the gallant Finns galvanized their fellow Scandinavians, who were still maintaining neutrality in an increasingly deadly neighborhood. Eight thousand volunteers from Sweden signed up to go to the front, where the Finns' David-like defiance of the Goliath Russians was an inspiration but also a reproach to the neutral government in Stockholm. Posters sprang up with this motto:

NOW THE WORLD KNOWS WHAT IT MEANS TO BE A FINN —
IT IS YOUR DUTY TO SHOW WHAT IT MEANS TO BE A SWEDE!
JOIN THE SWEDISH VOLUNTEERS!

Fifteen hundred Norwegian and Danish volunteers also joined the pilgrimage to fight alongside the Finns, as did 350 Finnish Americans and others for whom the fight against Communism, or just to support an underdog, was irresistible. The war became popular in America, particularly among Scandinavian Americans, as kids in the Midwest (as my father did in the suburbs of Minneapolis) divided up into teams of Russians and Finns, built snow forts, and pelted each other with snowballs in place of Mauser and Mosin-Nagant rifles.

Finns found admirers far outside the heavily Scandinavian Midwest. New York's mayor, Fiorello LaGuardia, organized a "Help Finland" rally in Madison Square Garden, and FDR authorized a government loan for $10 million. Although the money was not supposed to be used for arms (the United States in 1939 was still maintaining a policy of strict neutrality), the Finnish government used it to buy foodstuffs, which it promptly sold for pounds sterling, which it then used to purchase arms—from the United States. In the end, FDR released fifty Brewster Buffalo fighters to be sent to the Finnish Air Force, but only five made it in time to fight in what was becoming known as the Winter War.

At last the Soviets were able to bring all their weight to bear, and the unfortunate Finns were overwhelmed. Only the possibility that Britain and France might come to the rescue at the last minute, and land troops, kept Prime Minister Tanner and the Finnish government fighting on. By early March, however, those hopes were dashed. A final peace was signed in Moscow on March 13, 1940. The terms were humiliating. A large swath of border territory was lost to the Russians, including the Karelian peninsula, as well as the islands in the Gulf of Finland, which Stalin had demanded in the first place. Almost half a million Karelians had to flee their homes. But Finland was spared the fate of the Baltic republics, Lithuania, Latvia, and Estonia: complete absorption into the Soviet Union.

It was left to General Mannerheim to convey the news to his exhausted soldiers. By then nearly twenty-five thousand Finnish troops had been killed and forty-five thousand wounded — one of every three who served. His words summed up Finland's triumph but also its tragedy in the 105-day Winter War better than any historian could: "Soldiers! I have fought on many battlefields but I have never yet seen your equals as warriors. I am proud of you as if you were my own children . . . In spite of all the courage and self-sacrifice the government has been compelled to make peace on harsh terms. Our army was small, and both its resources and regulars insufficient. We were not equipped for a war with a great power."

That last sentence summed up the dilemma of every Scandinavian nation that terrible spring.

Then it was Norway's turn.

Seven months before that fateful March 1940, as Germany, France, and Britain geared up for war — and Finland and Russia came to blows — one Norwegian saw the rising tide and made his move. Rather than boldly lead Norway into the next great war as a hero, however, Vidkun Quisling dragged his home country into the fray as a traitor. His grab for power came at an incalculable cost.

Vidkun Quisling was born in Fyresdal in 1887, the son of a Lutheran pastor. He entered the Norwegian Military Academy at the age of eighteen and graduated with the highest-ever score since the academy's founding, in 1817. His intellectual promise led to a posting on the Norwegian General Staff in 1911. From there he became the Norwegian army's point man in revolutionary Russia and its leading expert on all things Russian. Quisling even married a Russian, Alexandra Andrevina Voronina, while working on famine relief in Ukraine with Fridtjof Nansen and later in Armenia. Nansen told him, "It is a great comfort for me to know that I have you." Later Nansen was quoted as saying that Quisling's work was "absolutely indispensable."

Despite such promising beginnings, in the 1920s Quisling was increasingly drawn to extremist political ideologies, including Hitler's fledgling Nazism.

The political party Quisling launched as his vehicle to command Norwegian politics, the Nasjonal Samling, or National Union Party (NS for short), proved a disaster. Norwegians failed to respond to its blend of socialist nationalism and racist politics borrowed from the Nazi agenda, even though the Germans spoke of the Nordic nations as fellow "Aryans" and used Viking symbols, like the swastika and the runic letters SS for Hitler's elite bodyguard.

In the national elections in 1933 and 1936, Quisling and the NS barely cleared 2 percent of the vote. Only an acute national crisis could possibly give him the influence he desired.

That crisis came with war in Europe in 1939. Quisling convinced himself that Norway's only salvation lay with Hitler himself. Three months after war broke out, Quisling arranged for a meeting in Berlin with the German dictator. He offered to hand over Norwegian military bases to Germany and promised that Norway, under Quisling, would become Germany's full-fledged ally.

Afterward, on December 14, 1939, Hitler set his army high command to work, preparing a plan for a secret invasion of Norway. On April 4, 1940, German ships entered the Bay of Oslo shortly after midnight. The plan was to swoop in and occupy the Norwegian capital, where Quisling would be waiting for them. Only one man stood in their way: Colonel Birger Erickson, commander of the Oscarsborg Fortress, which sat on a rocky island at the narrowest point of the bay.

Erickson's military career had been solid but hardly distinguished. He had graduated from the Norwegian Military Academy in 1896, when Norway was still part of Sweden. It took him five years to rise to the rank of captain, another fourteen to become a major, then sixteen more to be promoted to colonel, in 1931. (Armies of neutral countries make rapid promotion tough to achieve.)

In 1933 Erickson was assigned command of the Oscarsborg Fortress, which had old, obsolete artillery guns with biblical names: Moses, Aaron, and Joshua. No one expected that those guns would ever be fired in anger, or that the torpedo batteries also attached to the fortress would ever be used, except in a routine drill. Erickson himself was expected to retire in a year or two.

But suddenly, out of the darkness, Erickson could see large shadows blocking the lights from the villages three miles down the bay. Ships were coming toward the fortress — unfamiliar ships. Erickson did not hesitate. He ordered the nearest battery to fire. A question arose: why had no one received orders to expect and prepare for a hostile advance up the bay? It wasn't even clear whose ships they were: German, British, or possibly even Norwegian.

Erickson simply said, "Either I will be decorated or court-martialed. Fire!"

Two 255-kilogram heavy explosive shells leapt from the guns and arced across the darkened sky to land on the lead ship, which turned out to be the German heavy cruiser *Blücher*.

Now it was the Germans' turn for an unpleasant surprise. One shell hit the cruiser amidships and set it alight. The second hit the base of the forward gun turret, blowing parts into the fjord and starting a fire, while also knocking out the electrical system, so that the *Blücher* couldn't shoot back.

Considering that the Oscarsborg gunners had been virtually firing blind, they were amazingly accurate. Soon a major blaze was underway on the *Blücher,* fed by cans of oil, boxes of smoke dispensers, incendiary shells, and other combustibles. As luck would have it, shrapnel from one of Erickson's hits had also put out the cruiser's fire control system, so soon the ship was merrily ablaze, almost from stem to stern. But the *Blücher*'s anti-aircraft guns could still fire, forcing one of Erickson's gun batteries to evacuate, albeit with no Norwegian casualties.

Incredibly, Erickson and his men still didn't know who exactly they were shooting at until they heard crewmen on the blazing cruiser raise their voices in song. Erickson listened intently to the words: "Deutschland, Deutschland, über alles . . ." So they were Germans after all! Erickson realized the crippled ship might still be able to slide past the fortress and reach Oslo when another Norwegian officer took a hand in the matter. Kommander Kapitan Andreas Anderssen had been called back from retirement that same evening to oversee the fortress's torpedo battery. The torpedoes were forty years old, and no one knew if they would work.

But Anderssen ordered them to fire on the approaching cruiser anyway. The first struck home but did only incidental damage. The second hit the *Blücher* amidships and blew out a section of bulkheads as water poured in; the fire on deck was still raging.

At 5:30 a.m. the flames reached the midship ammunition magazine, triggering a massive explosion. At 6:22, just as first glimmers of dawn were appearing on the eastern horizon, Erickson watched as the *Blücher* sank, bow first. Then it rolled over on its side and plunged to the bottom of the bay, along with more than two thousand Germans. The rest of the German fleet turned back and headed out of the bay.

The Norwegian triumph, and Erickson's, was short-lived. The other German invaders landed farther down the bay, and by afternoon they had swarmed by land over the Oscarsborg Fortress, taking Erickson and his men prisoner. Airborne troops seized Oslo. But King Haakon and his government were not there. Erickson's bold action, worthy of any Norwegian warrior of the past, had given the king and his ministers time to leave the capital for the north. Eventually they would summon resistance to the Nazi invaders and welcome British aid in repelling them.

But at that moment, Norway's situation couldn't be bleaker. Its king and government were gone. The British and French had fled, leaving Hitler and the Nazis in complete control. Even worse, the Nazis had found, in Vidkun Quisling, a Norwegian puppet to help them. After enjoying independence for just thirty-five years, Norway was once again under the thumb of a foreign power. A darkness descended on the Norwegians, as bleak as any midwinter night.

Denmark came under occupation at the same time. Unlike the confrontation in Norway, when the German invasion caught the Danes by complete surprise, no one responded with strength and speed. There was no Danish Colonel Erickson. King Christian and his government had no time to escape.

Instead, the king was awakened at 5:30 a.m. on the ninth for a meeting of the emergency state council. He learned that German troops had landed in fifteen different locations across the country, and German bombers could be heard circling over Copenhagen. Denmark's commander in chief proposed mounting a stiff defense, but King Christian turned him down. To his thinking, it was pointless to fight a war that was, in his mind, lost before it could even begin.

The German minister in Copenhagen offered the king and his prime minister a strange and, at first sight, rather generous deal. Germany would accept

Denmark's surrender and take the country "under protection." It would continue to respect Denmark's neutrality and its territorial integrity. That included the 1920 border with Germany: for the first time Germany recognized that southern Slesvig was now to be considered part of Denmark.

The current government could remain in place, as would Denmark's control over its internal affairs. All the Danes had to do was submit to a "peaceful occupation" under the Third Reich. However reluctantly, the king and his government felt they had no choice but to agree to this — and make do with their unexpected but ineluctable fate as the unwilling partners of the Nazis as they gained control over more and more of Europe.

Denmark's North Atlantic dependencies, however, fared differently. The British navy quickly occupied the Faroe Islands on April 12, and Iceland likewise came under British protection on May 10. The United States, meanwhile, worried that Greenland might pass into the hands of Britain or Canada, both combatants in the war in Europe. The US Navy and Coast Guard took control of the big island, ostensibly to preserve its neutrality. Yet Greenland and Iceland would come to play a significant role in the war. The Germans tried three times to install secret weather stations in Greenland after the United States entered the war. Each time, the US Navy had to drive them out, with significant German casualties. In the end, however, inhabitants of the Faroes, Iceland, and Greenland passed the war in relative calm.

That left Sweden. The Swedish government had no stomach for the fate of either Norway or Denmark, let alone that of Finland. Its leaders decided the only way forward was to adhere to a policy of strict neutrality. Interestingly, Hitler and the Germans agreed to this. On the one hand, occupying Sweden had no strategic significance for Germany and might antagonize Stalin, who was still Hitler's nominal ally. In addition, the Swedish army, although small, was prepared to fight on a front that would otherwise tie up German resources and inflict casualties just when Hitler was about to launch a massive offensive in the west, against France.

On the other hand, Sweden enjoyed a brisk trade in iron ore with the industrial heartland of Germany, which sent much-needed coal to the Swedes; Norway's northern city Narvik had built its prosperity as the entrepôt between

Sweden's ore cars and Germany's colliers. So as long as Swedish iron continued to flow to Germany, and as long as the Nazi occupation of Norway and Denmark went unhindered, Hitler was willing to give, on April 25, his personal assurance to Sweden's king, Gustav, that Germany would respect Swedish neutrality. A month later, as German panzers swarmed over France and the British army was trapped at Dunkirk, Sweden's decision seemed presciently prudent.

According to Wilhelm Carlgren, a leading analyst of Swedish foreign policy between the world wars, "A small state on the edge of Europe, reviewing its policy in the last weeks of May 1940, could not possibly avoid taking into consideration the German army's overwhelming victories in the West and the prospect of an ultimate [Nazi] victory." It was this pragmatic perspective on events that forced Sweden, following the fall of France, to join Denmark and then Norway as part of the Nazi "new order." Hitler's lightning victories and the complete isolation of England opened vistas for him. Europe had not seen the rise of a lone ruler dominating the Continent since the time of Napoleon. An empire stretching from Poland to the Pyrenees, with a combined GDP greater than that of the United States or the British Empire, seemed to be within Hitler's grasp.

Scandinavia was pegged to play an important part in this Nazi order. Denmark and, to a lesser extent, Norway provided vital resources to the Third Reich, from dairy and pork products to wheat and fish; freezing plants installed in Norway made it easier to export fish to Germany. Neutral Sweden's supply of iron was invaluable to the Nazi war machine. In 1940 it supplied more than 83 percent of Germany's iron imports, making up more than 50 percent of the country's overall iron and steel needs. Indeed, without Sweden, Germany would have had a much harder time sustaining the war effort.

Allowing Sweden formal neutrality was the price Hitler was willing to pay to keep the country cooperative and within the perimeter of his European empire. Yet, like Switzerland in those early years, Sweden was neutral in name only. By contrast, Denmark and Norway felt the full impact of the German jackboot.

Denmark paid the heaviest moral price. Its successive parliamentary governments, although still traditional in their constitutional makeup, did their best to pretend to be willing participants in "The New Order in Europe" (the title of an article by the Danish prime minister, Erik Scavenius, in the *Berliner Börsenzeitung*). Denmark even joined the anti-Comintern Pact that Hitler had signed with Right Wing authoritarian governments, such as Italy and Japan, and several others, in November 1941. The Finns also decided it would be prudent to sign.

Anxious not to displease its Nazi overlords, the Danish government rounded up Communists and banned the Communist Party, imposed press censorship to prevent the publication of anti-German articles, and allowed the German navy to use Danish ports and other facilities — anything to avoid provoking the Germans to clamp down harder on Denmark's last remaining freedoms. More controversially, Danish police helped the Gestapo round up those who had taken refuge in Denmark to escape the Nazi regime, including foreign Jews. This was disastrous for some 50 to 100 refugees, including 21 stateless Jews, who were killed in the death camps. But Scavenius, prime minister from 1942 to 1943, and other Danes did manage to keep Denmark's own Jews safe from Nazi depredation — at least for the time being.*

Norwegian Jews were not so fortunate. What was left of normal parliamentary government there had been swept away by November 1940. Quisling and his NS now ran virtually everything that the Nazis' *Reichskommissar*, Josef Terboven, was willing to leave in their control. Posters for the NS appeared everywhere, as did posters of Vidkun Quisling, who had taken for himself the title Forer, or Führer, like his idol, Adolf Hitler. The Norwegian version of the Nazi salute became a standard greeting, and the flying eagle insignia and "sun cross," Quisling's Viking-based variant on Hitler's swastika, became the new

---

* Six persons the Nazis were unable to arrest were the six sisters of William Knudsen, Roosevelt's master architect of the arsenal of democracy. Whereas their brother had immigrated to America, they had remained in Denmark. Although not Jews, they would have been persons of interest to the Gestapo; in an occupied country they could have been easily arrested. What effect would this have had on Knudsen and his role in the war effort? Denmark's relatively independent status made the question moot.

national symbols of a Norway eager to become part of Europe's new Aryan order.

Nazi propaganda stressed the link between Nazism and Norway's Viking past. Images of blond and blue-eyed SS men, with dragon-prowed longships in the background, were rife, and young Norwegians were encouraged to join units of the Waffen SS, such as the "Viking" division, the SS Nordland Regiment (later the Nordland Division), and Den Norske Legion, Quisling's homegrown version of the SS. To his disappointment, however, the numbers remained tiny in proportion to Norway's population. Even Quisling's own NS remained unpopular, its membership stubbornly low, even though everyone knew membership was an easy ticket to success in government or industry. Finally, Quisling tried to disguise his frustration with this failure by announcing, on June 21, 1942, that the "NS has so many members now, it doesn't need any more." That provoked many a guffaw in Norway's cafés and workshops.

What wasn't funny was Quisling's willingness to cooperate with the Nazis' roundup of Norway's (very tiny) Jewish population. In 1941–42 there were perhaps 2,170 persons of Jewish identity in Norway. Starting in 1941, at least 775 were arrested, detained, and deported to the Third Reich. Of those, 742 perished in the Nazi death camps. Twenty-three others either were murdered or committed suicide. In all, 765 Norwegian Jews died in the Holocaust, including 230 complete families: father, mother, and children.

As for the rest, almost two-thirds managed to escape. Some 900 were smuggled out of Norway by the Norwegian resistance. When Josef Terboven, the German *Reichskommissar,* and Hellmuth Reinhard, the head of the Gestapo, ordered the first big roundup of Jewish men, on October 26, 1942, even Norwegian Nazis were warning Jewish families to leave the country to avoid a terrible fate. Most wound up finding refuge in Sweden, but some few made it to Great Britain. Quisling tried to extend the roundup to include the Sámi in Norway's far north. He argued that they too were an inferior race. But the project got nowhere.

It turned out that Norwegians are not very good at hating. At the end of the day, they just didn't respond to the blandishments of Nazism any more than they did to those of Communism, either before or after the war. Whatever compromise a government was prepared to make to protect what was seen as the national interest, ordinary Danes, Swedes, Norwegians, and Finns found that Nazi and race-based ideologies left them cold. The deep insecurities, the sense of alienation, and the desperate need to find meaning in a supposedly meaningless world that drove others to turn to violent extremist creeds like Nazism and Communism didn't reflect the thoughts and feelings of most Scandinavians. By and large, it was second nature for those men and women to experience a sense of security, of belonging, of spiritual freedom and meaning in life. These qualities are the foundation of what we are calling the Viking heart. Its wellsprings of courage can inspire acts of bravery and daring self-sacrifice. And when governing elites have failed to act, ordinary Scandinavians have often taken the lead themselves.

So while Norway suffered under Nazi occupation and a collaborationist rule, a handful of intrepid resistance fighters there changed the course of World War II.

In October 1941 a Norwegian refugee named Leif Tronstad arrived in London. It had been a harrowing journey. After slipping across the border into neutral Sweden using fake papers, Tronstad had managed to cadge a flight from Stockholm to Scotland, and then the train to London, where he demanded a meeting with Commander Eric Welsh of the Secret Intelligence Service. Welsh was English, but his wife was Norwegian; as it happened, she was also a relative of the composer Edvard Grieg. Welsh himself spoke fluent Norwegian. And what Tronstad now told him filled him with barely disguised alarm.

Tronstad was no ordinary refugee. A chemist by day, he was by night the living link between British intelligence and the Norwegian resistance movement — a risky job that earned him the code name "The Mailman." The message he had to deliver this time was so important, he told Welsh, he felt he had to deliver it in person.

A friend of his was the chief engineer at the Norwegian hydro-electric plant at Vemork, the largest hydro-electric plant in the world. Far in the remote north of Norway, Vemork generated so much electricity that some of it was used to power certain industrial processes inside the plant — processes that would be prohibitively expensive without the bountiful free electricity.

One of the products produced there was deuterium, an isotope of hydrogen with a nucleus consisting of one proton and one neutron, which is double the mass of the nucleus of ordinary hydrogen. Deuterium had little use in industry or commerce, but Tronstad's engineer friend had said that certain German companies were ordering huge amounts of the stuff — almost four kilograms a day.

Tronstad had heard the distinguished British physicist Lord Rutherford once say that substituting deuterium for ordinary hydrogen in water — thus creating "heavy water," with its larger hydrogen atom — could be useful in creating a moderator to slow and control a nuclear fission reaction, to prevent it from blowing everything up. Tronstad had quickly put two and two together: the Germans had to be ordering the deuterium as part of an all-out effort to produce an atomic bomb. Separate intelligence had confirmed Tronstad's hunch that the Nazis were working on this project. Now, if Great Britain planned to slow or even stop that effort, Vemork was the place to start.

But how? After mulling over Tronstad's intelligence, Britain's Air Ministry dismissed the idea of a long-range bombing raid as too risky. Besides, there was no guarantee that a nighttime run, if it managed to evade German detection, would do serious enough damage to the plant. There was talk of flying in a special team of British commandos, but Vemork's harsh mountainous terrain and remote location posed enormous problems for this kind of special operation.

Tronstad had the answer. They should send in commandos, all right, but only Norwegian ones: volunteers conditioned from birth to endure and even prosper in stark mountainous wilderness and intense sub-Arctic conditions. Those recruited to the mission would have to be intensely — even fanatically — committed to ensuring that this facility in their homeland did not become the key to Nazi victory.

Tronstad soon became part of the elite training outfit for the Norwegian volunteers known as Kompagnie Linge, named after Martin Linge, a Norwegian commander killed by the Nazis. Training for the Kompagnie meant weeks of rigorous mental and physical conditioning at remote locations in the British Isles — training that stretched many to the breaking point. But the deceptively bookish Tronstad soon rose to the rank of captain and proved himself as tough as the men he was going to lead.

One of the three stars of the Kompagnie Linge was Knut Haukelid, an enthusiastic outdoorsman who had been born in Brooklyn, New York. His engineer father had been part of the Great Migration to America earlier in the century and had helped in the building of the New York City subway. When the Haukelid family returned to Norway, Knut had turned down a lucrative career in banking to run a mountain lodge for skiing and fishing in the remote Norwegian wilderness — just the sort of man who could survive, and even thrive, in the sub-Arctic environs of Vemork.

The second star was Einar Skinnarland, who had grown up in a wood-planked cabin his father had built by hand thirteen miles west of Rjukan — as it happened, very close to the dam that powered the Vemork plant. From November until early summer, the Skinnarland home was accessible only by skis. In fact, while growing up, Einar had spent as much time on skis as he had on foot, and both his older brothers were championship ski jumpers and racers. Twenty-one when the Germans invaded, he had served briefly in the Norwegian army before the country surrendered. Afterward he had taken a job as a dam-construction supervisor at Vemork. Few people knew the Vemork facility as well as Skinnarland. When the opportunity arose to contribute his knowledge to the Norwegian resistance (he had already been arrested by the Gestapo on suspicion of harboring weapons but was released), he helped steal a freighter and sail across the North Sea to Aberdeen. Soon he was part of the Kompagnie Linge, a key member of the mission to destroy the plant at Vemork.

The third crucial member of the team was Odd Starheim, a shipowner's son who had run dangerous spying missions along the Norwegian coasts — including spotting the breakout of the German battleship *Bismarck*. He had more than once escaped the clutches of the Gestapo and SS. In fact, it was Starheim who had brought Skinnarland out of Vemork; they climbed down six-thousand-foot glaciers to reach the coast, where they commandeered that freighter for the trip to England. If the Linge group needed a ship, Skinnarland was their man.

It was a team worthy of any Viking chieftain's most dangerous voyage, honed like steel and ready for the adventure of their lives in the cause of Norway's national honor.

During the eleven-day crash course in atomic physics, spy craft, and sabotage, Tronstad sketched out the plan to his team. The first step was getting

Skinnarland back to his home turf. He was secretly parachuted back into Norway, where he picked up his job without missing a beat — he had been sick, he told his German supervisors. Then he began preparing for the operation, which was so secret and vital, the information he passed on was not entrusted to radio transmission but to microdot (miniaturized text), sent via couriers in Sweden.

But by the time Skinnarland was back at work, the world, and the war, had changed. Pearl Harbor had brought America into the conflict, and in June 1942 Winston Churchill flew to the United States to brief President Roosevelt on how and why atomic weapons spelled the future of warfare; he shared what British intelligence had found out about the German program. Churchill and FDR struck a deal to conduct a joint Anglo-American effort to win the atomic race; it would blossom into the Manhattan Project. They also agreed that the German attempt to develop an atomic weapon had to be slowed at all costs.

That decision moved Vemork to the front and center of this secret effort. In September a hand-picked team of four members of the Kompagnie Linge — Poulsson, Helberg, Kjelstrup, and Haugland, who was their radio operator — were flown to a drop zone near Barren Mountain. Twice bad weather drove their plane back. On the third try they parachuted safely onto a mountain plateau separated by peaks and glaciers from the Norsk Hydro plant.

As the legendary head of British intelligence, William Stephenson, later said, "The fate of the world seemed to hang on those four young agents." They were perched on the Hardanger Vidda, an area of six thousand square miles at a height of four thousand feet. The area, perpetually covered with snow and ice, was inhabited by only the occasional reindeer herd. Every message and bit of information that the team, code-named SWALLOW, sent back to London was scrupulously analyzed for any indication that the Nazis were another step closer to building an atomic bomb.

At one point, in desperation the War Ministry decided to dispatch, via two gliders towed by planes, a thirty-four-man British commando team to carry out the destruction of Vemork. The mission, code-named FRESHMAN, was a disaster. One glider crashed when ice formed and broke its tow rope. Only eight of the seventeen commandos on board managed to crawl out from the glider's wreckage. Caught by the Germans, the four most badly injured were murdered (counter to Geneva Convention guidelines for the treatment of prisoners of war) by the Nazi physicians who were in attendance; they injected air bubbles into the men's blood vessels. The other four survivors were executed out of hand. The second glider also crashed when its towing aircraft smashed into a mountain. Even though the survivors, like the other commandos, were wearing British uniforms and thus subject to the Geneva Convention, they were all shot, and their bodies tossed in an unmarked common grave.

The mission was proof enough — the Norwegians were the Allies' only hope. A fresh team was quickly put together to reinforce the SWALLOW team already on Barren Mountain. This group of six was to be led by Joachim Rønneberg with Knut Haukelid, the tough Norwegian from Brooklyn, as his second-in-command. For this effort, code-named GUNNERSIDE, Rønneberg, Haukelid, and the others had undergone even more rigorous training at the so-called gangster school near Southampton. They were to parachute in, join forces with the SWALLOW team, and sabotage the Vemork heavy water plant.

After final farewells from Tronstad, they set out on the frigid night of February 16, 1943, in an Avro Lancaster bomber. As they crossed the Norwegian coast, a local fishing boat flashed a light as a kind of greeting, imparting "a feeling of comradeship with the first Norwegians we had met on our way home," Haukelid wrote later.

Dressed in white camouflage suits, they were so loaded down with heavy equipment, including explosives and Thompson machine guns, they could barely move. They could feel the plane gain altitude as it headed north along the coast, staying low enough to avoid German radar, until they were over the Hardanger Vidda.

The cargo door opened to the freezing air. Joachim Rønneberg was the first out the door. Then came two packages of supplies, followed by Haukelid. Seconds later, his chute opened with a powerful but reassuring jerk. "While I hung in the air," Haukelid later remembered, "I saw the plane disappearing northwards, returning to England — to rain, to nice hot tea, to a party tomorrow. Beneath me was nothing but snow and ice. Here lay Hardanger Vidda, the largest, loneliest, and wildest mountain area in Northern Europe."

It took the men of GUNNERSIDE almost a week to locate the SWALLOW team. That winter had been one of the harshest in living memory. Poulsson and his men were half-starved and half-frozen; every member of the team suffered from frostbite. But they had remained vigilant and kept up their radio transmissions without a break. Now with the GUNNERSIDE men on hand, the two groups could begin preparing for their final objective.

The ten Norwegian commandos split into two groups, one to blow up the heavy water facility and the other to cover their retreat. Rønneberg took charge of the first, Haukelid the second. Every man carried two "L" pills, or potassium cyanide. As the final operational order had stated, "Any man about to be taken prisoner will take his own life."

There was more at stake than failure of the mission and possible capture and torture. If a team member cracked under pressure and revealed the plan to destroy the facility at Vemork, Hitler would gain two important pieces of information. First, the Allies were hot on the trail of his development of the atomic bomb, and second, they believed an atomic bomb could actually be built.

As the commandos descended the steep glacier on skis, they enjoyed one advantage. "The Germans considered Vemork so well protected by nature that it would be difficult for attackers to reach it," Haukelid wrote later. Because of this, a force of only thirty soldiers had been assigned to guard the facility. Although they had machine guns and searchlights and mines, a vulnerability remained. The railway line, cut through the solid rock, had been left largely unguarded. It looked like the perfect point of entry for the Norwegian team.

Rønneberg and his men painstakingly crept through the ice-laden cable-intake tunnel, into the electrolysis cellar, where the heavy water was made. There they carefully placed their charges, set their timers, and began creeping back.

Meanwhile, outside, Haukelid and the covering team were surprised when a German guard appeared. It was a tense moment for the men, fingers on triggers. But the guard didn't see them. Soon he turned back from the dark frigid cold and returned to the light and warmth of the guardhouse.

They were safe. Then Haukelid heard passwords being hissed in the dark. Rønneberg and the demolition team were back. So far, so good. They all waited to hear their explosives detonate. Only then, in the resulting confusion, would they make a dash for it.

They waited. And waited. Finally they heard a soft bang somewhere inside the building—then nothing. They sighed—frustration. The charges had been duds. Crestfallen, the ten men scrambled back to their skis and set out, convinced their mission had been a failure.

They were wrong. When the Germans inspected the damage the next morning, they found that the electrolysis containers were hopelessly wrecked. It would take months to repair the damage. Furious orders went out: find the saboteurs at all costs.

The Norwegian team now began the most difficult part of the entire mission. They were forced to hide out in the mountains to evade the constant patrols, including Quisling's *hird* militias. Five men were designated to head back, an option almost as dangerous as remaining: crossing 350 miles of towering snow-covered peaks and treacherous ravines in order to reach Sweden. For the rest, it was months of physical deprivation (they had to make do with the food they had brought, and one could live only so long on melted snow) and psychological hardship. Every human figure that came into view against the snow and ice was possibly a member of the Norsk Legion or a German soldier. The daily routine was grueling to say the least: staying on the move by day and sleeping out in the open by night, with only their sleeping bags to keep them from freezing to death.

They remained on the scene because London had discovered that their mission, although successful, had only partially dismantled the plant. A year later, the Germans were able to resume the production of heavy water. The British sent in bombers to smash the plant, and the Americans followed suit with a daylight raid—all without result, except the loss of bomber crews and innocent Norwegian civilians. Maddeningly, the bombs did not damage Vemork, which remained in full production.

The climax of the mission to dismantle Vemork finally came in 1944, when London learned that a massive shipment of heavy water from Vemork would soon be headed for Germany by steamer. Again, Haukelid and his team went in and struck. It was a grim undertaking. They sabotaged the ferry steamer as it was leaving port, knowing full well that when the ship sank, Norwegian lives would be lost. On February 21, 1944, the ferry steamer *D/F Hydro* left its dock on Lake Tinn, blew up, and sank, consigning a six-month supply of heavy water —and twenty-six Norwegian civilians—to the bottom of the deepwater lake.

The steamer D/F Hydro *on Lake Tinn, Telemark, in about 1940.* UtCon Collection / Alamy

Thus the Norwegian commandos delivered the coup de grâce to the German effort to make an atomic bomb. After the ferry sank, the Germans decided Norway was too dangerous for their heavy water operations. They ordered the Vemork electrolysis containers dismantled and moved to Germany, but it was too late to complete. By now the Manhattan Project had achieved a lead in atomic fission that it would never lose. And when a bomb similar to the one Germany was building finally was dropped, it would be over Nagasaki, not London or New York.

The secret operation had lasted three years. It had cost the lives of eighty-seven Allied servicemen, and more than a hundred Norwegian civilians were killed in air raids, in the sinking of the ferry, or by vengeful Nazis. One of those had been Haukelid's father, who had been captured, tortured, and executed by the Gestapo. Despite the human cost, "if it had not been for Haukelid's resolve" and that of the other Norwegians, Stephenson wrote soberly, "the Germans would have had the opportunity to devastate the civilized world. We would be either dead or living under Hitler's zealots."

Historians still debate how close the Germans really had come to developing a bomb and how crucial the interruption to the supply of heavy water really had been. Certainly if the Germans had had unfettered access to deuterium, they would have been one major step closer to an atomic bomb. Kurt Diebner, the head of the Nazi program, believed that if he had been able to get the supply of heavy water he needed, a German nuclear reactor would have been producing plutonium by the end of 1943.

In any case, the Norwegian "heroes of Telemark," as they became known, had helped prevent what was happening to their country from happening to the rest of the world. As Winston Churchill famously said of the RAF pilots in the Battle of Britain, "Never have so many owed so much to so few." Perhaps the same could be said for Haukelid, Rønneberg, and the intrepid Norwegian whom the British called the Mailman: Leif Tronstad.

By the time the first Norwegian team struck at Vemork, the tide of war was running against the Third Reich.

Rommel's defeat in North Africa, the failure of the Kursk offensive in the east, the steadily growing aerial bombardment of Germany's largest cities and industrial centers by British and US air forces — all signaled that those who had expected Nazi Germany's ultimate victory had been wrong. Even among senior leaders of German industry, according to reports by Himmler's secret police, by the middle of 1943 not one believed Germany could win.

The leaders of the Scandinavian countries were beginning to realize this too and needed to adjust to the reality.

Finland was one of the first. Gustav Mannerheim, now prime minister, led the shift in perspective for his country, changing adroitly from its role as Germany's ally in 1942–43, which had placed two Finnish divisions under German command after Hitler's invasion of Russia (many hoped that Germany's defeat of the Soviet Union would mean liberation for the parts of Finland lost in the Winter War), to secretly and then openly seek an armistice with Stalin by 1944. Part of the deal Mannerheim struck with the Allies was that he would turn Finnish forces loose on driving the Germans out of his own territory and out of northern Russia.

Mannerheim did not hesitate to turn on his former ally, now that Hitler was headed for defeat. Desperate times bear desperate measures, and the Finnish people agreed. By the time the last German soldier surrendered, in 1945, Mannerheim had emerged as a national hero, Finland's greatest. Finns would remember what Mannerheim's critics sometimes do not: he had saved his country from extinction three times. Twice from the Soviets, in 1917–19 and 1940, and once from the Nazis.

Sweden showed a similar agility in the face of changing events. The Swedish government secretly negotiated a deal with the Allies to wind down its support for the Nazi war effort by cutting the supply of iron ore by 30 percent and dropping by 50 percent the value of ball bearings that Sweden exported to Germany. More remarkably, the government set up camps for training Norwegian and Danish resistance fighters under the guise of training "police cadets." All of this had to happen without alienating the Third Reich. If Sweden's tilt toward the Allies became known, a full-scale German occupation might ensue, almost certainly followed by the extermination of Sweden's Jews.

The Danes were already working to protect their Jewish population. The Danish government was in a far more difficult position than Sweden was — they were, after all, under German occupation already. Although both they and the Nazis recognized that, under their agreement, Denmark was formally neutral and in charge of its own domestic affairs, that situation could change at any moment.

From the start of the German occupation, the Danish government had found a unique way to prevent the roundup and deportation of its Jews, which the Germans had undertaken in every other country they occupied. From the beginning they insisted that the *Jews were not Jews* as such, but full Danish citizens and therefore fully protected by law like any other citizen. The Danes, from King Christian on down, believed that "if Denmark embarked on a differentiation between Jews and other Danish citizens, it would be betraying a fundamental pillar of its democracy — and thus of what was 'Danish.' As the government saw it, there was no 'Jewish question' in Denmark" — certainly none the Nazis could exploit.

While it wasn't true that King Christian went about in public wearing a yellow star to show his solidarity with Denmark's Jews, this apocryphal story is true to his fundamental attitude, and those of Scavenius and other Danes: our Jews are part of "us," and therefore we won't hand them over to anyone, least of all the Nazis (who, interestingly, the Danes did not think of as part of that "us"; Danish Nazis, in fact, were ostracized and scorned in Danish society the same way that Communists had been in the 1930s).

This policy had some awkward repercussions. For one, it meant that although Denmark was adamant about protecting its own Jews, it was equally adamant about keeping foreign Jews out. Denmark did not serve as a haven for refugees during those years the way Sweden did, though Danes certainly could predict the fate of those denied asylum. As one politician, Jan Steinecke, put it before the war, "One does not want to be inhumane, and one dares not be humane because of the consequences." But for Denmark and its Jewish minority, their unusual arrangement worked for almost three years.

That is, until 1943, when Himmler and the other architects of the Holocaust lost patience with Denmark and decided that its policy of tolerance had to go. In August the Germans declared martial law in Denmark. Bands of SS men and other enforcers crossed the border to begin rounding up Danish Jews, as well as the fifteen hundred or so Czech, Austrian, and German Jews who, despite Denmark's restricted immigration policy, had found refuge in Denmark and received residence permits.

The Danes responded by taking the protection of the Jews into their own hands — and not only the government, but private citizens across the country. In every town and neighborhood and village, Danes carefully hid Jewish families from marauding Nazi patrols and smuggled them one by one to the coast, in a kind of Danish Underground Railroad. Once at the coast, Danish fishing boats and other small craft volunteered to take the Jewish refugees across the Sound to Sweden — and to safety.

While Danish citizens were engaged in this heroic enterprise (in some cases breaking into buildings where the Nazis had rounded up Jewish families, to set them free), the Danish government kept up a steady drumbeat of protests to the German authorities about the inhumane detention and treatment of Danish citizens — meaning the Jews — which was contrary to Danish law and mutual agreements. The Swedish press did the same (Denmark's was handcuffed by martial law), publishing news stories and editorials that highlighted what was happening in Denmark. "Pogroms in Copenhagen," read one editorial, "this is the unfathomable, which has to arouse even the most complacent, open the eyes of those who have been willing to keep them closed harder and longer than the rest . . ."

Another in the prestigious *Svenska Dagbladet* bore the title "Against Divine and Human Order," and stated, "With deepest disgust and outraged feelings the Swedish people learn the racial hatred against the Jews, which last year led to such terrible scenes in Norway, has now been unleashed on Danish soil." It denounced the attacks for their "sinister and ruthless disregard for humanity's advances through the long centuries of Western history, which these persecutions of Jews demonstrate." At the same time, Sweden announced that it would now provide safe haven for all Jews fleeing Denmark.

The Swedish announcement, together with the Danish resistance and rescue operations, put German officials on the ground in a difficult spot. On the one hand, Himmler and the SS in Berlin were insistent that the Jews be rounded up and deported, no matter what the cost. On the other, the SS *Reichsprotektor* in Copenhagen, Dr. Werner Best, had to live with the Danes and maintain civil order. Denmark, like Sweden, was supposed to be a model of Germany's new order and its cooperation with other nations; Hitler himself had said so. By turning Denmark into something like Poland, or even occupied France, Best had everything to lose — including the respect of Erik Scavenius, whom Best treated almost like a father — and very little to gain.

It would be a serious historical mistake to say that the SS man Werner Best helped save Denmark's Jews. But he did close at least one eye to what was happening around him, while also giving the Danish government repeated assurances that Jews who had married Aryans, or were only half Jewish themselves, would not be arrested.

In this strange manner, 95 percent of Denmark's Jews were spared from the extermination camps and gas ovens. As the story's recent chronicler Bo Lidegaard puts it, "The way in which the civilian population assisted both Danish and stateless Jews in October 1943 remains without precedent or parallel."

This was more than a mass display of humanitarianism. It sprang from the simple belief that everyone who was part of the Danish community and believed in democracy and lived under its laws deserved the protection of those laws, regardless of race, creed, or religion. For Danes, there was simply no question about it. To save another Dane was second nature: without an instinct for community, there could be no democracy — even no humanity.

By October–November 1943, the Swedes had also declared their stance on "the Jewish question." Some Swedish diplomats were actively involved in organizing an even more dangerous enterprise: helping Jews escape from Nazi-occupied Hungary.

This was among modern history's most poignant displays of the Viking heart in action.

In many ways, Hungary — although a German ally — had been the last holdout against the Holocaust. Unlike the Scandinavian countries, Hungary's Jewish population was large, more than 800,000 strong. They were an essential part of Hungarian urban life. More than half of the lawyers and doctors in Budapest were Jews, as was a sizable portion of the business community. Thousands more had become Hungarian citizens not by choice but by conquest, as Hitler's ally, the Hungarian dictator Miklós Horthy, scooped up portions of Slovakia and Transylvania as part of Greater Hungary. Anti-Semitic messages and measures began to creep into Hungarian politics as a response to Hitler's demands for extending the Final Solution into the country. Overall, the Budapest government was not so much actively cooperating with the Nazis as resigning to their wishes in order to avoid something worse.

But in August 1943, almost simultaneous with the crackdown on Jews in Denmark, Hitler made it clear to Horthy that Hungary needed to take decisive action against the Jews. In the spring of 1944 came the first formal ordinances against Hungarian Jews, including the requirement to wear the infamous yellow star.

Sweden's diplomats encouraged their king, Gustav, to send a note to Horthy denouncing the change in policy. Horthy and the Hungarian government dismissed it with a shrug. But a small group of diplomats in the Swedish embassy, led by Ivan Danielsson, decided to act. One of their first efforts involved a Jewish family in the city of Pécs that was about to be deported. The Swedes arranged for them to take temporary visas to Sweden, saving them from arrest.

But this was a straw blowing in a hurricane. The next day, the rest of the Jews in Pécs were rounded up and shipped to Poland for extermination. Soon the roundup spread to Budapest. The Swedes began taking steps to save whomever they could, however they could. They started with provisional Swedish passports. Then, when the Hungarian government refused to recognize new documents of Swedish citizenship after March 19, 1944, the embassy began issuing fake certificates. The number of families saved by these certificates swelled to more than seven hundred. Still a tiny number, but the Swedes believed it could be the start of something more significant.

Danielsson and his team then asked for help from Stockholm. The foreign ministry sent them someone who happened to know Hungary well, and who, in status-conscious Sweden, had impeccable political connections. His name was Raoul Wallenberg.

The Wallenbergs had produced generations of politicians, bankers, and leading churchmen. Raoul came from the less wealthy side of the dynasty: his father had been a naval officer, and he had studied architecture at the University of Michigan before reluctantly accepting work in his family's bank and its far-flung offices in South Africa and Palestine. Then he became involved in a trading company (one of his ventures had been trying to corner the market on Portuguese sardines), a job that took him several times to Budapest on business.

His experience and administrative skills were well known. What remained unknown, however, was the burning sense of mission he brought to this new work with the Swedish legation. He revealed it to a small circle of friends at an intimate dinner just before his departure.

"I am going to leave you now for one reason," he said, "to save as many lives as possible; to rescue Jews from the claws of those murderers."

Wallenberg's name has become forever associated with the effort to rescue the Jews in Budapest, and rightly so. But he had help: his fellow embassy officials, such as Per Anger, Ivan Danielsson, and Waldemar and Nina Langlet from the Swedish Red Cross; the International Red Cross; and the American

War Refugee Board. What made Wallenberg stand out was his level of personal commitment. The risks he ran required superhuman devotion.

He arrived in Budapest on July 9, 1944. His colleague Per Anger was surprised at his kit: two knapsacks, a sleeping bag, a thin windbreaker, and a revolver. "This revolver is just to give me courage," he told Anger sheepishly. "I hope I'll never have to use it."

The staff then brought him up to date with the effort to get Jews out, or at least postpone their deportation. "Everything depends on what the Germans have in mind," Wallenberg was told. "It's hardly believable that they will go along with sparing the Jews of the capital for good."

"What documents have you issued the Jews?" Wallenberg wanted to know.

Anger showed him the provisional passports and other documents the Swedes had been handing out. He thought for a moment, then said, "I think I've got an idea for a new and maybe more effective document."

That was how the famous protective passport came about: identification papers colored in blue and yellow, the Swedish national colors, with the three crowns of Sweden emblazoned at the top. This passport would save tens of thousands of Hungary's Jews, and others, as Raoul Wallenberg turned into a powerful diplomatic weapon for fighting the Holocaust.

Wallenberg also set up a separate bureau, financed in part by the War Refugee Board in Washington, DC, through the American legation in Budapest, to carry out the issuance of protective passports even as the war grew ever closer — and the Nazis more determined than ever to wipe out every last Jew in Hungary.

But would the passports work? German officials soon caught on to what Wallenberg was up to. But as with Denmark, what slowed the German response to the Swedish initiative was the desire to maintain good relations — not with Hungary, where the Horthy government had been toppled by a pro-Nazi coup, but with Sweden. Again and again, Wallenberg and other Swedish diplomats would call on the head of the German legation to make a protest when Jews were arrested or about to be deported. And again and again the Germans and their Hungarian allies were forced to back down.

The most important goal in those crucial weeks of late 1944 was to buy time, enough time for the Russians to arrive from the east and for German resistance to collapse. Every day was a race to see whether Wallenberg and his colleagues could delay the deportation program another twenty-four hours, or even another forty-eight. They also had to prevent a breakdown of law and order in the streets of Budapest, which might spill over into violent pogroms. When safe houses where Jews were quartered were threatened, Wallenberg arranged a separate "ghetto" for Jews being temporarily sheltered by other foreign legations, including the Americans, where Jews could go to receive protection under the Swedish flag. Even the Germans had to respect the protected "ghettos" Wallenberg set up. In the end, some thirty buildings in Budapest came under official Swedish protection — as were the refugees taking shelter there.

Then, when Russian bombs began to fall on Budapest, Wallenberg recognized that, despite the destruction, an advantage lay in this development. The Germans, struggling to hold the city, weren't likely to have time or energy to think about the Jews still in their midst.

But Wallenberg did more, much more. He himself went to train stations where the Germans were loading Jews for the journey to extermination camps, and handed out passports right and left, warning the Nazi guards that these Jews had been arrested by mistake and needed to be released. When word reached him that the sealed ghetto, where seventy thousand Jews were kept, was about to be the scene of a systematic massacre, Wallenberg demanded that the German general in charge, General Schmidhuber, prevent the slaughter — which Schmidhuber did, intimidated by Wallenberg's threats to go over his head.

When asked about the dangers he was running, Wallenberg told Anger, "Sure it gets me a little scared, sometimes. But for me there's no choice. I've taken on this assignment and I'd never be able to go back to Stockholm without knowing inside myself I'd done all a man can do to save as many Jews as possible."

The day they spoke was January 10, 1945. The Germans were on the run from the city, and Wallenberg said he was packing up to cross the river into Pest, to meet the advancing Russians. Anger never saw Wallenberg again.

In the end, he and his Swedish colleagues had saved at least fifty thousand Jews from extermination, plus the seventy thousand in the official ghetto. Even so, the Swedish government nearly blew it by refusing to recognize

Hungary's last pro-Axis government. Though the morally correct gesture, it might have triggered what Wallenberg and the Swedes in the city feared most: a general massacre of them all, both Jews and Swedes. But the arrival of the Russians saved the day.

When the Russians took the city, the Swedish rescuers were reunited as they emerged from their hiding places. But Wallenberg, who had moved to offices across the river in Pest, had disappeared.

What happened to him remains a mystery. Years later, the Soviets released one bit of information about his fate. They admitted that they had taken Wallenberg into protective custody in January 1945. They may have assumed he was an American spy. Documents recently released under the Freedom of Information Act have revealed that Wallenberg had working relations with, and served as a source for, the OSS, America's wartime secret service. This was hardly surprising. In addition to receiving money from the War Refugee Board, Wallenberg was committed to getting help wherever he could find it. To return the favor by passing information to the OSS about what was happening on the ground in pro-Axis Budapest would have seemed a bargain with little downside.

The Soviets, of course, would see any such collaboration in a very different light. They also knew that the Swedes, at war's end, were not in a position to push, at least not very forcefully, for Wallenberg's release, or information regarding his fate. Although unproved theories abound, what really happened to Raoul Wallenberg after he crossed into Russian lines remains one of the great unsolved mysteries of World War II.

What isn't a mystery is what he managed to accomplish in the six months he was working to save Hungary's Jews. The numbers may seem small in comparison to the 560,000 or so who were exterminated. But in moral terms, the accomplishment was titanic. It also underlines a paradox. The two European countries, Denmark and Sweden, that most compromised their formal neutrality to cooperate with the Third Reich also did the most to save Jews within their own borders and beyond.

With World War II over, it was time to take stock of what the conflict had meant for the Nordic countries — and what the future held.

Sweden, which did manage to remain neutral, got the most grief for its collaboration with Germany, including supplying the Nazis with vital war matériel such as iron ore and ball bearings. But it should be remembered that Sweden publicly announced that it would provide safe haven for all Jews fleeing Denmark, and that Wallenberg, a Swede, made a heroic effort to save Hungary's Jews, which justifiably became humanitarian legend.

Sweden also took on responsibility for caring and feeding more than 180,000 refugees after the war — roughly the equivalent of the state of Virginia taking the same number of foreign refugees today. More than half of them were Finns displaced by five years of seesaw warfare, as well as 18,000 Danes and 43,000 Norwegians. Yet when comparing the Swedish wartime record to Norway's brave resistance to the Nazis and Denmark's effort to save its own Jews, most Swedes preferred to look to the future.

In a way, Sweden's most important contribution to the recovery of the region, and of greater Europe, was its economy; prosperity became its hallmark after the war. Sweden's growth surge at first looked less impressive than that of other western European countries. France and Italy, for example, were readily bounding back from the deprivations of war. Still, unemployment in Sweden plummeted to a 2 percent average, where it stayed through the 1960s. From 1958 to 1964, the Swedish economy reached its all-time peak, with a yearly GDP growth average of 5.1 percent and a productivity growth average of 5.6 percent per year. Almost half its output was in the form of exports, especially finished manufactured goods, which helped fuel growth in other Scandinavian countries as well.

Sweden's postwar economic success soon spread to its Nordic neighbors. Norway's was comparable to Sweden's until 1964, Denmark's until 1965.

Finland too saw a comfortable expansion of economic growth, as did Iceland. In fact, all five Nordic countries had, by the late 1960s, become the envy of the world, due to their admirable growth rate and their constantly expanding welfare state. The Nordic way became the so-called Scandinavian model, a prototype for other countries as to how social democracy could survive, and even prosper, in the modern world. Scandinavian furniture and interior design, literature and cinema (especially the path-breaking films of the Swedish director Ingmar Bergman) grew in popularity.

It was forgotten, however, that Scandinavia's model of social democracy was built on twin foundations: a long period of free-market economic growth, dating back to the 1890s, and strong communities built on common cultural bonds, dating back to the Viking era. As the sociologist Nima Sanandaji has put it, "High levels of trust, a strong work ethic, and social cohesion are the perfect starting-point for successful economies. They are also the cornerstones of fruitful social democratic welfare policies."

What's striking, in fact, is how powerfully those same bonds can be seen at work among Scandinavia's offspring in the United States.

America's prosperity after World War II has become the stuff of legend and envy. There is no doubt that the affluence all Americans experienced has been a tribute to the nation's status as the world's biggest economy. Yet when we look at the experience of Scandinavian Americans, we see a substantial difference in their overall economic performance and status that simply living in the United States can't explain.

In the 2010 US Census, for example, the median income for American households was $51,914. For Norwegian Americans, however, it was $60,935. For Swedish Americans: $61,549. Danish Americans came in at $61,921, and Finnish Americans, traditionally the least affluent of the Nordic immigrant groups, have a median income more than seven thousand dollars upwards of the American average, at $59,379. Likewise, poverty levels for Scandinavian Americans are between one-half and one-third of those of Americans in general. In fact, Scandinavian Americans actually have lower poverty levels *than the inhabitants of the Nordic countries their ancestors left,* despite the welfare state there.

In short, Danish Americans have a 55 percent higher standard of living than the Danes themselves, and Swedish Americans enjoy a 53 percent higher standard than native Swedes. With Finnish Americans the gap is even greater, at nearly 60 percent. Norwegian Americans still edge out Norwegians in standard of living by three percentage points, even though their Norway-born counterparts enjoy the benefits of a generous welfare state and an oil-rich economy.

In other words, the right cultural ingredients, plus the kind of environment in which the qualities of the Viking heart can flourish, add up to a powerful socioeconomic advantage. With the exception of Finnish Americans, all Scandinavian immigrant groups also score higher in per capita income than the people of any Nordic country. Finnish Americans still finish higher than Danes, Swedes, and Finns themselves, and are bested only by Norwegians.

So although cultural differences have nothing to do with race or inherited genes, they do have a great deal to do with the legacy that most Scandinavian immigrants brought with them to America and passed along to their descendants. The belief in the virtue of hard work, the "instinct for workmanship," the commitment to personal integrity and truthfulness, and the will to lend aid to your fellow humans as a measure of who you are — when these cultural qualities are unleashed in a relatively free economy, with a smaller overall tax burden and fewer welfare-state giveaways to disincentivize hard work and personal savings than Scandinavian countries see today, the result can be extraordinary.

This reveals another basic historical truth, which Nicolaj Grundtvig first stumbled on in the early nineteenth century: Scandinavians flourish best where freedom is the most. Belatedly, Nordic countries are realizing this. Starting in the 1990s, and after Sweden experienced a real economic depression in 1990–93, with a 12 percent dip in employment, Scandinavians introduced free-market reforms, with some success, to revive sputtering economic growth. The consensus-driven politics that enabled the Nordic countries to launch social welfare programs also allowed them to unwind those same programs and thus lower taxes, instead of constantly raising them. That system has also enabled the Nordic countries to survive the COVID-19 pandemic ordeal with minimal disruption of normal life, in ways that intrigue yet also baffle outside observers.

This sort of adaptability is a reminder of what has made the Nordic countries so special. The proof, I would argue, is what their descendants have accomplished in America. With median incomes 20 percent higher than average US incomes, with a poverty rate half that of the US average — even lower than the rate of poverty among the Scandinavians who stayed home — their experience underlines the fact that Scandinavians are what makes Scandinavia extraordinary, along with the culture of the Vikings that shaped them.

It is truly the culture of the Viking heart.

CONCLUSION

The Viking Heart and the Land Beyond

Happiness is the struggle towards a summit and, when it is attained, it is happiness to glimpse new summits on the other side.

— Fridtjof Nansen

THE LEGACY OF the Vikings is one of history's greatest. It reaches across time, places, peoples, and cultures, right down to today. And driving it all is the courage, daring, loyalty, and resilience that have sustained the Scandinavian people — that cluster of human qualities I call the Viking heart. Though some historians claim that the Scandinavian conquest of the world was a brief episode within the grand scheme of things, actually it has more relevance to our times than perhaps even its most devoted admirers realize.

The original Norsemen's voyages reshaped the cultural and political contours of Europe for more than three hundred years, and we can still see traces of Viking influence in the places they settled and conquered, as seen in the archaeological remains of Norse sites: the museum at Bygdøy in Oslo, where the Oseberg and Gokstad ships rest in graceful majesty; the excavation of the farming village at Vorbasse in Jutland; the Tower of London; the magnificent Cappella Palatina in Palermo; or even the remains of the settlement at L'Anse aux Meadows in Newfoundland. All remind us of the extraordinary men and women from Scandinavia who became masters of the known world — the original pioneers of globalization.

The Viking era demanded extraordinary things from ordinary farmers and families, along with the great warriors and outsized leaders like King Canute of Denmark, Harald Bluetooth, and William the Conqueror. Much more three-dimensional than the superwarriors of legend, these men and women achieved great feats of courage and military enterprise by adapting to a violent, savage world, thus becoming Europe's dominant power culture — a role disproportionate to their numbers and resources.

The Viking world was never just about violence and pillaging. It was about daring to reach for more than the universe had gifted you, no matter the odds and the obstacles.

Thanks to modern science — most notably, the study of DNA and modern genetics — we can see proof of this in the lasting mark that the Scandinavian diaspora has left on places like the British Isles and northern France. The Vikings came not only to conquer but to make new homes for themselves and their families. Coupled with breakthroughs in archaeology, DNA studies have given us a much fuller picture of the mainsprings of the Viking era, from Greenland and Russia to the British Isles. The DNA investigation of the Vikings' genetic legacy has only just begun. But what we already know has dispelled forever the old theories about the Norsemen's achievements based on exclusivist racist assumptions.

The history of Europe would undoubtedly be very different without the presence of the German tribes after their wanderings from Scandinavia, followed by the Vikings and the Normans. In the nineteenth century, that ethnographic legacy became overblown as part of the Aryan myth, in an era when intellectuals and scholars assumed cultural traits had to have a genetic, and therefore racial, basis. We know better now. Nonetheless, the cultural and political impact of those peoples from the North is undeniable.

And it's not limited just to western Europe. The entire history of Russia, and eastern Europe as a whole, would be entirely different without the arrival of Rurik and his fellow Vikings from Sweden. It was they who founded the principality by which Novgorod, Kiev, and eventually Moscow became the key power centers of central Asia and eastern Europe. One could even argue that the history of the Middle East would have taken a very different direction if the Vikings hadn't acted as middlemen to supply the Arab ascendancy with the slaves it needed to sustain the golden age of the caliphates, including the Umayyad caliphate in Spain. Likewise, the entire religious history of Europe in the modern era would look very different if King Gustavus Adolphus of Sweden hadn't halted the Catholic Habsburg juggernaut in its tracks — and made the world safe for Lutheranism and, more broadly, Protestantism.

Then the Viking heart found a new home in America in the nineteenth century. Norwegian, Swedish, Danish, and Finnish immigrants descended on the new republic across the Atlantic and strove to shape its future while preserving their past. The impact of those immigrants and their children has proved indelible, from how we follow sports and wage war in the skies, to how we care for the poor and hungry in our own cities and abroad.

It is this philanthropic, even altruistic turn of the Viking heart that Scandinavian Americans, and Scandinavians at home, have become most known for today, whether we're talking about figures like Alfred Nobel and Fridtjof Nansen or organizations like the Ahmanson Foundation and the American-Scandinavian Foundation. This legacy is the direct result of the impact of Christianity, and the Lutheran Reformation, on the Viking heart. The coming of Christianity and the Lutheran work ethic also reveals that the Viking heart was never a fixed human quality but rather something that constantly evolves. It proves, once again, that biological explanations for Scandinavian or Germanic accomplishments, rooted in deep-seated racism, simply don't stand up to scrutiny.

As for Scandinavians and the Nordic countries today — where the direct descendants of the Vikings still live — history bears witness to their shift from conquering the world by force to contributing to it through more peaceful means, all while keeping the Viking heart alive during times of turmoil and crisis.

Today we see people taking newfound interest in the qualities of the Viking spirit. It permeates what many call the Nordic revival in fashion, food, and design. Even the most superficial admirers of Scandinavian culture have come to realize that Denmark, Norway, Sweden, Finland, and Iceland seem to have discovered some secret about how to live and thrive together that has eluded most of the modern world. That secret has nothing to do with race or ethnic origin. It has everything to do with culture and community. It is precisely the sense of community and shared values that binds citizens of the Nordic countries together, and shapes their societies even in our global age.

In its truest form, the Viking heart represents the bonds that hold a nation, *any* nation, together. It may be controversial, in some quarters, to cast Scandinavian nationalism in a positive light. The concept of nationalism took on evil connotations in the twentieth century, after the traumas of Nazism and fascism, not to mention Quisling's Norway and even today's racist neo-Nazis. But recently scholars, sociologists, and political observers have begun to see that a mindful sense of cultural solidarity and national belonging can serve positive ends. It could be the social cement that modern society needs.

Thanks to thinkers like Pierre Manent and Yoram Hazony, the notion of nation has shed some of its stigma. As Manent, a French political scientist, put it in a recent interview, "What I'm sure about is that to live a fully human life you need a common life and a community." This general sociological truth holds the secret of the continuing success of Scandinavian societies today — welfare state or no welfare state.

This secret has its origins in their deep shared history. The Norsemen lived in a world of physical hardships that demanded the strength of much more than just the individual, or even a handful of elites. In peace or war, all had to depend on one another to survive. Wherever a Viking warrior journeyed — even into the unknown, at the risk of life itself — that warrior went with a community of the spirit as well as flesh and armor.

And when that journey ended, that warrior returned to a community to hunt and fish and farm and join in the fabric of everyday life. For the Viking, the battlefield was an extension of society, and vice versa. Success in both was built on values of solidarity and trust that permeated all activity, whether it was digging out a new field for planting from bog and forest, or fishing off a rocky coast, or sailing to the farthest corners of the world.

That bond has undoubtedly left its mark, and not just in the Nordic countries. By tracing its true roots and understanding its true character, we can better understand the need for stronger community bonds in our own lives.

Indeed, the notion of the "tribe" as the building block of national identity has gained new purchase in modern discourse. It bears a certain relevance when talking about the Vikings and the Viking heart. As Sebastian Junger has written, "The earliest definition of community — of tribe — would be the group of people you would both help feed and help defend. A society that doesn't offer its members the chance to act selflessly in these ways isn't a society . . . it's just a political entity that, lacking enemies, will probably fall apart on its own."

This insight has achieved a new relevance in the age of COVID-19. Young and old in America, and around the world, have discovered how important, even essential, the family and the community of neighbors and friends has become, as the crucial anchor for people undergoing this crisis. Together they supply one another with the food and company that enable individuals to survive an ordeal, even one as disruptive as the COVID pandemic.

Family, tribe, community, nation: we now recognize that these institutions offer something missing from much of modern culture in the age of globalization. A sense of belonging, of common identity, of sharing in the dangers as well as the rewards of our common life: these are the human qualities that an entirely liberal, Enlightenment-based view of civilization has tended to overlook or even dismiss. But the need for them hasn't disappeared. On the contrary — where the value of those qualities is not respected, they can break out in destructive ways, in the communities formed by gangs, for example, and among violent extremists of all stripes. Racist fringe groups in Scandinavia and Europe, as the author Ryan Smith has pointed out, are actively seeking to co-opt the Viking "tribal" legacy to serve their own agenda.

In fact, the real Vikings' lives teach how shared culture and community — the foundation of the Viking heart — can empower us all in the midst of disruptive change and even chaos. Modern Scandinavians have retained those teachings as they adapt to the modern world without being devoured by it. They've forged a path that points the way forward for everyone, including those of us in America.

At the end of this historical journey, how can we define the qualities of the Viking heart?

Clearly it began with physical courage, sometimes to the point of recklessness. With that came a fierce loyalty to family and community, and a personal resourcefulness born from a society built on perpetual scarcity in a harsh and unforgiving environment, and a trust in others raised in those same circumstances.

Then and now, the Viking heart also demands a commitment to help sustain a cultural identity and its traditions, which represent the valuable lessons needed for survival and passed from one generation to the next. One could describe its attitude toward the past as essentially conservative, but it conserves only what is needed for survival, and to sustain a sense of confidence in the face of the unknown — which is easier to sustain when supported by the wisdom and experience of parents, grandparents, and generations gone by.

From their earliest traces, Viking and Scandinavian culture also revered what the Norwegian American sociologist Thorstein Veblen had called "the instinct of craftsmanship." It draws its strength from a deep respect for nature and the material world as it is presented to us, and as it is steadily shaped by the force of human character and needs.

As time passed, new qualities were added to the Viking heart. Christianity brought compassion, conscience, and a sense of moral discipline, which Scandinavians adopted and built upon without completely obliterating their vital pagan roots.

The Reformation then birthed the Lutheran work ethic, a form of altruistic service that (unlike so many other versions) actually works. Meanwhile, immigration to America gave Scandinavia's poorest but also most determined the scope to exercise their belief in the power of individual freedom — combined with a commitment to preserving the best of the culture they had left behind.

But what has undergirded the Viking heart from the beginning, and gives its history a vividness and intensity like no other, has been a constant willingness to strive toward unknown frontiers in order to find a place for oneself and one's family. It is a journey in which human ingenuity and resourcefulness can overcome whatever obstacles nature or the gods put in front of us.

So where do we find the Viking heart today?

For one thing, we certainly *don't* find it in today's racist and neo-Nazi fringe. Various groups have sprung up in Scandinavia, Europe, and North America, trying to appropriate the Vikings for their own nefarious purposes. Instead, they've wound up with a historical and cultural travesty, a caricature of primeval savagery that represents a decisive wrong turn in the evolution of the West today — just as it did in the twentieth century, when the Viking legacy fell into the hands of Adolf Hitler and his followers. As we've seen in its works, from the Holocaust to the massacre in Norway in 2011, this warped take on the Viking lineage results in the destruction of the best by the worst.

Instead, I would argue that we can look for the presence of the Viking heart at a much deeper and more universal level — it includes today's Scandinavian culture but also has a wider embrace. We need only look to the popular media image of the Norsemen, which still captivates millions around the world.

A clue to this truth can be found in a lecture given at Oxford University in 1939 by the celebrated scholar and author J.R.R. Tolkien.

Today of course we know him best as the author of the *Lord of the Rings* trilogy, and creator of a world of hobbits, elves, wizards, and warriors: the master fantasist and one of the most influential writers in the modern world. In 1939, however, he was still known only as a professor and scholar of Old English. His academic expertise had sprung from a fascination, at an early age, with the Vikings and the Old Norse sagas. As a young professor at the University of Leeds he had been cofounder of the so-called Viking Club, which was made up of philologists, scholars, and historians immersed in Germanic and Scandinavian studies. They would meet at a local club to share drinks and read aloud from Icelandic studies. They also composed original poems and songs in Old English, Gothic, and Old Norse (the collection was privately published as *Songs for the Philologists;* only a few copies survive). These were the prototypes of the songs and poems Tolkien would later incorporate into his trilogy, just as the club was the precursor of a more famous gathering of scholars of which Tolkien became part, at Oxford: the Inklings.

In any case, the Viking Club meetings formed the backdrop for Tolkien's own original venture into the fictional realm of myth and epic, the stories that would spawn *The Hobbit,* and then the volumes that make up the *Lord of the*

Rings. It was, however, in the 1939 Oxford lecture that Tolkien first revealed what he thought was the real value of fantasy literature and fairy tales for modern audiences. It is also gives us a striking insight into the imagination of the Viking heart.

The date was significant. It was the eve of World War II, when a twisted ideology based on a false reading of Viking culture and Aryan myth was about to engulf Europe. At this critical moment, Tolkien's title was "On Fairy Stories."

For his listeners Tolkien explored why people of all ages, not just children, have been perennially captivated by the fables and myths running from Greek myth to the epic works in which Tolkien took a professional interest, such as *Beowulf* and *The Saga of the Volsungs*. Tolkien's answer was that what we call fairy tales, with roots in primeval religion, are more than just fanciful entertainment. They enable us to refresh our sense of reality, by allowing us to see the familiar world around us in clearer, more universal terms. Our own personal journey through life, for example, takes on a more luminous significance when seen in the shape of a hero's journey, such as that of Sigurd in *The Saga of the Volsungs*, or Egil in *Egil's Saga*, or Leif Erikson in *The Saga of the Greenlanders*. Such stories dramatize and ritualize life's journey in ways that give it a universal meaning.

Historically and culturally, of course, epics and journeys go together — and not just for Vikings. As Tolkien explained, the entire literary realm of the fairy tale is wide open to "a wandering explorer (or trespasser)," whether a child or an adult. It is a fictional realm and home of "all manner of beasts and birds," from elves and dwarves to dragons and giants, plus "shoreless seas and stars uncounted," where the listener or reader can find a meaning that strikes deep as well as wide. Tolkien added that the genre of fairy stories and their modern offspring (including his own as yet unpublished fictional works) "does not seek delusion nor bewitchment and domination; it seeks shared enrichment, partners in making and delight, not slaves."

Here is the key passage: "Fantasy is a natural human activity. It certainly does not destroy or even insult Reason ... On the contrary. The keener and the clearer is the reason, the better fantasy will it make. If men were ever in a state in which they did not want to know or could not perceive truth (facts or evidence), then Fantasy would languish until they were cured."

Indeed, if human beings come to a point at which the Vikings and their deeds and myths no longer fascinate or matter, our future will be very dim indeed.

Tolkien knew very well that Nordic myth and legend had made a decisive impact on the shaping of European culture in the nineteenth century. It had inspired the writers of Denmark's golden age, including Hans Christian Andersen. It had inspired the operas of Richard Wagner and the brooding meditations of Friedrich Nietzsche. He knew that some of those myths had fed the minds of the worst, as in Nazi ideology. But they were also capable of feeding the imagination of Europe's best, including (we can confidently conclude) Tolkien himself.

In fact, Tolkien saw his *Lord of the Rings* trilogy as the literary and intellectual antidote to the nazification of Norse myth and the Viking legacy. As he wrote to his son Michael in 1941, in the midst of the war against Hitler, "There is a great deal more force (and truth) than ignorant people imagine in the 'Germanic' ideal . . . I have in this war a burning private grudge . . . against that ruddy ignoramus Adolf Hitler. Ruining, perverting, misapplying, and for ever accursed that noble northern spirit, a supreme contribution to Europe, which I have ever loved."

We can see how that "noble northern spirit" and Viking myth resonate throughout Tolkien's trilogy, from its setting in Middle Earth (the Vikings' Midgard); its main narrative, lifted from *The Saga of the Volsungs,* of a search for a ring that offers the power to rule the world; and even its final apocalyptic battle, with obvious echoes of Ragnarok. The trajectory of *The Lord of the Rings* contains key elements of Viking myth and epic captured in literary amber, as it were, and passed on to generations of devoted Tolkien readers, not to mention the millions who have flocked to see the film adaptations by Peter Jackson.

For example, the trolls, elves, and dwarves that appear in Tolkien's works come directly from Norse myth, specifically the *Eddas*. The dwarves of these stories are the master forgers and work underground, just as in Richard Wagner's operas — or in the story of Snow White and the seven dwarves. Likewise, the *Eddas* contain the story of the world's first literary werewolf, Fenrir: half man, half wolf, who plays a sinister role on the day of Ragnarok as the slayer of

Odin himself. Werewolves and their evil kin reappear again and again in European myth and literature, including the direwolves in George R. R. Martin's series of fantasy novels, *Game of Thrones,* set in a Viking-like Nordic setting. Likewise, J. K. Rowling borrows the name Fenrir for one of her most sinister characters in the Harry Potter series, Fenrir Greyback, who also happens to be a werewolf.

And so on. Dwarves, elves, giants, dragons, ravens (Odin's two messengers, Huginn and Munnin, are both ravens), and one-eyed Odin-like wizards have populated the pages of northern European literature from the Middle Ages until today. In fact, after World War II Tolkien's work triggered a massive fascination with these mythical beasts and demigods. They later would swirl to life in the pages and scenes of the Harry Potter books and the *Game of Thrones* novels. They have inspired tabletop games like Warhammer, Dungeons & Dragons, and an ever-growing repertoire of movies and TV series, including no fewer than four blockbuster movies about the embodiment of Norse manhood himself: the god of thunder, Thor.

But the connection between Norse myth and modern popular culture runs even deeper. A large portion of George Lucas's *Star Wars* films was clearly inspired by Tolkien's *Ring.* We also know that after finishing the original *Star Wars* movie, Lucas planned to do a film version of *The Lord of the Rings.* The project fell through, as film projects often do. Instead it fell to a New Zealander, Peter Jackson, to bring Tolkien's novels — with their Nordic-inspired characters and overtones *and* their universal messages — to the cinema.

All these works, both literary and cinematic, are proof of the staying power of the original Norse sagas. But I would argue that they are also proof of the persistent value of the Viking heart itself, and what it represents in Western culture. Because behind their façade of fantasy and magic, dwarfs and gods and dragons, these works explore the moral dilemmas we all face — ones that require the qualities of the Viking heart if we are to confront and overcome them.

The same is true of the entire fantasy realm inhabited by video gamers and admirers of comic book superheroes, from Batman and Spider-Man to the X-Men and the Avengers, with *Star Trek* and *Teenage Mutant Ninja Turtles* in between. This is the realm of what the author A. D. Jameson has called "geek culture." It's a world (in Jameson's words) filled with "giant robots, witches and wizards, dystopian futures, superheroes, dragons, and talking apes." To outsiders, it can appear ridiculous and juvenile, maybe even mildly toxic. There's a lot of gratuitous violence associated with these video game and cinematic exploits. But the Nordic roots of geek culture are clear, and not only in their characters and similar subject matter.

It's a world in which ancient weapons — swords, daggers, shields, and wands — can take on a magical, even mystical meaning. It's a world in which heroes, even superheroes, have human flaws and failings like the heroes of Norse myth — and whose struggle with their own dark side, including fear and self-doubt, reflects the struggle that is part and parcel of the universal human journey.

These are our contemporary equivalent of fairy tales. They offer the same mix of fantasy and enchantment that Tolkien ascribed to the traditional fairy tale, holding that same transformative power. I would even assert that for "geeks," that is, the men and women inhabiting a universe defined by computer screens and impassive algorithms, the world of superheroes and fantastic enchantment reinforces the sense that there can still be a world of heroic achievement: here, they lie within a keyboard's reach.

And what is today's world of artificial intelligence, nanotechnology, quantum computing, and blockchain but a venture into the unknown — a place where the instinct of workmanship boldly reaches toward seemingly unattainable objectives in order to build a new home for humanity, or to bring back fantastic treasure after slaying a terrible dragon?

At first glance there may not seem to be much similarity between Silicon Valley and the world of the Vikings. But at their best both are the story of daring individuals willing to take enormous risks in order to realize a personal goal that will benefit family and community, faith and tribe. The heroic journey, which the author Joseph Campbell once identified as archetypal for all cultures and peoples but particularly for Nordic culture, is resolved into a series of acts of individual daring, all of which are expressions of a desire for individual freedom — even the desire to venture into the complete unknown — but which still requires a reservoir of support from family, community, and culture to be strong and stable.

This is not to take away from the significance of Greek myth and other folktales, including the Celtic legends surrounding King Arthur, to the shaping of modern fantasy, or the universal significance reflected in all myths as described by Joseph Campbell and the historian and philosopher Mircea Eliade, among others.

But the persistence of Nordic myth through its various modern epic forms points to some quality that has kept the Vikings relevant—and resonant. Their story, and their sagas and legends, epitomizes the bravery and perseverance every human being, every child, needs in order to overcome danger and adversity, to find a path to happiness. *That* is the Viking heart.

Not only in fiction. The achievements of the Norwegian explorer Thor Heyerdahl, and his 1947 expedition to sail from Peru to French Polynesia in a simple, home-built raft, captured the imagination of millions and seemed to demonstrate that the Vikings' extraordinary ocean voyages could be duplicated by someone with the skill, daring, and determination to risk it today.*

And it expresses itself still in the extraordinary careers of two Scandinavian women, Liv Arnesen and Ann Bancroft, both intrepid polar explorers and outspoken advocates for humanity's role as guardians of the planet. Born in Baerum, Norway, Liv was the first woman to cross the Greenland icecap, in 1992, following almost literally in the footsteps of the great Fridtjof Nansen. Later, in 2003, she and Ann Bancroft, another inductee in the Scandinavian-American Hall of Fame, were the first people to ever cross Antarctica on foot. Their company, Bancroft Arnesen Explore, is dedicated to seeking out, promoting, and celebrating women's and young girls' achievements in exploration: a mission that harks back to the earliest wanderings of their Norse forebears—and one my grandmother Anna reflected, in her own humble way.

Whatever one might think about her political views, we can even see Greta Thunberg's eight-week voyage across the Atlantic in 2019, to raise awareness

---

* Ironically, Heyerdahl's thesis—that intrepid ancient voyagers had traveled from South America to Polynesia—would be disproved by the science of DNA. The lesson: what's physically possible may not be historically plausible.

about climate change, in the same heroic light, evoking the spirit of her ancestors to face a universal crisis.

If we look hard enough, all these examples reveal the hidden history of the Viking heart as well as the history of the Scandinavian experience in America. What drew the Scandinavian immigrant was less the promise of wealth or the escape from religious or political persecution, which was fairly mild, compared to the experience of other immigrants from around the world. It was much more a belief that this new United States of America — since almost all the Scandinavian migration came in the nineteenth century, starting in the 1830s and building to a climax just before World War I — offered every immigrant the freedom they needed to live their lives the way they wanted to live them. The move to America wasn't a rejection of the old country but a better way to integrate the best of the past and the present in order to build a better future for everyone.

In that sense, the story of Scandinavian immigration *is* truly a universal story, like that of the Vikings. Both radiate the human quality that Arnesen and Bancroft embody, and that the Norwegian explorer and humanitarian Fridtjof Nansen pioneered. Nansen himself described its ultimate vision — the ultimate vision of the Viking heart — in a speech he gave in 1924, after receiving the highest honor Scots can bestow on any non-Scot, becoming rector of the University of St. Andrews. At his inaugural speech, titled "A Land of Beyond," Nansen said:

"We all have a Land of Beyond to seek in our life— what more can we ask? Our part is to find the trail that leads to it. A long trail, a hard trail maybe; but the call comes to us, and we have to go. Rooted deep in the nature of everyone is the spirit of adventure — the call of the wild, vibrating under all our actions, making life deeper and nobler."

The Land of Beyond was Nansen's reference to a poem by Robert Service of the same name, which contains this passage:

> *Have you ever heard of the Land of Beyond,*
> *That dream at the gates of the sky?*
> *Alluring it lies at the skirt of the skies,*
> *And ever so far away . . .*

Have you ever stood where the silences brood,
And vast the horizons begin;
At the dawn of the day to behold far away
The goal you strive for and win? . . .
Thank God! There is always the Land of Beyond
For us who are true to the trail,
A vision to seek, a beckoning peak,
A fairness that never will fail;
A proud in our soul that mocks at a goal,
A manhood that irks at a bond,
And try how we will, unattainable still,
Behold it, our Land of Beyond!

So where are the Vikings today?

They live in our minds as well as our hearts, preserved in myth but also made real through the journey that each of us must make, as part of life.

ACKNOWLEDGMENTS

This book has been a deeply personal as well as historical journey. I want to take a moment to point out the key stops along the way.

At the very start of the journey was a question that my late uncle Norman Flaaten asked in the winter of 2001–2, after my *How the Scots Invented the Modern World* became a *New York Times* bestseller and was celebrated by critics and readers on both sides of the Atlantic.

He asked, "How about a book about Vikings?" He was thinking about our shared Norwegian heritage, through his parents and my maternal grandparents, but he was also raising a larger question: how to move the story of the Vikings out of the realm of caricature and stereotyping on one side, and that of academic specialists on the other, into the mainstream of history. I kept pondering this idea for almost two decades, while writing six other books in between. My single greatest regret is that Uncle Norm is no longer with us to see the final result of his bold urging.

Working on *The Viking Heart* also meant recovering memories of my Norwegian-born grandparents Carsten Flaaten and Anna Carlson Flaaten, each of whom reflected different facets of the book's main theme. My parents were helpful in helping to find documentary and physical fragments of that shared experience. These included photos, my grandparents' naturalization papers, and the invaluable privately printed Sorlie family history — not to mention the minié ball taken from my great-great-grandfather's knee during those dismal December days outside Murfreesboro, Tennessee, in 1862.

The Vikings constantly haunted my college undergraduate years, when I assumed I would be a Middle Ages specialist. My history mentor at the University of Wisconsin–Stevens Point, Professor Rhys Hays, first exposed me to the legal and economic intricacies of the Viking settlement of England and the Danelaw; Professor Imogen de Smet of the English Department introduced me to Old English studies and the shared linguistic heritage of Viking and Anglo-Saxon.

Fast-forward almost forty years later, when my thoughts for a book on the Vikings and the Scandinavian contribution to history, especially American history, began to take shape. My literary agents Keith Urbahn and Matt Latimer of Javelin DC were suitably enthusiastic, as was my wife, Beth, and a phone conversation between the four of us in the summer of 2019 convinced me this would be a valuable, and vital, project.

My friend of two decades Tom Veblen shared his thoughts in multiple discussions of his illustrious ancestor Thorstein Veblen, and helped me to keep perspective on growing up in Scandinavian American communities in Minnesota and the Midwest. So did eavesdropping as a boy on conversations between my father and his mother, Helen Sorlie Herman, on life among the Norwegians who settled in the Red River Valley in Buxton, North Dakota.

Thanks are also due to my editor Alex Littlefield and publisher Bruce Nichols at Houghton Mifflin Harcourt and the HMH staff, especially Zach Phillips, for their patience and professionalism. Similar thanks go to copyeditor Susanna Brougham for her diligence and attention to detail.

I owe a debt of gratitude to the Hudson Institute for the time they allowed me to work on the book, and also to my colleagues at the National Security Council who, at unexpected times, found they had to listen to me discuss the difficulties of translating *Beowulf* from Old English or grappling with alarming features of the Nazi obsession with Nordic culture.

The person to whom I owe the greatest debt, however, is my wife, Beth, to whom the book is lovingly dedicated. Writing *The Viking Heart* has been a long and sometimes complicated journey, and Beth has been my trusted and supportive companion the entire way. Her love and support made the journey worthwhile, and added value to the final result in ways that only she and I can appreciate.

APPENDIX: RUNES AND THE VIKINGS

The German tribes who migrated from their Scandinavian homes in the pre- and early Christian eras had a profound impact on their Nordic cousins who stayed home — the ancestors of the Vikings — through trade routes and cultural exchange.

Probably their most valuable legacy was the system of writing known as runes. Its name seems to be derived from the Old Norse word *runar,* meaning "secret," and the Saxon word *rna,* meaning "whisper." This unique form of writing, with its combinations of vertical and diagonal notches, was easy to carve on wood or stone. The German peoples learned to use it as early as the second century CE, probably learning it from their mercenary soldiers fighting in the Roman army who adopted it from an Old Italic alphabet used by the Etruscans. At first it may have been a convenient way to send secret messages, as the name implies — ones their Roman officers couldn't read. Eventually it became a common form of writing, although clearly it also had occult and magic properties.

Runes were never meant to be read horizontally, like Greek or Latin letters. They were made to be arranged vertically or twisted into shapes, like the back of a carved dragon or flower, or to fit on a particular stone or piece of wood.

The earliest extant runic inscriptions come from Scandinavia and date from circa 200 CE. The earliest version of the runic alphabet, Elder Fuþark, used twenty-four different runes for writing proto-Norse inscriptions, arranged in three groups of eight runes each. The Anglo-Saxon tribes in England, meanwhile, developed their own system of runes using twenty-nine to thirty characters, as did another German tribe, the Marcomanni, whose runes can be found in eighth- and ninth-century manuscripts from Bavaria.

But the most famous by far of the runic scripts was one used by the Vikings dating from the ninth through the eleventh century, using a shorter alphabet of only sixteen characters, dubbed the Younger Fuþark. The reduction in the number of characters was accompanied by a simplifying of the shapes of certain letters, making the alphabet easier to carve. Without doubt this shift also reflected the switch from the proto-Norse language, which early Scandinavians had shared with their German cousins, to Old Norse: the unique language of the Vikings.

Younger Fuþark inscriptions are harder to read than their paleographic forebear, however, because characters represented multiple sounds or meanings. The k-rune, for example, can be read as a *k* — or a *g* or an *nk* or an *ng*. Inscribers also introduced other symbols to mark a break between sentences or between individual words. These complications make some runes all but impossible to decipher.

In Scandinavia runes are found everywhere, including on the walls and floors of later churches. The sheer range of their use suggests that rune literacy was fairly widespread. Perhaps not everyone in the Norse lands could read a complicated runic inscription (just as today's experts are stumped by some), but the evidence suggests that lots of ordinary people used runes as a kind of Viking Twitter or Instagram: a way to casually carve their name or coin a phrase as part of daily life.

The most important (or at least the most durable) runes are those that form stone inscriptions, such as the Jelling stone monument to King Harald

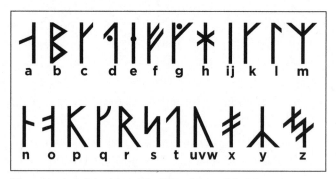

Runes diagram adapted from The Viking Network by Mapping Specialists, Ltd.

Bluetooth and to other prominent Nordic figures. These include the so-called Tirsted stone from Lolland, Denmark, which was raised in memory of a warrior named Frathi, "the terror of men" and "first in Friggir's retinue of all Vikings" — almost the only use of the word *Viking* by Vikings themselves.

It is striking that, of the 220 Danish runic inscriptions in stone, approximately 45, or nearly one-fifth, mention women. Even more striking, almost half of those were sponsored and raised by the women themselves. A fascinating Norwegian example is this memorial inscription from Dynna: "Gunnvor Thidrik's daughter made a bridge in memory of her daughter Astrid, she was the handiest maiden in Hadeland."

Runes were also used more casually to mark personal possessions or attach a maker's name to an object, like the comb case found in Lincoln that proudly reads "Thorfast made a good comb." Among the most common runic inscriptions that archaeologists have found, especially on wood carvings, look like nothing more or less than Nordic graffiti, such as "Tholfir Kolbeinsson carved these runes high up." Or "Ingibjorg had sex with me when I was in Stavanger." Many were irreverent, like "Ivor was f*cked. Helga made this." (*Þorný sarð. Helgi reist.*) Others take a stab at misogynist humor: "Ingigerth is the most beautiful of all women" — a runic inscription accompanied by a drawing of a dog.

Still others are positively poetic, like this one at Gripsholm, sponsored by a woman named Tola in memory of her son Harald and his companions:

> *They went gallantly*
> *Far for gold*
> *And in the East*
> *Fed the eagle.*
> *They died in the south*
> *In Saracenland.*

With time, rune carving was raised to a fine art, especially in Sweden, around Uppsala and north of Stockholm. This is where archaeologists and linguists have located the most numerous runic finds: some 2,500, in fact, compared to 220 in Denmark and only 50 in Norway (outside Scandinavia, the most are found on the Isle of Man, a leading Viking settlement, which accounts for half of the 60 or so extant in the non-Scandinavian world).

The most prolific of all rune carvers — truly a runic Rembrandt — was an Upplander named Asmund. He signed at least nineteen monument stones; another thirty have been attributed to him on the basis of style. Asmund's heyday was somewhat late in the Viking Age proper, probably the 1050s, when Christianity was bringing Latin into prominence in Scandinavia for the first time. But there's no denying that Asmund and his fellow artists were embellishing a form of communication that originally linked the Viking tribes to their German kinsmen.

At the same time, the association of runes with religious or mystical meanings never died. A fragment of a human skull recovered from Ribe, Denmark, bears this runic inscription: "Odin." Was it part of a religious ceremony involving the father of the gods? Or was the skull supposed to represent the great Odin? There is no way to know. We do know from the *Edda*s that runes were thought to have been invented by Odin himself and that they were engraved on the teeth of Odin's horse, Sleipnir, and on the fingernails of the fategoverning sisters, the Norns.

With the advent of Latin writing, runes eventually faded from the scene. The Germans themselves had given up runes for Latin script by 700 or so, as part of their integration into mainstream civilization. In Scandinavia runes survived as a rough-and-ready way for ordinary people to send short messages (one of the most popular being a fragment of bone or a stone with the inscription "kiss me") until well into the Middle Ages. Then they dropped out of use, and folk memory, for at least four centuries. The ability to read their meanings was lost.

Then, in the eighteenth century, the Swedish scholar Anders Celsius, the inventor of the thermometer, was able to decipher runes. Romantic interest in all things Viking triggered a new fascination with runic writing, and a host of elaborate theories arose, linking the inscriptions to mystical meanings and symbolic power. The most notorious of the theorists would be the Nazis, who incorporated runes into their racist propaganda; they used the letters *SS* as the symbol for their most notorious elite racist organization, Himmler's SS.

But runes were redeemed in the works of J.R.R. Tolkien and *The Lord of the Rings* trilogy. Tolkien was too good a linguist to overlook the link between writing and language and the evolution of culture, whether in the fictional or historical realms. Therefore he turned to the runic alphabet to create his own version, called Cirth. This pseudo-rune script was, according to the story, invented by the Grey Elves for their language, Sindarin, and then was adopted for the host of languages Tolkien created for his imaginary Middle Earth.

Similarly, his invention of the Common Tongue — the early common language, like proto-Norse — was accompanied by distinct Elvish lettering, which is engraved on the all-powerful Ring itself, "in a flowing script" of "fiery letters." Although the gracefully curved strokes of Elvish lettering are very different from the stiff, angular strokes of the Viking runes, they are redolent of the magical power associated with the original, and most mysterious, Nordic inscriptions.

NOTES

PREFACE

PAGE

xv *"a knack for being in"*: R. W. Southern, *The Making of the Middle Ages* (New Haven: Yale University Press, 1953), 28.

1. THE WRATH OF THE NORSEMEN

1 *"Hungry wolves take"*: Quoted in Gwyn Jones, *A History of the Vikings* (Oxford, UK: Oxford University Press, 1984), 220.
    "They came to the church": Dorothy Whitelock, ed., *English Historical Documents, c. 500–1042*, 2nd ed. (London: Routledge, 1979), 273.

2 *A church record from 792*: Peter Sawyer, ed., *The Oxford Illustrated History of the Vikings* (Oxford, UK: Oxford University Press, 1997), 3.
    "those valiant, wrathful, purely": Quoted in Kenneth Clark, *Civilisation* (New York: Harper and Row, 1969), 13.
    "spread on all sides": Simeon of Durham, quoted in Dorothy Whitelock and David C. Douglas, eds., *English Historical Documents, Volume I, c. 500–1042*, 2nd ed. (London: Cambridge University Press, 1975), 273.

3 *"Never before has such"*: Quoted in Dorothy Whitelock, ed., *English Historical Documents*, 1st ed. (London: Eyre and Spottiswoode, 1955), 193.

4 *"When we reflect"*: Winston Churchill, *A History of the English-Speaking Peoples*, vol. 1.1 (1956; New York: Bloomsbury Academic, 2015).
    "a world unto itself": W. R. Mead, *An Historical Geography of Scandinavia* (London: Academic Press, 1981), 10.

5 *the name "North Way"*: Peter Foote and David M. Wilson, *The Viking Achievement* (New York: Praeger, 1970), 36.
    Only 3 percent of Norway: Else Roesdahl, *The Vikings* (1987; New York: Penguin Books, 2016), 28.
    In the remote past: Roesdahl, *The Vikings*, 30.

6 *six hundred islands*: Jones, *History of the Vikings*, 23.

7   *strips of leather:* Yves Cohat, *The Vikings: Lords of the Seas* (New York: Abrams, 1992), 14.

    the Storegga Slide: Neil Oliver, *The Vikings: A New History* (New York: Pegasus Books, 2014), 10.

8   *made the American frontier:* Mead, *An Historical Geography,* 13.

11   *"They set about destroying":* Orosius, "History of the World," quoted in Jones, *History of the Vikings,* 21.

    same Scandinavian stock: Jones, *History of the Vikings,* 22; J. B. Bury, *The Invasion of Europe by the Barbarians* (London: Macmillan, 1928), 5–6.

12   *"They spend all their lives":* Julius Caesar, *The Conquest of Gaul,* trans. S. A. Hanford (Harmondsworth, UK: Penguin Books, 1965), 35–36.

    "No business, public or private": Tacitus, *On Britain and Germany,* trans. H. Mattingly (Harmondsworth, UK: Penguin Books, 1965), 112.

    "The power even of the kings": Tacitus, *On Britain and Germany,* 109–10.

    "It stands on record": Tacitus, *On Britain and Germany,* 107.

13   *great restless conglomerations:* J. M. Wallace-Hadrill, *The Barbarian West: The Early Middle Ages, A.D. 400–1000* (New York: Harper and Row, 1962), 21.

    Frisian and Frankish longships: Peter Brown, *The World of Late Antiquity* (New York: Harcourt Brace Jovanovich, 1971), 22–24.

15   *Scandinavian tribal name:* Jones, *History of the Vikings,* 31–33.

    Belgium their homeland: Wallace-Hadrill, *Barbarian West,* 66–67.

16   *"treated those to whom":* Einhard, "The Life of Charlemagne," in *Einhard and Notker the Stammerer: Two Lives of Charlemagne,* trans. David Ganz (New York: Penguin Books, 2008), 32–33.

    version of ethnic cleansing: Wallace-Hadrill, *Barbarian West,* 102–3.

17   *"a rampart, so that":* Quoted in Peter Sawyer, *Kings and Vikings: Scandinavia and Europe, AD 700–1100* (London: Routledge, 1984), 73.

18   *possible for Scandinavian merchants:* Sawyer, *Kings and Vikings,* 77.

    organize a personal summit: Jones, *History of the Vikings,* 98.

19   *"intoxicated by the hope":* Einhard, "Life of Charlemagne," in *Einhard and Notker,* 28.

    "But I am sad at heart": Notker the Stammerer, "The Deeds of Charlemagne," in *Einhard and Notker,* 105.

20   *"Wolf-battening warrior":* *Egil's Saga,* trans. W. C. Green, *Icelandic Saga Database,* Sveinbjorn Thordarson, ed., chapter 47, http://www.sagadb.org/egils_saga.en.

21   *series of rearguard campaigns:* Wallace-Hadrill, *Barbarian West,* 137.

22   *the archbishop of Rheims:* Jones, *History of the Vikings,* 225.

    decided to hang all 111: Jones, *History of the Vikings,* 212.

    "The number of ships": Quoted in Oliver, *The Vikings,* 147.

23   *"Guazelin, have compassion":* Abbo de St. Germain chronicle, quoted in Robert Ferguson, *The Vikings: A History* (New York: Penguin Books, 2004), 105.

24   *"On every side arrows":* Ferguson, *The Vikings,* 106.

25   *see a Viking fleet again:* Jones, *History of the Vikings,* 225.

27 *hub of Norse activity:* John Haywood, *The Penguin Historical Atlas of the Vikings* (New York: Penguin Books, 1995), 70–71.

28 *"between the dykes":* Quoted in Sawyer, *Kings and Vikings,* 103.
    agreed by formal treaty: G. O. Sayles, *The Medieval Foundations of England* (New York: Barnes and Co., 1961), 94–96.

2. BEING VIKINGS

30 *"When spring came":* Egil's Saga, trans. W. C. Green, chapter 19.

31 *The ship lay under:* Beowulf, verses 210–24. The translation is mine.

32 *tiny silver hammer of Thor:* Oliver, *The Vikings,* 174–75.
    very recent finds: https://www.world-archaeology.com/features/estonia-salme-ship-burials/.

33 *"tall as date palms":* Ibn Fadlan, c. 922, quoted in Haywood, *Historical Atlas,* 108.
    "swarthy and ugly": Egil's Saga, trans. Bernard Scudder (New York: Penguin Books, 2004), 4.
    "The findings from ancient": David Reich, *Who We Are and How We Got Here: Ancient DNA and the New Science of the Human Past* (New York: Pantheon, 2018), 286.

34 *almost spontaneous movement:* Sawyer, *Kings and Vikings,* 4.
    "They were seeking adventures": Georges Duby, *The Early Growth of the European Economy* (Ithaca, NY: Cornell University Press, 1974), 114.

35 *the Hjortspring boat:* Oliver, *The Vikings,* 52–53.

36 *backward when necessary:* Roesdahl, *The Vikings,* 88.

37 *could still go great distances:* Foote and Wilson, *Viking Achievement,* 236.
    guide to latitude: Jones, *History of the Vikings,* 192–93; Haywood, *Historical Atlas,* 40–41.
    Vikings' staying power: Sawyer, *Kings and Vikings,* 65–77.

38 *"the free peasant":* Jones, *History of the Vikings,* 150.
    changed location: Roesdahl, *The Vikings,* 103–7.
    "Ulf is said to have": Egil's Saga, trans. Bernard Scudder, 4–5.

39 *new chapter in life:* Eirik the Red's Saga, in *The Vinland Sagas,* trans. Keneva Kunz (New York: Penguin Books, 1997), 26–27.

40 *In these meetings:* Alexandra Sanmark, "Administrative Organization and State Formation: A Case Study of Assembly Sites in Sodermanland, Sweden," *Medieval Archeology* (2009): 53; Marie Odegaard, "State Formation, Administrative Areas, and Thing Sites," *Journal of the North Atlantic* 5 (2013): 42–63; Tacitus, *On Britain and Germany,* 109–11.
    "They have no king": Quoted in Cohat, *Vikings: Lords of the Seas,* 94–95; Jesse Byock, *Viking Age Iceland* (New York: Penguin Books, 2001), 174–76.

41 *"have the right to elect":* Quoted in Jones, *History of the Vikings,* 152.

42 *"was equated with the":* Jones, *History of the Vikings,* 150.
    numbered only 4,560: Sawyer, *Kings and Vikings,* 59.

the Latin term for "slaves": Duby, *Early Growth of European Economy,* 121.

both of Scottish origin: Eirik the Red's Saga, in *The Vinland Sagas,* 41.

43 *"Women have the right":* Ibrahim ben Yaqub, tenth century, quoted in Judith Jesch, *Women in the Viking Age* (Woodbridge, UK: Boydell Press, 1991), 91.

    "the sources preserve": Foote and Wilson, *Viking Achievement,* 114.

44 *a woman became a widow:* Foote and Wilson, *Viking Achievement,* 109, 110.

    "Our women stay with": Quoted in Jesch, *Women in the Viking Age,* 94.

    "The good farmer Holmgaut": Quoted in Jesch, *Women in the Viking Age,* 64.

45 *Red Girl or Red Maiden:* Jesch, *Women in the Viking Age,* 176–77.

    "was too important": Jones, *History of the Vikings,* 396.

46 *Hedenstierna-Jonson's DNA:* "A Female Viking Warrior Confirmed by Genomics," in *American Journal of Physical Anthropology,* December 2017, 853–60.

    "The women in The Saga*":* Introduction, *The Saga of the People of Laxardal,* trans. Keneva Kunz, in *The Sagas of Icelanders* (New York: Penguin Books, 2001), 274.

47 *substantial defensive wall:* Roesdahl, *The Vikings,* 136–37.

48 *no fewer than fifteen towns:* Haywood, *Historical Atlas,* 42–44.

    every salable commodity: Jones, *History of the Vikings,* 3.

49 *slave-trade superhighway:* H. Trevor-Roper, *The Rise of Christian Europe* (New York: Harcourt Brace Jovanovich, 1971), 89–90.

    Luitprand of Cremona: Trevor-Roper, *Christian Europe,* 92.

50 *growing political stability:* Oliver, *The Vikings,* 48–52; Southern, *Making of the Middle Ages.*

    the element of surprise: Paddy Griffith, *The Viking Art of War* (London: Greenhill Books, 1995), 109.

51 *the Arab traveler's account:* Cohat, *Vikings: Lords of the Seas,* 154.

52 *might call on a half levy:* Griffith, *Viking Art of War,* 138.

    "In the lives of the most": Duby, *Early Growth of European Economy,* 121.

53 *Scandinavia's social order:* Griffith, *Viking Art of War,* 137–38.

    scholars understand: Ryan Lavelle, *Alfred's Wars: Sources and Interpretations of Anglo-Saxon Warfare in the Viking Age* (Woodbridge, UK: Boydell Press, 2010), 26–27; B.P.C. Molloy and D. Grossman, "Why Can't Johnny Kill? The Psychology and Physiology of Interpersonal Combat," in B. Molloy, ed., *The Cutting Edge: Studies in Ancient and Medieval Combat* (London: Stroud, 2007), 188–202.

    "bashing the hell out": Foote and Wilson, *Viking Achievement,* 283.

54 *"such men were prized":* Foote and Wilson, *Viking Achievement,* 285.

    "I fought, nor feared vengeance": Egil's Saga, trans. W. C. Green, chapter 60.

55 *the Gothic word gudja:* Byock, *Viking Age Iceland,* 13–14.

56 *"what a great and generous":* Egil's Saga, trans. Bernard Scudder, 16.

    "On the day the king": Egil's Saga, trans. Bernard Scudder, 19.

    shrouded in legend and myth: Jones, *History of the Vikings,* 86–87.

57 *wait until 1100 or so:* Foote and Wilson, *Viking Achievement,* 29–31; Jones, *History of the Vikings,* 38–39, 45–49; Sawyer, *Kings and Vikings,* 18–19.

    until the tenth century: Jones, *History of the Vikings,* 113–14.

As Paddy Griffith details: Griffith, *Viking Art of War,* 27.

59 *his own coins at Sigtuna:* Jones, *History of the Vikings,* 380–81.

3. THE WORLD THE VIKINGS MADE, PART ONE:
FROM RUSSIA TO THE BRITISH ISLES

60 *"The island of St. Patrick":* The Annals of Clonmacnoise from the Creation to A.D. 1408 (Dublin: Royal Antiquaries of Ireland, 1893–95), I, 28.

61 *part of a "culture war":* Compare Lucien Musset, "The Vikings in Frankia," in J. M. Wallace-Hadrill, ed., *Early Medieval History* (Oxford, UK: Oxford University Press, 1975).

62 *"They then left to sail":* Saga of the Greenlanders, in *The Vinland Sagas,* 10.

63 *returned to circulation:* Duby, *Early Growth of European Economy,* 126.

  western Europe's access: H. Pirenne, *Mohammed and Charlemagne* (1939; New York: Barnes and Noble, n.d.), 239–41.

64 *Birka's affluence apparently:* Foote and Wilson, *Viking Achievement,* 205–9.

  not far from Uppsala: Ferguson, *The Vikings,* 98.

65 *eight major silver hoards:* Sawyer, *Kings and Vikings,* 123–26.

  twelve grams of silver: Ferguson, *The Vikings,* 112–13.

66 *"the men who row":* Jones, *History of the Vikings,* 246–47, note.

  alternate route: Roesdahl, *The Vikings,* 302–3.

  "he investigated the reason": Quoted in Haywood, *Historical Atlas,* 103; Sawyer, *Illustrated History,* 23.

67 *the Finnish majority:* Ferguson, *The Vikings,* 112.

  a truly intrepid Viking: Foote and Wilson, *Viking Achievement,* 399.

  "Here was no law": Serge Zenkovsky, ed., *The Nikonian Chronicle,* vol. 1 (Princeton, NJ: Kingston Press, 1984), 15, and n. 46.

68 *"Do you recollect":* Quoted in Edward Luttwak, *The Grand Strategy of the Byzantine Empire* (Cambridge, MA: Belknap Press, 2009), 154; compare Zenkovsky, *Nikonian Chronicle,* 17.

69 *Then the raids extended:* Oliver, *The Vikings,* 148.

70 *The most sensational tale:* Jones, *History of the Vikings,* 205–6.

  area is now Wood Quay: Oliver, *The Vikings,* 156–57.

71 *a highly developed arm:* Oliver, *The Vikings,* 136.

  "Forty Years' Rest": Haywood, *Historical Atlas,* 74; Roesdahl, *The Vikings,* 237.

  "a flourishing international": Roesdahl, *The Vikings,* 237–38.

72 *tribute money to Irish rulers:* Roesdahl, *The Vikings,* 237–38; Foote and Wilson, *Viking Achievement,* 218.

  a Gaelic literary culture: Sawyer, *Illustrated History,* 105–6.

  Two very recent studies: Julian Richards, *Blood of the Vikings* (London: Hoddard and Stoughton, 2001); https://www.rcsi.com/dublin/news-and-events/news/news-article /2017/12/unique-study-provides-the-first-genetic-map-of-the-people-of-ireland.

Indeed, archaeological remains: Roesdahl, *The Vikings,* 220.

73 *virtual Norwegian colonies:* Foote and Wilson, *Viking Achievement,* 157.
The real prize, however: Ferguson, *The Vikings,* 63.

74 *single most powerful man:* Jones, *History of the Vikings,* 396–97.

75 *were called* birlinns: Oliver, *The Vikings,* 190.

76 *"the wealth of Viking":* Roesdahl, *The Vikings,* 226.
Isle of Man's Tynwald: Roesdahl, *The Vikings,* 227–28.
grave does offer proof: https://www.ancient-origins.net/ancient-places-europe/peel
-castle-0011772.

77 *One of them displays:* Roesdahl, *The Vikings,* 230.
"It was a time when he": Southern, *Making of the Middle Ages,* 86.

78 *In swift order:* Sayles, *Medieval Foundations of England,* 98–99.
less than seven years: Jones, *History of the Vikings,* 234–35.
"Egil and his men": Egil's Saga, trans. Bernard Scudder, 98–99.

79 *"The two brothers":* Anglo-Saxon Chronicle, quoted in Ferguson, *The Vikings,* 225.
"was a greater slaughter": Anglo-Saxon Chronicle, quoted in Ferguson, *The Vikings,*
225.
eight hundred place names: Sayles, *Medieval Foundations of England,* 133.

80 *original Viking owners:* Sawyer, *Kings and Vikings,* 103.
hie, heira, and him: Roesdahl, *The Vikings,* 255.

81 *heart of the Danelaw:* Sayles, *Medieval Foundations of England,* 132–33.
only one place on earth: Roesdahl, *The Vikings,* 254.
Four hundred years later: Sayles, *Medieval Foundations of England,* 134.

82 *These expanded rights:* Sawyer, *Kings and Vikings,* 107.
half of the population: Sayles, *Medieval Foundations of England,* 136.

83 *"a woman with no husband":* Richard Maitland, *English Law,* vol. 1, 482, quoted in
Alan Macfarlane, *The Origins of English Individualism* (Cambridge, UK: Cambridge
University Press, 1978), 132.
part of the Danelaw: Macfarlane, *English Individualism,* 127–29.

4. THE WORLD THE VIKINGS MADE, PART TWO:
NORMANDY, THE ATLANTIC, AND NORTH AMERICA

85 *"Then that decree":* Quoted in Byock, *Viking Age Iceland,* 341.

86 *an additional claim:* Ferguson, *The Vikings,* 177, 179.
granted the Viking leader: David Douglas, *The Norman Achievement, 1050–1100*
(Berkeley: University of California Press, 1969), 22–23.
axis for Rollo's possessions: David Douglas, *William the Conqueror* (Berkeley: University
of California Press, 1967), 17.

87 *Old Norse was still spoken:* Douglas, *Norman Achievement,* 25.
Old Norse word tomt: Ferguson, *The Vikings,* 191–92.

"eager thirst of wealth": Geoffrey Malaterra, quoted in Douglas, *Norman Achievement*, 26.

88 *responded to this insult*: Douglas, *Norman Achievement*, 26.

   as a "pirate chief": Ferguson, *The Vikings*, 194; Douglas, *Norman Achievement*, 24.

   major local trading centers: Haywood, *Historical Atlas*, 80–81; Douglas, *William the Conqueror*, 18–19.

   "I will never bow": Quoted in Ferguson, *The Vikings*, 192.

89 *historical figures at all*: Griffith, *Viking Art of War*, 31–34.

90 *to cast serious doubt*: Sawyer, *Kings and Vikings*, 13.

91 *in the other direction*: Byock, *Viking Age Iceland*, 82–83.

   another three centuries: Foote and Wilson, *Viking Achievement*, 25.

92 *official list of rulers*: Foote and Wilson, *Viking Achievement*, 32.

   a single unified nation: Jones, *History of the Vikings*, 79.

   reasonable to believe: Jones, *History of the Vikings*, 114–17; Oliver, *The Vikings*, 226–29.

   Trelleborg and Fyrkat: Haywood, *Historical Atlas*, 34–35.

93 *the crucified Christ*: Roesdahl, *The Vikings*, 71.

94 *betrays his Irish origin*: Jones, *History of the Vikings*, 270.

95 *"When he loosed the first"*: The Saga of the Settlements, quoted in Ferguson, *The Vikings*, 154–55.

   "active volcanoes spewing": Oliver, *The Vikings*, 202.

96 *the Landamabok*: Roesdahl, *The Vikings*, 277.

97 *role in religious functions*: Byock, *Viking Age Iceland*, 13–14; Sawyer, *Kings and Vikings*, 58–59.

   "Each of the wise": Quoted in Byock, *Viking Age Iceland*, 233.

98 *"Never kill in the same"*: Njal's Saga, trans. Robert Cook (New York: Penguin Classics, 1997), 94.

   The skalds' poems: Sawyer, *Kings and Vikings*, 14.

   "Iceland is the first": Richard Tomasson, *Iceland: The First New Society* (Minneapolis: University of Minnesota Press, 1980).

99 *certainly lusher than Iceland*: Ferguson, *The Vikings*, 282.

   "a green land": "Erik the Red's Saga," in *The Vinland Sagas*, trans. Keneva Kunz (New York: Penguin Classics, 1997), 28.

100 *three thousand hardy souls*: Jones, *History of the Vikings*, 293.

   the men five foot eight: Roesdahl, *The Vikings*, 283–84.

101 *"like a single flat slab"*: The Saga of the Greenlanders, in *The Vinland Sagas*, 7.

102 *identified with Baffin Island*: "Suggested locations of places mentioned in the *Vinland Sagas*," chart in *The Vinland Sagas*, 66–67.

   hardly an all-male: Erik Wahlgren, *The Vikings and America* (London: Thames and Hudson, 1986), 128; Roesdahl, *The Vikings*, 285; Oliver, *The Vikings*, 217–18.

103 *to treeless Greenland*: Ferguson, *The Vikings*, 296–97.

   when a ship stopped at: Oliver, *The Vikings*, 218; Haywood, *Historical Atlas*, 96.

5. TWILIGHT OF THE GODS:
VIKINGS, KINGS, AND CHRISTIANITY

105 *"I see the Earth"*: Jackson Crawford, ed. and trans., *The Poetic Edda: Stories of the Norse Gods and Heroes* (Indianapolis: Hackett Publishing, 2015), 15.

106 *Scandinavians had been*: Sawyer, *Illustrated History*, 146.
another armed assault: Zenkovsky, *Nikonian Chronicle*, 35.
"Oleg commanded his warriors": Zenkovsky, *Nikonian Chronicle*, 36; Ferguson, *The Vikings*, 119.

107 *the central axis*: Zenkovsky, *Nikonian Chronicle*, 39–42.
"long-standing amity": Zenkovsky, *Nikonian Chronicle*, 39.
bear Scandinavian names: Ferguson, *The Vikings*, 122.
the Rus's main water routes: Sawyer, *Illustrated History*, 149.

109 *The Nordic version of Genesis*: T. Birkett, *The Norse Myths* (London: Quercus, 2019), 13–14.
"[Odin's] men went": Hilda Davidson, *Shape Changing in Old Norse Sagas* (Totowa, NJ: Rowan and Littlefield, 1978).
"Odin owns you all!": Daniel McCoy, *The Viking Spirit: An Introduction to Norse Mythology and Religion*, 33.

110 *gods almost as equals*: Birkett, *The Norse Myths*, 70.

111 *"Brother will fight one"*: Crawford, *Poetic Edda*, "Voluspa," stanza 44, 12.
"The sun turns black": Crawford, *Poetic Edda*, "Voluspa," stanza 55, 14.

112 *"I see the Earth"*: Crawford, *Poetic Edda*, "Voluspa," stanza 57, 15.
"myth of the eternal return": Arthur Herman, *The Idea of Decline in Western History* (New York: Free Press, 1997), 105.

113 *"I see a hall standing"*: Crawford, *Poetic Edda*, "Voluspa," stanza 62, 16.
"an Odinic wanderer": Letter 181 (1946), in *The Letters of J.R.R. Tolkien*, ed. Humphrey Carpenter (New York: Mariner Books, 2000), 252.

114 *"Even dogs and horses"*: Adam of Bremen, quoted in Jones, *History of the Vikings*, 326.

115 *"Drinking is the joy"*: Simon Franklin and Jonathan Shepard, *The Emergence of Rus, 750–1200* (London–New York: Longman, 1996).
"We no longer knew": Zenkovsky, *Nikonian Chronicle*, 98.

116 *also opened the way*: Janet Martin, *Medieval Russia, 980–1584*, 2nd ed. (Cambridge, UK: Cambridge University Press, 2007), 6.
the custom of grave goods: Duby, *Early Growth of European Economy*, 53.
Previously, all Vikings: Wallace-Hadrill, *Barbarian West*, 57–58.

117 *made virtually no impact*: Dorothy Whitelock, *The Beginnings of English Society* (1954; Harmondsworth, UK: Penguin Books, 1972), 42–44.

118 *shift from piracy to trade and settlement*: Sawyer, *Kings and Vikings*, 145.
"and you'll have the good": Eirik the Red's Saga, in *The Vinland Sagas*, 34–35.

119 *of driving Olaf out*: Jones, *History of the Vikings*, 135.

"*Christ's men*": Jones, *History of the Vikings,* 384, n.

Olaf's title: Rex Sv: Foote and Wilson, *Viking Achievement,* 32.

120 "*If he wished to be*": Jones, *History of the Vikings,* 74.

"*the bodies hang in*": Adam of Bremen, quoted in Jones, *History of the Vikings,* 326.

were hardly very large: Alexandra Sanmark, *Power and Conversion: A Comparative Study of Christianization in Scandinavia* (Uppsala, Sweden: Department of Archaeology and Ancient History, Uppsala University, 2002).

121 "*those who have already*": Quoted in Jones, *History of the Vikings,* 326.

Scandinavians weren't quite: H. R. Ellis Davidson, *Myths and Symbols of Pagan Europe: Early Scandinavian and Celtic Religions* (New York: Syracuse University Press, 1988).

123 *along the Bay of Biscay:* Southern, *Making of the Middle Ages,* 26.

124 *ceased almost altogether:* Sawyer, *Kings and Vikings,* 126.

"*Bows were drawn*": Singing the Song: The Battle of Maldon, trans. by the author.

125 *eighteen thousand pounds:* Haywood, *Historical Atlas,* 118.

another exorbitant danegeld: Jones, *History of the Vikings,* 368–69.

cash nexus was being forged: Sawyer, *Kings and Vikings,* 127.

126 *an economic powerhouse:* Whitelock, *Beginnings of English Society,* 68.

158,000 pounds in silver: Sayles, *Medieval Foundations of England,* 142.

127 *his army was destroyed:* Haywood, *Historical Atlas,* 119.

128 *career as a great monarch:* Sayles, *Medieval Foundations of England,* 145.

most underrated king: Jones, *History of the Vikings,* 371; Sayles, *Medieval Foundations of England,* 143–44.

129 "*There is no doubt that*": Sayles, *Medieval Foundations of England,* 147–48.

man of superior rank: Duby, *Early Growth of European Economy,* 130.

130 *greatest Viking ruler:* Jones, *History of the Vikings,* 381.

6. CONQUERORS: THE NORMAN TRANSFORMATION

131 "*When under the rule*": Quoted in Douglas, *Norman Achievement,* 26.

133 *murderous anarchy:* Douglas, *William the Conqueror,* 37.

Hubert's son Eudo: David Howarth, *1066: The Year of the Conquest* (New York: Viking, 1978), 65; Douglas, *William the Conqueror,* 48.

134 *to be ruled by Normans:* Howarth, *1066,* 68.

135 *churchman Robert of Jumièges:* Douglas, *William the Conqueror,* 169.

met and acclaimed: Frank McLynn, *1066: The Year of the Three Battles* (London: Jonathan Cape, 1998), 177.

Harald eagerly agreed: McLynn, *1066,* 188.

136 *spoke fluent Norse:* Howarth, *1066,* 54.

some would claim: Jones, *History of the Vikings,* 404.

burning towns and villages: Jones, *History of the Vikings,* 406–8.

137 *had no ships or navy:* Howarth, *1066,* 81–82.

some contemporary sources: For example, William of Jumièges, in S. Morillio, ed., *The Battle of Hastings: Sources and Interpretations* (Bury St. Edmunds, UK: Boydell Press, 1996), 18.

138 *"the venture had been":* Douglas, *William the Conqueror,* 188.

"*at last the long-awaited":* William of Poitiers, quoted in Morillio, *Battle of Hastings,* 8.

139 *"To take a large seagoing":* Howarth, *1066,* 132.

"*we march forward in":* McLynn, *1066,* 203.

140 *Harold generously allowed:* Howarth, *1066,* 140.

satellite of the dukes: Haywood, *Historical Atlas,* 81–82.

141 *According to one version:* Howarth, *1066,* 161.

"*He grew pale and for":* William of Poitiers, quoted in Morillio, *Battle of Hastings,* 11.

142 *"Now you must prove":* William of Poitiers, quoted in Morillio, *Battle of Hastings,* 12.

143 *"With the strength of Hercules":* Carmen de Hastingae, quoted in Morillio, *Battle of Hastings,* 49.

144 *see King Harold himself:* Douglas, *William the Conqueror,* 201.

145 *as one out of three:* Howarth, *1066,* 188.

"*By the duke's command":* Carmen de Hastingae, quoted in Morillio, *Battle of Hastings,* 51–52.

146 *an outbreak of dysentery:* Douglas, *William the Conqueror,* 205.

mercenaries thought a riot: McLynn, *1066,* 232.

147 *From 1073 until 1085:* Douglas, *William the Conqueror,* 211.

beg the Normans to stay: G. A. Loud, *The Age of Robert Guiscard* (Harlow, UK: Pearson Education, 2000), 60–61.

completely different story: Loud, *Age of Robert Guiscard,* 65–68.

148 *"They saw that their own":* Quoted in Loud, *Age of Robert Guiscard,* 6.

149 *sons of Guimund des Moulins:* Loud, *Age of Robert Guiscard,* 84, 89.

one of those knights: Richard Fletcher, *The Quest for El Cid* (Oxford, UK: Oxford University Press, 1989), 77–78.

"*he had a ruddy":* For example, Anna Komnene, *The Alexiad,* trans. E.R.A. Sewter (Harmondsworth, UK: Penguin Classics, 2003), 30.

150 *"By the middle of":* Douglas, *Norman Achievement,* 53.

Normans were so strong: Loud, *Age of Robert Guiscard,* 186–87.

151 *"did not exile anyone":* Quoted in A. Cilento and A. Vanoli, *Arabs and Normans in Sicily and the South of Italy* (New York: Riverside Books, 2007), 186.

complex iconographical program: Cilento and Vanoli, *Arabs and Normans in Sicily,* 270.

152 *many of the Muslim ways:* Cilento and Vanoli, *Arabs and Normans in Sicily,* 255.

153 *"By 1085 Robert had":* Loud, *Age of Robert Guiscard,* 4.

154 *Kenneth Clark has asserted:* K. Clark, *Civilisation: A Personal View* (New York: Harper and Row, 1969), 35.

155 *"was the exact replica":* Komnene, *Alexiad,* 42–43.

with a magnificent effort: Douglas, *Norman Achievement,* 61.

156 *"They wear the badge": Gesta Francorum,* in Christopher Tyerman, ed., *Chronicles of the First Crusade* (New York: Penguin Books, 2004), 72–73.
offered the Normans: Peter Frankopan, *The First Crusade* (Cambridge, MA: Harvard University Press, 2012), 109.
The men he brought: Tyerman, *Chronicles of the First Crusade,* 73n.

157 *"I was afraid he":* Quoted in Frankopan, *The First Crusade,* 129.
according to one chronicler: That is, Anna Komnene, in Frankopan, *The First Crusade,* 123.
"howling like wolves": Fulcher of Chartres, quoted in Frankopan, *The First Crusade,* 147–48.

158 *one of the signal victories:* Douglas, *Norman Achievement,* 67.
keep Antioch for himself: Frankopan, *The First Crusade,* 160.
the archbishop of Pisa: Douglas, *Norman Achievement,* 66.

159 *the solid gold shackles:* Douglas, *William the Conqueror,* 209.
Sven's troops were feted: Douglas, *William the Conqueror,* 219.

160 *he stayed until 1087:* Douglas, *William the Conqueror,* 356.
"They can endure with": Quoted in Douglas, *Norman Achievement,* 26.

161 *"We were sprung":* Quoted in Douglas, *Norman Achievement,* 128.
"they rend each other": Quoted in Douglas, *Norman Achievement,* 26.

7. VIKINGS INTO SCANDINAVIANS: FROM GAMES OF THRONES TO MIGHTY FORTRESSES

163 *first European monarch:* Jonathan Riley-Smith, *The First Crusade and the Idea of Crusading* (Philadelphia: University of Pennsylvania Press, 1996), 132; "Heimskringla: Saga of Sigurd the Crusader," quoted in Gary B. Doxey, "Norwegian Crusaders and the Balearic Islands," *Scandinavian Studies* (1996): 10–11.

164 *nobles like Earl Birger:* T. K. Derry, *A History of Scandinavia* (Minneapolis: University of Minnesota Press, 1979), 7.
dream of a Baltic empire: Derry, *History of Scandinavia,* 52–53.

165 *late as the twelfth century:* Jones, *History of the Vikings,* 71.
the Hanseatic League: Denys Hay, *Europe in the Fourteenth and Fifteenth Centuries* (London: Longmans, 1966), 207.

166 *this principle made:* Derry, *History of Scandinavia,* 45.

167 *remained a viable institution:* Jones, *History of the Vikings,* 285–86.

168 *primary export industries:* Sawyer, *Kings and Vikings,* 14.
from the eleventh century: Sawyer, *Illustrated History,* 222.

169 *"a sense of closure":* Walter J. Ong, *Orality and Literacy: The Technologizing of the Word* (London: Routledge, 1982), 129.
Jane Smiley has said: Jane Smiley, Preface, *The Saga of Icelanders* (New York: Penguin Books, 2000), xiii.

170 *"People are always making"*: Smiley, Preface, *Saga of Icelanders,* xi.
Snorri was no bookworm: Jesse Byock, Introduction, *The Prose Edda* (New York: Penguin Classics, 2005), xiii.

171 *"In the 1230's the number"*: Byock, Introduction, *Prose Edda,* xiii–xiv; Byock, *Viking Age Iceland,* 60.
Haakon IV was laboring to secure: Derry, *History of Scandinavia,* 50.

172 *checks and balances:* Derry, *History of Scandinavia,* 58–59; Michael Roberts, *Essays in Swedish History* (Minneapolis: University of Minnesota Press, 1976), 40–41.
no hereditary fiefs: Derry, *History of Scandinavia,* 58; Roberts, "Aristocratic Constitutionalism," in *Essays in Swedish History,* 5–7.

173 *the status of slaves:* Derry, *History of Scandinavia,* 57.
Norway, Denmark, and Sweden: Derry, *History of Scandinavia,* 64.

174 *some of their freedoms:* Foote and Wilson, *Viking Achievement,* 112–14.
such as April DeConick: April DeConick, *Holy Misogyny: Why the Sex and Gender Conflicts in the Early Church Still Matter* (London: Bloomsbury Academic, 2013).
practice of infanticide: https://www.researchgate.net/publication/225030359 _Christianization_Female_Infanticide_and_the_Abundance_of_Female_Burials_at _Viking_Age_Birka_in_Sweden.
become a lady-in-waiting: Derry, *History of Scandinavia,* 68.
she was only thirteen: "St. Bridget," *Catholic Encyclopedia* (http://www.newadvent.org /cathen/02782a.htm).

175 *a Swedish crusade:* Derry, *History of Scandinavia,* 68.

176 *"I want to explain"*: St. Bridget, *Revelations,* Chapter 4, http://www.saintsbooks.net /books/St.%20Bridget%20(Birgitta)%20of%20Sweden%20-%20Prophecies%20and %20Revelations.html.

177 *rumors were confirmed:* Hay, *Europe,* 209.
only one with a seat: Grete Authén Blom, "Ingebjørg med Guds misskunn Kong Håkons datter," in *Hertuginne i Sviarike: Brudstykker av. et politisk kvinneportrett* (Oslo: Norsk Historisk Tidskrift, 1981), 425.

178 *her dream of carving out:* Hay, *Europe,* 208.
the nation's wealth had: Derry, *History of Scandinavia,* 65.

179 *still maintained fully half:* Derry, *History of Scandinavia,* 65.
By midcentury, it owned: James Larson, *Reforming the North: The Kingdoms and Churches of Scandinavia, 1520–1545* (Cambridge, UK: Cambridge University Press, 2010), 6.

180 *that she marry Haakon VI:* Derry, *History of Scandinavia,* 70.
"for that lady's wisdom": Lübeck Chronicle, quoted in Derry, *History of Scandinavia,* 71.

181 *"A statesman cannot"*: Quoted in A.J.P. Taylor, *Bismarck: The Man and the Statesman* (1955; New York: Knopf, 1967), 115.
Albrecht's forces at Falköping: Vivian Etting, *Queen Margrete I, 1353–1412: And the Founding of the Nordic Union* (Leiden, Netherlands: Brill Publishing, 2004), 61–63.
as "Lady King": Derry, *History of Scandinavia,* 72.

182 *"the most intensely"*: Jerker Rosen, *Svenska Historia,* vol. 1 (Stockholm: Svenska Bokförlaget, Bonniers, 1961), 198.

Kalmar continues to baffle: Harald Gustafsson, "A State That Failed?," *Scandinavian Journal of History* (2006): 205–20.

"This very cunning woman": Quoted in Derry, *History of Scandinavia,* 73.

183 *historians give her credit:* Etting, *Queen Margrete;* Derry, *History of Scandinavia,* 74.

Whether her death was: For example, Sophia Elizabeth Higgins, *Women of Europe in the Fifteenth and Sixteenth Centuries,* vol. 1 (London: Hurst and Blackett, 1885), 69.

184 *Engelbret Engelbretsen:* Derry, *History of Scandinavia,* 76–77.

took these serial depositions: Hay, *Europe,* 210.

186 *Luther had swept aside:* Arthur Herman, *The Cave and the Light: Plato Versus Aristotle and the Struggle for the Soul of Western Civilization* (New York: Random House, 2013), 307–9.

187 *first monarchs in Europe:* Ewan Cameron, *The European Reformation* (Oxford, UK: Clarendon Press, 1991), 272.

a series of changes: Derry, *History of Scandinavia,* 83–84.

not have entirely understood: Cameron, *European Reformation,* 272–73.

188 *translations of the Bible:* Derry, *History of Scandinavia,* 91–93.

189 *but the early translation:* Derry, *History of Scandinavia,* 94.

"useful book for the ordinary": Luther, *Preface to the Book of Jesus Sirach* (1533), http://beggarsallreformation.blogspot.com/2010/11/luther-and-book-of-sirach.html.

190 *"the valuation of the"*: Max Weber, *The Protestant Ethic and the Spirit of Capitalism* (1904–5; New York: Scribners, 1976), 80.

"Labor in a calling": Weber, *Protestant Ethic,* 81.

a calling ultimately focuses: R. H. Tawney, *Religion and the Rise of Capitalism* (London: John Murray, 1922).

191 *a fierce critic of usury:* Weber, *Protestant Ethic,* 82.

8. VIKING HEART EMPIRE: KING GUSTAVUS ADOLPHUS AND THE SCANDINAVIAN CENTURY

192 *"You may earn salvation"*: Quoted in Christian Potholm, *War Wisdom: A Cross-Cultural Sampling* (Lanham, MD: University Press of America, 2015), 81.

193 *Dutch East Indies two years:* Alex Jack, ed., *Hamlet: Volume 2, History and Commentary* (Becket, MA: Amber Waves, 2005), 53.

chronicler Saxo Grammaticus: Oliver Elton, trans., *Saxo Grammaticus' "Amleth, Prince of Denmark"* (London: David Nutt, 1894), books 1–10.

He was just fifteen: Michael Roberts, *Gustavus Adolphus and the Rise of Sweden* (London: The English University Presses, 1973), 21–22; T. K. Rabb, *The Struggle for Stability in Early Modern Europe* (Oxford, UK: Oxford University Press, 1975).

194 *the greatest prize of all:* Roberts, "Of Swedish History in General," in *Essays in Swedish History,* 8–9.

195 *massive pine forests:* Arthur Herman, *To Rule the Waves: How the British Navy Shaped the Modern World* (New York: HarperCollins, 2004), 366.

for support and protection: Barbara Stolberg-Rilinger, *The Holy Roman Empire: A Short History* (Princeton, NJ: Princeton University Press, 2018), 91–92.

executed in Denmark: Michael Bailey, *Historical Dictionary of Witchcraft* (Lanham, MD: Scarecrow Press, 2003).

in Norway, only 2 percent: Peter Leeson and Jacob Russ, "Witch Trials," *Economic Journal* 128, no. 613 (2018): 2066–105.

196 *especially the older ones:* Jesch, *Women in the Viking Age,* 142–43, 207–8.

James's entire reign: G.P.V. Akrigg, *Jacobean Pageant: The Court of King James I* (New York: Atheneum, 1967), 79–83.

197 *modern states everywhere:* M. Roberts, "Of Swedish History in General," in *Essays in Swedish History,* 8–9.

198 *"be humane toward":* Roberts, *Gustavus Adolphus,* 20–21.

199 *the gates of Vienna:* A.J.P. Taylor, *The Habsburg Monarchy, 1809–1918* (1948; University of Chicago Press, 1976), 13.

200 *in money and support:* Roberts, *Gustavus Adolphus,* 60.

typical Renaissance monarch: Derry, *History of Scandinavia,* 102–3; 114–16.

pleased to say yes: C. V. Wedgewood, *The Thirty Years War* (1938; New York: New York Review Books, 2005), 196.

201 *"king or emperor, prince":* Quoted in Wedgewood, *The Thirty Years War,* 243.

202 *When "Gustavus came":* Michael Howard, *War in European History* (Oxford, UK: Oxford University Press, 1976), 58.

army unique for its time: Henrik Lunde, *A Warrior Dynasty: The Rise and Fall of Sweden as a Military Superpower, 1611–1721* (Oxford, UK: Casement Publishers, 2014), 75–79.

"My troops are poor": Quoted in Lunde, *A Warrior Dynasty,* 59.

ranks firing at once: Roberts, "Gustav Adolf and the Art of War," in *Essays in Swedish History,* 66–68.

203 *"it's necessary for me":* Quoted in Lunde, *A Warrior Dynasty,* 31.

9.4 artillery pieces: Roberts, "Gustav Adolf and the Art of War," *Essays in Swedish History,* 69–70.

Swedish forces in Livonia: Roberts, *Gustavus Adolphus,* 115.

204 *"I've not thoughtlessly":* Quoted in Wedgewood, *The Thirty Years War,* 259.

205 *"The legend embodies":* Wedgewood, *The Thirty Years War,* 260.

"a signal-flare for rebellion": Quoted in Roberts, *Gustavus Adolphus,* 130.

206 *"This fellow will rob":* Quoted in Wedgewood, *The Thirty Years War,* 287.

207 *the shattering news:* Roberts, *Gustavus Adolphus,* 142–43.

One Protestant town after: Wedgewood, *The Thirty Years War,* 296.

geopolitical power network: Roberts, "The Political Objectives of Gustaf Adolf in Germany," *Essays in Swedish History,* 92–93; Wedgewood, *The Thirty Years War,* 302.

208 *"From Constantinople to":* Roberts, *Gustavus Adolphus,* 147.

general Alexander Leslie: Steve Murdoch, ed., *Scotland and the Thirty Years' War, 1618–1648* (Leiden, Netherlands: Brill, 2001); Roberts, *Gustavus Adolphus,* 149.

"*Means must be devised*": J.F.C. Fuller, *Military History of the Western World,* vol. 2, quoted in Lunde, *A Warrior Dynasty,* 107.

209   *It included a chancery:* Roberts, "Gustav Adolf in Germany," *Essays in Swedish History,* 98–99; Roberts, *Gustavus Adolphus,* 155–56.

    took this outcome for granted: Roberts, "Gustav Adolf in Germany," *Essays in Swedish History,* 99.

210   *bellicum et politicum:* Roberts, "Gustav Adolf in Germany," 99–100; Roberts, *Gustavus Adolphus,* 164.

    His factories and estates: Geoff Mortimer, *Wallenstein: The Enigma of the Thirty Years' War* (London: Palgrave and Macmillan, 2010).

    "*Where's your king?*": Quoted in Wedgewood, *The Thirty Years War,* 305.

211   *received a kiss from:* Wedgewood, *The Thirty Years War,* 307.

    leaving four thousand: Lunde, *A Warrior Dynasty,* 147.

212   "*God is with us*": Quoted in Walter Harte, *The History of the Life of Gustavus Adolphus, King of Sweden* (London: G. Hawkins, 1859), 335.

213   *their king had fallen:* Lunde, *A Warrior Dynasty,* 159–60.

    "*He thinks the ship cannot*": Quoted in Wedgewood, *The Thirty Years War,* 319.

214   "*would have to be placed*": Quoted in Lunde, *A Warrior Dynasty,* 174.

    The change in mood: Rabb, *Struggle for Stability,* 68, 79.

215   *evolution of modern warfare:* Howard, *War in European History,* 61: Roberts, "Gustav Adolf and the Art of War," *Essays in Swedish History,* 74–75.

    "*the king among kings*": Quoted in Wedgewood, *The Thirty Years War,* 269.

9. SCANDINAVIANS INTO AMERICANS

217   "*We recall with gladness*": Quoted in Theodore Blegen, *Land of Their Choice: Immigrants Write Home* (Minneapolis: University of Minnesota Press, 1955), 203, 379.

218   *half the money for:* Adolph Benson and Naboth Hedin, *Americans from Sweden* (Philadelphia: Lippincott, 1950), 23.

219   *they had enough goods:* Benson and Hedin, *Americans from Sweden,* 27.

    "*A remarkably beautiful country*": Quoted in Benson and Hedin, *Americans from Sweden,* 30.

    a single black slave: Benson and Hedin, *Americans from Sweden,* 33.

220   *the "lost colony":* H. Arnold Barton, *The Old Country and the New: Essays on Swedes and America* (Carbondale: Southern Illinois University Press, 2007), 9.

221   *Sweden was no longer:* Herman, *To Rule the Waves,* 367; Derry, *History of Scandinavia,* 203.

    able to wrest control: T. K. Derry, *A History of Modern Norway* (Oxford: Clarendon Press, 1973), 15–16.

222   *the surge in population:* Derry, *History of Scandinavia,* 225.

    the rural working poor: Derry, *History of Scandinavia,* 225–26.

    life in a strange land: For example, Arthur Herman, *How the Scots Invented the Modern World* (New York: Crown Books, 2001), 198–99.

223   *a spiritual depth:* Dorothy Burton Skardal, *The Divided Heart: Scandinavian*

Immigrant Experience Through Literary Sources (Lincoln: University of Nebraska Press, 1974), 110.

224 *he gave his name:* Brian Andersson, "The Bronx, a Swedish Connection," *Ancestry Magazine* 16, no. 4 (1998): 36–41.

a church of its own: George Nielsen, *The Danish Americans* (Boston: Twayne Publishers, 1981), 52–53.

relative freedom of America: Helge Rønnow, "Danish Moravian Mission," from *Brødremenigheden — en levende tradition,* side 77 f; Published by Savanne, 1980 (www.bdm-dk.dk).

225 *baron from Pomerania:* Benson and Hedin, *Americans from Sweden,* 60.

set off for America: Henry J. Cadbury, "The Norwegian Quakers of 1825," *Harvard Theological Review* 18, no. 4 (1925): 293–319.

"A Viking who was born": Alfred Hauge, *The True Saga of Cleng Peerson* (Dallas: Special Projects Committee, Norwegian Society of Texas, 1982), 8.

226 *what was awaiting them:* Ingrid Semmingsen, *Norway to America: A History of the Migration* (Minneapolis: University of Minnesota Press, 1978), 17.

"God had never forbidden": Quoted in Kendric Babcock, *The Scandinavian Element in the United States* (1914; New York: Arno Press, 1969), 30.

227 *carried Swedish iron ore:* B. Boëthius, "Swedish Iron and Steel, 1600–1955," *Scandinavian Economic History Review* 6, no. 2 (1958): 144–75.

aristocrat in their midst: Babcock, *Scandinavian Element,* 52.

228 *"Like a flock of frightened":* Quoted in Benson and Hedin, *Americans from Sweden,* 94.

Jamestown became the largest: Benson and Hedin, *Americans from Sweden,* 92, 93–95.

Jansson had taught: Benson and Hedin, *Americans from Sweden,* 107; Barton, *The Old Country,* 31–33.

229 *sixty acres of land:* Benson and Hedin, *Americans from Sweden,* 106.

"I take now pen": Quoted in Barton, *The Old Country,* 35.

230 *formally disbanded:* Benson and Hedin, *Americans from Sweden,* 112–13.

231 *biggest in San Francisco:* Rudolph M. Lapp, *Blacks in Gold Rush California* (New Haven, CT: Yale University Press, 1977), 10; http://www.sfmuseum.net/bio /leidesdorff.html.

quantities of gold: Nielsen, *Danish Americans,* 156–58.

232 *Less than 10 percent:* Nielsen, *Danish Americans,* 61.

single largest Danish-born: Nielsen, *Danish Americans,* 59.

233 *the quickest to assimilate:* S. F. Jorgensen, L. Schering, and N. P. Stilling, *From Scandinavia to America* (Odense: University Press of Southern Denmark, 1987), 24.

took more than ninety: Nielsen, *Danish Americans,* 68–69.

houses in Navajo country: Nielsen, *Danish Americans,* 67–69.

234 *"covered with buffalo grass":* Quoted in Howard Shaff and Audrey Karl Shaff, *Six Wars at a Time: The Life and Times of Gutzon Borglum, Sculptor of Mount Rushmore* (Sioux Falls, SD: The Center for Western Studies, 1985), 11.

"The first thing I remember": Quoted in Shaff and Shaff, *Six Wars at a Time,* 21.

235 *their cozy welcome:* Semmingsen, *Norway to America*, 74.

236 *a cholera outbreak:* Semmingsen, *Norway to America*, 76.

"A great many are lying": Quoted in Lars Ljungmark, *Swedish Exodus* (Carbondale: Southern Illinois University Press, 1979), 4–5.

"the noble thought": Quoted in Semmingsen, *Norway to America*, 51.

237 *praised the new land:* Semmingsen, *Norway to America*, 32–33, 51.

nine-tenths of them: Ljungmark, *Swedish Exodus*, 11; Jerry Rosholt, *Ole Goes to War: Men from Norway Who Fought in America's Civil War* (Decorah, IA: Vesterheim Norwegian-American Museum, 2003), 22–23.

"So we rowed up": Quoted in Theodore Blegen, *Norwegian Migration to America* (1940; New York: Haskell House Publishers, 1969), 9.

built no fewer than six: Blegen, *Land of Their Choice*, 9, 13.

Thirty to sixty dollars: Rosholt, *Ole Goes to War*, 26.

238 *a ship from Arendal:* Blegen, *Land of Their Choice*, 20.

"It brought them a": Quoted in Skardal, *Divided Heart*, 78.

"filled with rafts of logs": Quoted in Blegen, *Land of Their Choice*, 378.

239 *"a tall, powerful young":* Quoted in Blegen, *Land of Their Choice*, 376–77.

a new wave had come: Blegen, *Land of Their Choice*, 492–93.

10. "WE ARE COMING, FATHER ABRAHAM": SCANDINAVIANS IN THE AMERICAN CIVIL WAR

240 *"That which we learned":* Quoted in Theodore Blegen, ed., *The Civil War Letters of Colonel Hans Christian Heg* (1936; Northfield, MN: Minnesota Historical Society Press, n.d.), 23.

241 *"with men and money":* Bruce Catton, *The Coming Fury* (1961; New York: Fall River Press, 2009), 268–69.

inspired J. A. Johnson: Blegen, *Civil War Letters*, 20–21.

242 *was not until 1858:* Derry, *History of Modern Norway*, 76–77.

early as April 1861: Blegen, *Civil War Letters*, 20.

those who signed up: Benson and Hedin, *Americans from Sweden*, 76–77, 158.

243 *"The government of our":* Quoted in Blegen, *Civil War Letters*, 23.

244 *born Iver Jacobsen Sorlie:* Myra Jenson Sorlie, *Sorlie: A Family History* (privately printed, n.d.), 1–2.

"perhaps the most versatile": Quoted in Sorlie, *A Family History*, 12–13.

245 *recruits from Illinois:* Rosholt, *Ole Goes to War*, 39.

Clausen's Guards: Blegen, *Civil War Letters*, 25.

246 *"God knows what kind":* Quoted in Skardal, *Divided Heart*, 93.

"Den Gang Jed Drog": Rosholt, *Ole Goes to War*, 43.

247 *Jansson's own son, Eric:* Benson and Hedin, *Americans from Sweden*, 121–22.

was born in Värmland: James T. deKay, *Monitor: The Story of the Legendary Civil*

War Ironclad and the Man Whose Invention Changed the Course of History (New York: Ballantine Books, 1997), 9–10.

248 *technological revolution:* Herman, *To Rule the Waves,* 449–50.

249 *navy brass ignored it:* deKay, Monitor, 19.

to build a prototype: deKay, Monitor, 21–22.

"a semi-globular turret": deKay, Monitor, 28–29.

French emperor's response: deKay, Monitor, 26, 27.

250 *"No craft that ever":* Quoted in deKay, Monitor, 78.

single most difficult: deKay, Monitor, 86.

251 *nicknamed "soda bottles":* Robert Schneller, *Quest for Glory: A Biography of Rear Admiral John A. Dahlgren* (Annapolis: Naval Institute Press, 1995).

252 *almost disappointed:* deKay, Monitor, 91–92.

for underwater toilets: deKay, Monitor, 112.

253 *"I never saw a vessel":* Quoted in deKay, Monitor, 141.

most powerful warships: Bruce Catton, *Terrible Swift Sword* (1963; New York: Fall River Press, 2009), 209–10.

254 *steaming up the Potomac:* Catton, *Terrible Swift Sword,* 210.

"a huge, half-submerged": deKay, Monitor, 164.

"He saw more of the": John Quarstein, *The* Monitor *Boys: The Crew of the Union's First Ironclad* (Charleston, SC: The History Press, 2011), 295.

255 *Congressional Medal of Honor:* Quarstein, Monitor *Boys,* 296–97.

photograph after the battle: Rosholt, *Ole Goes to War,* 28–29.

Norwegian-born men: Rosholt, *Ole Goes to War,* 89.

256 *nearly seventy-five men:* Rosholt, *Ole Goes to War,* 41.

"He always calls me Heck": Letter of November 2, 1862, in Blegen, *Civil War Letters,* 152.

"Eleven years ago": Letter of December 11, 1862, in Blegen, *Civil War Letters,* 154.

"I hope you will not": Letter of December 25, 1862, in Blegen, *Civil War Letters,* 158.

257 *"under the heaviest fire":* Letter of January 6, 1863, in Blegen, *Civil War Letters,* 165.

"two solid volleys": Blegen, *Civil War Letters,* 165.

"Don't you know we": Sorlie, *A Family History,* 18.

258 *streamed toward the rear:* Bruce Catton, *Never Call Retreat* (1965; New York: Fall River Press, 2009), 41.

"Lt. Col. McKee fell here": Blegen, *Civil War Letters,* 166.

"the Rebels came pouring": Blegen, *Civil War Letters,* 166.

eighty-five killed or wounded: Catton, *Never Call Retreat,* 45–46; Blegen, *Civil War Letters,* 166, 169.

259 *invalided out of the army:* Sorlie, *A Family History,* 19–22.

260 *"The rebels are in":* Letter of September 18, 1863, Blegen, *Civil War Letters,* 245.

"I was glad the Fifteenth": Blegen, *Civil War Letters,* 41.

261 *including forty-nine soldiers:* Rosholt, *Ole Goes to War,* 48–49.

"a braver man than General": Benson and Hedin, *Americans from Sweden,* 131–33.

262 *"Lincoln said the dream":* Catton, *Never Call Retreat,* 457.

11. "MORE WONDERFUL THAN RICHES":
AMERICAN FEVER AND THE GREAT MIGRATION

263 *"Farewell, O Mother":* Quoted in Skardal, *Divided Heart,* 270.

the Swedish Great Migration: Barton, *The Old Country,* 54.

Norwegian immigration: Martin Ulvestad, *Norwegians in America, Their History and Record,* trans. Olaf Tronsen Kringhaug and Odd-Steinar Dybvad Raneng (1907; Waukon, IA: Astri My Astri Publishing, 2012); Derry, *History of Modern Norway,* 216.

264 The next two decades: Nielsen, *Danish Americans,* 32.

to more than a third: Odd Lovoll, *The Promise of America: A History of Norwegian-American People* (Minneapolis: University of Minnesota Press, 1984), 35.

265 some fifty thousand left: Kristian Hvidt, *Danes Go West: A Book About the Emigration to America* (Denmark: Rebild National Park Society, 1976), 158.

"All through the winter": Siri Lee, "Amerikarise I 1866," *Samband* 69 (1914): 130–34, quoted in Blegen, *Norwegian Migration to America,* 7.

"We harbor no hopes": Quoted in Lovoll, *Promise of America,* 72.

266 the pre–Civil War era: Lloyd Hustvedt, *Rasmus Björn Anderson: Pioneer Scholar* (Northfield, MN: Norwegian-American Historical Association, 1966), 13; Semmingsen, *Norway to America,* 65.

the issue of slavery: Hustvedt, *Rasmus Björn Anderson,* 47–49.

267 *"the myth is the oldest":* Hustvedt, *Rasmus Björn Anderson,* 318–19.

"Live for truth and": Quoted in Hustvedt, *Rasmus Björn Anderson,* 82–83.

268 *"to present the reader":* R. B. Anderson, *America Not Discovered by Columbus* (1891 edition, n.p.; London: Forgotten Books, 2012), 35.

"Let us remember": Anderson, *America Not Discovered,* 93.

269 as many as twenty-one: Hustvedt, *Rasmus Björn Anderson,* 314.

within shouting distance: Anderson, *America Not Discovered,* 81–82; Hustvedt, *Rasmus Björn Anderson,* 312–13.

"Let us praise Leif": Anderson, *America Not Discovered,* 94.

270 *"Where now the western":* Anderson, *America Not Discovered,* 63, 94.

271 By 1875 every ship: Lovoll, *Promise of America,* 28.

"The result was that": Blegen, *Norwegian Migration to America,* 5.

272 *"If you have decided":* Holger Rosenberg, *100 nyttige Raad for Udvandrere* (*100 Pieces of Advice for Emigrants*) (Copenhagen: Tillge, 1911), 1, https://www.danishmuseum.org/pdfs/danish/100-pieces-of-advice.pdf.

273 contract labor arrangements: Otis Graham, *Regulating Immigration in the National Interest* (Cummer Hill, Oxford, UK: Rowman & Littlefield, 2001), 100.

"A Danish newspaper": Rosenberg, *100 nyttige Raad,* 11.

274 *"Travel home to old":* Rosenberg, *100 nyttige Raad,* 100.

"Dress warmly for": Rosenberg, *100 nyttige Raad,* 13.

as fine as a palace: Skardal, *Divided Heart,* 67.

275 herring for snacks: Skardal, *Divided Heart,* 67.

birth of the hamburger: Paul Kriwaczek, *Yiddish Civilisation: The Rise and Fall of a Forgotten Nation* (New York: Vintage, 2006), 311.

lubricated by vomit: Glen Seaborg, *Adventures in the Atomic Age: From Watts to Washington* (New York: Farrar, Straus and Giroux, 2001), 4.

276 *"They saw it not as"*: John Higham, *Send These to Me: Immigrants in Urban America* (1975; Baltimore: Johns Hopkins University Press, 1984), 75.

"this new divinity": Quoted in John Higham, *Send These to Me*, 75.

at Ellis Island: Lovoll, *Promise of America*, 39; Skardal, *Divided Heart*, 70.

their money ran out: Ljungmark, *Swedish Exodus*, 82.

"New York City itself": Skardal, *Divided Heart*, 73.

278 "In form how big": Quoted in Skardal, *Divided Heart*, 73.

service in the 1850s: Lovoll, *Promise of America*, 34; Ljungmark, *Swedish Exodus*, 62.

279 as big as elephants: Skardal, *Divided Heart*, 75.

"make a beeline": Quoted in Jon Gjerde and Carlton Qualey, *Norwegians in Minnesota* (Minneapolis: Minnesota Historical Society Press, 2002), 22.

"The loyalty of the Scandinavians": Babcock, *Scandinavian Element*, 111.

By 1893 one student: Babcock, *Scandinavian Element*, 112.

280 "one of the most densely": Gjerde and Qualey, *Norwegians in Minnesota*, 10–11.

281 "a round Puritan head": Quoted in Gjerde and Qualey, *Norwegians in Minnesota*, 26.

urban-oriented skills: Rosenberg, *100 nyttige Raad*, 79.

282 One writer remembered: Gjerde and Qualey, *Norwegians in Minnesota*, 30–31.

"The Norwegian exploitation": Blegen, *Norwegian Migration to America*, 504–5.

"We watched the [prairie]": Quoted in Blegen, *Norwegian Migration to America*, 506.

Native American tribes: "Gunlög Fur," "Indians and Immigrants — Entangled Histories," *Journal of American Ethnic History* 33, no. 3 (Spring 2014): 55–76.

283 was half Norwegian: Sorlie: *A Family History*, 103; Blegen, *Norwegian Migration to America*, 510.

"What a country, this": "Knut Hamsun's Early Years in the Northwest," *Minnesota History* 20, no. 4 (December 1939), 405.

however, an angry man: Skardal, *Divided Heart*, 51.

284 more than $150: Skardal, *Divided Heart*, 76.

285 shortage of Danish women: Nielsen, *Danish Americans*, 35–36.

"The sentiment of patriotism": Quoted in Nielsen, *Danish Americans*, ii.

"Half the store signs": Quoted in Skardal, *Divided Heart*, 79.

286 "one of the best": Babcock, *Scandinavian Element*, 111.

287 "If this process of leveling": Quoted in Skardal, *Divided Heart*, 110.

"There is a middle way": Quoted in Skardal, *Divided Heart*, 103.

289 He slept in doorways: J. Riis, *The Making of an American* (1901; Project Gutenberg, 2005), Chapter 3.

Riis's fortunes suddenly: Luc Sante, Introduction, in Jacob Riis, *How the Other Half Lives* (1890; New York: Penguin Books, 1979), xvii.

by trial and error: Riis, *Making of an American*, 174.

291 with C. S. Peirce: Herman, *The Cave and the Light*, 521.

292 *"workmanship is"*: Charles Camic and Geoffrey Hodgson, eds., *Essential Writings of Thorstein Veblen* (London: Routledge, 2011), 554.

"a disposition to do": Camic and Hodgson, *Writings of Thorstein Veblen*, 555.

"shows at its best": Camic and Hodgson, *Writings of Thorstein Veblen*, 555, 558.

293 *"The instinct of workmanship"*: Camic and Hodgson, *Writings of Thorstein Veblen*, 557; 550.

294 *key to all his thinking:* Tom Veblen, *Imagining an Inland Empire: And Other Myths of Endeavor* (privately printed, 2018), 64.

12. LAND OF WONDERS: HOW TWO SCANDINAVIAN ICONS TRANSFORMED JAZZ AGE AMERICA

295 *"Choose any American"*: Alexis de Tocqueville, *Democracy in America*, ed. J. P. Mayer, trans. G. Lawrence (New York: Doubleday, 1969), 401.

"the world must be": Quoted in Arthur Herman, *1917: Lenin, Wilson, and the Birth of the New World Disorder* (New York: HarperCollins, 2017), 149.

296 *"We have needed the new"*: Randolph Bourne, "Trans-National America," *Atlantic Monthly,* July 1916.

became "Liberty steak": Herman, *1917,* 245–46.

297 *"We are strangers to"*: Quoted in Skardal, *Divided Heart,* 328.

among American Progressives: Herman, *Idea of Decline,* 182–84.

298 *"God damn the continent"*: Quoted in Paul Johnson, *Modern Times: The World from the Twenties to the Eighties* (New York: Harper and Row, 1983), 215.

denounced the Scandinavian: Higham, *Send These to Me,* 56.

299 *"something which does not"*: Tocqueville, *Democracy in America,* 406.

"a land of wonders": Tocqueville, *Democracy in America,* 407.

buggy maker to royalty: Jerry Brondfield, *Knute Rockne: The Coach, the Man, the Legend* (New York: Bison Books, 2009), 36.

300 *a small Norwegian colony:* Lovoll, *Promise of America,* 48.

only sixth or seventh: Babcock, *Scandinavian Element,* 73.

the Chicago Daily News: Brondfield, *Knute Rockne,* 36.

301 *"the face of a battered"*: Quoted in Michael Bohn, *Heroes and Ballyhoo: How the Golden Age of the 1920s Transformed American Sports* (Washington, DC: Potomac Books, 2009), 147.

Rockne later recalled that: Brondfield, *Knute Rockne,* 39.

302 *announced to his family:* Brondfield, *Knute Rockne,* 42.

the competitive sport: John J. Miller, *The Big Scrum: How Teddy Roosevelt Saved Football* (New York: Harper Perennial, 2012).

303 *"Win this one for"*: Bohn, *Heroes and Ballyhoo,* 142.

most famous photos: Brondfield, *Knute Rockne,* 122–23.

304 *"I try to make every"*: Quoted in Brondfield, *Knute Rockne,* 83, 159.

"We knew he knew": Quoted in Brondfield, *Knute Rockne,* 158.

"He had us on our": Quoted in Brondfield, *Knute Rockne,* 159.

305 *"a national loss":* Quoted in the *New York Times,* April 2, 1931.

306 *he rigged up a special:* A. Scott Berg, *Lindbergh* (New York: Putnam, 1996), 14.

307 *Norwegian-born politician:* Wisconsin Historical Society, https://www
.wisconsinhistory.org/Records/Article/CS8559.

sudden death in 1909: Benson and Hedin, *Americans from Sweden,* 261.

308 *would have recognized:* Minnesota Historical Society's Governors of Minnesota
http://collections.mnhs.org/governors/index.php/10004150.

The exemption has lasted: Biographical Directory of the Congress of the United States,
http://bioguide.congress.gov/scripts/biodisplay.pl?index=v000114.

bootlegger's crime spree: Benson and Hedin, *Americans from Sweden,* 263.

309 *It was even said:* Lovoll, *Promise of America,* 193.

the highest office in: Biographical Directory of the Congress of the United States
Congress, http://bioguide.congress.gov/scripts/biodisplay.pl?index=l000241; Benson
and Hedin, *Americans from Sweden,* 268–69.

"If everything goes well": Benson and Hedin, *Americans from Sweden,* 267.

310 *"a Swede who dreams":* Quoted in Berg, *Lindbergh,* 35.

many Nordic Americans: Herman, *1917,* 152.

"driven from one town": H. Salisbury, quoted in Berg, *Lindbergh,* 45.

311 *a 2-to-1 margin:* Berg, *Lindbergh,* 50.

"If you are for America": Quoted in Berg, *Lindbergh,* 49.

312 *"vaguely outlined forms":* Berg, *Lindbergh,* 124.

313 *"I was astonished at":* Quoted in Berg, *Lindbergh,* 136.

Fog, Snowstorm, and Sleep: Berg, *Lindbergh,* 150–51.

"for the second time": Berg, *Lindbergh,* 243.

314 *emotional cliff-hanger:* Ludovic Kennedy, *The Airman and the Carpenter: The
Lindbergh Kidnapping and the Framing of Richard Hauptmann* (New York: Penguin
Books, 1986).

"I wonder why my": Quoted in Berg, *Lindbergh,* 10.

"as much as I disagree": Quoted in Berg, *Lindbergh,* 367.

first working helicopter: https://www.armedforcesmuseum.com/germanys-wwii-era
-focke-wulf-fw-61/.

315 *a secret meeting:* Arthur Herman, *Freedom's Forge: How American Business Produced
Victory in World War II* (New York: Random House, 2012), 289–91.

"I will never give": Quoted in Arthur Herman, *Joseph McCarthy: Reexamining
the Life and Legacy of America's Most Hated Senator* (New York: Free Press, 1999),
29.

the preservation of our: Quoted in Herman, *Joseph McCarthy,* 29.

"continuation of the old": Quoted in Berg, *Lindbergh,* 395.

316 *"The army meant so much":* Anne Morrow Lindbergh, *War Within and Without, 1939–
1944* (New York: Harcourt Brace Jovanovich, 1980), 159.

"their greatest danger": Quoted in Berg, *Lindbergh,* 427; Speech Delivered in Des Moines, September 11, 1941, at www.charleslindbergh.com.

317 *"Is Lindbergh a Nazi?":* Quoted in Berg, *Lindbergh,* 424, 428.
"I am not attacking": Quoted in Berg, *Lindbergh,* 427.
"to the same extent": Winston Groom, *The Aviators: Eddie Rickenbacker, Jimmy Doolittle, Charles Lindbergh, and the Epic Age of Flight* (Washington, DC: National Geographic, 2013), 299.

318 *For Charles, she wrote:* A. M. Lindbergh, *War Within and Without,* 220–25.

319 *"where the man Hitler":* Berg, *Lindbergh,* 464–65.
his growing fear: Herman, *Freedom's Forge,* 292–93.

320 *"Science, freedom, beauty":* Charles Lindbergh, *The Spirit of St. Louis* (New York: Scribners, 1953), 261.

13. MEN AT WORK: THE VIKING HEART AND AMERICAN DEMOCRACY

321 *"We can do anything":* Quoted in Herman, *Freedom's Forge,* 58.
"No civilized man": Shaff and Shaff, *Six Wars at a Time,* 108.

322 *"Gutzon believed the Jew":* Shaff and Shaff, *Six Wars at a Time,* 108.

323 Death of the Chief: Shaff and Shaff, *Six Wars at a Time,* 39–40.

324 *three more sculptures:* http://www.artcyclopedia.com/artists/borglum_gutzon.html.
an honorary member: Herman, *Idea of Decline,* 184.

325 *"He was one of those":* Felix Frankfurter, "Recollections," quoted in Shaff and Shaff, *Six Wars at a Time,* 88.
left Georgia for good: Shaff and Shaff, *Six Wars at a Time,* 215.

326 *"Would it be possible":* Quoted in Shaff and Shaff, *Six Wars at a Time,* 210.
"which I have had for": Shaff and Shaff, *Six Wars at a Time,* 212.

327 *the purchase agreement:* https://www.nps.gov/moru/learn/historyculture/the -entablature-idea.htm#:~:text=Original%20plans%20for%20the%20carving,%2C %20three%2Dfoot%20tall%20letters.

328 *death toll of ninety-six:* Herman, *Freedom's Forge,* 53.
"Of course what Hitler": Quoted in Shaff and Shaff, *Six Wars at a Time,* 350.
"There is one single": Quoted in Shaff and Shaff, *Six Wars at a Time,* 353.

329 *became a national hero: American National Biography,* vol. 12 (Oxford: Oxford University Press, 1999), 843; Norman Beasley, *Knudsen: A Biography* (1947; Roswell, GA: Canton Street Press, 2013), 1–2; Herman, *Freedom's Forge,* 16.

330 *interchangeable parts:* David Hounshell, *From the American System to Mass Production* (Baltimore: Johns Hopkins University Press, 1984), 222.
assembly line flow: Hounshell, *From the American System,* 224.

331 *automobile of choice:* Herman, *Freedom's Forge,* 31–32.
modification and change: Hounshell, *From the American System,* 266–67; Herman, *Freedom's Forge,* 33.

first phone call went: Herman, *Freedom's Forge,* 67.

332 *"I'm not a soldier":* Quoted in Herman, *Freedom's Forge,* 83.
war matériel worth: Richard Overy, *Why the Allies Won* (New York: W. W. Norton, 1995); Herman, *Freedom's Forge,* 336.

333 *make entire airplanes:* Herman, *Freedom's Forge,* 221; Charles E. Sorensen, *Forty Years with Ford* (New York: W. W. Norton, 1956), 280–82.
the long-range B-24s: Herman, *Freedom's Forge,* 243–44.

334 *Operation Warp Speed:* "Politics, Science and the Remarkable Race for a Coronavirus Vaccine," November 22, 2020, https://www.nytimes.com/2020/11/21/us/politics/coronavirus-vaccine.html.
I and others invoked: Compare Arthur Herman, "Make America the Medicine Chest of the World," *Wall Street Journal,* March 20, 2020.
his Swedish Bible: Carl Sandburg, *All the Young Strangers* (1953; New York: Harcourt Brace Jovanovich, 1981), 19.

335 *"De tar en poijke":* Penelope Niven, *Carl Sandburg: A Biography* (New York: Charles Scribner's, 1991), 3–4.
"the calluses inside": Sandburg, *Strangers,* 18.
"in the old country": Sandburg, *Strangers,* 16.

336 *"The trees stood out":* North Callahan, *Carl Sandburg: Lincoln of Our Literature* (New York: New York University Press, 1970), 17.
"The Civil War was": Quoted in Sandburg, *Strangers,* 25; Niven, *Carl Sandburg,* 4.
"He is blowing out": Quoted in Callahan, *Carl Sandburg,* 23.
"I read [those words]": Carl Sandburg, *Prairie Town Boy* (New York: Harcourt, Brace, and World, 1953), 135–36.

337 *"A man was building":* Quoted in Callahan, *Carl Sandburg,* 43.

338 *"If it were possible":* Quoted in Callahan, *Carl Sandburg,* 41.

339 *"The damp air chilled":* Quoted in Callahan, *Carl Sandburg,* 89.

340 *650 pages each:* Callahan, *Carl Sandburg,* 119.
"famous flyer who has": Quoted in Niven, *Carl Sandburg,* 546.

342 *a life of Jesus:* Niven, *Carl Sandburg,* 689, 699.
"Lincoln arose before": Alfred Kazin, *On Native Grounds* (1942; New York: Harcourt Brace, 1982), 508.

343 *"Life is a river":* Quoted in Niven, *Carl Sandburg,* 703.
"a landscape at once": Charles Mann, *The Wizard and the Prophet: Two Remarkable Scientists and Their Dueling Visions to Shape Tomorrow's World* (New York: Knopf, 2018), 97.
"The new arrivals built": Mann, *Wizard and Prophet,* 98.

344 *northeastern Iowa chose corn:* Noel Vietmeyer, *Borlaug, Volume 1: Right Off the Farm, 1914–1944* (Lorton, VA: Bracing Books, 2009) 1, 17–18.
"I was born in that era": Quoted in Vietmeyer, *Borlaug,* vol. 1, 75; 74.
"That was true hell": Quoted in Vietmeyer, *Borlaug,* vol. 1, 35.

345 *collections of poems, Cornhuskers:* Vietmeyer, *Borlaug,* vol. 1, 78.
their parent strains: Mann, *Wizard and Prophet,* 122–24.

346 *results were spectacular:* Mann, *Wizard and Prophet,* 154.
     "Ours is the first": Quoted in Mann, *Wizard and Prophet,* 155.
347 *"Not just poor, but":* Quoted in Mann, *Wizard and Prophet,* 440; 438.
     "gives more people": Quoted in Niven, *Carl Sandburg,* 547.

14. THE VIKING HEART COMES HOME

348 *"Yes, you sons":* N.F.S. Grundtvig, Foreword, *Scandinavian Mythology* (1832), quoted in
     Bruce Kirmmse, *Kierkegaard in Golden Denmark* (Bloomington: Indiana University
     Press, 1990), 223.
349 *language of government:* Derry, *History of Scandinavia,* 237; Taylor, *Bismarck,* 70.
     an international crisis: Neil Kent, *The Soul of the North* (London: Reaktion Books,
     2000), 243.
350 *standstill the next day:* Tom Buk-Swienty, *1864: The Forgotten War That Shaped
     Modern Europe,* trans. Annette Buk-Swienty (London: Profile Books, 2015),
     19–20.
     more than five thousand: Buk-Swienty, *1864,* 311.
     farther west, to America: Kent, *Soul of the North,* 246.
351 *Norway's prime minister:* Derry, *History of Scandinavia,* 246–47.
     written stirring pamphlets: Derry, *History of Scandinavia,* 248.
352 *took them to his house:* "Golden Horns of Gallehus," https://traffickingculture.org
     /encyclopedia/case-studies/golden-horns-of-gallehus/.
353 *the modern age had lost:* Arthur Beer, "Hartner and the Riddle of the Golden Horns,"
     Journal for the History of Astronomy 1 (1970): 139.
     one of the first to see: Sawyer, *Illustrated History,* 234–35.
     a forgery and a fake: Herman, *How the Scots Invented the Modern World,* 249–51.
354 *"Ye days long past":* Adam Oehlenschlager, "The Golden Horns," trans. George Borrow
     (London: privately printed, 1913), 10–14.
355 *Geatish (or Gothic, in English) Society:* Sawyer, *Illustrated History,* 236.
     Norse goddess Idunn: Snorri Sturluson, *The Prose Edda,* trans. Jesse Byock (New York:
     Penguin Books, 2005), 6.
     entire suburban district: Patrick Kingsley, *How to Be Danish: A Journey to the Cultural
     Heart of Denmark* (New York: Marble Arch Press, 2012), 24.
     "matchless discovery": Kirmmse, *Kierkegaard in Golden Denmark,* 221.
356 *enemy of papal Rome:* Kent, *Soul of the North,* 60.
     "We are one people": https://www.facebook.com/1313736618667054/posts/hans
     -christian-andersens-poem-i-am-a-scandinavianjeg-er-en-skandinavwe-are-one-p
     /1317199228320793/.
357 *"The German language":* Quoted in Kent, *Soul of the North,* 245.
     The twin discoveries: Derry, *History of Modern Norway,* 136–71.

358 *"Already in Dresden":* Quoted in Introduction, *The Saga of the Volsungs,* trans. Jesse Byock (New York: Penguin Books, 1999), 2.
"Although the glorious": Quoted in H. F. Garten, *Wagner the Dramatist* (Totowa, NJ: Rowan and Littlefield, 1977), 81, 80.

359 *"with restless activity":* Der Niebelungen-Mythus, quoted in Garten, *Wagner the Dramatist,* 82.

360 *vanguard of world revolution:* Compare Herman, *Idea of Decline,* 72; Garten, *Wagner the Dramatist,* 84.
not being radical enough: Herman, *Idea of Decline,* 74–75.
"Any attempt to tell": Charles Morris, *The Aryan Race: Its Origins and Its Achievements* (Chicago: S. C. Griggs and Company, 1888), v.
"the Scandinavian scheme": Morris, *The Aryan Race,* 229.

361 *"Their existence is a crime":* Quoted in Herman, *Idea of Decline,* 72.
through the Thule Society: David Luhrssen, *Hammer of the Gods: The Thule Society and the Birth of Nazism* (Dulles, VA: Potomac Books, 2012); Nicholas Goodrick-Clarke, *The Occult Roots of Nazism: The Ariosophists of Austria and Germany, 1890–1935* (New York: New York University Press, 1992).

362 *"The hour of freedom":* Quoted in Arnold Barton, *A Folk Divided: Homeland Swedes and Swedish-Americans, 1840–1940* (Carbondale, IL: University of Southern Illinois Press, 1994), 152.
commission's recommendations: Barton, *A Folk Divided,* 153–54; Derry, *History of Scandinavia,* 252–53.
had the sixth highest: Nima Sanandaji, *Scandinavian Unexceptionalism: Culture, Markets, and the Failure of Third-Way Socialism* (London: Institute of Economic Affairs, 2015), 16, 18.

363 *experienced faster growth:* Nima Sanandaji, *Debunking Utopia: Exposing the Myth of Nordic Socialism* (Washington, DC: WND Books, 2016), 88.

364 *outside the laboratory:* Kenne Fant, *Alfred Nobel: A Biography,* trans. Marianne Ruuth (New York: Arcade Publishing, 1993), 78.
a global enterprise: Daniel Yergin, *The Prize: The Epic Quest for Oil, Money, and Power* (New York: Free Press, 1992), 58–60.

365 *"the merchant of death":* Quoted in Fant, *Alfred Nobel,* 207.
"has done the most": Quoted in Fant, *Alfred Nobel,* 310.

366 *"A more humane way":* Quoted in Fant, *Alfred Nobel,* 312.
like Roald Amundsen: Stephen Brown, *The Last Viking: The Life of Roald Amundsen* (New York: Da Capo, 2013).

367 *"Our ancestors, the old":* Fridtjof Nansen, *Farthest North* (New York: Harper Brothers, 1897), 3.
the seal-hunting ship Jason: Fridtjof Nansen, *The First Crossing of Greenland* (London: Longmans, 1919), 72.

368 *from the North Pole:* Nansen, *Farthest North,* passim.

"Never in my life": Quoted in E. E. Reynolds, *Nansen* (Harmondsworth, UK: Penguin Books, 1949), 221.

369 *"The human mind"*: Frederick Stang, Nobel Prize Ceremony Speech, 1922, https://www.nobelprize.org/prizes/peace/1922/ceremony-speech/.

370 *"Every good cause"*: Quoted in Reynolds, *Nansen,* 276.

371 *more Swedes arrived:* Ljungmark, *Swedish Exodus,* 13.
   determining policy: Derry, *History of Scandinavia,* 265–67.

372 *a royal crown prince:* Marquis Childs, *Sweden: The Middle Way* (New Haven, CT: Yale University Press, 1936), 6.
   "If the test of the good": Childs, *Sweden,* xvi.
   "A European war": E. D. Simon, *The Smaller Democracies* (London: Victor Gollancz, 1939), 191.

15. THE VIKING HEART IN WAR AND PEACE

373 *"A people who submissively"*: Quoted in Geirr Haarr, *The German Invasion of Norway, April 1940* (Annapolis, MD: Naval Institute Press, 2012), 177.

374 *Finnish, not Russian:* Derry, *History of Scandinavia,* 218–19; 232–34.
   crossing the Finnish border: William Trotter, *Frozen Hell: The Russo-Finnish War of 1939–40* (Chapel Hill, NC: Algonquin Books, 1991), 3.

375 *Molotovin koktaili:* Gordon Sander, *The Hundred-Day Winter War* (Lawrence: University Press of Kansas, 2013), 131–32.
   the hero of the war: Sander, *Hundred-Day Winter War,* 46–47.

376 *lost only 900 soldiers:* Trotter, *Frozen Hell,* 169–70.

377 *"NOW THE WORLD KNOWS"*: Quoted in Trotter, *Frozen Hell,* 195.
   Fifteen hundred Norwegian: Derry, *History of Scandinavia,* 332.
   but only five made it: Trotter, *Frozen Hell,* 198.

378 *"Soldiers! I have fought"*: Quoted in Sander, *Hundred-Day Winter War,* 331–32.
   "It is a great comfort": Quoted in Hans Fredrik Dahl, *Quisling: A Study in Treachery,* trans. Anne-Marie Stanon-Ife (Cambridge, UK: Cambridge University Press, 1999), 67.

379 *tough to achieve:* "Birger Eriksen" in *Norsk Biographisk Leksikon,* https://nbl.snl.no/Birger_Eriksen.

380 *"Either I will be decorated"*: https://web.archive.org/web/20081016061047/http://www.lofotenkrigmus.no/april2.htm.

381 *aid in repelling them:* George Lukacs, *The Duel, 10 May–31 July 1940: The Eighty-Day Struggle Between Churchill and Hitler* (New York: Ticknor and Fields, 1990), 31–32.

382 *fate as the unwilling partners:* Bo Lidegaard, *Countrymen: How Denmark's Jews Escaped the Nazis,* trans. Robert Maas (New York: Atlantic Books, 2013), 17–18.
   Germans tried three times: Ole Guldager, *Americans in Greenland in World War Two,* Greenland Historical Series, vol. 2 (Arhus: Arctic Sun, 2019), 45–46.
   the only way forward: W. Carlgren, *Swedish Foreign Policy Between the World Wars,* trans. Arthur Spencer (New York: St. Martin's Press, 1977), 61–62.

383 *"A small state on":* Carlgren, *Swedish Foreign Policy,* 65.

a combined GDP: A. Tooze, *The Wages of Destruction: The Making and Breaking of the Nazi Economy* (New York: Penguin Books, 2006), 383.

more than 83 percent: Tooze, *Wages of Destruction,* 380–81.

384 *killed in the death camps:* Lidegaard, *Countrymen,* 23.

385 *Den Norske Legion:* Kathleen Stokker, *Folklore Fights the Nazis: Humor in Occupied Norway, 1940–1945* (Madison: University of Wisconsin Press, 1997), 105.

"NS has so many": Quoted in Stokker, *Folklore Fights,* 126.

765 Norwegian Jews died: Lidegaard, *Countrymen,* 36–37.

900 were smuggled out: Dahl, *Quisling,* 287.

386 *"The Mailman":* Neal Bascomb, *The Winter Fortress: The Epic Mission to Sabotage Hitler's Atomic Bomb* (New York: Houghton Mifflin Harcourt, 2016), 27–29.

387 *the rank of captain:* Bascomb, *Winter Fortress,* 43.

388 *just the sort of man:* Knut Haukelid, *Skis Against the Nazis* (1954; Minot, ND: North American Heritage Press, 1989).

the Kompagnie Linge: Bascomb, *Winter Fortress,* 48.

389 *Churchill and FDR:* Bascomb, *Winter Fortress,* 67–69.

"The fate of the world": William Stevenson, *A Man Called Intrepid: The Secret War* (New York: Harcourt Brace Jovanovich, 1976), 422.

390 *they were all shot:* Bascomb, *Winter Fortress,* 116–17, 119–23.

"a feeling of comradeship": Haukelid, *Skis Against Nazis,* 15.

"While I hung in the air": Haukelid, *Skis Against Nazis,* 82.

391 *"Any man about to be":* Quoted in Stevenson, *Intrepid,* 426.

"The Germans considered": Haukelid, *Skis Against Nazis,* 100.

392 *had been a failure:* Haukelid, *Skis Against Nazis,* 112–13.

the deepwater lake: Bascomb, *Winter Fortress,* 306.

393 *"if it had not been for":* Quoted in Stevenson, *Intrepid,* 427.

394 *by the end of 1943:* Bascomb, *Winter Fortress,* 320.

Himmler's secret police: Tooze, *Wages of Destruction,* 603.

turn Finnish forces loose: Derry, *History of Scandinavia,* 349.

395 *training "police cadets":* Derry, *History of Scandinavia,* 348.

"if Denmark embarked on": Quoted in Lidegaard, *Countrymen,* 11.

396 *"One does not want":* Quoted in Lidegaard, *Countrymen,* 13.

397 *"Against Divine and Human":* Quoted in Lidegaard, *Countrymen,* 221.

very little to gain: Lidegaard, *Countrymen,* 234, 362.

"The way in which": Lidegaard, *Countrymen,* 363.

398 *the spring of 1944:* Per Anger, *With Raoul Wallenberg in Budapest,* trans. David Mel Paul and Margareta Paul (New York: Holocaust Press, 1981), 21.

399 *temporary visas to Sweden:* Anger, *With Raoul Wallenberg,* 40–41.

"I am going to leave": Quoted in Frederick Werbell and Thurston Clarke, *Lost Hero: The Mystery of Raoul Wallenberg* (New York: McGraw-Hill, 1982), 25.

400 *"This revolver is just":* Quoted in Anger, *With Raoul Wallenberg,* 50.

powerful diplomatic weapon: Anger, *With Raoul Wallenberg,* 50–51.

401 *buildings in Budapest:* Anger, *With Raoul Wallenberg,* 67.
     prevent the slaughter: Anger, *With Raoul Wallenberg,* 92–93.
     "Sure it gets me a little": Quoted in Anger, *With Raoul Wallenberg,* 86.
     never saw Wallenberg: Anger, *With Raoul Wallenberg,* 86.
402 *remains a mystery:* Werbell and Clarke, *Lost Hero,* passim.
403 *More than half of them:* Derry, *History of Scandinavia,* 339, 353.
     Denmark's until 1965: Walter Lacquer, *Europe Since Hitler* (New York: Pelican Books,
     1971), 230.
404 *"High levels of trust":* Sanandaji, *Debunking Utopia,* 54.
     Likewise, poverty levels: Sanandaji, *Debunking Utopia,* 63–65.
     edge out Norwegians: Sanandaji, *Debunking Utopia,* 62.
405 *consensus-driven politics:* Sanandaji, *Scandinavian Unexceptionalism,* 112–13.
     intrigue yet also baffle: e.g., https://www.healthcareitnews.com/news/europe/covid-19
     -lessons-nordics.

CONCLUSION:
THE VIKING HEART AND THE LAND BEYOND

406 *"Happiness is the struggle":* Rectorial Address at St. Andrews University, November 3,
     1926, in Fridtjof Nansen, *Adventure and Other Papers* (London: Hogarth Press, 1927).
407 *exclusivist racist assumptions:* Richards, *Blood of the Vikings.*
409 *Pierre Manent and Yoram Hazony:* Pierre Manent, *A World Beyond Politics?: A Defense
     of the Nation-State* (New French Thought Series), trans. Marc LePain (Princeton:
     Princeton University Press, 2006); Yoram Hazony, *The Virtue of Nationalism* (New
     York: Basic Books, 2018).
     "What I'm sure about": Quoted in "How Nationalism Can Solve the Crisis of Islam,"
     Wall Street Journal, 5-27/8-2018.
410 *"The earliest definition":* Sebastian Junger, *Tribe: On Homecoming and Belonging* (New
     York: Twelve, 2016), 110.
     the Viking "tribal" legacy: Ryan Smith, *The Way of Fire and Ice: The Living Tradition of
     Norse Paganism* (Woodbury, MN: Llewellyn Publications, 2019), esp. 161–67.
412 *so-called Viking Club:* Gloriana St. Clair, "An Overview of the Northern Influences
     on Tolkien's Works," Proceedings of the J.R.R. Tolkien Centenary Conference,
     Keble College, Oxford, 1992 (Pittsburgh, PA: Carnegie Mellon University Research
     Showcase, 1995); Humphrey Carpenter, *J.R.R. Tolkien: A Biography* (New York:
     Houghton Mifflin, 2000).
413 *"Fantasy is a natural":* J.R.R. Tolkien, *On Fairy Stories,* ed. Verlyn Flieger (New York:
     HarperCollins, 2008), 18–19.
414 *"There is a great deal":* Quoted in David Day, *An Encyclopedia of Tolkien: The History
     and Mythology That Inspired Tolkien's World* (San Diego: Canterbury Classics, 2019),
     526.

dwarves of these stories: Day, *Encyclopedia,* 110–11.

416 *"giant robots, witches":* A. D. Jameson, *I Find Your Lack of Faith Disturbing: Star Wars and the Rise of Geek Culture* (New York: Farrar, Straus, and Giroux, 2018), 8.
Campbell once identified: Joseph Campbell, *The Hero with a Thousand Faces* (1949; Novato, CA: New World Library, 2008).

417 *she and Ann Bancroft:* Liv Arnesen and Ann Bancroft, *No Horizon Is So Far: Two Women and Their Extraordinary Journey Across Antarctica* (New York: Penguin Books, 2003).

418 *"We all have a Land":* Rectorial Address, in Nansen, *Adventure and Other Papers.*
"Have you ever heard": Robert W. Service, *Rhymes of a Rolling Stone* (New York: Dodd, Mead and Co., 1912).

APPENDIX: RUNES AND THE VIKINGS

423 *Old Norse word* runar: Gwyn Jones, *A History of the Vikings* (Oxford, UK: Oxford University Press, 1984), 419; https://www.wordsense.eu/r%C3%BAnar/; Lauraian Gallardo, "Violence, Christianity, and the Anglo-Saxon Charms," Master's Thesis, Eastern Illinois University, 2011.
an Old Italic alphabet: Jones, *History of the Vikings,* 420.
extant runic inscriptions: Else Roesdahl, *The Vikings* (New York: Penguin Books, 2016), 50.

424 *are harder to read:* Roesdahl, *Vikings,* 51.

425 *use of the word* Viking: Robert Ferguson, *The Vikings: A New History* (New York: Penguin Books, 2009), 203.
mention women: Judith Jesch, *Women in the Viking Age* (Woodbridge, UK: Boydell Press, 1991), 49.
inscription from Dynna: Jesch, *Women in the Viking Age,* 71.
case found in Lincoln: Jesch, *Women in the Viking Age,* 46.
Many were irreverent: Mark Mancini, "11 Samples of Authentic Viking Graffiti," Mental Floss, February 24, 2015, https://www.mentalfloss.com/article/61841/11-samples -authentic-viking-graffiti.
this one at Gripsholm: Jesch, *Women in the Viking Age,* 61.
most numerous runic finds: Peter Sawyer, *Kings and Vikings: Scandinavia and Europe, AD 700–1100* (London: Routledge, 1984), 29.

426 *Upplander named Asmund:* Sawyer, *Kings and Vikings,* 30–32.
engraved on the teeth: Neil Price, *A History of the Vikings: Children of Ash and Elm* (New York: Basic Books, 2020), 190.
the inscription "kiss me": Roesdahl, *The Vikings,* 52.

427 *"in a flowing script":* J.R.R. Tolkien, *The Fellowship of the Ring* (New York: Ballantine Books, 1955), 74–75.

INDEX

Page numbers in *italics* refer to illustrations.

inheritance of property, 43–44
Instinct of Workmanship, The (Ve-
    blen), 292–94
Iona, 73
Iowa, migration to, 227
Ireland, 69–72, 74
Irish Potato Famine, 343
iron-plated warships, 247–55
Islam, 115, 132
Island No. 10, 255–56
Isle of Man, 76–77, 163
Italy, 147–51, 152–54

Jackson, Peter, 414, 415
Jackson, Stonewall, 325
Jacobsen, Iver, 244–45, 258–60
Jacobsen, Oscar, 257
Jakob (son of Olaf Sköttkonung),
    120
James, William, 292
James I of England, 196, 199–200
Jameson, A. D., 415–16
Jamestown, New York, 228
Jansson, Erik, 228–30, 246
Jefferson, Thomas, 327, 353
Jelling stones, 92–93, *93*, 118
Jeremiah, 3
Jesus Sirach, Book of the All-Virtu-
    ous Wisdom of Yeshua ben
    Sira, 189–90
Jewish population during World
    War II, 384, 385, 395–402
Johnson, J. A., 241
Johnson, John, 307

Johnson, Kirsten, 233
Johnson, Ole, 260
Johnson, Olof, 230
Johnson, Philip, 320, 333
Jon Loptsson, 170–71
Jones, Gwyn, 38, 41–42, 45
Jordanes, 12
Joscelin (bishop of Paris), 23–24
Joyce, James, 72
Judaism, 115. *See also* anti-Semitism;
    Jewish population during
    World War II
Julius Caesar, 12
Junger, Sebastian, 410
justice system, 40
Jutland, 5, 6, 17

Kalm, Peter, 224
Kalmar, Union of, 181–82
Kalmar Nyckel, 218–19
Karl Knutsen, 184
Kazin, Alfred, 342–43
Keel mountains, 5
keel, 36
Ketil Flatnose, 74
Khazars, 115
kings, early, 56–58. *See also individ-
    ual kings*
Kjelstrup, 389
knarr, 36–37
Knox, John, 190
Knudsen, William "Big Bill," 299,
    321, 329–32, 333, 334, 340, 347,
    373, 384